From
HUE AND CRY
to
HUMBLE PIE

From
HUE AND CRY
to
HUMBLE PIE

Curious, Bizarre and Incomprehensible
Expressions Explained

JUDY PARKINSON

with a Foreword by
ADAM HART-DAVIS

Special edition for PAST TIMES® Oxford, England

First published in Great Britain in 2000 by
Michael O'Mara Books Limited
9 Lion Yard, Tremadoc Road
London SW4 7NQ

A CIP catalogue record for this book
is available from the British Library

ISBN 1-85479-841-3

3 5 7 9 10 8 6 4 2

Designed and typeset by Martin Bristow

Printed and bound in Finland by WS Bookwell, Juva

PAST TIMES®

FOREWORD

by ADAM HART-DAVIS

Believe it or not, the customer is always right, but don't buy a pig in a poke; look before you leap, or at least take a dekko inside this book. However, I won't beat about the bush; I don't have to sail close to the wind to say it's the bee's knees, the cat's whiskers, the full Monty. It certainly passes the acid test by a long chalk, and the bottom line is that while some of it may be over the top, overall it's finger-lickin' good!

Scientifically, this collection of phrases and sayings is interesting because each one is a 'meme', and a highly successful meme at that. Memes are little bits of information that are passed on from one person to another by imitation; they include phrases, hairstyles, recipes, and tunes. When I sing in my shower, I don't make up my own song, but do my best to imitate one I have heard, perhaps on the radio or from a Beatles album. A song is one kind of meme, and successful songs are the ones we can't get out of our heads.

The world is full of bits of information; think how many words you have read or heard in the last week, on the radio, on television, in newspapers, magazines, and books – thousands of them. All these words and groups of words are memes, and all compete to get into our brains and to get passed on to other people. The fittest memes survive, and the most successful are those that go on being used for years. Clever advertisers are always looking for sparkling new memes, such as 'Liquid engineering' and 'All because the lady loves Milk Tray'. Every phrase in this book, from 'hue and cry' to 'humble pie', is a brilliantly successful meme.

Memes used to be spread only by word of mouth, but then came writing and printing, the telephone, the photocopier and the fax machine, radio and television, and finally the computer and the Internet. Each step has allowed memes to spread faster, further and wider, and some people would go so far as to say that the memes in our brains have driven us to create these pieces of technology – that the Internet is not for our benefit, but for the benefit of the memes, because it allows them to multiply with amazing speed. And yet to create a successful meme still needs a human brain.

I was interested to see in this book that many of the great advertising lines were written by copy-writers who went on to become great authors. Some people seem to have an extraordinary skill in manipulating words so that when they put thousands together they write wonderful books, and when they put a few together in a phrase it acquires exceptional memorability, for that is what makes a great meme. As a result this book is great fun to dip into, and a mine of intriguing information.

So don't fiddle while Rome burns or go off at half-cock; for Pete's sake go for it! Strike while the iron is hot, boldly go, cross the Rubicon, bite the bullet, and put your money where your mouth is. If you buy this book you'll be happy as a sandboy and as pleased as Punch, while if you don't you'll be sick as a parrot and possibly as mad as a hatter. Are you sitting comfortably? Then clear the decks and find out why the curate's egg didn't cut the mustard, why the man on the Clapham omnibus might have a bee in his bonnet, and why the origin of the Elephant and Castle still isn't as plain as a pikestaff.

ADAM HART-DAVIS
June 2000

About one's ears

This colloquialism, which means to be in a very bothersome situation in which one might sustain some pain or trouble, is a shortened form of the proverb, 'To bring a hornets' nest about one's ears'. A hornet is a type of large wasp which can inflict a savage sting; like wasps, but unlike honey bees, hornets can sting repeatedly without damage to themselves. It is well known that bears are very fond of honey, and like Winnie the Pooh have a tendency to make mistakes, and they often get their noses stung by

poking their snouts into a hornets' nest mistaking it for a bees' nest. The expression 'To stir up a hornets' nest' implies the same degree of trouble and pain.

According to Cocker

This describes a statement or calculation that is reliably correct. Edward Cocker (1631–75) was a London schoolmaster who published over a hundred editions of his *Arithmetick*, which first appeared in 1678. The phrase was popularized by Arthur Murphy in his farce *The Apprentice* (1756). The American equivalent of the phrase is 'According to Gunter', used to describe a task carefully and correctly done with no chance of a mistake. The English mathematician and astronomer Edmund Gunter (1581–1626) invented 'Gunter's chain', a device used by surveyors to measure distances. A chain is an imperial unit of length equal to 22 yards (66 feet), the actual chain being divided into 100 links each of 7.92 inches; a cricket pitch is 1 chain in length.

According to plan

A well-used expression which is often taken to mean the exact opposite of its apparent meaning. It derives from optimistic communiqués issued during the First World War, often after a particularly bloody or shambolic operation, with the result that the phrase became associated with official attempts to cover up military incompetence and confusion. In true British style, it was thus employed ironically to describe things that did *not* go according to plan. Use of language in this way implies a kind of coded understanding between those in the know, strengthening the sense of camaraderie among those who suffer from such plans.

Acid test, to pass the
Said of someone or something that has been subjected to a conclusive or severe test. Gold is not attacked by most acids, but reacts to nitric acid, also known as *aqua fortis*, which is therefore the acid used in the 'acid test' for gold. To 'put on the acid' is probably derived from 'to pass the acid test' and is Australian slang meaning to exert pressure on someone when asking for a favour or a loan.

Affluent society, the
A phrase, in fashion from the late 1950s, used to describe the growth in material wealth of British society during the decade after the Second World War, with the increasingly widespread ownership of houses, cars, televisions, and items now known as 'white goods' – washing machines, refrigerators, and so on. Health care and other social services were also newly available to all. The term was popularized in JK Galbraith's book *The Affluent Society* in 1958: 'In the affluent society no useful distinction can be made between luxuries and necessities.'

Alive and kicking
Active and in good health. The expression probably refers to a healthy baby either while still in the womb or just after birth. Appropriately, it is the title of a popular Saturday-morning children's show broadcast by BBC Television.

All because the lady loves . . .
A highly successful advertising catch line, originating in the 1960s, for Cadbury's Milk Tray chocolates, which survived all but unchanged for over twenty years and is still quoted today.

Television commercials for Milk Tray featured a mysterious black-clad stunt-man in exotic locations, *au* James Bond, risking life and limb in daring feats to deliver the box of chocolates to his lady love. The clip has been much parodied over the years, perhaps because this series of lavish commercials was used to sell rather ordinary chocolates.

All Greek to me
'It's all Greek to me' is often used to mean that something is completely unintelligible, or is written in a foreign language unknown to the speaker, Greek being particularly tricky to grasp because of its different alphabet. It probably comes from Shakespeare's *Julius Caesar* (1599) in which Casca says, ' For mine own part, it was Greek to me.' Nowadays something incomprehensible is sometimes described as being 'rocket science', while the opposite, 'It's not rocket science,' is often used to indicate that something is simple to grasp. It is also common now to see someone simply passing a hand over his or her head if they find something difficult to understand, a new kind of sign language indicating that something is 'over their head'.

All in a day's work
Said of an unusual or unexpected task that can be obligingly included in the normal daily routine. The expression was common by the eighteenth century, but it is uncertain when it was first coined. A character in Sir Walter Scott's novel *The Monastery* (1820) says, 'That will cost me a farther ride . . . but it is all in the day's work.'

All over bar the shouting
This expression is firmly rooted in the world of sport, and means that victory is in the bag, only the cheering of the crowd at the end of the game or contest being lacking. The phrase may perhaps be derived from boxing, the shouting being the noisy appeal from the supporters of one of the boxers against the referee's decision. It is

also often applied to political elections in which the outcome is certain even before the ballot papers have been counted. In a famous reference to the phrase, an excited Kenneth Wolstenholme, the BBC's commentator at the 1966 World Cup final at Wembley, when England won against West Germany, said, 'There are people on the pitch . . . they think it's all over . . . it is now!' In extra time, Geoff Hurst scored a last goal making the final score 4-2 and sealing the Germans' fate. *They Think It's All Over* is now the title of a popular BBC Television sports quiz show.

All singing, all dancing

This piece of popular phraseology was inspired by the first Hollywood musical, *Broadway Melody* in 1929, the era in which sound first came to the movies, which was advertised with posters proclaiming:

The New Wonder of the Screen!

ALL TALKING

ALL SINGING

ALL DANCING

Dramatic Sensation!

The phrase caught on immediately, and two rival studios adopted the same sales pitch in the same year for *Broadway Babes* and *Rio Rita*.

In about 1970 the computing world adopted the phrase to hype up new software, so that by the mid-1980s every kind of organization

seemed to boast that their computers and systems packages had some quality that was 'all singing, all dancing'. Also from the mid-1980s the financial world embraced the phrase with enthusiasm to describe the stock market at the time of the 'Big Bang', the major modernization of the London Stock Exhange that came into effect in October 1986. Subsequently the expression has been linked with anything from savings plans, pensions and mortgages to machines – especially electronically controlled machines – of almost any kind. It can just as easily be substituted with the older phrase, 'All bells and whistles', bestowing the 'Wow' factor on almost anything.

All that glitters is not gold

Appearances are not what they seem. A saying that must have been in use for a thousand years or more and a favourite of poets, it is thought to be Latin in origin. It is a well-known note of prudence in Shakespeare's *The Merchant of Venice* (1596):

> All that glisters is not gold,
> Often have you heard that told.

This implies that the proverb dates from earlier wisdom; certainly it was used by Chaucer in *The Canterbury Tales*, for in 'The Canon's Yeoman's Tale' (*c.* 1387) he wrote:

> However, all that glitters is not gold,
> And that's the truth as we're often told.
>   (Modern translation by Nevill Coghill, 1951)

Thomas Gray (1716–71) wrote in his 'Ode on the Death of a Favourite Cat, Drowned in a Tub of Gold Fishes'(1747):

> Not all that tempts your wand'ring eyes
> And heedless hearts, is lawful prize;
> Nor all that glisters gold.

While, more cynically, Ogden Nash (1902–72) observed in 'Look What You Did, Christopher':

> All that glitters is sold as gold.

Alternative medicine

The concept of turning away from traditional forms of medicine took hold in the late 1960s. Many people think that there are other ways to treat illnesses and injury other than by long-accepted 'doctor's' methods employing drugs, surgery and so on, and such remedies as homeopathy and acupuncture are widely used today. The word 'alternative' has been applied since the late 1960s to describe some cultural or other value that is different from the norm. Earlier in the decade, in what came to be known as the 'counter-culture' or 'underground', there was much experiment into creating alternative societies, which attempted to exist without most of the accepted appurtenances of modern life. 'Alternative' was applied in the 1980s to a style of comedy which, with its subversive and surreal themes and anti-establishment tone, became widely popular – to the extent that 'traditional' comedy is arguably now 'alternative' itself.

And now for something completely different

An almost ubiquitous British catchphrase of the 1970s that came from *Monty Python's Flying Circus*, a cult comedy television series of the 1960s and 1970s, first broadcast in 1969, which had a huge following of youthful fans who would quote its lines in schools and colleges and at work on the day after each screening of the programme. The phrase was also the title for the *Monty Python* team's first feature film in 1971. In the television show the line was spoken by John Cleese, wearing a dinner jacket and seated at a desk behind a microphone, in a parody of the early BBC announcers, although Cleese's desk would be set in absurd surroundings such as on a beach or hillside. The expression had previously been used on television magazine programmes as a jolly link between two unconnected items, but scriptwriters had to think of something completely different to say after *Monty Python*.

Annus horribilis

A particularly bad or miserable year, the phrase being Latin for 'horrible year'. It owes its popularity to the Queen, who used it in a speech at a banquet in the Guild Hall, London, in 1992, the year which saw the divorce of the Princess Royal, the separations of the Prince and Princess of Wales and of the Duke and Duchess of York, and the devastating fire at Windsor Castle. The next day, the punning headline writers had a **field day** (q.v.), with the *Sun* proclaiming on the front page, 'One's Bum Year'. Conversely, a glorious year can be described as *annus mirabilis*, used to describe 'a year of wonders, catastrophes or other notable events'. One such (for the British, at least) was 1757, which marked Britain's final conquest of Canada and the foundation, again by force of arms, of her Indian empire. Philip Larkin wrote a poem entitled 'Annus Mirabilis' about the year 1963 – see **The birds and the bees** (q.v.).

Ants in one's pants

Said of an excessively restless or eager person, someone displaying such behaviour can also be described as a 'fidget-bottom'. The expression was popularized by Hugh S Johnson, the dynamic former US Army general who was in charge of the National Recovery Administration in 1933–4, when the national reconstruction policies of President Franklin D. Roosevelt's 'New Deal' were implemented. ('Pants' in this case has the American meaning of trousers.) In Britain nowadays the word 'pants' is often used colloquially to mean naff or not very good, possibly harking back to the grubby English sense of the word 'pants'.

An apple a day keeps the doctor away

A popular panacea that holds that to include an apple in the daily diet will guarantee good health. The proverb is said to be of nineteenth-century origin and has no particular medical support, although apples do contain vitamins and fibre, which are part of the daily dietary requirements. However, the American statesman, writer, philosopher and scientist, Benjamin Franklin (1706–90) is credited with quoting the phrase, if not with inventing it, in the eighteenth century.

Apple of one's eye
The Bible has:

> He kept him as the apple of his eye
>> Deuteronomy 32: 10

and:

> Keep me as the apple of the eye, hide me under the shadow of thy wings
>> Psalms 17: 8

and:

> For he that toucheth you toucheth the apple of his eye
>> Zechariah 2: 8

while in Shakespeare's *A Midsummer Night's Dream* (c. 1594) we find:

> Flower of this purple dye,
> Hit with Cupid's archery,
> Sink in apple of his eye.

The earliest recorded examples of the phrase's use in this country can be found in the works of King Alfred, dating from the end of the ninth century. At this time, the pupil of the eye was thought to be a solid object, and was known as the 'apple', presumably because an apple was a common spherical object. (Interestingly, the fruit of the Tree of the Knowledge of Good and Evil, which brought about the downfall of Adam and Eve, and which gave rise to our expression 'forbidden fruit' meaning any illicit indulgence or pleasure, has for centuries been represented as an apple. In fact, the Book of Genesis, where the tale is found, does not describe the fruit at all.)

Our modern word 'pupil' comes from Latin and appeared in English in the sixteenth century. It is figurative in origin; the late Latin original was *pupilla*, little doll, which is a diminutive form of pupus, boy, or *pupa*, girl (the source for the other sense of 'pupil', meaning a schoolchild, is the classical Latin *pupillus*, *pupilla*, meaning an orphan or ward, and hence a student taught by a teacher). The word might have been applied to the dark central portion of the eye within the iris because of the tiny image of oneself, like a puppet or marionette, that can be seen when looking into another person's eye.

'The apple of one's eye' is what one cherishes most. As has been said, the pupil of the eye has long been referred to as the 'apple' because it is perfectly round and appears solid. Because sight is so precious, someone who was called this as an endearment was similarly precious, with the result that the phrase took on the figurative sense we still retain.

Apple-pie order
Said of something that is perfectly ordered or set out, or in perfect condition. It is uncertain how this phrase entered the language, although there are various theories. It may have originated as a corruption of the French *cap à pie*, meaning 'head to foot', used to describe a correctly dressed or armed gentleman or soldier. Another suggested French source is *nappes pliées*, 'folded linen', which could therefore be extended to mean 'in perfect order', but it is more likely that it refers to the prank of making an 'apple-pie bed'. Equally, however, the phrase may come from America, where apple pie, the family favourite 'just like Mom used to bake', symbolizes all that is wholesome and homely.

Are you sitting comfortably?
The cosiest question known to the generation that grew up in the 1950s, when radio was still much more common than television. 'Are you sitting comfortably? Then I'll begin . . .' was the line that introduced the regular story in the BBC children's radio programme *Listen with Mother*, and it continued in use until 1982.

Julia Lang, the original presenter, first broadcast the programme in 1950, although there is some dispute as to whether the question was formulated by Lang herself or by Frieda Fordham, an analytical psychologist and adviser to the BBC.

As every schoolboy knows
This is a rather condescending put-down, said as a rejoinder to someone who has said something that is already considered common knowledge. The expression is particularly associated with Lord Macaulay (1800–59), although it had been recorded much earlier. In 1840 one of Macaulay's contemporaries, Lord Clive, wrote:

> Every schoolboy knows who imprisoned Montezuma, and who strangled Atahualpa.

It is, however, doubtful whether many schoolboys today would actually know these facts. In *The Anatomy of Melancholy* (1621) Robert Burton (1577–1640) wrote, 'Every schoolboy hath . . .', while Bishop Jeremy Taylor (1613–67) used the expression 'Every schoolboy knows it' in 1654. Later Jonathan Swift (1667–1745) wrote in his 'The Journal' (1727):

> How haughtily he lifts his nose,
> To tell what every schoolboy knows.

Curiously, 'school' derives from the Greek word *skhole*, meaning 'leisure spent in the pursuit of knowledge', since only those who enjoyed a life of leisure had the time to attend a school. The archetypal prep-school boy, Nigel Molesworth, the inspired creation of Geoffrey Willans and Ronald Searle who first appeared in *Down With Skool!* in 1953, tends to use the expression 'As any fule kno . . .'

Ass in a lion's skin, an
An old saying to describe a cowardly person who blusters or tries to bully others; otherwise, a fool with groundless aspirations to wisdom. The ass in this context represents a fool, an ass or donkey being often used figuratively to symbolize ignorance or stupidity. (In American usage, however, 'ass' equates with English 'arse' – see next.) The legendary allusion is to the fable of the ass that dressed in a lion's skin, but betrayed itself by its braying.

Ass, to cover one's
A slang term, American in origin, meaning to make up an excuse or prepare an alibi in advance, in order to avoid being blamed if something goes wrong. The phrase originated in the 1960s among US troops in Vietnam, and later became part of colloquial American language. It came to Britain in the 1980s, and was probably popularized by its use in the vulgar banter of 'get-rich-quick' financial traders. It is commonly used today in the planning of business ventures or in contracts, in which 'ass-covering clauses' are often included as a means of safeguarding the signatory against the unexpected, and thus blame. The phrase originally derives from military tactics, when one soldier provides covering fire for another as the latter advances; US black slang often uses 'ass' for the self, as in 'I'm going to whup your sorry ass.'

At this moment in time
This roundabout expression, beloved of journalists, commentators and pundits of all shades since the 1960s, is a classic example of a speaker or writer going round the houses and using a circumlocution to make a point with as many words as possible when one word would do – and that word is 'now'.

Aunt – My giddy aunt
An exclamation of surprise, a mild oath. There seems to have been a fashion at the end of the nineteenth century for using the word 'giddy' in a hyperbolical sense. In Kipling's *Stalky & Co* (1899) we find:

> King'll have to prove his charges up to the giddy hilt.

However, it has also been suggested that the expression derives from the archetypal saga of giddy-auntdom, the classic farce *Charley's Aunt* by Brandon Thomas (1856–1914), first performed in 1892:

> I'm Charley's aunt from Brazil – where the nuts come from.

This use of 'giddy' in the phrase ('Oh my sainted aunt' is another variant) suggests something or someone lightheartedly or exuberantly silly, a sense of the word that dates from the sixteenth century, as in the expression 'to act the giddy goat'. Although 'giddy' has been used for hundreds of years in this sense, at first it literally meant to be possessed by a god, and only later shifted to its modern sense of experiencing vertigo or dizziness.

Aunt Sally
An 'Aunt Sally' is a name for anyone or anything that is an object of ridicule or abuse, or of an unreasonable attack. This somewhat cruel term comes from a game, often found at fairgrounds and village fêtes, in which short sticks are thrown at a wooden figure of an old-woman's head mounted on a pole, the fun being to knock off its nose or break the pipe stuck in its mouth. The word 'aunt' was traditionally applied to any old woman; hence in Shakespeare's *A Midsummer Night's Dream* (*c.* 1594) Puck speaks of, 'The wisest aunt telling the saddest tale'. As an aside, an 'Aunt Emma' is someone who is an unadventurous croquet player.

Awkward age, the
The age of adolescence, when one is no longer a child but not quite an adult, a time when the hormones are said to be jumping. (A modern lighthearted description of teenagers suggests that they are 'hormonally challenged', a parody of many terms derived from

'political correctness'.) Henry James wrote a novel of this title, published in 1899, about a young Englishwoman's emergence from this age into maturity and understanding (though what was particularly awkward for her was that she and her mother were rivals in love for the same young man). The word awkward is applied to other situations involving the young. The 'awkward squad' is the term used to describe young untrained military recruits not yet ready to take their place in the ranks.

Back burner, to put on a (*or the*)
To put off or postpone. A very useful expression in business if a decision cannot be made immediately, meaning that an idea, proposition, course of action or project can be put aside and kept in reserve for use when necessary, or when circumstances are more propitious. (An almost diametrically opposed metaphor is also used, for an idea or project can be also 'put on ice', to be figuratively defrosted at a later date.) The back burners, or rings, on a cooker are used for simmering, while the front burners are usually the hottest and are used for fast cooking. There is now even a verb form gaining increasing usage, with people talking of 'back-burnering' something.

Back of beyond, the
This is an Australian expression, nineteenth-century in origin, which is now commonly used to describe any remote area, but which originally referred to the vast spaces of the interior of the country, the Great Outback. The 'back', reduced from 'back

country', is the outlying territory behind the settled regions, and the term 'backblock' is found in 1850, referring to those territories of Australia split up by the government into blocks for settlement. The more isolated and sparsely populated areas of the Australian interior are also known as 'the bush'.

Back to basics
This infamous phrase, meaning to go back to the ground rules, to 'traditional values', was first heard in politics in the 1950s. It probably derived from the expression, used in mathematics and physics, 'to go back to first principles', with its implication that any calculation, however complicated, has its origin in just a few essential basic rules. 'Back to basics' was taken up by the Conservative Party in 1993 as an all-embracing political slogan designed to promote family values. John Major, the Prime Minister, launched this ill-fated phrase, albeit with the best of intentions, in a speech to the Conservative Party Conference in 1993:

> The message from this conference is clear and simple. We must go back to basics. The Conservative Party will lead the country back to these basics, right across the board: sound money, free trade, traditional teaching, respect for family and the law.

The campaign soon backfired, not least because of a number of widely publicized sex scandals, characterized as 'sleaze' by the press, within Mr Major's party. In America the phrase 'Back to the basics' was used in the mid-1970s as a government-education slogan to promote better teaching of reading, writing and arithmetic.

Back to square one
To begin again, or, less formally, 'Back to where you started, sunshine!' This colloquialism possibly derives from board games in which players, through bad luck or bad judgement, have to move their pieces back to the starting point. Another suggestion is that it comes from the early days of radio football commentaries, for which diagrams of the pitch divided into numbered squares were printed in radio listings magazines so that listeners could follow the game. The meaning is similar to 'Back to the drawing board', which means to go back and rethink a complete project or

scheme. Aircraft designers during the Second World War used the latter phrase when a concept or even a whole design for a new machine proved unworkable and had to be started all over again.

Bacon, to save one's

To have a narrow escape, to emerge from some dire situation without injury or loss. This expression may date from the late seventeenth or early eighteenth century, long before refrigeration, when the meat of the pig was cured and preserved for use during the winter months, and may refer to the need for cured bacon to be protected from any thieving dogs. In his unfinished epic *Don Juan* (1819–24), Lord Byron makes reference to this:

> But here I say the Turks were much mistaken,
> Who hating dogs, yet wish'd to save their bacon.

Bacon was a significant ingredient in the diet of the eighteenth century and the expression 'To bring home the bacon', meaning to earn the money to maintain the household, describes the custom at country fairs of greasing a live pig and letting it loose among a group of blindfolded contestants. He who successfully caught the greased pig could keep it and so 'bring home the bacon'. According to Nathan Bailey's *Universal Etymological English Dictionary* of 1720, 'bacon' was a slang term to describe booty of any kind which fell to beggars, shoplifters, highwaymen and the like in their enterprises; 'to save one's bacon', therefore, was to save something that was valuable both literally and figuratively.

Ballpark figure

Another North Americanism that has taken hold in Britain, this is an estimate, or a budget figure, which might better be described as a 'guesstimate'. A ballpark is a large stadium in America or

Canada built specifically for the game of baseball. The original reference in financial quotations to two or more figures as being 'in the same ballpark' means that they are of roughly the same amount; even so, given that actual ballparks are vast, the variation between such figures may be correspondingly large. 'Ballpark' is also used to describe a situation or state of affairs, as in 'This is a whole new ballpark for me.'

Ban the bomb

This simple, alliterative and easily remembered political slogan first became current in the early 1950s in America. It was taken up in Britain by 1958, when it was used to promote the Campaign for Nuclear Disarmament (CND) during the years of the perceived global threat from nuclear weapons following the increased nuclear tension during the period, known as the Cold War, which succeeded the end of the Second World War. It entered public consciousness by its simplicity, the political correctness of its message, and the striking symbol that went with it, which was seen on almost every surface during the 1960s from T-shirts to brick walls. Both the phrase and the symbol are still in active use today, linked with support for campaigns for nuclear disarmament all over the world.

Bandwagon, to climb on the

To declare support for a popular movement or trend with the intention of profiting or reaping some sort of easy material gain, usually without believing in the movement or trend. The expression is believed to have originated in the Southern States of America, probably dating from the first presidential campaign of William Jennings Bryan (1860–1925) in 1892, when candidates for political elections would parade through the streets led by a band of musicians performing on a large horse-drawn dray. As a publicity stunt the local candidate would mount the wagon as it passed and ride through his constituency with the band as they played, in an attempt to gain personal support from the voters. Bryan never won the presidency, losing to McKinley in 1896 and

1900, and to Taft in 1908; he was, however, appointed Secretary of State in 1913, but resigned from the government in 1915, believing that President Wilson's policies would bring the United States into the First World War, a bandwagon he did not wish to climb on.

Bank – To laugh all the way to the bank

The original expression was 'To cry all the way to the bank', which was a popular catchphrase in the 1950s. It is an ironic comment, usually made about someone who has done something questionable, or produced something kitsch or tasteless or for some other reason generally disapproved of, while making a great deal of money from it. It may have been first said by the high-camp pianist and entertainer Liberace (born Wladziu Valentine Liberace, 1919–87), after a critic had savaged his playing – which was extravagantly ornamented with trills and arpeggios – and his embellished stage act. Liberace was the highest-paid entertainer in the United States during the 1960s and 1970s, and his income averaged $5 million a year for more than twenty-five years. 'To laugh all the way to the bank' was, for him, an obvious twist to the original phrase, as well as a derisive riposte to the critic.

Bark up the wrong tree, to

To be totally off the mark, to waste energy following the wrong course of action, or to have one's attention diverted off the subject in hand. The phrase comes from the American sport of racoon hunting, which generally takes place at night. The hounds of the hunting pack are trained to mark the tree in which the racoon they are pursuing takes shelter, and then to howl at its base until their master arrives to shoot the animal. The hounds will frantically bark up at the wrong tree, however, if they mistake it in the dark. The expression neatly puns a dog's bark and tree bark, and first became popular in the early nineteenth century, appearing in the works of James Hall, Davy Crockett – a great racoon hunter – and Albert Pike.

Bath – To take an early bath

This euphemism comes from the sports pitch, and means to retire early to the dressing room after being injured, or sent off by the referee, during a match of football or rugby. The phrase was popularized from the 1970s by the television sports commentator Eddie Waring in his descriptions of Rugby League matches, and is now often used to describe any situation in which someone is obliged to pull out of the action before it is over. In America, and increasingly in this country, 'To take a bath' means to suffer any kind of defeat or serious loss, as in 'He took a bath in the stock-market collapse.'

Be like Dad, keep Mum

The British weakness for puns ensured that this expression gained wide currency during the Second World War. 'To keep mum' means to keep a secret or simply to keep quiet, not giving away what you know. In its original context the word 'mum' represented an inarticulate sound made with sealed lips, and 'mumble' probably has the same derivation. In *Henry VI*, Part II Shakespeare has:

Seal up your lips and give no word but mum.

By the same token, mumchance is a game of dice during which complete silence is maintained. In its other meaning, 'Mum' is a diminutive of 'Mummy', a child's affectionate word for 'mother'.

The slogan itself originated in 1941 on a poster issued by the British Ministry of Information, the body largely responsible for issuing wartime propaganda. The aim was to make sure that people remembered national security and did not engage in idle gossip, which might be overheard by spies. Similar slogans of the war years were 'Careless talk costs lives' and **'The walls have ears'** (q.v.). Unlike the other slogans, however, the five words paint a picture of a bygone age and the sort of life Dad might have expected to lead with Mum, provided she stayed at the kitchen sink.

Beam ends, to be on one's
To be destitute, or nearly so. This is one of many English phrases that describe an extremely impecunious state; others include 'boracic', from Cockney rhyming slang 'boracic lint', meaning 'skint'; to be 'in Carey Street', that street being the site of the old Bankruptcy Courts in the City of London; and to be 'on one's uppers', the upper being the part of the shoe above the sole which covers the upper part of the foot, the phrase implying extreme destitution because one cannot afford to replace the worn-out sole, much less the whole pair of shoes. The origin of the phrase 'on one's beam ends' is not altogether certain, but it probably refers to the beams of a wooden ship, which run across the vessel from side to side, supporting the deck. If the beams are 'on end', then the ship has turned over on its side and cannot right itself – a desperate plight (as is being flat broke).

Beam me up, Scotty
A catchphrase, widely used and held in great affection, this comes from the popular television science-fiction series *Star Trek*, first shown in 1966. Whenever one of the intrepid adventurers from the Starship *Enterprise* found himself in a spot of trouble while away from the ship, he would call up Scotty, the *Enterprise*'s chief engineer, to transfer him, as 'matter', back to base. The expression is still widely used, always humorously and often ironically, to mean 'I don't want this task' or 'I don't want to be here'. It enjoys wide currency largely because the TV series is repeated regularly, and also because *Star Trek* has a huge following of fans, who are known as 'Trekkies'.

Beans, to spill the

The expression means 'to let on', to tell all, perhaps prematurely, to an eager audience, to give away a secret or to let the cat out of the bag (see **A pig in a poke**, q.v.). There are various explanations for the derivation, one of the most likely being that it may have originated at the turn of the twentieth century as a colourful American euphemism for vomiting, because beans represented basic food.

The phrase thus roughly equates to 'Cough it up' or 'Spit it out', said when someone is having difficulty in finding the right words, and meaning, 'Be clear, let's have it'. This expression, with its overtones of there being a juicy piece of gossip in the offing, obviously alludes to hiding something in the mouth, and being reluctant to reveal it. Beans appear in various expressions: 'to be full of beans' means to be in high spirits or full of energy, and was originally said of lively horses; beans used to be slang for money or property, so that 'I haven't got a bean' means that one is broke.

Beat about the bush, to

To approach a matter indirectly or in a roundabout way. The reference is probably to a form of hunting in the fifteenth-century, known as 'batfowling', in which one hunter held a light to dazzle the birds roosting in thickets while another went in to seize them – normally the noise of men crashing about in undergrowth would scare the birds out long before the hunters could get near them. Other ancient methods were to disturb the roosting birds in the bush and then catch them in a net as they fluttered out. The hunters would literally beat about all the bushes in order to catch just a few birds.

Bed of nails, to lie on

A situation or position, usually self-inflicted, that is fraught with a multitude of painful or difficult problems. The phrase refers to the spiked bed of the Hindu fakir (ascetic or holy man), but while the spikes may not hurt the fakir, they would be unbearable for most normal mortals. The saying is sometimes used in it variant form, 'to lie on a bed of thorns'. It is thought that the expression first received wide notice in a modern context when it was used by the Labour government in 1966.

Bee in one's bonnet, to have a

To be obsessed with a particular idea or notion, as though mentally all a-buzz. The expression, in the variant 'to have bees in the head', implying scattiness, was in circulation in the sixteenth century, for a reference to bees and crazed thought was recorded by the English poet, Court musician and entertainer John Heywood (c. 1497–c. 1580) in 1546 in one of his collections of English proverbs. A slightly worse accusation current then was 'to have maggots in the head', which meant to suffer complete madness. It is thought that bees met bonnets in the poem 'Mad Maid's Song' by Robert Herrick (1591–1674), written in 1648:

> For pity sir, find out that bee,
> Which bore my love away.
> I'll seek him in your bonnet brave,
> I'll seek him in your eyes.

Beer and sandwiches

This is a political snack, originally consumed during informal negotiations with the Labour ministers and Prime Ministers of the 1960s and 1970s. During the then frequent industrial disputes the phrase became associated with last-ditch talks held between trade-unionists and politicians at No. 10 Downing Street in an effort to avert a threatened strike. This proletarian-style 'pub grub' was looked upon as indicating the high seriousness and impeccable Socialist credentials of the politicians, as well as being thought – rather patronizingly – as being eminently suitable for the 'cloth-cap' negotiators, a sort of working-man's 'champagne and chicken'. A 'beer-and-sandwich' meeting implied (or so it was hoped) that here were honest men in their shirtsleeves, too busy and too honourable to indulge in the lavish and bibulous feasts enjoyed by lesser politicians and union leaders. These days the 'rubber-chicken circuit' describes the usual menu for the rounds of dinners prospective MPs attend in order to woo local party workers and other supporters.

Before you come up
Used in the context, 'I'd stuck my bayonet up twenty-five Jerries before you come up', this was one-upmanship at its worst. With this not altogether hospitable welcome, First World War veterans would attempt to put down greenhorns, young soldiers new to the front line. The phrase implied that the target of the remark was utterly wet behind the ears and would be unlikely to cope with the unpleasant conditions in the trenches. Variations included, 'Before your number [painted on your kitbag] was dry' and 'Before you knew what a button stick [issued to each new recruit] was'.

Believe it or not!
This catchy slogan originated as the title of a cartoon strip created by the American writer Robert Leroy Rinpley (1893–1949) in 1923, with which it is always associated. The concept of the series was to illustrate amazing but allegedly true facts and stories. Later spin-offs from the strip were a radio and television series, and even a museum at Niagara Falls. The phrase is often used ironically, implying that the listener won't believe what is said anyway, whether it is true or not.

Bell – As the bell clinks, so the fool thinks
A foolish person believes what he desires. In the fifteenth-century tale of Dick Whittington, the young poor boy came to London because he believed its streets to be paved with gold and silver. Running away from his cruel master, he reached Highgate Hill where, hungry and tired, he did not know whether to continue his flight from the city. Bow Bells began to ring and the boy imagined that they said, 'Turn again, Whittington, thrice Lord Mayor of London.' The bells clinked their answer to his thoughts and he returned to prosper as a merchant and to become mayor three times. The story is based on a certain Richard Whittington (c. 1358–1423) who came from Gloucestershire to achieve fame and fortune as a merchant and as Lord Mayor

of London – and, not least, ultimately to become a pantomime legend. Dying childless, he left all his money to charity, while the legend of his cat is a long-established part of English folklore.

Best bib and tucker
This is probably an old wives' expression, and one that has been addressed to women and children for two or three hundred years. To put on one's best bib and tucker means to don one's 'Sunday best', to make oneself smart and spruce. A bib is familiar to children as a piece of cloth put under the chin to protect clothes while eating, while a tucker was an ornamental frill of lace or linen worn by women in the seventeenth and eighteenth centuries over the bodice to cover the neck and shoulders. This meaning predates the Australian slang word 'tucker' for food, referring to the contents of a tuck box, although there is also a close connection with 'bib and tucker' in this sense.

Best of British luck
Often shortened to 'Best of British', this is an ironic quip as if to say, 'You can get on with it, but leave me out.' It was frequently heard during the early days of the Second World War, when the Allies were losing confidence in their ability to win the war and British luck was hard to come by. It compares with an ironic line from a First World War soldiers' song:

Over the top with the best of luck
Parley voo . . .

(see **Over the top**, q.v.). In the 1960s, 'And the best of British' took on a less sarcastic and more positive meaning, especially with the government-supported 'I'm Backing Britain' campaign. The expression became one of comedian Frankie Howerd's (1917–92) innuendo-laden catchphrases. For instance, when introducing a mock opera he would say,

. . . Vera would pause for breath before a high C and as she mustered herself for this musical Everest I would mutter, 'And the best of British luck!'

Bets – To call off all bets

A summons to cancel all wagers in certain circumstances, deriving from the race track and the betting shop; for instance, a bookmaker may call off all bets if he suspects that a race or other contest has been rigged. In a widening of its meaning, the phrase is used to mean rejecting a complicated or disadvantageous issue. In American black slang of the 1940s, however, it meant to die – indeed, the most final way of calling off all bets.

Big Apple, the

The well-known nickname for New York City. The name was first coined in the 1920s by John J Fitzgerald, a reporter for the *Morning Telegraph*, who used it to refer to the city's race tracks and who claimed to have heard it used by black stable hands in New Orleans in 1921. Black jazz musicians in the 1930s took up the name to refer to the city, especially Harlem, as the jazz capital of the world. The epithet was revived in 1971 as part of a publicity campaign by Charles Gillett, in charge of a push to attract tourists to New York, who was possibly inspired by the name of the Beatles' trading company, the Apple Corporation, founded in 1968. The general allusion is to a city that is the 'big apple' sought as the ultimate location for anyone seeking world fame. There are many classical references to apples, such as the golden apples given by Venus to Melanion so that he could beat, by trickery, the fleet-footed Atalanta in a race; the girl stopped to pick up the apples, and so lost the race and married Melanion. The sentiment behind 'The Big Apple', however, is more likely to be the idea of an apple as a symbol of the best, as in **the apple of one's eye** (q.v.), meaning someone or something that is very precious.

In the eighteenth century, the writer and politician Horace Walpole (1717–97) referred to London as 'The Strawberry', impressed by its freshness and cleanliness compared with foreign cities; he named his estate at Twickenham, Middlesex, Strawberry Hill, and founded there the Strawberry Hill Press.

Big Brother is watching you
This term is popularly applied to an individual or establishment that exercises dictatorial control, supposedly for everyone's benefit. 'Big Brother' is the invisible state machinery that sees all, from which there is no hiding place, even at home. It is one of the key phrases from George Orwell's (1903–50) *Nineteen Eighty-Four* (1949). Aspects of Orwell's fictional Ministry of Truth were derived not only from the BBC, where he once worked, but also from the experiences of his first wife, Eileen, who worked at the Ministry of Food during the Second World War preparing *Kitchen Front* broadcasts. (See also **Black-coated workers**, q.v.) One campaign to promote potatoes with the slogan 'Potatoes Are Good For You' was so successful that it led to shortages, so it was followed by a 'Potatoes Are Fattening' promotion. In 1984 Orwell was alluding to the Soviet Union of the day, then under Stalin's brutal control; in this country nowadays, however, closed-circuit television has most of our movements covered.

Big enchilada, the
The leader, the top man or woman, the Boss. A phrase that crops up in the Watergate tapes referring to the US Attorney-General, John Mitchell (1913–88), who led President Nixon's re-election campaign in 1972, and who was later indicted on charges that he had conspired to plan the burglary of the Democratic National

Committee's headquarters in the Watergate office-hotel-apartment complex in Washington, DC, and had then obstructed justice and perjured himself during the subsequent cover-up. He was convicted in 1974 and sentenced to a gaol term for 'associated offences' uncovered during the investigation into the scandal. Enchilada is a Mexican speciality, and consists of a tortilla filled with meat and dressed with chilli sauce. It can only be surmised that, since Mexican food is ubiquitous in America, it was the Attorney-General's favourite dish on the hotel menu. Since the mid-1970s, 'the big cheese' is also occasionally used to describe a VIP, especially in business, while a group of them may sometimes be facetiously described as *les grands fromages*. In an echo of Watergate terminology, Monica Lewinsky would sometimes refer to President Clinton as 'the big creep' when she was annoyed with him during their on-off liaison in 1996; by another coincidence, she too lived in the Watergate complex for a time.

Big-stick diplomacy
A political catchphrase which refers to the conduct of negotiations or the carrying out of policy backed up by the threat of military force. The term was brought to public attention in 1901 when US Vice-President Theodore Roosevelt revealed in a speech his fondness for the West African proverb 'Speak softly and carry a big stick'. Later, as President, he used such practices successfully in the Alaskan boundary dispute of 1902–4.

Birds and the bees, the
A euphemism for human procreation which was probably inspired by Cole Porter's 1954 song, 'Let's Do It':

Birds do it, bees do it
Even educated fleas do it
Let's do it, let's fall in love.

The phrase was used, often by embarrassed parents or teachers, as a means of avoiding dangerous words like 'sex' or 'sexual intercourse'; nowadays it tends to be used ironically. In his poem 'Annus Mirabilis' (1967), Philip Larkin (1922–85) wrote that 'Sexual intercourse began in nineteen sixty-three', so in the buttoned-up 1950s roundabout phrases sounding as though they came from the nursery were extremely useful for the unmentionably grown-up subject of sex.

Biscuit – That takes the biscuit
An exclamation to indicate shock and surprise that some action has gone beyond the bounds of acceptable behaviour and implying that the speaker is affronted by this outrageousness. Specially spiced biscuits and cakes were formerly prized as small treats and were given as rewards in a variety of competitions.

Bish-bash-bosh
A Yuppie phrase, mainly current in the 1980s, full of bravado, to describe something done well, quickly and efficiently. It was later shortened to 'bosh' and widely used by manual workers, as if to say, 'Just like that', or 'Sorted'. It gained wide circulation through its use by one of the characters portrayed by the comedian Harry Enfield, the loutish but high-earning plasterer 'Loadsamoney'.

Bishop – As the bishop said to the actress
A rejoinder to a perfectly innocent statement intended to create a sexual *double entendre*, sometimes inverted to become 'As the actress said to the bishop'. Typical comments that might encourage such a retort would be, 'I didn't know I had it in me', or 'I'd bend over backwards to please you', or 'I've never seen a female "Bottom" . . .'. The phrase was popular in the 1940s in the RAF, although it is thought to have originated in the music-hall era, when the staple fare of stand-up comedians included many stories of potentially scandalous couplings between bishops and actresses. In *Educating Archie*, the popular BBC radio

33

show of the 1950s, Beryl Reid as Monica, an upper-class schoolgirl friend of Archie Andrews, the ventriloquist's dummy, used an alternative phrase, '. . . As the art mistress said to the gardener'.

Bitter end, to the

To the last extremity, to the final defeat, or to the death. An affliction can be born until the bitter end, meaning to the last stroke of bad fortune. Despite appearances, the phrase has nothing to do with bitterness. 'Bitter end' is a mid-nineteenth-century nautical term for the end of a rope or chain secured in a vessel's chain locker, or 'abaft the bitts'. When there is no windlass the cables are fastened to bitts, that is, pairs of bollards fixed to the deck, and when the rope is let out until no more remains, the end is at the bitts – hence the bitter end.

In Captain Smith's *Seaman's Grammar* (1627) we read:

> A Bitter is but the turne of a Cable about the Bitts, and vear it out by little and little. And the Bitters end, is that part of the Cable doth stay within boord.

However, the phrase appears in the Old Testament in the context that we use today:

> Her end is bitter as wormwood, sharp as a two-edged sword.
>
> Proverbs 5:4

Black is beautiful

This slogan was adopted in the 1960s by supporters of black civil rights in America in an attempt to destroy the negative associations that the word 'black' had had until then. The West Indian-born civil-rights activist Stokely Carmichael (born Kwame Toure, 1941) coined the phrase in 1966 at a civil-rights rally in Memphis, Tennessee, and Martin Luther King, Jr (1929–68), the leader of the Civil Rights Movement, took it up the following year when he used it in a poster campaign. The expression may have biblical origins:

> I am black, but comely.
>
> Song of Solomon 1:5

Carmichael was the leader of black nationalism in America during the 1960s, and also the originator of its rallying cry, 'Black power'.

Black-coated workers

A euphemism for prunes, in reference to their laxative qualities. The phrase was coined by Charles (later Lord) Hill, the BBC radio doctor in the 1940s, in early-morning radio broadcasts of a programme called *The Kitchen Front* (see **Big Brother is watching you**, q.v.). The expression is a neat counterpoint to the terms 'white-collar workers' – management who sit at desks – and 'blue-collar workers' – the employees in overalls who get their hands dirty. However, the politician and diarist Sir Henry 'Chips' Channon used the phrase literally when writing about the Old-Age Pensions Bill in 1937, referring to those in clerical and professional jobs as 'black-coated workers'.

Blarney Stone, to kiss the

A popular term used of someone who speaks in persuasive or seductive terms; the verb 'to blarney', meaning to employ persuasive flattery, and the noun 'blarney', for flattering talk, have the same derivation. The provenance for this expression can be found, literally, at Blarney Castle, near Cork, in south-west Ireland. Set high in the south wall of the castle is an almost inaccessible triangular stone bearing the inscription, *Cormac Macarthy fortis me fieri fecit*. In 1602, the same Macarthy, Lord of Blarney, was defending the castle against the English, who were fighting to force him to surrender the fortress and transfer his allegiance to the English crown. However, Macarthy smooth-talked the British emissary, Sir George Carew, with flattery and sweet promises and stood his ground, much to the fury of the Queen Elizabeth I; it is said that the Queen herself coined the term 'blarney' to show the worthlessness of Macarthy's promises. The tradition of kissing the Blarney Stone to improve one's eloquence and persuasive abilities – which can only be done by hanging, with one's feet securely held, head-down from the castle's battlements – dates from the eighteenth century. 'To blarney' is also a slang American term meaning to pick locks.

Blood, sweat and tears

The phrase comes from Winston Churchill's speech to the House of Commons upon taking over as Prime Minister, 13 May 1940, and is used to describe a task that will be hard and difficult, demanding great sacrifice with few if any compensations. At the time British morale was at a low ebb: Nazi forces had overrun Denmark, Holland and Belgium, and were in the process of conquering Norway and France. The prospect of victory over Germany looked increasingly grim. Churchill's actual words were, 'I have nothing to offer but blood, toil, tears and sweat,' and he revisited this phrase several times during the war years. It has since been reduced to just three words, making it easier to remember, without losing any of its emphatic meaning of selfless hard work and dedication.

Some three centuries earlier, John Donne (c. 1572–1631) wrote in 'An Anatomy of the World' (1611):

> Mollify it with thy tears, or sweat, or blood.

While Lord Byron (1788–1824) observed in *The Age of Bronze* (1823):

> Year after year they voted cent per cent,
> Blood, sweat and tear wrung millions – why? For the rent!

In 1882 the Italian patriot Giuseppe Garibaldi (1807–82) made this speech to his followers in the struggle for Italian nationhood, which may well have inspired Churchill:

> Soldiers, I'm getting out of Rome. Anyone who wants to carry on the war against the outsiders, come with me. I can't offer you either honours nor wages, I offer you hunger, thirst, forced marches, battles and death. Anyone who loves his country, follow me.

Blood Sweat and Tears was also the name of an American jazz/rock band in the 1960s and 1970s.

Blow hot and cold, to

To be inconsistent, to have fluctuating opinions, or simply to be unable to make up one's mind. The allusion is to the classical fable of a traveller who accepted the hospitality of a satyr, one of the gods of the forest, a creature part goat and part man. The chilly traveller blew on his cold fingers to warm them and then blew on his hot broth to cool it. The indignant satyr ejected him because he blew both hot and cold with the same breath.

Blow the gaff

A slang phrase meaning to reveal a secret, which may derive from French *gaffe*, a blunder, but it is more likely to come from 'gab', the informal English word for speech, which in turn derives from 'gob', meaning mouth or beak (the expression 'gift of the gab' comes from the same source). Current in the eighteenth century was a slang expression, 'to blow the gab', meaning to betray a secret. A more colourful derivation, however, may be that the phrase refers to a concealed device, known as a gaff, used to cheat at cards. This was a small hook set in a ring worn on the finger and used by the crooked player to grip the cards. In America and Canada, the expression 'to stand the gaff' means to withstand problems, scorn and other troubles. 'Gaff' is also archaic English slang for someone's home, as in 'Let's go round to his gaff'.

Blue-rinse brigade, the

Although this phrase has a military ring, it is used to describe women of a certain age with conservative tendencies. It is a slightly derogatory description that refers to the colour of the rinse used to conceal grey hair; conveniently, blue is the Conservative Party colour. The collective term 'brigade' was obviously applied because of the formidable presence these ladies make at political meetings, party conferences and other rallies of the faithful, but the term can be extended to encompass any group of well-groomed, socially active, usually well-off, elderly women.

Bogart – Don't Bogart that joint

A widely used phrase that comes from the film *Easy Rider* (1969), which featured a song by Holy Modal Rounders called 'Don't Bogart That Joint'. It means to take too long to pass the joint, or cannabis cigarette, to the next person. The term 'to bogart' was obviously inspired by the film actor Humphrey Bogart (1899–1957), who more often than not appeared on screen as well as in public with a cigarette hanging from his lip; perhaps unsurprisingly, he died from lung cancer.

Bone to pick, to have a
This is a desire to discuss a difference of opinion, settle a misunderstanding about something disagreeable, or express a complaint. The bone is probably the bone of contention, metaphorically tossed between two dogs fighting over it. Usage goes back to the middle of the sixteenth century, but the expression may well have come from an earlier phrase, 'to have a crow to pluck', which was used at least a hundred years earlier, the crow in this instance symbolizing discord. In Howell's *Proverbs* (1659) the phrase 'to have a goose to pluck with you' is used in the same sense.

Bone up on, to
To study intensively, to engage in serious research into a particular subject, or to revise a subject comprehensively. It has been said that the allusion is to whalebone in a corset, which sculpts the shape and stiffens the garment, as a metaphor for the gaining of 'hard knowledge'. However, in the nineteenth century Bohn's, a publishing firm owned by Henry Bohn (1796–1884), produced English translations of Greek and Latin classics that were widely used by students cramming for their exams. The expression 'to Bohn up' soon became 'to bone up', while there is also a certain satisfaction to be had from 'bone' as a pun on 'bonehead'.

Bones, to make no
To be honest and direct without any risk that the statement may be misunderstood, but also sometimes used to mean to have no scruples about something. A possible derivation for this phrase is that it comes from the world of gambling, a pursuit that has been popular since the eighteenth century. Dice were often known as

'bones', perhaps because in play they are rattled together and sound like castanets, which in turn used to be known as bones (from which they were made). Once dice have been thrown the score is a gamble; therefore if you make no bones, you will incur no risk – a situation that cannot be misinterpreted. Dice are said to have been invented in China by Chen Su-Wang in the third century AD, so the phrase may well have been in use for hundreds of years. Another derivation, however, suggests a reference to the simple pleasure of drinking a bowl of soup in which there are no bones, and thus nothing to complain about.

Born-again Christian
A person who has undergone a spiritual conversion and become a fervent and sometimes evangelizing Christian; by extension, 'born-again' is now used of anyone newly converted to some activity or cause, as in 'born-again Socialist'. The phrase was originally applied to fundamentalist Christians in the Southern United States and has been in use since at least the 1960s, although the term originates in the New Testament with the story of Christ and Nicodemus (John 3: 3):

> Except a man be born again, he cannot see the kingdom of God.

Originally the phrase took on a figurative meaning of zealousness, and especially the zealousness of the newly converted, at about the time when Jimmy Carter, from a born-again Baptist background in the South, was running for the American presidency in 1976. The epithet 'born-again' is usually, but not necessarily, religious. A born-again golfer is one who, having played golf occasionally over the years, becomes a regular player on retirement. Currently, with divorce becoming relatively common, many ex-wives describe themselves, somewhat profanely, as 'a born-again virgin'.

Bottom line, the
The main point of an argument, the basic characteristic of something or the actual value of a financial deal, the nub or truth of the matter. The phrase gained wide currency during the 1970s possibly, because of its frequent use by the US Secretary of State,

Henry Kissinger. He spoke of 'the bottom line' as the eventual outcome of a negotiation – ignoring the distraction of any inessential detail. The phrase itself is an accounting term, and refers to the figure on the line at the end of a financial statement indicating the net profit or loss of a company.

Break a leg!

The theatre is notoriously superstitious, and among actors it is deemed bad luck to wish a colleague 'good luck' before going on stage. Instead, this phrase, a traditional, if somewhat black, euphemism, is employed to wish someone good luck in a performance, especially on a first night. The expression, which seems to have originated in America, is said to come from the assassination of President Abraham Lincoln in his private box at Ford's Theatre, Washington, DC, on 14 April 1865. The murderer, John Wilkes Booth, a reputable Shakespearian actor, escaped after firing the shot by leaping down on to the stage, breaking his leg in the process. 'Break a leg!' may derive from a German expression for good luck, *Hals und Beinbruch* ('May you break your neck and your leg'), with which the Kaiser's pilots used to wish each other luck during the First World War.

Breakfast of Champions, the

An American advertising slogan associated since the 1950s with Wheaties, whose television commercials featured sporting champions endorsing the cereal. In what is known as a chiastic twist, this phrase can also be inverted to read, 'The champion of breakfasts'. Perhaps in acknowledgement of the slogan's success, Kurt Vonnegut (1922–) published a novel entitled *The Breakfast of Champions* in 1973.

Bridesmaid – Always a bridesmaid, never a bride

The phrase actually originated as 'Often a bridesmaid . . .', and was coined to advertise Listerine mouthwash in 1923. It was created by Milton Feasley of the advertising agency Lambert & Feasley, although it is reminiscent of the British music-hall song 'Why Am I Always a Bridesmaid?' made famous by Lily Morris. A screen title in the newsreel sequence of Orson Welles's film *Citizen Kane* (1941) proclaims of Kane, 'In politics, always a bridesmaid never a bride'. The bridesmaid advertisement was succeeded by an even more famous line used to promote Listerine: 'Even your best friends won't tell you . . .' (that is, that your breath smells).

Bright young things

A typically sparkling phrase invented by the prolific romantic novelist and former journalist Barbara Cartland (1902–2000) to describe the young socialites of the years following the First World War. As a counterpoint to the horrors of war it was all the rage to dance the night away in a riot of frivolous partying, possibly in a subconscious attempt to deny that the war had ever happened, or at least to try to forget the bloody conflict. In the 1920s young women in their teens, and especially those who were unconventional in their dress, manner or behaviour, were known as 'flappers' – many of them wore their hair in a plait tied with a bow, which flapped when they danced. They came to epitomize the meaning of the phrase 'Bright young things'.

Buck – The buck stops here

A slightly self-important declaration meaning 'This is where ultimate responsibility lies'. 'Buck' is slang for the American and Canadian dollars, and possibly derives from deer hunting, the bucks (males) being more valuable than the does (females). As well as being a male deer, hare or rat (among other animals), a high-spirited young man, a young dandy or, in a more derogatory sense, a male Native American or African-American, a 'buck' is also an article placed as a reminder before a player whose turn it is to deal at poker, and it is very likely that the slogan actually originated at the poker table (see next entry), and has nothing to do with dollars. The phrase was made famous by US President Harry S Truman (1884–1972; President 1945–53), who had it hand-written on a sign on his desk at the White House to remind himself and those around him that he alone had the ultimate responsibility for every decision of his administration. Some twenty-five years later President Jimmy Carter had the legend reinstated with the same idea in mind. In a perceived lowering of public respect for the morals of certain American presidents, however, the phrase was later modified in common usage to 'The f**k stops here' (see also **The big enchilada**, q.v.). The original phrase is now generally applied to the boss of any organization.

Buck – To pass the buck
To evade blame or responsibility and shift all criticism elsewhere. An American phrase from the game of poker, the 'buck' being the token object that is passed to the person who wins a jackpot, to remind him that when it is his turn to deal the next hand he must start another jackpot. Originally the token was a buckhorn knife, so called because its handle was made from the horn of a buck, or male deer; although some sources argue that the buck was either a piece of buckshot or a buck's tail, which early hunters carried as a lucky talisman. The earliest recorded use of the phrase is by Mark Twain (born Samuel Langhorn Clemens; 1835–1910) in 1872, in the first decade after the end of the Civil War, when poker or 'stud poker' – the stake was probably originally a stud horse – were played in bars by lumberjacks, miners and hunters, those being the days before it became known as a 'gentleman's' game. (See also entry above.)

Bullet – To bite the bullet
To seize the moment when one undertakes a feat of endurance, to face danger with courage and fortitude, to behave stoically, to knuckle down to some difficult or unpleasant task. The expression probably originated in field surgery before the use of anaesthetics. A surgeon about to operate on a wounded soldier would give him a bullet to bite on, both to distract him from the pain and to reduce his ability to scream.

Business as usual
This self-explanatory expression was widely used in Britain in the Second World War, and especially during the London Blitz and the blitzes on other major cities, when shops and businesses continued to open, and stay open, in spite of bomb damage. In the capital, 'Business as usual' and 'London can take' it were commonly scrawled defiantly on the walls of damaged buildings. Winston Churchill popularized the phrase in 1941 in a speech at the Guild Hall in London when he said, 'The maxim of the British people is "Business as usual".' A later Conservative Prime Minister, Margaret (now Lady) Thatcher, memorably evoked the fighting spirit behind these words after the IRA bomb attack on the Grand Hotel in Brighton during the Conservative Party Conference of 1984.

By a long chalk
This expression comes from the athletics or sports arena, and means to win easily, far ahead of the competition. The allusion is probably to chalk marks made on the floor to record the score of a player of team, and the phrase sounds as if it originated with the long jump or throwing the javelin, or some sport of that nature where the greatest distance determines the winner. Before lead pencils became common, merit marks or scores used to be made with chalk. A long chalk, therefore, is a high score.

C'est la guerre
An ironic phrase employed to accompany an excuse or an explanation for anything that has not gone quite to plan. Originally a French military catchphrase from the First World War, it was used as a somewhat fatalistic excuse for any failure to perform properly. By 1915 it had been taken up by British soldiers, although after the Armistice its use declined until its revival in the next war. It was then widely used in a civilian, as well as a military, context to account for anything that had been affected as result of the war. It is nowadays used, especially in business, to indicate acceptance of matters beyond one's control, and naturally prompts the use of the similar phrase of gritty acceptance, *C'est la vie* ('That's life').

Camp – As camp as a row of tents

An expression used to describe something – a man, a theatre performance, an outfit, and so on – that is blatantly homosexual or wildly and effeminately affected, especially anything that is in questionable taste. The phrase, which is sometimes seen as 'As camp as a row of little pink tents', is a pun on the double meaning of the word camp and is a variation on other euphemisms for homosexual, like 'As bent as a lighthouse staircase' or 'As queer as a nine-bob note'. The adjective 'camp' does not necessarily mean homosexual, although it invariably has those overtones; it also carries with it a strong hint of self-parody. The colour pink may be associated with gay men because in Hitler's Germany known homosexuals were forced by the Nazis to wear a triangle of pink cloth as a means of identification. The spending power of gays, especially in an area, like London's Soho, where there is a substantial gay community, is called the 'economy of the pink pound'.

Cards – To ask for (or be given) one's cards

To ask for or be given one's cards is to resign from or be dismissed from a job. The cards in question are the National Insurance cards and other documents kept by the employer as a record of income tax and insurance contributions deducted from an employee's pay. In a sporting extension of this phrase, if a player, particularly in football, is shown a card by the referee, he is in breach of the rules; a yellow card represents a warning and red card means the player is sent off the field.

Carpe diem

Do not put off until tomorrow what can be done today, or enjoy the present while you have the chance. This has been for centuries a popular poetic theme or motif, urging the young to grasp the joys of life, especially love, before it is too late. The phrase is Latin for 'seize the day' and probably first appeared in literature in the first century BC; the Roman poet Horace (Quintus Horatius Flaccus, 65 BC–8 BC) wrote in his *Odes* (c. 23–13 BC):

Carpe diem, quam minimum credula posterio.
Seize the day, put no trust in the future.

The same spirited call to enjoy the pleasures of life was expressed by many later poets, among them Robert Herrick (1591–1674), whose 'To the Virgins, to Make Much of Time' (1648) enjoins maidens to abandon their virginity and live life to the full:.

Gather ye rosebuds while ye may,
Old Time is still a-flying:
And this same flower that smiles today,
Tomorrow will be dying.

Saul Bellow's (1915–) novella *Seize the Day* (1956) treats the theme ironically, portraying the effects of failure to follow one's authentic impulses. The phrase gained increased popularity after the Oscar-winning film *Dead Poets Society* (1989), directed by Peter Weir and starring Robin Williams as the passionate and inspiring teacher John Keating, who calls to his class, '*Carpe diem*, lads. Seize the day. Make your lives extraordinary!' Nowadays, the expression is often used of any opportunity that should be seized before it is too late.

Case the joint, to
An American slang expression from the criminal fraternity meaning to inspect or reconnoitre a building carefully before attempting to rob it, or to break into it for some other nefarious purpose. 'Joint' in this context means a building, an early twentieth-century colloquial Americanism for a sleazy dive where opium could be smoked or, during the Prohibition era (1920–33), where illicit spirits could be bought and drunk. National prohibition, which resulted from the Eighteenth Amendment to the US Constitution forbidding the manufacture, sale, transportation and consumption of alcoholic beverages, was known – by its supporters, at least – as 'the Noble Experiment',

prohibitionists believing that alcohol was a dangerous drug that destroyed lives and communities. In the event, however, illegal trading in alcohol made many fortunes, and gave a tremendous boost to organized crime. The word 'joint' has since come to be generally applied disparagingly to almost any more or less disreputable establishment, especially less than salubrious public meeting places like certain clubs, pubs or restaurants.

Cast pearls before swine, to
To offer something precious or of quality to someone who is perceived to be too ignorant or uncultured to understand or appreciate it. To show, for example, a brilliant idea or a work of art or literature to, or to bring one's 'pearls of wisdom' before, an unappreciative audience or the kind of person known as a Philistine. Philistines were warlike immigrants to Philistia in ancient Palestine, who fought the Israelites for possession of the land, and hence came to be stigmatized as an uneducated, heathen enemy; the term has since by extension come to mean anyone unreceptive or hostile to culture, especially someone who is smugly and boorishly so.

The phrase itself comes from the New Testament (Matthew 7: 6):

> Give not that which is holy unto the dogs, neither cast ye your pearls before swine, lest they trample them under their feet.

Cat – All cats love fish but fear to wet their paws
A traditional saying, dating back to at least the sixteenth century, used to describe a person who is keen to obtain something of value, but who is not bold enough to make the necessary effort or to take the risk. It is to this saying that Shakespeare referred in *Macbeth*:

Letting 'I dare not' wait upon 'I would',
Like the poor cat i' the adage.

Cat – No room to swing a cat

A commonly used description for a restricted or cramped space.
There are various suggested origins for this phrase, of which the most
likely is not as cruel to cats as it sounds, but was not much fun for the
metaphorical cat's human victim. 'Cat' was an abbreviation for 'cat-
o'-nine tails', a whip of nine knotted lashes or 'tails' which from the
eighteenth century was used in the army and navy, as well as on criminals in gaol, and was not formally banned in England as an instrument of punishment until 1948. It was a popularly held superstition
that lashing with a 'trinity of trinities', that is nine, was a a more effec-
tive punishment. Since space was restricted on the old sailing ships, it
may be that it was the amount of elbow room available that determined when the cat was swung. However, while this may seem the
most likely origin, 'cat' is also an old Scottish word for a rogue, and if
the expression derives from this, the swing is that of the condemned
criminal hanging from the gallows. Equally, suspending live cats in
leather sacks and then swinging the sacks as moving targets for
archers was once a popular, if barbaric, amusement, and this too has
been suggested as a source for the phrase.

Cat – The cat's pyjamas

This colloquialism first surfaced in
America in the 1900s and has
retained its meaning over the last
hundred years. It became current in
England in the 1920s and 1930s as a
phrase meaning something or someone superlatively good, top-notch or
extremely enticing, the last perhaps because of some saucy link
between pyjamas and bedtime.

'The cat's whiskers' and 'the bee's knees' are also used in the
same way. In the first crystal wireless sets of the 1920s, the fine
wire that made contact with the crystal was known as the cat's
whisker, alluding to the sensitivity of cats' whiskers. At about the
same time, people played with phrases that linked animals to

humans, and we find 'the kipper's knickers', 'the snake's hips', 'the elephant's instep' and so on. However, in the last ten years modern imagination has taken the idea further, and we now have more ribald phrases such as 'the dog's bollocks', which is sometimes abbreviated to just 'the dog's'.

Cat – To fight like Kilkenny cats
This is a fight to the end, no holds (as in wrestling) barred. The connection between fighting and Kilkenny cats is obscure. From the Norman period until 1843, Kilkenny was divided into Englishtown and Irishtown, with much strife between the two. One theory harks back to a legendary battle between a thousand cats from Kilkenny and a thousand cats from other parts of Ireland. In the night-long battle all the Kilkenny cats survived victorious, while all the others perished. Another more popular theory dates fom about 1800, when Kilkenny was occupied by a group of Hessian mercenaries in British government service, some of whom, bored and with nothing better to do, tied two cats to a clothes line by their tails and sat back to enjoy the feline fight. The soldiers had no time to release the cats when an officer approached to investigate the noise, so they cut the animals free by severing their tails. The officer was told that the cats had fought so fiercely that only their tails remained.

Catch-22, a Catch-22 situation
This is a lose-lose situation; whichever alternative you choose you can't win. It is the title of former advertising copywriter Joseph Heller's (1923–99) highly regarded satirical novel published in 1955. The story centres on Captain Yossarian of the 256th US Army Air Force bombing squadron in the Second World War, whose main aim in life is to avoid being killed. The best way for a pilot to achieve this was to be grounded due to insanity.

> There was only one catch and that was Catch-22 which specified that concern for one's own safety in the face of dangers that were real and immediate was the process of a rational mind. Orr was crazy and could be grounded. All he had to do was to ask and as soon as he did he would no longer be crazy and would have to fly more missions.

48

Century of the common man, the
The twentieth century is known as 'the century of the common man', the age of democracy. The phrase comes from the 1940 book of the same name by Henry A Wallace (1888–1965), New Dealer and FD Roosevelt's Vice-President, 1940–45. He subsequently used the phrase after America had joined the Allied forces in the Second World War, in an address entitled 'The Price of Free World Victory' on 8 May 1942:

> The century in which we are entering – the century which will come out of this war – can be and must be the century of the common man.

The phrase speedily became popular on both sides of the Atlantic and was much favoured by Nancy, Viscountess Astor (1879–1964), outspoken Conservative and, although American born, first woman MP to sit in the House of Commons, which she did from 1919 to 1945. In the late 1930s, she supported an appeasement policy toward Nazi Germany. When Britain declared war, however, she strongly supported the war effort.

The American composer, and prominent champion of American music, Aaron Copland, appropriately born in 1900, wrote *Fanfare for the Common Man*.

Changes, to ring the
This phrase is often used incorrectly as meaning to make changes. It actually means to repeat the same thing in a different way, and comes from the world of bell ringing, which was at its most popular in Britain in the seventeenth century. A change is the order in which a series of bells is rung. Thus with a series of four bells, as in the Westminster chimes, it is possible to ring twenty-four changes without once repeating the order in which the bells are struck. With five bells 120 changes can be rung, and with twelve bells 479,001,600 are possible. The greatest number of changes ever actually rung is reported to have been 16,000 changes, which took about nine

hours. Someone who repeats the same statement or idea, *ad nauseam* and with only minor variations, rings 'all' the changes.

Charity begins at home

This old proverb, meaning 'look to yourself and those close to you before helping others', is listed in the *Concise Oxford Dictionary of Proverbs*, which dates it from 1383, although it has a biblical counterpart:

> But if any widow have children or nephews let them learn first to shew piety at home.
>
> 1 Timothy 5:4

Writers have played with it ever since; for instance, in 1732 Fuller wrote, 'Charity begins at home, but should not end there', and Charles Dickens in *Martin Chuzzlewit* has, 'Charity begins at home and justice begins next door.' Other cultures have sayings alluding to acts of charity, one Russian proverb advising, 'Don't collect straw for your neighbour's roof while your own is leaking'.

Charlie's dead

A slang euphemism used to indicate that a woman's petticoat is showing, or that a trouser zip is undone. This expression has been in use since the 1950s, though the origin and identity of Charlie can only be guessed at. 'Charlie' is English slang for a fool and may come from Cockney rhyming slang for Charlie Hunt (i.e. c**t), used euphemistically, as 'Charlie's come', to describe anything that is unmentionable or unwelcome, such as the onset of menstruation. In Australian rhyming slang a Charlie is a girl, derived from Charlie Wheeler – 'sheila'.

Chattering classes, the

A wry description of journalists, political pundits and the like, members of the so-called 'classless society', who discuss current affairs and social issues. More generally, this is a slightly derogatory term for groups of would-be or pseudo-intellectuals pontificating on subjects of which they have perhaps incomplete knowledge, and certainly no control. Such types used to be called 'armchair philosophers'. The term was first coined some twenty years ago, at the beginning of Margaret Thatcher's reign as Prime Minister, as a disparaging description of the liberal middle classes who impotently raged against Thatcherite policies around the dinner tables of London.

Cheque-book journalism

A phrase first heard in the mid-1960s to describe the activities of the highly competitive press when trying to secure exclusive rights to stories from notorious personalities and criminals, in the latter case sending out a rather misleading message that crime does pay. Sex scandals, for instance, known as 'kiss-and-tell' stories, involve scorned ex-partners being tempted by the tabloid press, particularly, to sell their salacious accounts. The freedom of the press is a highly valued privilege in Britain and there remains a fierce debate about the ethics of paying for lurid stories, however colourful, the invasion of privacy being set against the press's need to provide the public with what they want to read.

Chickens – Don't count your chickens until they are hatched

To assume something is certain before it is proved to be so. It is well known that, in modern parlance, 'assumption is the mother of all f**k ups', and it is wise to heed this when planning ahead. The phrase has certainly been around for thousands of years, since it appears in Aesop's fable of the 'Milkmaid and Her Pail'. Indeed, there are probably more versions of this proverb than any other.

> The man that once did sell the lion's skin
> While the beast liv'd, was kill'd with hunting him,

wrote Shakespeare in Henry V, while a Hindu proverb urges, 'Don't bargain for fish which are still in the water', and an ancient Egyptian saw cautions, 'Do not rejoice over what has not yet happened'. A colloquial modern alternative from the betting shop is, 'Don't count your winnings until the bookie has put the money in your hand.'

Chip on one's shoulder, to have a

To display an inferiority complex, to perceive oneself as an underdog, to have a grievance, often unjustifiably. The expression is believed to have originated in America in about 1840 and may allude to a game of dare in which a man challenges another to dislodge a chip – as in piece of wood, not French fry – he carries on his shoulder. In American parlance a chip was also a figurative term for consequences, and so the phrase may be a warning to an adversary not to aim too high. There is an ancient proverb 'Hew not too high lest chips fall in thine eye'. By the late sixteenth century this health-and-safety warning had become something of a challenge, a dare to a fearless woodcutter to look high up without regard to any falling chips of wood.

Chips with everything

This comes from the days when Britain was over-concerned with social class, and is a snobbish comment on the perceived less adventurous appetites of the working classes. It implies a British taste for everything to be served with chips, usually drenched in vinegar or ketchup, and neatly describes the sort of British tourist who travels abroad and demands chips with everything, from pizza to curry. In 1962 Arnold Wesker (1932–) wrote a play entitled *Chips With Everything* about class attitudes among National Servicemen in the RAF. Nowadays, the phrase takes on a slightly different meaning with the increasing significance of computer chips in our lives.

Chuck out your chintz

A catchy alliterative phrase used by the Swedish-owned chain Ikea in 1999 to persuade people to buy new furniture from their stores. Chintz is a hybrid word, first heard in Britain in the seventeenth century when cotton fabric with floral designs was imported from the East. The Hindi word *chint* means variegated. The many chint fabrics soon became chints, and, in time the spelling was changed to chintz.

Clean, bright and lightly oiled

This is an army slogan that goes back to the First World War, and describes the approved state for a soldier's rifle. Between the wars, 'slightly oiled' came to mean to be a bit tipsy, alluding to the property of oil as a lubricant. By the same token, 'well oiled' means drunk. In the next war, the phrase took on military connotations again, and Gerald Kersh used it as the title of a book of wartime short stories in 1946.

Cleanliness is next to godliness

This homely phrase comes from a sermon given by John Wesley in a sermon in 1791, although it is thought to have its origins in the writings of an ancient Hebrew rabbi, Phinehas ben Yair. A British advertising agent, Thomas J Barratt (1842–1914), seeking an endorsement for Pears Soap in America in the 1880s, was naturally shy of approaching former President Grant and instead asked the eminent American cleric, Henry Ward Beecher, to say a few kind words about his product. Beecher wrote a text including the phrase, which entered the lexicon of English both as an unforgettable advertising strap-line and as a moral statement or injunction.

Clean round the bend

Completely crazy, eccentric, in the sense of being out of alignment. The phrase was described by FC Bowen in the *Oxford English Dictionary* in 1929 as 'an old naval term for anybody who is mad'. The word 'clean' is used in many different ways to describe something complete, pure, or unreserved, for instance 'clean bowled', 'to make a clean break' or 'to make a clean breast of it'. In a neat play on words the phrase has been used to advertise the lavatory cleaner Harpic since the 1930s – 'It cleans right round the bend'.

Clear the decks, to

To remove everything not required, especially when preparing for action; hence, to prepare for some task by removing the extraneous or irrelevant. As it sounds, this is a nautical phrase and alludes to a sailing ship preparing for battle, when anything in the way of the guns and their crews, or that might burn or splinter, or that was not lashed down, was removed from the usually cluttered decks, so that no untethered articles would roll about and injure the seamen during the battle. This saying is used in many contexts, such as clearing the table of food and dishes, or preparing the house to receive guests. 'Deck' appears in many commonly used phrases, among them 'to hit the deck', to fall over, usually to escape injury, or 'to deck someone', to hit them and knock them to the floor.

Cleft stick, to be in a

A figurative phrase meaning to be in a tight place or dilemma, with no room for manoeuvre either backwards nor forwards. The phrase may be an ancient pun on the verb 'to cleave' which has two directly opposite meanings, one being to stick to or adhere, and the other to split, chop or break along a grain or line of cleavage.

The form of torture inflicted on Ariel by the witch Sycorax in Shakespeare's *The Tempest* (1611) was to imprison him in the trunk of a cleft pine tree.

Cloak and dagger
Any operation that involves some intrigue, especially the melodramatic undercover activities of those involved in espionage or other secret work. Cloak-and-dagger plays were swashbuckling adventures popular in the seventeenth century. In France a performance of this type was known as a *comédie de cape et d'épée* and this is the direct source of the English phrase, 'cloak and dagger'. The name also appears in the Spanish *comedias de capa y espaded*, literally comedies of cloak and sword, particularly those by the Spanish dramatists Lope de Vega (1562–1635) and Calderón (1600–81), although these plays were dramas of merely domestic intrigue.

Clockwork orange
A person who has been brainwashed to alter his or her personality, particularly someone whose individuality has been suppressed by conditioning. The term comes from the title of the novel *A Clockwork Orange* (1962) by Anthony Burgess (1917–93) which was popularized by Stanley Kubrick's controversial and violent film of the same title (1971). The story tells of the state's attempts to punish its criminal hero, Alex, by turning him into a 'mechanical man' through sinister forms of therapy and brainwashing. In spite of its success the film was taken out of circulation by Kubrick and Warner Brothers after it was blamed for a number of copycat crimes as reported by the police and the courts; Kubrick himself also received several death threats. Following the director's death in 1999 the film was re-released in 2000. Burgess took his title from a little known Cockney expression from the 1950s, 'as queer as a clockwork orange', that is, homosexual, which may derive from the phrase 'as odd as an orange'.

Closet, to come out of the
To declare one's homosexuality, to come out into the open about it. This was the slogan of the American gay rights organization known

as the Gay Liberation Front from about 1969. In the days when homosexuality was a criminal offence, gay men had to hide the nature of their sexual preferences. (Lesbianism has never been criminalized in Britain, since at the time the legislation was formulated Queen Victoria refused to believe that sexual relations between women could ever occur.) They became known as closet queens, the closet being a private room; closet plays, for instance, are written to be read, not acted. When anti-homosexual laws were repealed, the need for secrecy receded and gays were able 'to come out', although many, fearful of society's disapproval, remained 'in the closet'. The expression is now used generally to mean to declare one's real position. The phrase 'to come out' was used in the first half of the twentieth century of debutantes, upper-class young women who were presented at Court, so making their official debut in society.

Cloud nine, on
To be on cloud nine means to be in a state of elation, very happy indeed, or feeling 'as high as a kite'. This fanciful twentieth-century expression comes from the terminology used by the United States Weather Bureau. The Bureau divides clouds into classes, and each class into nine types. Cloud nine is cumulonimbus, a cumulus cloud that develops to a vast height, with rounded masses of white vapour heaped one on the other, the upper parts resembling the shapes of domes, mountains or towers, while the base is practically horizontal.

Coat – To cut your coat according to your cloth
This metaphorical proverb is all about good
housekeeping and living within one's means.
It is self-evidently sensible advice to keep
to one's budget and restrict expenditure
to the amount of one's income; in
other words, simply to live within
one's means. It is often shortened,
becoming simply 'to cut your coat'.

Cock-and-bull story
A rambling or incredible tale; a tall story invented as an excuse; a
lie. There are various possible explanations for the derivation for
this term. In the coaching days of the seventeenth century the
London coach changed horses at the Bull Inn and the Birmingham
coach at the Cock Inn. From the exchange of travellers' stories
and jokes between the waiting passengers of both coaches the
'Cock-and-Bull' story is said to have originated.

The phrase may derive, however, from ancient fables in which
cocks and bulls and other animals conversed. In his Boyle Lecture
of 1692, Richard Bentley (1662–1742) stated:

> That cocks and bulls might discourse, and hinds and panthers hold
> conferences about religion.

While in his novel *Tristram Shandy* (1759–67) Laurence Sterne
(1713–68) wrote:

> 'L—d! said my mother, what is all this story about?
> 'A Cock and Bull,' said Yorick – 'And one of the best of its kind,
> I have ever heard.'

A Scottish satire or lampooning story is known as a 'cockalane',
which is taken directly from the French phrase of the same
meaning as 'cock and bull', *coq et l'âne*, cock and ass, donkey or
fool. Today both words are commonly employed separately in a
slang or vulgar context. 'Bull' is used as in 'What a load of bull',
politely avoiding saying the word 'bullshit' – while 'cock' speaks
for itself.

Cold enough to freeze the balls off a brass monkey
This means that the weather is extremely cold, and although the expression sounds delightfully vulgar, it is not in fact a reference to monkeys' testicles. A brass monkey is a type of rack in which cannon balls were stored. Being brass, the 'monkey' contracted in cold weather, resulting in the cannonballs being ejected. The expression has also mutated to a shortened form, again a comment on the temperature, as 'brass-monkey weather', which is almost universally understood.

Come up and see me sometime
This sexy phrase was immortalized by Hollywood screen actress and siren, Mae West (1892–1980). The line first appeared in the play *Diamond Lil* (1928), but probably reached a wider audience in the film version, *She Done Him Wrong* (1933), in which Mae West played a saloonkeeper who falls for the young Cary Grant's undercover cop. In one scene she says to Grant:

> You know, I always did like a man in uniform. And that one fits you grand. Why don't you come up sometime and see me? I'm home every evening.

The original order of the words has been rearranged to make them easier to say, and subsequently this is how WC Fields quotes them to Mae West in *My Little Chickadee* (1939). The American author Gelett Burgess (1866–1951) is credited as the originator of the phrase in his 1907 book *Are You a Bromide?*

Corridors of power, the
A collective expression to describe the ministries in Whitehall and their high-powered civil servants. The phrase was first coined by CP Snow (1905–80) in his novel *Homecomings* (1956):

The official world, the corridors of power, the dilemmas of conscience and egotism – she disliked them all.

Snow later used it as the title of his 1964 novel, and the phrase quickly caught on with the public and newspaper-headline writers.

Couch potato

American slang from about the late 1980s, used to describe a 'telly addict', someone who indulges in the habit of lounging at home watching television all day and night, eating and drinking, but never taking exercise. The expression is now used in most English-speaking countries, particularly with the increase in the number of television channels to choose from. Perhaps the potato featured in the metaphor because the blemishes on its skin are known as eyes, or possibly because it is the tuber of the potato plant, thus punning with 'the tube' – the television. Couch potatoes indulging in the habit of 'channel hopping' use the remote control or 'zapper', in many homes affectionately known by the name of 'Frank' after the zany pop artist Frank Zappa.

Coughs and sneezes spread diseases

A public-health slogan proclaimed by the Ministry of Health during the early days of the Second World War, in an effort to reduce the number of working days lost by workers taking sick leave for minor ailments. This was a zealous campaign to persuade people not to sneeze in close proximity to each other, especially on public transport and in air-raid shelters, and the phrase is still used today. Tony Hancock, in his classic *Hancock's Half Hour*

episode, 'The Blood Donor', reads the health poster bearing this legend while he waits to give his 'armful' of blood. The sister slogan was 'Trap germs in your handkerchief'.

Crazy mixed-up kid
An American term for the first post-Second World War generation of teenagers. Without the pressures of war, many teenagers found they could relax and turn their backs on responsibility, sometimes pretending to suffer from post-war trauma, or otherwise showing such symptoms as confusion, inability to make moral distinctions, and occasionally displaying mild psychological traits. Some argue that many of these went on to become hippies, although it is more likely that they have settled down and are now running the country.

Credibility gap
The space between the truth and fantasy; the disparity that exists between a claim or statement on one hand, and the reality of the situation on the other. If such claims are repeated it naturally results in a loss of confidence in those making such exaggerations. The phrase is generally attributed to Gerald Ford in 1966, while he was still a US Congressman, referring to the escalating involvement of America in the Vietnam War, an assertion that was strongly disputed by Lyndon Johnson's administration. Modern office jargon has bred a new buzz phrase, 'gap analysis', which means the assessment of untapped business opportunities.

Cropper, to come a
To fall heavily, head over heels, or to fail ignominiously. The origin probably lies in the old barber's term for a short haircut, 'neck and crop', which came to be used colloquially to mean headlong or bodily. So to fall to the ground neck and crop is to 'come a cropper', a phrase which has distinctly Cockney overtones with its alliteration and abbreviation.

Cross my heart
To make a firm promise or a pledge that will not be broken, with religious overtones. The words are often accompanied by a sign of the cross made over the heart, and to emphasize the seriousness of

the pledge to add a note of mortality, as quoted in Rose Macaulay's *Crewe Train* (1926):

Let's both swear,
Cross my heart and hope to die.

Curate's egg, the
This phrase is one of many from Mr Punch and it is one his most famous punch lines (see **as pleased as Punch,** q.v.). 'Good in parts, like the curate's egg' is proverbial. An elaborate cartoon from 1895 shows a timid young curate at his bishop's breakfast table, too nervous to say that the egg is bad. The phrase is often misquoted to mean that some parts of a thing are good. In fact, the curate was too shy to tell the bishop the truth about the egg.

I'm afraid you've got a bad egg, Mr Jones.

To which the curate stammers, 'Oh, no my Lord, I assure you! Parts of it are excellent!'

Curse of *Hello!*, the
The popular magazine *Hello!* features glowing and obsequiously uncritical celebrations of the lifestyles of the rich and famous. It has been noticed that some of the happy couples who appear on the front cover do not remain so for many months to follow. Such couples whose marriages have run into trouble include the Duke and Duchess of York and Mr and Mrs Paul Gascoigne. The phrase was probably invented by the satirical magazine *Private Eye*, deriving from its irreverent column, 'The Curse of Gnome'.

Customer – The customer is always right
The idea behind this famous trading slogan may have been suggested by the hotelier César Ritz (1850–1918), who said in

SELFRIDGE'S London's New & Wonderful
Shopping Centre ∗ ∗ ∗
Dedicated to Woman's Service - devoted to the Children's
Needs - the Man's Best Buying Place - with best assorted
Stocks at London's Lowest Prices:
NOW OPEN TO THE WORLD   OXFORD STREET
LONDON.W.

"London receiving her
Newest Institution"

1908, 'Le client n'a jamais tort' ('The customer is never wrong'). The American, Gordon Selfridge (1856–1947) is credited as the author of this ubiquitous statement. He came from Chicago and brought the concept of the large department store to Britain, and his shop opened in Oxford Street in 1909, adopting such slogans as 'This famous store needs no name on the door' and 'Complete satisfaction or money cheerfully refunded'. Gordon Selfridge is also credited as inventing the concept of so many 'shopping days until Christmas'.

Cut the mustard, to

A zesty and confident phrase meaning to do something well and efficiently, to prove oneself beyond all expectations at completing a task or occupation. The expression probably derives from mustard as slang for the best, possibly because it is hot or spicy; a line from O Henry's *Cabbages and Kings* (1894) reads,

> I'm not headlined in the bills but I'm the mustard in the salad just the same.

To cut, in this phrase, might refer to the harvesting of the plant, but it also might be used as in the expressions to 'cut a dash', 'cut up rough' or 'cut capers'.

Dear-John letter

A 'you're dumped' note from a wife or girlfriend breaking the news that the relationship with the recipient is over. The expression originated during the Second World War and is thought to be American. The unfortunate objects of Dear-John letters were usually members of the armed forces overseas, whose female partners at home had made new liaisons, proving that absence sometimes did not make the heart grow fonder.

Dekko, to take a
To glance at, or to have a quick look at. This is one of the many phrases that were brought back from India by the British Army in the colonial days in the late nineteenth century. In Hindi *dekho* is the imperative form of the verb *dekhna*, meaning to look at.

Devil – Between the devil and the deep blue sea
Between two evils, in a dilemma with nowhere to turn, to be between two equal dangers. The expression may be of nautical origin, the devil being a seam in the hull of a ship that ran along the waterline. Equally it could have been inspired by the phrase 'to steer or sail between Scylla and Charybdis'. In Homer's *Odyssey* Scylla was a six-headed monster that lived in a cavern overlooking a narrow channel off the coast of Sicily, who seized sailors from every passing ship with each of her six mouths. On the opposite rock Charybdis lived under a huge fig tree from where he sucked in and regorged the sea, forming a treacherous whirlpool. Odysseus sailed between these two perils, losing his ship in the whirlpool and the crew to Scylla. Only he survived by clinging to the fig tree.

A commonly used modern phrase with a mythical ring is 'between a rock and a hard place'.

Devil – Talk of the devil
This proverb, thought to have appeared in the seventeenth century should read, 'Talk of the devil and he's sure to appear', and 'Speak of the devil and he comes in person.' It is superstitious, as with most references to the devil, referred to in the Christian and Jewish faiths as the supreme spirit of evil, tempter of mankind and enemy of God. It means that if you talk about someone, they are

likely to appear unexpectedly. Most people now shorten the phrase to 'Talk of the devil'. The phrase may have come from an old proverb, 'Talk of the Dule and he'll put out his horns'.

Forthwith the devil did appear,
For blame him, and he's always near.
                    Matthew Prior (1664–1721), *Hans Carvel* (1701)

And a more modern and optimistic version is, 'Talk of an angel and you'll hear the fluttering of its wings'.

Diamond – A diamond is forever

In 1939 the South African company De Beers launched an advertising campaign to promote the tradition of diamond engagement rings, using this as a catch line. It was created by copywriter BJ Kidd from the NW Ayer agency in Chicago, perhaps inspired by a line in Anita Loos's novel *Gentlemen Prefer Blondes* (1925; filmed in 1953): 'Kissing your hand may make you feel very, very good, but a diamond and sapphire bracelet lasts forever.' Ian Fleming put a new twist on the phrase in the title of his 1956 James Bond novel, *Diamonds are Forever*. The theme tune of the film, memorably sung by Shirley Bassey, has helped to perpetuate the phrase.

In fact diamonds are not forever, as they consist of pure carbon and will burn at extremely high temperatures.

Diamond – Diamond of the first water

An especially fine diamond, one of the greatest value for its size. The degree of brilliance or lustre of a diamond is called its water; and in the seventeenth century diamonds were classified as first water, second water and so on, the highest-quality gems being of the first water, that is, as pure as clear, limpid stream water. This method of grading died out before 1850, but the phrase remained in common usage. Hence 'of the first water' denotes the finest, or an extreme of some kind surpassing all others, whether good or bad; for instance, an 'artist of the first water' or a 'thief of the first water' or a 'gaffe of the first water'.

Did she fall or was she pushed?

Originally this phrase was used to ask, flippantly, how a young girl had lost her virginity. In 1908 the phrase was used in a different context in the news about the mysterious death of a certain Violet Charlesworth, whose body was found on the beach at the base of the cliffs at Beachy Head, and Thorne Smith wrote a comic novel *Did She Fall* in 1936. It is now used by headline writers about women who lose their jobs in dramatic circumstances.

Dig for victory

Food shortages in the early days of the Second World War in 1939 prompted the Ministry of Agriculture to encourage people to 'grow their own'. Only a month after the outbreak of war, on 4 October the Minister, Sir Reginald Dorman-Smith, said in a radio broadcast:

> Let's get going. Let 'Dig for Victory' be the motto of everyone with a garden and of every able-bodied man and woman capable of digging an allotment in their spare time.

Within two years the number of allotments in Britain had doubled, and 'rearing your own' became popular – especially pig keeping, with nearly 7,000 Pig Clubs in existence by the end of the war.

DINKY (Double Income, No Kids)

This phrase of the 1980s, better known by its acronym DINKY, refers to a couple with well-paid jobs and no offspring to support. It was one of a variety of new terms created in New York during the high-spending, high-earning early years of the 1980s. As with most Americanisms, these newly invented words travelled to Britain to describe various social sub-groups and relationships. YUPPIE means 'young upwardly (or urban) mobile professional person', then the craze really caught on and in 1986 NIMBY was born, which means 'not in my back yard', referring to folk who did not want building development to take place which might spoil their view or their way of life. Today we have YETTIES, to describe those computer nerds who are 'young, entrepreneurial, technology-based'.

Divine Right of Kings, the

This is the hypothesis that kings reign by decree of God, notwithstanding the will of the people. This phrase was much used in the seventeenth century on account of the posturings of the Stuart kings. The idea that monarchs were answerable to God alone arose from the example of patriarchal rule set in the Old Testament. Monarchy based on primogeniture was held to be divinely anointed, and unquestioning obedience could therefore be demanded from the people. The theory was expounded in full by James I (1566–1635) in his True Law of Free Monarchies (1598) and Sir Robert Filmer's *Patriarcha* (1642, published 1680). Divine Right was suspended in Britain by Oliver Cromwell and his son Richard between 1649 and 1660. The phrase, however, remained in circulation and appears later from an early feminist voice.

> The divine right of husbands, like the divine right of kings, may, it is hoped, in this enlightened age, be contested without danger.
> Mary Wollstonecraft (1759–97),
> *A Vindication of the Rights of Woman* (1792)

Dog – A dog in a manger

A mean-spirited person who will not use something he has that is wanted by another, while not allowing the other to use it, or more

66

simply, someone who prevents another enjoying himself. The allusion is to Aesop's fable written in about 600 BC, of a dog that made his bed in a manger of hay. When an ox disturbed him he snarled and drove the ox away. He would not allow the ox to come near to eat the hay, but would not eat it himself. This story also suggests the wise advice of the old German expression 'Let sleeping dogs lie'.

Dog – A dog is for life not just for Christmas

An advertising slogan from the National Canine Defence League, probably from the 1980s, to promote the protection from cruelty of dogs given as Christmas gifts. This resilient phrase can be reworked in many convoluted ways such as 'A turkey is not just for Christmas, it's for Boxing Day, the day after, and the day after . . .', and from the *Independent* (1 February 1997), 'A Scottish parliament is not just for Christmas, it's for life'.

Dog – Every dog has its day

This is a commonly used phrase that seems to have appeared first in English in the writings of R Taverner in 1539 and subsequently in those of Shakespeare:

> Let Hercules himself do what he may,
> The cat will mew, and dog will have his day.

> *Hamlet* (1600)

It means that one may be enjoying good luck or success right now, but remember there's always a queue, so make way for the next person (see **Flavour of the month**, q.v.). This sentiment has been expressed for thousands of years. Rupert Brooke (1887–1915) gives the dog and his day a sentimental word in his poem, 'The Little Dog's Day'. The Latin proverb reads *Hodie mihi – cras tibi*, 'Today to me, tomorrow to thee'. And another ancient old wives' tale states that 'Fortune visits every man once, she favours me now, but she will favour you in your turn'.

Thus every dog at last will have his day –
He who this morning smiled, at night may sorrow,
The grub today's a butterfly tomorrow.

Peter Pindar (1738–1819), *Odes to Condolence*

Dog – The black dog has walked all over him

The metaphorical 'black dog' has various personalities. To be
walked over or to be cursed by the 'black dog' means to be suffering
from mental depression. Horace wrote that to see a black dog with
its pups was a bad omen, and the devil has been frequently
symbolized by a black dog. However, the phrase 'black dog' is
eighteenth-century slang for a counterfeit silver coin made of
washed pewter. Even then 'black' when applied to ill-begotten
money was a familiar term. There is another phrase, 'to blush like
a black dog', which means not to blush at all.

Dog – The dog days of summer

Very hot and oppressive summer days. The Romans called the
hottest weeks of the summer *caniculares dies*, not because dogs are
thought to go mad in the heat, although Noël Coward did write
in 1932, that 'Mad dogs and Englishmen go out in the midday sun'.
The theory was that the Dog Star, Sirius, the brightest star in the
firmament, rises with the sun. It is an ancient belief that the
combined heat of Sirius and the sun produced the stifling weather
of the dog days, from about 3 July to 11 August. The film *Dog Day
Afternoon* (1975) by Sidney Lumet, starring Al Pacino, is set on a
day during these weeks and tells a story of two incompetent bank
robbers, a tragi-comic tale based on a true newspaper story.

Dog – The hair of the dog that bit you

This phrase refers to a remedy usually administered to someone
with a hangover, after an overindulgence of alcohol the night
before. The theory is that the very thing that causes the malady is
the best cure or means of relief, so another drink in the morning
is considered by some the best pick-me-up, or by others a recipe to
make one feel worse, not better. The general principle that 'like
cures like' comes from Roman times, expressed in Latin as *similia
similibus curantura*. The peculiar 'hair of the dog' phrase perhaps

originated in the sixteenth century when if one was bitten by a mad dog, probably suffering from rabies, it was accepted medical practice to dress the wound with the burnt hair of the dog, as an antidote. Amazingly this cure was recommended for dog bites for about two hundred years until its efficacy was brought into question.

Dog – To see a man about a dog

This is a very shifty turn of phrase and suggests a cover-up. It is the excuse offered if one wishes to be discreet and avoid giving the true reason for leaving the room, the meeting or whatever social gathering. The phrase is often used as a euphemism for some unmentionable activity such as going to the lavatory or, worse, going to do something or meet someone one shouldn't. The phrase refers to betting on dog racing.

Do-it-yourself

A phrase that took hold after the Second World War during the boom in house ownership and the natural desire to carry out repairs and improvements cheaply. The phrase, commonly known by the mnemonic DIY, is the hobby if not obsession of the amateur builder, plumber or electrician. Nowadays householders are inspired by the 'do-it-yourself' television programmes such as the BBC's phenomenally popular *Changing Rooms*. The phrase is also used more widely to describe many other forms of self-help – including, jokingly, 'DIY brain surgery'.

Dragon's teeth, to sow

To stir up trouble, strife or war, to foster disagreement, or perhaps to act with the intention of putting an end to conflict, but to succeed only in starting it. The Philistines are supposed to have sown dragon's teeth when they captured Samson, bound him and put out his eyes. Ethelred II did the same in 1002 when he ordered the massacre of the Danes on St Brice's Day, which started such fierce reprisals that he was eventually forced to flee, as did the Germans when they took Alsace-Lorraine from France in 1871. The reference is to the Greek myth of Cadmus. Cadmus was supposed to have introduced the alphabet to Greece and according to legend he killed the dragon that guarded the fountain of Dirce, in Boeotia, and sowed its teeth. From these sprang up a horde of warriors intent on killing him. On Athene's advice Cadmus threw a precious stone among them. The warriors set upon each other in the struggle to retrieve the stone until only five remained alive, and with Cadmus they founded Thebes. The teeth which Cadmus did not sow came into the hands of Aetes, King of Colchis, and one of the tasks he gave the hero Jason was to sow them and slay the armed warriors that rose from them.

Drunk as a lord, as

This simile must have first been observed in the eighteenth century when the consumption of alcohol was something well-bred gentlemen liked to boast about. There was a certain amount of pride in the amount of wine or port that could be consumed in one session. Indeed, gin was safer to drink than water at the time, and gout was a common affliction among the gentry.

Dust, to bite the dust

To fall down dead, alluding to falling off a horse. This expression derives from Wild West stories of violence and desperadoes, from the unstable western frontier in nineteenth-century America, before orderly settlements were established. It was in common use during the Second World

War, especially in the RAF. The phrase is now often heard as a chant to the tune of the song by Queen of the same name, in the form 'Another one bites the dust', when one contestant beats another – especially by the live audience for the television contest *Gladiators*.

Easy as pie, as
Making a pie is not easy and this expression must apply to the eating of it. An easy task can also be described as a 'piece of cake' which is also easy to obtain and eat, as opposed to baking it. It could also refer to the Greek letter pi or P, which stands for the number 3.14 and forms part of a number of mathematical formulas – though not 'easy', pi does simplify the calculations.

Elephant and Castle
This is not only a district in south-east London, but also the sign of a public house at Newington Butts, the name of an Underground station and a pink shopping centre on a very busy roundabout in that area. A common sight in ancient times were the war elephants that were used to transport archers and armed knights who travelled in 'castles' (howdahs) mounted on the animals' backs. Another popular derivation is that the name is a corruption of the disparaging name, 'Infanta de Castile', referring to Eleanor of Castile, young wife of Edward I (1239–1307), who, incidentally, was known as 'Longshanks' because of his tall stature. The Elephant and Castle motif is used as the crest of the Cutlers Company, which traded extensively in ivory.

England expects every man to do his duty
Admiral Lord Nelson's famous signal to his fleet before the Battle of Trafalgar in 1805. The intended signal was 'England confides every man to do his duty', but much to the signalman's consternation, the word 'confide' was not included in the signal

book, so he sought permission to substitute the word 'expects', which meant that he did not have to hoist seven flags, one for each letter of the word 'confide'. The original meaning of the word 'confide' is to entrust knowledge of one's private affairs, so Lord Nelson meant to put his trust in his men to do their duty in his plan of battle. The sentiment of this slogan was later revived in many a Victorian bedroom, in a call to reluctant or shy wives, to be brave, do their patriotic duty and 'lie back and think of England'.

English disease, the
The poor old English have been blamed for many complaints and *malaises* over the years. Since Columbus's time the French have described syphilis as the English disease, and the English retort to this insult was to call it the French disease. The French term for the onset of menstruation is *les Anglais sont arrivés*. Later, after the Industrial Revolution the damp English climate combined with sooty smog meant that bronchitis was prevalent, and it became known as the English disease all over the world. Now some social ailments tend to be described as English, including class differences, poor industrial relations and economic stagnation. In the 1950s and 1960s under the all-powerful trade unions, industrial strikes were widely known as the English disease. More recently, football hooliganism, both at home and abroad, has been dubbed the English disease.

Every cloud has a silver lining
In every situation, no matter how seemingly hopeless and gloomy, there is always some redeeming brightness to be found if one takes the trouble to look for it – while there's life there's hope. This

optimistic guidance to look on the bright side has been around since Roman times (although one Latin proverb reads, 'After the sun, the clouds'). In a similar sixteenth-century proverb it all depends whose side you are on: 'The death of wolves is the safety of sheep' (see **Wind**, q.v.) – good news for sheep, bad news for wolves. In Milton's *Comus* (1634), the lady lost in the wood resolves not to give up hope, and says,

Was I deceived or did a sable cloud
Turn forth her silver lining on the night?
I did not err: there does a sable cloud
Turn forth her silver lining on the night.

And, not forgetting the cynic, Noël Coward included these lines in his 1952 song, 'There Are Bad Times Just Around the Corner':

There are dark clouds hurtling through the sky,
And it's no good whining
About a silver lining,
For we know from experience that they won't roll by.

Every picture tells a story
This is thought to be a modern proverb, although Charlotte Brontë alludes to it in *Jane Eyre* (1847):

The letter press . . . I cared little for . . . Each picture told a story.

In 1904 the phrase was used with a picture of a man bent over, clutching his back in pain to advertise Doan's Backache Kidney Pills. The pop singer Rod Stewart released an album with this title in the 1970s. The catchphrase has been adapted for many other situations, and in a development of the idea the well-used phrase 'One picture is worth a thousand words' rings true for some, although others might say, 'Pictures are the books of the unlearned' (1662; found in *Tilley's Dictionary of Proverbs*, 1950).

Everything in the garden is lovely
A colloquial phrase to say, all's well, there's not a worry in the world. The expression comes from George Le Brunn and JP

73

Harrington's song 'Everything in the garden's lovely' of 1898, made popular by Marie Lloyd (1870–1922). Gardens have symbolized paradise since biblical times and the Garden of Eden in which Adam was placed by God (Genesis 2:15). The name is Hebrew in origin and means 'place of pleasure', and the Garden of Eden was traditionally said to be situated in Mesopotamia. Fertile land tends to be referred to as a garden, such as Kent, the Garden of England; Italy is known as the Garden of Europe and Sicily is the Garden of Italy. In the 1920s the highly suggestive song 'Come Into the Garden, Maud' (a setting of Tennyson's poem of 1855) had something entirely different in mind. The phrase is still used today, and in these more cynical times, with an ironic tone, to indicate that perhaps everything in the garden is not quite as lovely as it could be.

Exception that proves the rule, the
This strange phrase has been in use since the seventeenth century. It seems to mean the very opposite of what it is actually trying to say, and it is often misused to mean that a particular exception proves the correctness of a rule, rather than putting it to the test. However, the word 'prove' here is used in its meaning to 'test'. So the phrase makes more sense, that an exception tests the truth of a rule. Alternatively perhaps 'prove' is used in the context of baking, as dough is left to 'prove' or rise before it is baked, and it might be meant that the exception must 'rise' to meet the demands of the rule in question. Because of the general confusion over the years, this proverb has embraced the additional meaning 'no rule is so general that it cannot embrace some exception'.

Eye for an eye, a tooth for a tooth, an
Punishment equal to the crime, retaliation in kind or simply getting even. The justification for this form of retribution comes from the Old Testament.

Eye for eye, tooth for tooth, hand for hand, foot for foot.

Exodus 21:24

Jesus referred to these words in the New Testament and put his own spin on their message, creating another commonly used expression, 'to turn the other cheek':

> Ye have heard that it hath been said, An eye for an eye, and a tooth for a tooth: But I say unto you, That ye resist not evil: but whosoever shall smite thee on thy right cheek, turn to him the other also.

Matthew 5:39–9

Face that launched a thousand ships, the

The face is that of the legendary beauty, Helen of Troy, and the ships were the Greek fleet, which sailed for Troy to avenge the King of Sparta. In Greek legend Helen was the daughter of Zeus and Leda, and wife of Menelaus, King of Sparta. She eloped with Paris, Prince of Troy, and the angry Menelaus sent a thousand ships to lay siege to the city of Troy. The fabled Helen is now an archetype of female beauty.

The phrase itself was first written by Christopher Marlowe (1564–93):

> Was this the face that launched a thousand ships,
> And burned the topless towers of Ilium?

Doctor Faustus (1604)

The story of Helen of Troy is father to other words of wisdom such as 'Beware Greeks bearing gifts', or 'I fear Greeks even when they offer gifts' (Virgil, *Aeneid*, 1 BC). After the ten-year siege of the city of Troy heroes had been slain on both sides, Achilles the Brave and Ajax the Proud lay dead, and the Trojan Paris was dead too. Only Helen remained as lovely as ever, a precious prize locked in Troy. One of the Greek survivors, Odysseus, devised an ingenious plan to invade the city by hiding all his men in a wooden horse, which the Trojans mistakenly took to be a tribute from their beaten enemy. Finally the victorious Greeks escorted Helen, ever since known as Helen of Troy, back to Greece and the house of King Menelaus.

Famous for fifteen minutes, to be

Meaning to have short-lived fame, of the type that is now quite possible in the modern, media-obsessed age. This expression comes from the celebrated words in a catalogue for an exhibition of Andy Warhol's work in Stockholm in 1968. Pop artist Warhol (1928–87) was concerned, amongst other subjects, with the nature of celebrity and he wrote, 'In the future everyone will be world famous for fifteen minutes.' Andy Warhol was described by Gore Vidal as the only genius he knew with an IQ of 60. The phrase struck a chord and can now be shortened to, 'He's had his fifteen minutes'. *Famous for Fifteen Minutes* was the title of a series of 'Where are they now?' programmes lasting fifteen minutes on BBC Radio 4 from 1990, which featured faded 'movers and shakers' who were recalled from obscurity to account for their decline.

Fast lane, to live life in the

This is a metaphor meaning to live dangerously, indulgently and expensively, and dates from the late 1970s, probably coined by newspaper headline writers. The fast lane is the outer lane of a motorway where traffic overtakes or travels at high speed. It is naturally associated with fast cars, and in an advertisement for Toshiba computers in 1989 the strapline read, 'Jackie Stewart lives life in the fast lane – like any businessman really'. The opposite metaphor, of course, is to be stranded on the hard shoulder of life.

Feather in one's cap, a

A personal achievement or honour to be proud of. The feather is a proud and visible emblem of victory and the gesture of putting a feather in your hat is almost universal in one form or another. The allusion is to the ancient custom, widespread in Asia, among American Indians and throughout Europe of adding a feather to the headgear to mark each enemy killed. Indeed, today's sportsman who kills his first woodcock puts a feather from the bird in his hat. At one time in Hungary the only person who could wear a feather was someone who had killed a Turk. When General Charles Gordon (1833–85), known as Chinese Gordon, quelled the Taiping rebellion in 1864 he was honoured by the Chinese government with the 'yellow jacket and peacock's feather'.

Field day, to have a field day

A figurative expression for a day or occasion or time of particular excitement, often a day away from the usual routine. The phrase is in fact a military term for a day when troops have manoeuvres, exercises or reviews – out in the field. (The military refer to the area or sphere of operations as 'the field'.) In the American Navy it is a day devoted to cleaning ship in preparation for inspection. School children enjoy field trips on which they travel away from school, particularly to study geography.

Fine fettle, in

To be in good order or condition – 'fettle' is an old word meaning condition, order or shape. Nowadays, it rarely appears on its own, being usually heard in the alliterative phrase. In the past we might have heard 'good fettle' or 'bad fettle', and in *John Barleycorn* by Jack London, published in 1913:

> Those fifty-one days of fine sailing and intense sobriety had put me in splendid fettle.

The origin of the word fettle is somewhat obscure. It probably comes from the Old English *fetel* for a belt, so fettle first meant to gird oneself up, as for a heavy task. It is related to the German *Fessel* for a chain or band, but not to the similar 'fetter', which actually comes from the same root as 'foot'. In English the word was most typically used as a verb meaning to put things in order, tidy up, arrange, or prepare. In Anne Brontë's *Agnes Grey* (1847), in the Yorkshire dialect speech of a servant:

But next day, afore I'd gotten fettled up – for indeed, Miss, I'd no heart to sweeping an' fettling, an' washing pots; so I sat me down i' th' muck – who should come in but Maister Weston.

In northern English dialects it is sometimes used in the sense of making or repairing something. In Australia, a 'fettler' is a railway maintenance worker. It is also used in some manufacturing trades – in metal casting and pottery it describes the process of knocking the rough edges off a piece.

Fingerlickin' good, It's

An enduring advertising slogan for Kentucky Fried Chicken, first used by the company in 1952. Many songs used the expression in the 1960s and 1970s, and Lonnie Smith had a hit with his album, *Fingerlickin' Good Soul Organ* in 1968. The description 'fingerlicking' is probably jargon used by Southern American black jazz musicians, most likely guitarists; however, the *OED* records the phrase as early as 1860.

Flavour of the month

A generic American advertising phrase of the mid-1940s attempting to persuade shoppers to buy a new flavour of ice cream each month and not just stick to their usual choice. Since then it has been used to describe any short-lived fashion, craze or person, popularly referred to as being 'flavoursome', and then quickly dropped after a period of being in demand.
The metaphorical possibilities of the word 'ambush' are currently catching on in several areas of activity in the USA, making it the lexical flavour of the month in American English.

Flynn – To be in like Flynn

A ribald phrase that means to take instant advantage of any chance that might be up for grabs. More particularly it means not to miss an opportunity of seducing a woman. Flynn of the phrase is the Tasmanian-born film star, Errol Flynn (1909–59), who led one of Hollywood's most adventurous lives, both on and off screen. His swashbuckling lifestyle enthralled millions of fans for twenty years, but it got the better of him by the end of his life. The phrase was widely used in the Second World War. It is said that Flynn himself was not flattered by it, despite his own tendency to boast about his sexual conquests.

Foot – To put one's foot in it

To make an inadvertent blunder, particularly to say the wrong thing and get yourself into 'deep doo-doo'. To make a *faux pas*, which literally means a false step. From the Irish 'bull', 'Every time I open my mouth I put my foot in it'. Bull is an old fashioned word for a verbal blunder, and the Irish seem to have been associated with this trait. Bull may have been named after the Irish Lawyer, Obadiah Bull, who worked in London in the fifteenth century and was notorious for his mistakes. Another explanation is that it comes from the contradiction in Papal Bulls in which the Pope humbly styles himself 'servant of servants', while asserting complete authority. Since the 1970s the habit of making verbal *faux pas* has been called 'foot-in-mouth disease' following a serious outbreak of foot-and-mouth disease, a contagious viral disease of cattle, sheep, goats and pigs. Prince Philip, with something of a reputation for saying the wrong thing at the wrong time, calls the affliction, 'dentopedalogy'.

Forty winks, to take

A colloquial term for a short nap or a doze. Quite why shutting one eye forty times has come to mean a quick snooze is unclear, but it could have something to do with the fact that the number forty appears frequently in the scriptures and used to be thought of as a holy number. Moses was on the Mount for forty days and forty nights, Elijah was fed by ravens for forty days, the rain of the Flood fell forty days and another forty days passed before Noah opened the window of the ark. Christ fasted for forty days and he was seen forty days after his Resurrection. Modern colloquialisms for a quick nap include a 'zizz', 'to catch a few zeds' alluding to the zeds drawn in cartoons indicating that the character is asleep, the zeds replicating the sound of their breathing. Busy people and politicians who work late into the night maintain their faculties by taking 'a power nap'.

Fourth dimension, the
The three known dimensions are length, breadth and height. The fourth dimension, or space–time continuum, is defined as reality. In the fourth dimension the infinite number of solids in the universe react with each other through time and energy. As a mathematical concept a hypothetical fourth dimension is related to the recognized three dimensions and exists in parallel with their relation with each other. In 1921 Albert Einstein (1879–1955) introduced time as the fourth dimension in his Theory of Relativity. And here we get very New Age; in the time domain, the fourth dimension continues the movement of the third dimension (the past) to form a wave, constituting fractally the space-time continuum. Not surprisingly, the expression is sometimes used to describe that which is beyond the limits of normal experience.

French leave, to take
This is leave of absence without permission or without announcing one's departure, particularly referring to soldiers taking unauthorized leave. Rivalry between the British and the French has lasted for hundreds of years and this phrase alludes to the eighteenth-century French custom of leaving without saying goodbye to one's host, if one had a pressing engagement, in order not to disrupt the party, or to disconcert the host. This was naturally interpreted by the British as extremely bad manners. Not to be outdone, the French later associated the habit with the English, however. Hence their equivalent for French leave is *s'en aller à l'anglaise*. An earlier

French insult was the sixteenth-century slang for a creditor, which was *un Anglais*. Even Shakespeare got in on the act:

> France is a dog hole.
>
> *All's Well That Ends Well*

Friend – A friend in need is a friend indeed

This is a Latin proverb from the sayings of Ennius (239–169 BC) and reads *Amicus certus in re incerta cernitur* – 'a sure friend is made known when (one is) in difficulty'. Whatever the truth of this wise old saying there have been numerous plays on its words over the centuries as it often transpires that 'a friend in need, is a pest indeed'. Or according to Kin Hubbard, 'A friend that ain't in need is a friend indeed'. And this witticism was seen on an old postcard: 'A friend in need is a friend indeed, but who needs a friend in need?'

Frying pan – To jump out of the frying pan into the fire

To leap from one bad predicament to another which is as bad or even worse. In short, to go from bad to worse. Most languages have an equivalent phrase, and the French have *tomber de la poêle dans le feu/la braise*, from which the English is probably translated. The Greeks have, 'out of the smoke into the flame'; the Italians and Portuguese, 'to fall from the frying pan into the coals'; and the Gaelic is, 'out of the cauldron into the fire'. The phrase can be traced back to about 1530 when, in the course of a religious argument, Sir Thomas More, Henry VIII's Lord Chancellor and author of *Utopia*, accused William Tyndale, translator of the Bible into English, that he 'featly conuayed himself out of the frying panne fayre into the fyre'. Unfortunately both men met a gruesome end. Sir Thomas More was hanged as a traitor in 1535 for not approving of the marriage between Henry VIII and Anne Boleyn, and Tyndale was publicly strangled and burned as a heretic in 1536.

Full Monty, the
Everything, the lot, the complete works. Said of anything done to the utmost or fullest degree. The origin of the expression is uncertain. It may derive from the 'full amount', or the Spanish card game *monte* (literally mountain or heap of cards), or it may refer to the full three-piece Sunday Best suit from the men's outfitters Montagu Burton. The full English breakfast – bacon, eggs, sausage, black pudding, beans, fried bread – that is, the works – was popularly known as the 'Full Monty' after the Second World War because Field Marshal Sir Bernard Montgomery, nicknamed 'Monty' (1887–1976), was said to have started every day with a full English breakfast when campaigning in North Africa. The British phrase became familiar generally in the English-speaking world from the 1997 film *The Full Monty*, directed by Peter Cattaneo, about a group of unemployed factory workers from Sheffield who raise money by staging a strip act at a local club.

Full tilt, at full tilt
At full speed or full force. The expression probably originated in the fourteenth century when 'tilting at the quintain' was a popular sport among medieval knights. A dummy head, often representing a Turk or Saracen, was fastened to rotate around an upright stake fixed in the ground. At full speed, the knight on horseback tilted towards the head with his lance and if he failed to strike it in the

right place it would spin round and strike him in the back before he could get clear. Londoners used to tilt from boats, the quintain being fixed to a mast erected in the Thames. Tilting at the quintain remained a rustic sport especially popular at wedding celebrations until the mid-seventeenth century. The similar phrase 'to tilt at windmills' has a rather different meaning, namely, to stand up to fanciful enemies. The reference is to the crazed knight Don Quixote (in Cervantes's novel, *Don Quixote*, 1605) who imagined the windmills to be giants and advanced to attack. The gentle, if mad, knight with his dreams of chivalry has given his name to the English language in the adjective 'quixotic', used to describe a romantic idealist with wildly unrealistic ideas of honour and doing good.

Game as Ned Kelly, as

To possess fighting spirit or energy for some dynamic activity, or in modern parlance, 'up for it'. The phrase refers to the infamous Australian desperado, bushranger and folk hero Ned Kelly (1855–80), who after legendary exploits including robbery and murder, was captured with his brother Dan wearing roughly made suits of armour, after a battle with the police, and hanged at Melbourne. True to form, his last words were 'Such is life'.

Garbage in garbage out

A term from typesetting and computing known by 1964 and sometimes abbreviated to GIGO, meaning that if you put incorrect data into a computer, however much you embellish it, what comes out will be meaningless and useless. In the wider sense it conveys the simple idea that you get back what you put in, reflected in the sixteenth-century proverb, 'There comes nothing out of a sack but what was in it.' It could never be argued that this phrase came from Roman times, but there is a charming Latin translation, *Purgamentum init, exit purgamentum*.

Genghis Khan – Somewhere to the right of Genghis Khan

This cliché describes someone whose views are extremely right wing. Genghis Khan (1162–1227) was the founder of the Moghul Empire. His original name was Temujin and he was given the title 'Genghis Khan', which literally means 'King of the Ocean'. He acquired a fighting force of some 20,000 tribesmen and through sheer brutality and relentless raping and pillaging, overcame the Mongolian and Tartar peoples, and by 1206 he was acknowledged overlord of Mongolia. Eventually his empire extended from China to the Adriatic Sea and his son reached the walls of Budapest.

Arthur Scargill, president of the National Union of Mineworkers said in 1982, 'Of course, in those days, the union leaders were well to the right of Genghis Khan.'

Giddy goat, to act the

To fool around. Goats are noted for their unpredictable behaviour. In the literal sense giddy means insane or to be 'possessed by a god'. In Latin goat is *caper* and goats are noted for their frivolous and frisky nature. To cut a caper means to skip or leap about playfully.

Go – To boldly go where no man has gone before

A claim made in part of the title sequence to the popular TV space adventure series, *Star Trek* (see **Beam me up Scotty**, q.v.). The mission of the Starship *Enterprise* to explore outer space still attracts millions of regular viewers all over the world. The expressed aim 'to boldly go' became possibly the most celebrated split infinitive of the twentieth century. Its wide use, often in parody, has meant that we all know how to break this particular rule of English grammar.

Go for it!

A very popular encouragement in wide use during the 1980s. It may come from the keep-fit exercise of aerobics, which was all the rage at the time. In Jane Fonda's book (1981) and video (1983) she exhorted, 'Go for the burn, go for it!' The burn is the sensation felt in the muscles during the workout. President Reagan said, 'America, go for it', in 1985, of tax reform. Victor Kiam, American razor entrepreneur, entitled his 1986 memoirs, *Going For It*. British Airways coined, 'Go for it, America' to persuade Americans to ignore current terrorist threats and visit Europe. Media mogul and, coincidentally, Jane Fonda's husband, Ted Turner, was called a 'Go-for-it guy'. 'To go for it' was also a vulgar Australian term from the mid-1920s meaning 'extremely eager for sexual intercourse'.

Go to work on an egg
The British Egg Marketing Board launched a high-profile advertising campaign in 1957 with this catch-line. Fay Weldon (1932–), later well known as a novelist and television playwright, was at the time a copywriter at the Mather & Crowther agency. She is modest about the authorship of the line, saying, 'It is perfectly possible that I put those particular six words together in that particular order, but I would not swear to it.'

Goal posts, to move the
A colloquial expression derived from football meaning to change the agreed conditions or rules for carrying out a plan, quite often in business when clients change their minds after work on a project has already begun. The implication is that 'to move the goal posts' involves some attempt to gain unfair advantage over an opponent, or generally to upset him.

Seen in the *Guardian*, 1 March 1989, about the imposition of a new railway line in Kent:

The people of Kent vote solidly for the Conservative Party . . . Why are these people, therefore, trying to move the goalposts after the football match has started?

Gone for a Burton

Absent, missing or lost, dead or presumed dead. The expression was common among service personnel in the Second World War. There are several theories as to its origin. One possibility is that it refers to the training of RAF wireless operators in a Blackpool Burton's clothing store. Those who failed their test were said to have 'gone for a Burton' and it was subsequently applied to those who were killed. Another popular theory is that the town of Burton is famous for its beer, and that to have 'Gone for a Burton' is a euphemism to explain someone's absence because they have gone for a beer. Extending this usage, the sea is known as 'the drink', so when sailors or airmen were killed at or over the sea, other servicemen referred to them, with a certain amount of black humour, as 'gone for a Burton'.

Gone with the wind

A wistful saying to describe events that have occurred, but have left no trace. The phrase comes from Ernest Dowson's poem 'Non Sum Qualis Eram', also known as 'Cynara' (1896):

> I have forgot much, Cynara! Gone with the wind,
> Flung roses, roses, riotously, with the throng.

It is the title of one of America's most widely read novels, written by Margaret Mitchell, published in 1936, and filmed by David O Selznick in 1939. The phrase refers to the Southern United States before the American Civil War (1861–5). The on-screen prologue of the film reads:

> There was a land of Cavaliers and Cotton Fields called the Old South. Here in this patrician world the Age of Chivalry took its last bows. Here was the last ever seen of the Knights and their Ladies fair, of Master and Slave. Look for it only in books, for its is no more than a dream remembered, a Civilization gone with the wind . . .

The story concerns an egotistical Southern girl, played by

Vivien Leigh, who survives the Civil War, but loses the only man she cares for.

Gordon Bennett
A mild oath, similar to, 'Oh God'. In fact, 'Gawd' and St Bennett (or Benet) have been put forward as the pair behind this expletive; St Benet is short for St Benedict. Shakespeare has in *Twelfth Night* (1600) 'the bells of St Bennet' possibly from the church, St Bennet Hithe, Paul's Wharf, opposite the Globe theatre. However, it seems more likely that the said Gordon Bennett was James Gordon Bennett (1841–1918), the editor-in-chief of the *New York Herald*, who was responsible for sending Henry Morton Stanley to find Dr David Livingstone in Africa. Extravagant and extrovert, he gave his name to a motor race held in France in the 1900s where he resided after a scandal in America. Such was his profile in society that there is a street in Paris named Avenue Gordon-Bennett. In English the similarity between Gordon and Gawd must have struck a chord and this expletive, which is still used today, was born. At the turn of the nineteenth century people shied away from blasphemy in the name of God, so 'Gorblimey' evolved instead of 'God blind me', and WC Fields used to cry out, 'Godfrey Daniel!' in place of 'God damn you!', but the identity of Godfrey Daniel can only be guessed at.

Great balls of fire!
A famous hit song for Jerry Lee Lewis in 1957 written by Jack Hammer and Otis Blackwell. It was first heard in public as a cry of surprise in the 1939 film **Gone With the Wind** (q.v.)and is presumably derived from the Deep South of America.

Green-eyed monster, the
To be jealous of or covet someone's beauty, achievements, attainment or wealth. The simile is commonly known as to be 'green with envy'. The monster was identified by Shakespeare in *Othello* (1602–4):

> IAGO: O! beware, my lord, of jealousy;
> It is the green ey'd monster which doth mock
> The meat it feeds on.

A greenish complexion was formerly held to be indicative of jealousy, not queasiness which is more likely, and it has been observed that all cats with green eyes 'mock the meat they feed on', so jealousy taunts its victim by both loving and hating it. However, to accuse someone of having 'green in their eye' is to suggest that they are inexperienced or easily bamboozled, as in 'greenhorn', which means to be a novice, green behind the ears, like the green horns of a young horned animal.

And Shakespeare again, in *Antony and Cleopatra* (1606–7):

> My salad days,
> When I was green in judgment . . .

Green wellie-brigade, the

A posse of Sloane Rangers, or those members of the upper classes who practise the country pursuits of hunting, shooting and fishing. Green Wellington boots as typically worn by country folk take their name from Arthur Wellesley, first Duke of Wellington (1769–1852). The term Sloane Rangers was coined by style commentator Peter York in *Harper's and Queen* in the 1970s, in a pun combining Sloane Street or Sloane Square, London habitats of these types, with 'Lone Ranger', from the popular television cowboy series of the 1960s. Sloane Rangers were also commonly known as 'Headscarf Harriets', and their men as 'Hooray Henrys', shortened to 'Hoorays'.

Half cock, to go off at

To be unsuccessful at doing something due to inadequate preparation, or being in too much of a hurry, reminiscent of the phrase 'more haste less speed', or simply 'be prepared'. This is probably an eighteenth-century expression when a musket which was cocked half-way had the hammer set in the safety position, to prevent accidental discharge. However, the mechanisms were sometimes faulty and the gun would fire, much to the surprise of the musketeer. It is thought that the term is simply related to hunting and shooting, though modern guns cannot in fact 'go off' when they are half cocked. However, a hunter, carried away in the thrill of the chase and sighting his quarry, may raise the gun and press the trigger while still at half cock, so the gun does not fire.

Hanged, drawn and quartered
The correct order for this form of torturous capital punishment was that the victim was 'drawn, hanged, drawn, beheaded and quartered'. The crime that merited this sort of punishment was high treason against crown and country. The guilty were to be drawn to the place of execution on a hurdle or dragged along by horse's tail. Drawn also meant to be disembowelled, and this was added to the punishment in between the hanging stage and the quartering stage. Thus the sentence passed on the Scottish patriot Sir William Wallace in August 1305 was that he should be drawn from the Palace of Westminster to the Tower of London, then hanged until nearly dead, disembowelled, then beheaded and finally quartered. His quarters were gibbeted at Newcastle, Berwick, Stirling and Perth.

Happiness is egg shaped
Still working on the egg account, Fay Weldon did write the phrase 'Happiness is egg shaped' (see **Go to work on an egg**, q.v.) although she was probably inspired by Charles M Schultz's title for a Peanuts cartoon book in 1962, *Happiness is a warm puppy* ('. . . with an empty bladder' was added by some wag). The advertising and greetings-card worlds were inspired and a host of strap-lines were born, most famously 'Happiness is a cigar called Hamlet' (1970). In typical style songwriters Lennon and McCartney emphasized the dark side when they wrote 'Happiness is a warm gun' (1970). For centuries man has tried to define the essence of this most elusive of sensations. Rousseau (1712–78) said:

Happiness is a good bank account, a good cook, a good digestion.

Samuel Johnson declared in 1766:

Happiness consists in the multiplicity of agreeable consciousness.

And more recently we see:

Happiness is just a state of mind . . . like insanity.

Happy – As happy as Larry

This is another expression that means to be extremely happy, but the question is, 'Who was Larry?' It is believed to be an Australian expression from the late nineteenth century, and Larry may have been the boxer Larry Foley (1847–1917). The word may also relate to 'larrikin', an Australian term for a young hoodlum given to acts of rowdiness. Larrikins were particularly active on the streets in the 1880s and wore distinctive neat and colourful clothing.

Happy – As happy as a sandboy

This means to be very happy or in high spirits. It is a traditional expression from the late nineteenth and early twentieth centuries, when sandboys or men drove their donkeys through the streets selling bags of sand taken from beaches. The sand was used by householders for their gardens, by builders, and by publicans for sanding their floors. The merriness of the sandboys was probably due, in some part, to the temptation of spending their takings in the hostelries to which they delivered the sand.

Hash, to settle someone's

To subdue or silence someone in no uncertain terms, or to sort out a muddle for them. A hash in this case is a jumble, mess or hotch-potch, from the dish of stewed mixed meat, potatoes and other vegetables. To 'make a hash of' means to bungle or make a mess of something. The verb 'settle' is often used to denote an active or somewhat forceful method of resolving a situation. Strictly speaking, to 'settle a score' is to settle accounts, and the phrase can be used to mean to settle financial debts, but it is more likely to be said when taking revenge for an injury or getting even with someone.

Another culinary expression with much the same meaning is to 'cook someone's goose'.

Hat – At the drop of a hat

On signal, instantly, without delay. The expression alludes to the American frontier practice of dropping a hat as a signal for a boxing or wrestling match to begin, usually the only formality observed. Athletics or horse races used to be started by the fast downward sweep of a hat. The expression has come to mean that one will do something with very little encouragement, or without delay. Hence the title of a revue, *At the Drop of a Hat*, starring Michael Flanders and Donald Swann, whose follow-up was entitled *At the Drop of Another Hat* (1963).

There are many sayings including the word 'hat', such as 'hats off to him', 'as black as your hat', 'I'll eat my hat' and many more that probably originated in the days when dress codes and social etiquette were more formal, requiring people in polite society to cover their heads.

Hat – To throw one's hat into the ring

To enter a contest or to become a candidate for office. This expression relates to the old custom of throwing one's hat into the boxing ring as the sign of accepting the pugilist's challenge.

Hatches, matches and despatches

A long-established and charmingly poetic colloquialism for a newspaper's announcements of births, marriages and deaths.

Have a banana

Britain became aware of the joys of bananas in the early 1900s, thanks to the efforts of a certain Roger Ackerley of Elders & Fyffes, banana importers, in 1898. This rhythmic phrase was never an official advertising slogan, but, 'Have a banana', was popularly added to the end of the first line of the song 'Let's All Go Down the Strand' (1904). The composer had not written it in, but it was so successful that the line was later added to the lyrics. Sales of bananas rocketed. Other banana songs soon followed. With undisguised innuendo the song 'Burlington Bertie from Bow' (1914) includes, 'I've had a banana with Lady Diana'. 'Yes, we have no bananas' was allegedly proclaimed by a Greek fruit seller, and in 1923 *Punch* described it as 'the latest catchword'. The suggestive nature of the banana was celebrated again in 1959 with the slogan, 'Unzip a banana'.

Heath Robinson, it's a bit Heath Robinson
A phrase applied to an absurdly complicated mechanical contraption, especially one performing a basically simple action – some fantastic and ingenious apparatus usually with moving parts joined by bits of string and held together with a lick and a promise. The name is that of the highly imaginative William Heath Robinson (1872–1944) whose amusing cartoons of daft inventions, which appeared in *Punch* and elsewhere, captured the public imagination. Heath Robinson's absurd gadgets were seen as a caricature of the age of the machine and the humour often came from the expressions of the solemn onlookers inspecting the machines.

Here's mud in your eye!
A drinking toast, the sentiments of which could be read either way. One interpretation is that it is to wish good fortune, originating in the trenches of the First World War when soldiers would naturally rather mud was thrown in their eye than anything more lethal. Another, somewhat less good-natured, theory comes from horse racing, in which, with one's own horse out in front, it will be kicking mud into the eyes of the slower runners behind.

High jump, for the high jump
English slang for being in big trouble, also known these days as 'deep doo-doo' or 'deep shit'. It usually implies that dismissal or serious punishment are on the cards. The allusion is to the hanging of a convicted criminal, the gallows being 'the high jump', which was the former British judicial method for capital punishment.

Hoist with one's own petard
To be beaten with one's own weapons, or to be caught in one's own trap. The modern equivalent relates to the sport of football, 'to

score an own goal'. Shakespeare puts the petard in context when he has Hamlet say:

> For 'tis the sport to have the engineer
> Hoist with his own petard.

Hamlet (1600)

In 1600 a petard was a newly invented iron device used for blowing up walls, barricades or gates with gunpowder. It was a metal bell-shaped grenade filled with five or six pounds of gunpowder, dug into a trench and set off by a fuse. The devices were often unreliable and went off unexpectedly, and the engineer who fired the petard might be blown up by the explosion. Hence the expression, in which 'hoist' means to be lifted up, is an understated description of being blown up by your own bomb. The name of the device came from the Latin *petare* meaning to break wind, and the phrase is perhaps an ironic comment on the noise of the explosion. The 1979 film *Le Pétomane* starred Leonard Rossiter (1926–84) as Joseph Pujol, the tuneful wind-breaker who gained something of a reputation all over Europe as a musical performer at the end of the nineteenth century.

Hold the mayo

This is one of many urban buzz phrases of the ubiquitous takeaway food and drinks culture of the 1990s. When ordering a sandwich to 'take out', or take away, the order 'hold the mayo' means to serve the burger or sandwich without mayonnaise. The American chain of coffee shops, Starbucks and the like, are spawning a whole new language with buzz phrases such as 'a tall decaff latte with wings', 'a large triple shot cappuccino to fly', or 'wake up and smell the coffee', which means 'get your brain in gear'.

Horse – Don't look a gift horse in the mouth

Do not question the value or something given to you; it is very bad form to inspect a gift for faults or defects, so be grateful for anything received and, as the old saying goes, 'it's the thought that counts'.

This is an old proverb that has probably been in use for hundreds of years. The phrase has been discovered in the writings of St Jerome, one of the Latin Fathers of the fourth century, who identified it as a common proverb. No doubt the phrase alludes to the method of assessing the age of a horse by inspecting the number and condition of its teeth. The proverb also occurs in French, German, Italian, Spanish and other European languages.

Horse – Straight from the horse's mouth
Some knowledge received direct from the highest authority, from the person whose word need not be doubted. The expression comes from horse racing and has to do with the age of the steeds. The only certain way of discovering the age of a horse is by examining its teeth, especially those of the lower jaw. The first permanent horse teeth appear in the centre of the jaw at the age of two and a half. A year later a second pair appears and at between four and five years, the third pair appears. So, no matter what an owner may say about a horse's age, the evidence is there, straight in the horse's mouth.

Hour – at the eleventh hour
Just in the nick of time, at the last moment, before the end of the day. The allusion is to Jesus's parable of the labourers hired to work in the vineyard in which those starting work at the eleventh hour, that is late in the afternoon at about 5 o'clock, were paid the same as those who had 'borne the burden and heat of the day' (Matthew 20:1–16). The armistice ending the First World War came into effect at the eleventh hour of the eleventh day of the eleventh month.

How to win friends and influence people
Self-improvement courses date back to the early 1900s, and this phrase summed up the principle of Dale Carnegie's (1888–1955)

courses aimed at business people in America. In 1936 the phrase caught on with a worldwide audience when it was the title of Carnegie's best-selling book about business psychology. Following Carnegie's lead, Sheperd Mead published a book entitled *How to Succeed in Business Without Really Trying* in 1953, which was made into a musical in 1961 and a film in 1967.

How's your father?

A purely rhetorical question that originated as a humorous catchphrase in the music halls before the First World War. It later came to be a synonym for 'nonsense' or meaningless ritual and it is a useful substitute for a collective noun when no other comes immediately to mind, and sounds a little more imaginative than just the word 'stuff'. After Bernadette Devlin's maiden speech in the House of Commons in 1969, she commented on the ritual, 'All this stand up, sit down, kneel down and how's-your-father was so funny.' More recently, the phrase has acquired a sexual connotation as in, with barely concealed innuendo, 'a bit of how's your father'. Similarly, 'hanky panky' has come to mean covert sexual activity, foolish or inadvisable behaviour; that phrase is derived from the magician's mock Latin 'hocus pocus', possibly a parody of *Hoc est corpus*. The word 'hoax' is thought to derive from 'hocus'.

Hue and cry

A noisy commotion over some spot of bother. Until the beginning of the nineteenth century 'hue and cry' was the old legal term for an official outcry made when calling out for assistance, 'with horn and with voice', in the pursuit of a suspected criminal escaping arrest. The phrase must have been in use since the beginning of the last millennium because the Norman French word *huer* means 'to shout'. Thieves failing to respond to the 'hue and cry' were liable to greater penalties once they were caught, hence the increased clamour, and cry of alarm in the case of the villain.

Humble pie, to eat

To make a humble apology or to submit oneself to a certain degree of humiliation, to climb down from a position one has assumed, to be obliged to take a lower station. Here humble is a play on the word 'umble', the umbles being the offal – the heart, liver and entrails – of an animal, usually the deer, considered a delicacy by some, although most thought them only fit for the servants. When the lord of the manor and his family dined on venison at high table, the huntsman and lower orders of the household took lower seats and partook of the umbles made into a pie. James Russell Lowell observed in 1864:

> Disguise it as you will, flavour it as you will, call it what you will, umble pie is umble pie, and nothing else.

I counted them all out and I counted them all back

During the Falklands War of 1982 Brian Hanrahan, a BBC war correspondent with the naval Task Force sent by Britain to recapture the Falkland Islands from Argentina, spoke these carefully considered words in order to report that no aircraft had been shot down during a mission, and so as not to reveal the military secret of the numbers. The Sea Harriers from HMS *Hermes* had just returned from a bombing raid against Argentinian positions at Port Stanley, the capital of the Falklands. The expression, so reassuring to people listening or watching anxiously 8,000 miles away in Britain, became a catchphrase for a time.

I have seen the future and it works

A widely used catchphrase that caught on immediately after it was first coined by American reformer and journalist Lincoln Steffans

(1879–1955), who was inspired by a visit to the Soviet Union and his meeting with Lenin in 1919. The phrase has been reworked by the Orange mobile-telephone company for its slogan 'The future is Orange'.

I'll have what she's having

A line from the 1989 film *When Harry met Sally*, whose central theme is whether a man and a woman can enjoy friendship without sex. The character played by Meg Ryan fakes an orgasm in a coffee bar. Her performance is so realistic that the woman at the next table, when approached by the waiter for her order says, 'I'll have what she's having.'

Imitation is the sincerest form of flattery

However peeved one may be that someone has copied one's style or work, one should keep calm and remember this sage advice and take it as a compliment. This phrase probably dates from the early nineteenth century. In the first century, Lucius Vitellius, father of Aulus Vitellius, Roman Emperor in AD 69, with the help of excessive flattery and general sycophancy made himself in turn a favourite of Tiberius, Caligula, Claudius and Nero. His name became a Roman synonym for one skilled in the art of flattery.

According to Benjamin Disraeli (1804–81):

> Everyone likes flattery; and when it comes to Royalty you should lay on with a trowel.

However, heard on television, 'Flattery is the floating cockroach in the milk of human kindness'. It is said that only two groups of people fall for flattery – men and women.

In extremis

To be in dire straits or at the point of death. The phrase is commonly used, probably with some exaggeration, and is Latin for 'in the furthest reaches'.

Insult to injury, to add
To hurt, by word or deed, someone who has already suffered an act of violence or injustice. During the Augustan era, the so-called Golden Age of Latin literature (27 BC–AD 14) Phaedrus translated Aesop's fables into Latin verse, peppering them with anecdotes of his own. He quotes the fable about a bald man who tried to kill a fly that had bitten him on the head, missed the insect and gave his pate a sharp slap. Whereupon the fly said, 'You wished to kill me for a mere touch. What will you do to yourself since you have added insult to injury?'

Iron Chancellor, the
The original Iron Chancellor was Prince Otto von Bismarck (1815–98), the creator of the German Empire. A century later Gordon Brown, Chancellor of the Exchequer in the Labour government elected in 1997, was so called for his characteristic frugality with the nations' budgets, no doubt overseeing the finances with an iron hand, that is, with severe or harsh control.

Iron Lady, the
Even before she became Prime Minister, the then Leader of the Opposition Margaret Thatcher was dubbed the Iron Lady by the Soviet Defence Ministry newspaper *Red Star* in January 1976, in an article accusing her of trying to rekindle the Cold War in what they interpreted as a viciously anti Soviet-speech. She had said, 'The Russians are bent on world dominance . . . the Russians put guns before butter.' She had, in fact, borrowed the phrase from a surprising source – one of the leaders of the Nazi Party. Hermann Goering (1893–1946) made a radio broadcast in 1936 in which he said, 'Guns will make us powerful; butter will only make us fat,' often misquoted as 'guns before butter'. The article mistakenly suggested that she was already known by this nickname in Britain, although Marje Proops had dubbed her 'The Iron Maiden' in the *Daily Mirror* in 1975. An iron maiden was a medieval instrument of torture in the form of a human-figure-shaped box with spiked doors which could be closed mechanically, slowly piercing its victim. Iron Maiden was also the name of a popular heavy-metal group of the 1980s.

Joneses – Keeping up with the Joneses

This phrase defines twentieth-century materialism as the never-ending struggle to keep up appearances, keeping up with the apparent affluence of one's neighbours, paying particular attention to the cars they drive, the holidays they take, the schools their children attend and all sorts of other lifestyle indicators. American Arthur R Momand ('Pop'), whose strip cartoon was first published in the *New York Globe* in 1913, probably invented the phrase. It was based on Momand's own experiences of living beyond his means in a prosperous neighbourhood and his realization that all his neighbours were doing the same as him. The phrase had spread to Britain by the 1940s, where its sentiments remain rampant.

Just when you thought it was safe to go back in the water

Following the worldwide popularity of Stephen Spielberg's epic shark thriller *Jaws* (1975), this phrase was used to promote *Jaws 2* (1978). It was much imitated and parodied, 'Jaws 3, just when you thought it was safe to go to the toilet' was seen as graffiti in London in 1979. Or 'The return of Julian Bream – just when you thought it was safe to go to the lute' (graffito on a poster Amsterdam, 1983). 'Just when you thought . . .' remains a commonly used phrase for headline writers or as an opening gambit in conversation.

Keep it real

This is the cry of contemporary youth and is one of many suburban catchphrases of the increasingly popular television character Ali G, who was asked by Channel 4 to interview a number of public figures for the *Eleven O'Clock Show*. The comic character Ali G is an irreverent Asian 'urban gansta' who comes from Staines – and is played by a white Jewish actor, Sacha Baron Cohen. Other buzz words include, 'booyakasha', and 'risspeck'. He has developed a much-imitated comic patois and describes himself, ' Me look iz South Central LA wiv a twist of Staines'. He now has his own show called *Da Ali G Show*.

Kilroy was here
The motto of the graffiti artist. During the Second World War, the phrase 'Kilroy was here' was found written or scrawled wherever US troops, particularly Air Transport Command, had been. Its origin is a matter of conjecture. One suggestion is that a shipyard inspector, James L Kilroy (d. 1962), at Quincy, Massachussetts, chalked up the words on material he had inspected. It was the title of a film in 1947. Kilroy, whoever he might be, is closely related to the British 'Chad' – drawn as a bald-headed figure with a large nose who appears looking over a wall with the words, 'Wot, no . . .' – the phrase was completed with the word to suit, as a protest or comment on shortages or shortcomings.

Kitchen-sink drama
A type of drama popular in the 1950s in which the plot centres on the more sordid aspects of working-class or lower-middle-class domestic life. Much of the action takes place in the kitchen or at the kitchen sink, which presumably is a metaphor to suggest drudgery and the dullness of dirty dishwater. Plays such as *Look Back in Anger* (1956; this play gave birth to the phrase, 'angry young men') by John Osborne (1929–94) were examples of these types of dramas and used such squalid settings to emphasize their message of protest against the established values of the time. More recently Joanna Trollope's stories of domestic dramas and upheavals feature the lives of the middle-class country set and her books are known as 'Aga sagas', because much of the action takes place near the comfort of this famous stove seen in most country kitchens worth their salt.

Kiss of death
This phrase derives from Judas Iscariot's kiss given to Christ in the Garden of Gethsemane before he betrayed him (Luke 23:48 and Matthew 26:49). Also known as a 'Judas kiss', meaning an insincere act of courtesy or false affection. In Mafia circles, a kiss

from the boss is no sign of affection, but a fatal omen that one's life expectancy is not looking too good. The phrase is often used in political or business contexts meaning that certain associations may not bode well.

Labour isn't working

Saatchi & Saatchi coined this pertinent phrase during the Conservative Party general-election campaign of 1978, and Margaret Thatcher's victory over the governing Labour Party is, in some part, credited to the strength of this play on words. The posters bearing the slogan showed a long queue outside an unemployment office. The sentiments were to ring rather hollow when unemployment continued to rise under the new Tory government.

Labour's double whammy

Another intriguing Saatchi & Saatchi strap-line for the Conservative Party's 1992 election campaign. Posters appeared showing a boxer with two huge boxing gloves with this legend, and the phrase caused considerable national bafflement, although the concept of the 'double whammy' has been well known in the States since the 1950s. Inspired by the 1992 posters, the idiom has gone into common usage. One source suggested that it was fighting talk from the Dick Tracy comic strip, another credited cartoonist Al Capp. Its dictionary meaning is 'a thing with supernatural power, especially bringing bad luck', but it is most likely that the derivation is from the boxing world and means a double blow.

Land fit for heroes, a

The actual phrase was the title of a verse by GK Chesterton (1874–1936) with its cynical undertones:

> They said (when they had dined at Ciro's)
> The land would soon be fit for heroes

And now they've managed to ensure it
For only heroes could endure it.

It was adapted from a semi-official political slogan from the time shortly after the First World War. When the war was over, Prime Minister, David Lloyd George (1863–1945) coined this phrase in a speech at Wolverhampton on 24 November 1918 when he said, 'What is our task? To make Britain a fit country for heroes to live in.' By 1921, with wages falling and a general economic depression, the sentiment was frequently mocked and ridiculed. F Scott Fitzgerald (1896–1940) quipped in *The Crack Up*:

Show me a hero and I will write you a tragedy.

Land of Nod, the

This was the land to which Cain was exiled after he had slain Abel (Genesis 4:16). The phrase refers to the gentle state of sweet dreams, and to nod off means to go to sleep, obviously derived from the fact that the head tends to fall forward when one feels drowsy. Jonathan Swift, the famous seventeenth-century satirist, (1667–1745), was the first to make the pun on the phrase from Genesis in his little-known work, *Complete Collection of Genteel and Ingenious Conversation* (1731–8) – usually referred to as *Polite Conversation* – in which he wrote that he was 'going to the land of Nod', meaning that he was going to sleep. The phrase has been used in that context ever since.

Legal, decent, honest, truthful
Think what you like about advertising, this is the mission statement of the Advertising Standards Authority. All British advertising should be all the above in order to uphold the essence of good advertising. The organization was founded in 1962 when the slogan was 'Legal, Clean, Honest, Truthful'. The phrase was used as the title of a Radio 4 comedy series about advertising, broadcast in the mid-1980s.

Lemon – The answer's a lemon

Ask a silly question, get a silly answer. This retort means 'no comment'. The phrase is a reasonable answer to an unreasonable or absurd request, or question. The expression probably originated in America at the beginning of the twentieth century, using the various meanings given to the word 'lemon'. The fruit with its sharp juice represents a tart reply to an unreasonable request. To describe something or somebody as a lemon is to mean it, he or she is somehow inadequate – an unattractive person, an unsatisfactory object such as an unreliable car, or a simpleton.

Life begins at forty

Now a rather dated catchphrase taken from the title of a book by the American professor William B Pitkin (1878–1953) published in 1932. The book defined the new-found leisure time that many people discovered they had after forty, and encouraged them to enjoy the second half of their lives, especially by taking up new interests. Jack Yellen and Ted Shapiro wrote a song with this title, and a gutsy rendition of it by singer Sophie Tucker at the age of fifty-three was a huge hit. Nowadays, people want to stay younger for longer and deny their so-called middle age, while economic pressures mean that most people have less spare time to take up new hobbies.

Life's a beach

A colloquial slogan probably originating in Australia in the late 1980s to celebrate the hedonistic lifestyle of sun, sea and surf. The phrase may have been a pun based on the cynical American expressions, 'Life's a bitch, then you die' or 'Life's a bitch, then you marry one'. In the summer of 1991 the Body Shop devised a clever slogan for suntan products with 'Life's a beach, then you fry', while 'Life's a binge, then you diet' was seen in the *Observer* in 1990.

Lightning never strikes the same place twice
In your dreams. This is a classic case of legend-as-wishful-thinking, for this commonly held belief just doesn't hold water. Many tall buildings and trees have been struck by lightning more than once. The statue of William Penn on City Hall in Philadelphia is struck by lightning about five times every year, and the Empire State Building in New York up to ten times. Nor are humans immune: an American Park Ranger from Virginia, Roy C Sullivan, claims to have been struck on seven different occasions between 1942 and 1977 although he has suffered only relatively minor injuries, but has a collection of singed hats as evidence. Thanks to lightning conductors, invented in 1752 by Benjamin Franklin (1706–90) who, after his famous kite experiment proved that lightning contained an electrical charge, designed a vertical copper rod attached to the top of buildings to earth the electricity and save the building. He fell out with King George III, patron of the Sciences in the eighteenth century, who favoured round lightning conductors.

Long time no see
A mock greeting, or verbal shorthand, originating from the pidgin-English phrases used by the colonial British and Americans in the Far East, dating back to the beginning of the twentieth century and still in use today. The variant 'long time no see, short time buckshee' ('free') was how servicemen dreamt they would be welcomed by their favourite prostitute after a long spell abroad. Expatriates and servicemen imported the phrase and it became well used on both sides of the Atlantic. In similar style, 'Who he?' is another shorthand term, this time from America. Harold Wallace Ross (1892–1951) founded the sophisticated literary magazine the *New Yorker* in 1925 and, with his keen eye for detail and perfection, would write pertinent notes on typescripts, such as 'Hogwash', 'Transcends credulence' or 'Who he?'

Love means never having to say you're sorry
A line taken from the successful 1970 film, *Love Story* by Eric Segal. Ryan O'Neill says it to Ray Milland, playing his father-in-law. He is quoting his student wife (Ali MacGraw) who has just died. Unusually, Segal wrote the novel after the film screenplay, in which the penultimate sentence is 'Love means *not ever* having to say you're sorry'. The phrase was much used and abused in the decade to follow. At the end of the 1972 film *What's Up Doc?* Ryan O'Neal in self-parody quotes the line to his co-star, Barbra Streisand. A graffito from 1974 reads, 'A vasectomy means never having to say you're sorry'.

Lovely jubbly
'Jubbly' is one amongst many euphemisms for money. Jubbly was originally the trade name for an orange drink in the 1950s and 1960s, probably because it rhymes with bubbly, which used the slogan 'Lovely Jubbly'. It came to national prominence with the popularity of the BBC comedy series *Only Fools and Horses,* as it was a catch-all catchphrase of Del Boy, the lovable wide boy played by David Jason. Other slang words for money include 'dosh' possibly derived from the African colonial word for a tip – 'dash'; 'lids' and 'lolly' may have developed from the L or £ symbol for a pound.

Luck – A lorra lorra luck
This phrase has been exaggerated by the woman who first coined it, in self-parody of her pronounced Liverpudlian accent. Cilla Black, singer and presenter of the successful television programme *Blind Date*, wishes her contestants a 'lorra lorra luck', meaning 'good luck', that is, 'a lot of luck', before they play the dating game. She also used the phrase 'a lorra, lorra laffs' when she presented another television show, *Surprise, Surprise.* It is a key phrase used by impressionists.

Mad – As mad as a hatter
A renowned simile ever since Lewis Carroll's (1832–98) *Alice in Wonderland* (1865), although it can be found in WM Thackeray's

(1811–63) *Pendennis* (1850) and is recorded in America as early as 1836. The likely reason for linking hat makers with madness is that hatters used the chemical mercurous nitrate in the making of felt hats, and its side effects can produce trembling symptoms as those suffered in St Vitus's Dance. It is believed that Lewis Carroll based his character on Theophilus Carter, a furniture dealer who was known locally as the 'mad hatter' because he wore a top hat and devised fanciful inventions such as an alarm-clock bed which tips the sleeper to the floor when it's time to wake up. It has also been suggested that the original mad hatter was Robert Crab, a seventeenth-century English eccentric who gave all his belongings to the poor and only ate dock leaves and grass.

Mad – As mad as a March hare
Lewis Carroll also refers to the madness of the March hare in *Alice in Wonderland* because hares run wild in March, the beginning of their rutting season.

> The March hare will be much the most interesting and perhaps, as this is May, it won't be raving mad – at least not so mad as it was in March.

Make do and mend
Official morale-boosting slogan which has a special place in the language for people of a certain age, meaning to make do with what you already have and repair it rather than buying a replacement. It was in common use by 1943 and set the tone for British life during the Second World War, and for many years after

while food and clothing continued to be rationed. It may have derived from 'make and mend', which was a Royal Navy term for an afternoon free from work when the time was spent mending clothes and darning socks. There were even 'make do and mend' departments in stores. The phrase was designed to encourage thrift and the repairing of old garments and furniture rather than buying new and using up scarce resources. This slogan struck a chord in the British psyche, although it seems somewhat quaint to young members of today's consumer society, and the old sentiment to 'waste not, want not' lives on in recycling. Sadly, the art of darning is no more, not least because young Brownies are not taught such skills these days.

Make hay while the sun shines

To act promptly when the opportunity presents itself (see **Carpe diem** and **Strike while the iron's hot**, q.v.). One today is worth two tomorrows, while, as seen on a postcard, 'There's many a lemon dries up unsqueezed'. The phrase originated when many people worked on the land, and appeared in the sixteenth century. 'To make hay' is an old phrase meaning to disorganize and throw things into confusion and disorder. Before the days of the baler hay was tossed about with a pitchfork before being gathered in.

> The sun shines hot, and we use delay,
> Cold biting winter mars our hop'd for hay.
>
> Shakespeare, *Henry V*

I made hay while the sun shone.
My work sold.
Now, if the harvest is over
And the world cold,
Give me the bonus of laughter
As I lose hold.

Sir John Betjeman (1906–84), 'The Last Laugh'

Man – A drowning man will clutch at a straw

Someone in desperate circumstances will reach out and grab hold
of anything, however flimsy or inadequate, in the hope of surviving
the situation. The phrase is often shortened to 'clutching at straws'.
No one is sure of the origin of this unpleasant metaphor, nor of the
other well-known drowning phrase and common belief that 'His
whole life passes before the eyes of a drowning man'. The word
'straw' has been used as a metaphor for the insubstantial or
groundless for hundreds of years, such as a 'man of
straw', someone financially insecure or with a poor
credit rating; 'the last straw (that broke the camel's
back)', that little extra burden which
makes something no longer
bearable, as with the camel's
load, tipping the balance of
tolerance. A 'straw in the
wind' is a slight hint that
suggests much, but in the
event, delivers little.

Man – A man's gotta do what a man's gotta do

A macho expression used to emphasize the difficult and dangerous
actions a man is forced to take in his life. It may have come from
American strip cartoons of the 1930s in this style, and an early
example of its literary use appears in John Steinbeck's novel *The
Grapes of Wrath* (1939), evoking the Southern American dialect:

I know this – a man got to do what he got to do.

John Wayne first delivered the line on celluloid in the film
Stagecoach (1939), and it has been paraphrased ever since; or in a

108

play on the words, meaning to show great determination, 'a man's gotta chew what a man's gotta chew'.

Outside the context of the Wild West it is usually used facetiously. Shortly before the Gulf War in 1991 a US truck driver, William J Brown, from Sioux Falls, South Dakota, decided to embark on a one-man peace mission to see Saddam Hussein personally. After the meeting he was quoted in the *Independent*, 'In Sioux Falls a man's got to do what a man's got to do'.

Man – One man's meat is another man's poison

This is a very old adage that has inspired an endless stream of spin-offs and simply means that what is palatable or beneficial to one person is distasteful or harmful to another. The phrase 'different strokes for different folks' pretty well sums up the meaning. The rhythm and phrasing of this expression have given rise to an endless stream of imitations. To an adulterer, perhaps, 'One man's mate is another man's passion' or 'One man's Jill is another man's thrill', or to a vegetarian, 'one man's meat is another man's *poisson*'. 'One man's floor is another man's ceiling' is attributed to D Bloodworth (1967). In ancient times meat and bread were generic terms for food, so in Italy 'bread' stood for food and in Britain, once famous for eating roast meat, the use of the word meat in many proverbs simply meant food.

Man – The man on the Clapham omnibus

The man in the street. This typically ordinary person on the bus was invented by a law lord, Lord Bowen, in 1903. While summing up a case for negligence he told the jury, 'We must ask ourselves what the man on the Clapham omnibus would think.' In those days the omnibus was still a horse-drawn carriage and Clapham was a suburb that the judge obviously regarded as the home of common sense. Clapham is an area of south London that is light-heartedly pronounced 'clarm' because it has attracted many well-heeled, well-spoken residents who have snapped up property there.

Man – The man with the plan

The original man with the plan was the Labour Party leader, Hugh Gaitskell. This was the caption to his picture on general-election campaign posters in 1959, at which his party was defeated. The next man dubbed as such was Jonathan Ross, presenter of a highly successful, anarchic television chat show series in the 1980s.

Man – The man you love to hate

This man was the extravagant Austrian film director Eric von Stroheim (1885–1957) after he appeared as an actor in the First World War propaganda film, *The Heart of Humanity* (1918), in which he played an obnoxious German officer who not only tried to rape the leading lady, but nonchalantly tossed a baby out of a window. The phrase was used to publicize the film and it succeeded in whipping up public emotion. At the film's première in Los Angeles, von Stroheim was booed and jeered at when he appeared on stage. A 1979 film tribute to the work of von Stroheim was entitled *The Man You Love to Hate*. It is now a phrase in general use to describe any alluring or attractive villain.

Man from the Pru, Ask the man from the Pru

The Prudential Assurance Company Ltd was founded in 1848 and the phrase evolved long before the days of direct debit and telephone banking. 'The man from the Pru' was familiar to millions as the man who knocked at the door, to collect life-insurance premiums. It had become a music-hall joke by the end of the nineteenth century, but the phrase did not appear as an official company slogan until after the Second World War, when it was applied to advertisements.

Marie Céleste, Like the Marie Céleste

An eerily quiet and deserted place, somewhere normally occupied, but uncannily empty and quiet. The *Mary Céleste* was an American brigantine found abandoned, ready to sail, between the Azores and Portugal on 5 December 1872. The ship's one lifeboat, sextant, chronometer, register and crew were missing and no trace of any of them was ever found. It remains one of the unsolved mysteries of the high seas to this day. Hence the use of the ship's name to describe a silent, empty place. Why 'Mary' should be 'Marie' is open to conjecture, but it might be because of its association with the French 'Céleste'.

May the force be with you!

A phrase used to bid farewell, with overtones of a blessing, in the American film *Star Wars* (1977) by George Lucas, and in its prequels and sequels. The Force is the life force of the universe, the power of good. To millions of the film's fans it is almost the equivalent of 'May God go with you'. More parochially, the Cornish police used it in a recruitment campaign, and President Reagan, always at ease quoting from the movies, used it in a speech about his Star Wars weapons programme, named after the film, saying, 'The force is with us'. Radio disc jockeys are known to repeat it frequently every May the Fourth.

Men stand with their backs to the fire

This expression has no military connotations, as it might suggest at first sight, but has a tenuous link with Noah. This phenomenon is still observed, for men do seem to like to stand on the hearth rug facing out into the room, perhaps to hold court, in a lord-of-the-manor sort of way. Because open fires are less common these days, this expression is not heard quite so often, but an old explanation is that when the dog's nose proved to be too small to plug a leak in Noah's Ark, Noah sat on the hole to keep the water out. Ever since it has been observed that men seem to need to warm their backs and dogs have cold wet noses.

Mentioned in dispatches

To single out someone for particular congratulation or recommendation for carrying out a task with distinction. Dispatches are official communications sent or dispatched to the relevant government ministries from commanding officers during a military campaign. If an officer is listed or mentioned in British naval, army or air force dispatches commending his or her conduct in action, he or she is entitled to wear a small bronze oak leaf on the left breast or upon the medal ribbon for that particular campaign.

Milk has gotta a lotta bottle

Milk was remarketed as a macho drink, not just for kids, in 1985 with this fighting phrase. The word bottle denotes courage or guts and has been used in this sense since the late 1940s. To 'bottle out' or to 'lose one's bottle' means to shrink from. One suggestion is that bottle comes from Cockney rhyming slang, either 'bottle and glass' – arse; or 'bottle of beer' – fear; or 'bottle and glass' – class. The associations between either arse, fear or class with courage are not obvious, but links can be guessed at. Arse meaning bottom, which if you have a lot of you are brave; fear to mean provoking fear in others; or class which a boxer has; while if he loses it he has lost his bottle. Cockney slang was used increasingly during the 1970s, with the influence of numerous television crime dramas such as *The Sweeney* and *Minder*.

Miss is as good as a mile, a

Coming second is just not good enough. A failure is a failure by however small a margin. Conversely, though, a narrow escape is an escape. An old form of the phrase was 'an inch in a miss is as good as an ell'. An 'English ell' was an old unit of measurement equal to forty-five inches. Another old saying is 'give him an inch and he'll take an ell'; the 'ell' later evolved into 'mile'. It has also been said that 'a miss is as good as her smile'.

Miss Otis regrets

A very handy excuse in replying to an invitation to a function that one does not wish to accept. It originated in Cole Porter's 1934 song of the same name, in which Miss Otis's butler, with sublime understatement, gives his mistress's tragic reason for not being able to keep a lunch date. After being scorned by her lover, she has been hanged for his murder.

> She drew her forty-four pistol and shot the dirty rascal down,
> Now Old Lady Otis regrets she's disabled and can't lunch today.

Moon – To bay at the moon

'To bay, or bark, at the moon' is to crave for what is unattainable. This fanciful phrase means to fluster about pointlessly, aiming at something or some idea probably out of reach. It can be said of children with big ideas that they might 'cry for the moon to play with'. But a deranged dog may think he can frighten the moon by baying at it. It is an old superstition that when a dog howls at the moon it's an ill omen of death or bad luck.

Moon – To shoot the moon

This is an American expression meaning to leave without paying one's bills or rent, or to remove swiftly one's household goods under cover of night to avoid their seizure by a landlord or creditor, more colloquially known as 'to do a moonlight flit' and often shortened to 'do a moonlight'. Simply to 'moonlight' means to take a second job supposedly at night to supplement one's wages from the day job. References to the moon are often used to denote that something is fanciful: for instance, unrealistic ideas are known as 'moonshine'; 'to cry for the moon', mentioned above, means to crave for what is totally beyond one's reach. *Shoot the Moon* was the title of the 1981 Alan Parker film about a well-heeled family who split up.

Mother of all battles, the
This phrase entered the English language thanks to Saddam Hussein, Iraqi president since 1979. In 1990 Saddam invaded Kuwait and was repulsed by a coalition of Western and Arab forces during the Gulf War. Just before the beginning of Allied attacks in 1991 Saddam pronounced:

> The devil Bush and his treacherous gang, with criminal Zionism, have begun the great showdown, the mother of all battles between good and evil.
>
> Speech in Baghdad, 6 January, describing Operation Desert Storm. Quoted in the *Sunday Times*, 27 January 1991

The phrase has been adapted to describe something terrible or arduous and is used in such contexts as 'the mother of all rows'. Expressions such as 'the mother and father of all hangovers' were, however, commonly used in the English language well before the Gulf War.

Muster, to pass
To come up to an adequate standard, to pass inspection or to get by. Originally 'muster' was a military term for the gathering of

soldiers for inspection. To 'muster in' means to enrol, and to 'muster out' means that the group disperses or falls out.

My old Dutch

A colloquial term for a wife or, nowadays, long-term female partner. Although Dutch in English expressions often refers to a person or thing from Holland, or, especially in America, from Germany (as a corruption of *Deutsch*, German), in this instance the word is a contraction of 'duchess'. Cockney rhyming slang has it that wife is 'Duchess of Fife', shortened to 'Dutch'. The expression gained currency notably among Cockneys and costermongers from the late Victorian and early Edwardian music halls, and especially from the song 'My Old Dutch' performed by Albert Chevalier (1861–1923), the 'costers' laureate' known as Albert the Great, who was enormously popular in his day.

Nail – on the nail

This is a very old phrase meaning to pay immediately or on the spot and generally it means now, at once. In medieval times, a nail was a shallow vessel mounted on a post or stand and business deals were closed by payments placed in the 'nail'. It may have been so named from the resemblance of the stand to the shape of a nail. Outside the Bristol Corn Exchange such nails can still be seen in the form of four bronze pillars and it is said that if a buyer was satisfied with the sample of grain shown on the nail he paid on the spot. However, there could be another derivation for this phrase from the world of wine tasting. Latin for 'on the nail' is *supernaculum*, and this word also describes the very best wine, meaning that the wine is so fine that the imbiber only leaves enough in the glass to make a bead on a nail. And the French say of

115

first-class wine, *faire rubis sur l'ongle* – 'to make a ruby on the nail'. Thomas Nash (1567–1601) in *Pierce Penilesse* (1592) wrote that after a man had drunk from his glass it was customary to turn the cup upside down and let a drop fall on the thumbnail. If the drip rolled off the drinker was obliged to fill up and drink again, eventually ending up 'on the floor'.

Nail – another nail in the coffin
A depressing phrase which is applied to a further event in a situation that is getting progressively worse; one more factor to plunge a person into greater disfavour, to hasten his dismissal, or downfall, or death. The final nail can be compared with the 'last straw' (see **Man – A drowning man will clutch at a straw**, q.v.). Peter Pindar (Dr J Wolcot, 1738–1819) wrote in one of his *Expostulary Odes*:

> Care to our coffin adds a nail, no doubt.

The phrase came to be adopted by smokers – who, as early as the 1920s, referred to cigarettes as 'coffin nails' – becoming a stock response as someone accepted yet another cigarette. At the time, however, they were referring to the hazards of a smoker's cough. The links between smoking and cancer, and smoking and heart disease were recognized later (when cigarettes earned another nickname – 'cancer sticks').

Nation of shopkeepers
This was meant as an insult to the English people by Napoleon Bonaparte (1769–1821), who said 'L'Angleterre est une nation de boutiquiers', which he must have read in Adam Smith's *The Wealth of Nations* (1776):

> To found a great empire for the sole purpose of raising up a people
> of customers, may at first sight appear a project fit only for a nation
> of shop keepers.

Nation shall speak peace unto nation
The motto of the BBC from 1927 was put forward by Dr Montague John Rendall (1862–1950), a schoolmaster who became one of the first five governors when the original company was incorporated

and its coat of arms created. The words echo a passage in Micah 4:3: 'Nation shall not lift up a sword against nation'. In 1932, however, it was decided that the BBC's mission was not principally to broadcast to other nations, but to provide a service for a home and colonial audience. A new assertion was introduced by Dr Rendall – *Quaecunque* – 'Whatsoever' – when the new BBC headquarters at Broadcasting House in London was built, which reflected the spirit of the passage from Philippians 4:8: 'Whatsoever things are beautiful and honest and of good report'. In 1948, however, the BBC reverted to its first motto after its vital role in international broadcasting during the Second World War.

Naughty but nice

Between 1981 and 1984 the National Dairy Council used this alliterative and somewhat suggestive slogan in a campaign to promote fresh cream cakes. The novelist Salman Rushdie claimed to have created the phrase when he was the castaway on BBC's *Desert Island Discs*. Before achieving fame and fatwa Rushdie had been an advertising copywriter in London, but his claim was refuted by others who had worked on the account. The phrase was certainly not original, as it was the title for a 1939 film about a classical-music professor who accidentally wrote a popular song, starring Dick Powell and Ronald Reagan. It has also been an oblique phrase implying sexual intercourse since about 1900.

Necessity is the mother of invention

An imperative need will force one to summon extra creative forces to devise a solution, or to create something, to alleviate a problem. The phrase was probably first coined by Plato in the fourth century BC in *The Republic*. More modern derivations of the phrase are 'A guilty conscience is the mother of invention' and 'Boredom is the mother of invention'. And in a chiastic twist by one Thorstein Veblen (1857–1929), 'Invention is the mother of necessity'.

117

However, Daniel Defoe (1661?–1731) wrote in *Serious Reflections of Robinson Crusoe*:

> Necessity makes an honest man a knave.

Never knowingly undersold

The motto of the John Lewis stores since the 1930s. The founder of the John Lewis Partnership, John Spedan Lewis, formulated this line in about 1920 to declare the pricing policy which began with his father, John Lewis, who first opened a small shop in London's Oxford Street in 1864. It is thought that the slogan was used internally before it was given public expression in the 1930s with the promise, 'If you can buy more cheaply elsewhere anything you have just bought from us we will refund the difference.' 'Never knowingly undersold' still appears on carrier bags and on the sides of delivery vehicles and the 'If you can buy . . .' undertaking is printed on the reverse of sales bills. The firm does not advertise and the phrase has an almost mystical significance for the partnership. It is a tortuous phrase that requires some thought to work out its meaning.

News – No news is good news

The absence of information justifies continued optimism; that is, if all's quiet, then there is no cause for alarm. The phrase probably dates back to the early seventeenth century, and can be explained by Plutarch's phrase in about 100 AD that 'Bad news travels fast'.

> For evil news rides post, while good news baits.
> John Milton (1608–1674), *Samson Agonistes*

The word news, now understood as a singular noun, was still plural up to the nineteenth century:

> The news from Austria are very sad, and make one very anxious.
> Letter from Queen Victoria to the King of the Belgians,
> 20 August 1861

The word is short for 'new stories', and the old spelling was 'newes', a literal translation from the French *nouvelles*. (Seen as graffiti: 'No nukes is good nukes'.)

Nice one Cyril!

This enormously popular catchphrase was an advertising slogan that struck a chord with the public, who dropped it as quickly as they had embraced it. The line first appeared in a television commercial for Wonderloaf bread in 1972, written by Peter Mayle (author of *A Year in Provence*). Why the phrase was so popular is a mystery. It had a Cockney mateyness, it was fun to say and it could be applied to all sorts of situations, not least sexual ones. In 1973 it was chanted by Tottenham Hotspur football supporters who were fans of player Cyril Knowles, and who went as far as recording a song about him. The comedian Cyril Fletcher used it as the title to his 1978 autobiography. Suddenly the phrase became old hat and it did not make another public appearance until it was used on posters in 1989 advertising Access credit cards. It showed the corpulent figure of the politician, Sir Cyril Smith (1928–), trying to touch his toes.

Nineteenth hole, the

The bar at the golf clubhouse. The standard course has eighteen holes so the player who has played badly can drown his sorrows at the nineteenth. The term was first heard by American golfers in the 1920s.

Not my bag

A slang expression for something which is definitely not one's subject or style. It probably came from the American jazz scene, 'bag' meaning a personal style of playing; for instance, 'playing with a hip-hop band was not his bag'. This phrase came into general use, being applied to almost anything, in both America and Britain.

Not on your Nellie!

Not bloody likely, not on any account, on your life. One conjecture is that it derives from Cockney rhyming slang from around the 1930s, 'Nellie Duff'; 'duff' rhymes with puff, i.e. breath, that which keeps you alive. Another theory is that your 'nellie' is your stomach, your 'Aunt Nellie' – belly, something that in a more refined age you did not reveal to the world. The phrase was one of comedian Frankie Howerd's (1917–1992) catchphrases, which he popularized in the 1940s. Howerd referred to his many catchphrases as 'verbal punctuation marks' and his camp humour derived from the implied suggestiveness in his emphasis on certain syllables.

Not worth a tinker's damn

This is one of many phrases meaning that something is worthless. Tinkers were itinerant menders of kettles and pans and were a common sight on the streets in the eighteenth century. It has been suggested that the term comes from the tinker's custom of blocking up a hole in the article he was mending with a pellet of bread, thus making a 'dam', or plug, that would hold the molten solder. This pellet was discarded as unreusable when the job was finished. So a tinker's dam is a useless or negligible thing. However, the present spelling of 'damn' alludes to its meaning as a curse or oath, and the phrase is also heard as 'not worth a tinker's cuss', a cuss being slang for a curse. It can only be assumed that tinkers made such a bodged job of their repairs that they frequently uttered oaths of frustration at their own incompetence. It is still common 'to tinker about' with something, which means to fiddle in a clumsy fashion in an attempt to make repairs.

Nudge nudge, wink wink, say no more

A catchphrase understood by everyone during the 1970s, which came from the television comedy show *Monty Python's Flying Circus*, broadcast between 1969 and 1974. Laden with sexual innuendo, these words provided the accompaniment to rhetorical questions such as 'Is your wife a goer, then, eh, eh?' asked by a lewd character played by Eric Idle in a ridiculously suggestive manner, accompanied by much elbow jerking, embarrassed twitching and prodding.

Oil on troubled waters, to pour

A well-known metaphor meaning to mollify or soothe with gentle words, or to use tact and diplomacy to restore calm after an angry or bitter argument. It has been a well-known scientific fact since the first century AD that rough waves are calmed when oil is poured upon them. According to the Venerable Bede's (673–735) *History of the English Church and People* (731) St Aidan, an Irish monk of Iona, knew of this 'miracle' and gave a young priest a vessel of holy oil to pour on the sea when the waves became stormy on a voyage to fetch a maiden destined to be the bride of King Oswy. On his many Atlantic crossings between Pennsylvania and Portsmouth in the eighteenth century, the ever curious Benjamin Franklin (1706–90) observed not only the Gulf Stream, but also the calming effect of oil on the waves.

Old – As old as Methuselah
This means to be very old indeed. Methuselah is the oldest man referred to in the Bible, and it is written in Genesis (5:27) that he died at the impossibly great age of 969 years. 'As old as the hills' is probably a more realistic simile as hills are indeed extremely ancient features of the landscape.

Old Grey Whistle test, the
In Tin Pan Alley, the popular music-publishing district of New York around 14th Street, and in London's Denmark Street, off Charing Cross Road, songwriters would play their newly penned tunes to the 'old greys' – the elderly doorkeepers and clerks in the offices of music publishers. If the 'old greys' were still whistling the songs after few days, they might be worth publishing. It later became the title of a long-running rock-music programme on BBC television during the 1970s and 1980s.

Old-boy network
This is the art of using one's social connections to get on in life. To arrange something on the old-boy network is to fix it through a social contact or someone from one's old school, instead of through

less nepotistic channels. An old boy or old girl is a former pupil of a particular school, hence old boys' or old girls' societies through which former pupils reunite and reminisce about old times. The old-school tie worn by former pupils of the public and grammar schools is a distinguishing mark, recognized by members of the same privileged class. Nowadays, the practice of 'networking' in order to make contacts is referred to, describing going out to meet people in a similar field who can help advance one in business; that is, meeting those more successful than yourself in the hope that some of their success might rub off.

Once bitten, twice shy
A phrase meaning that one learns from previous experience. Having been caught out once, one is wary or cautious the next time, and you should therefore learn from your mistakes. 'He that stumbles twice at the same stone deserves to have his shins broke', appears in R Taverner's list of *Proverbs and Adages* of 1539 while the American humorist Josh Billings (1818–95) said that 'nobody but a fool gets bit twice by the same dog.'

> I'll trust by leisure him that mocks me once.
> Shakespeare, *Titus Andronicus* (1590)

One sandwich short of a picnic
A derogatory description of someone who is not terribly bright. It is one of many such almost cartoon-like expressions, such as 'one prawn short of a cocktail' and other variations. 'The lights are on but on one's at home' and 'the lift doesn't go to the top floor' have very much the same meaning.

Out for the count
Said of someone who is fast asleep, dead drunk or completely demoralized. It is a boxing and wrestling term meaning to be defeated by being counted out by the referee. If a fighter is floored and does not find his feet within ten seconds counted out loud he has lost the bout, much to the excitement of the audience, who usually raucously accompany the referee while he counts down the seconds. To say 'count me out' means 'do not include me in this.'

Over a barrel

To be stuck in a helpless position, powerless to get yourself out of it, or to be at someone's mercy. The phrase is probably nautical in origin and is said to derive from the practice of draping over a barrel someone who has been rescued from the water when close to drowning, so encouraging the ejection of water from the lungs. A more likely derivation, however, may be a form of punishment or torture in which the victim is bent over a barrel and beaten.

Over the top

An expression that describes something that goes way beyond the bounds of good taste or good sense, or which is outrageously inappropriate. It came from the trenches of the First World War when soldiers were described as going 'over the top' when they scrambled out of the trenches to attack the enemy. *Over The Top* was the name of a bawdy television show in the 1980s, which became known only by its initials, OTT, which are still used in many colloquial contexts. For example, a particularly impassioned verbal outburst, or a person who behaves or dresses outrageously, might be described as OTT.

Oyster – Never eat an oyster unless there's an R in the month

An old maxim that served as sensible advice to avoid the eating of native oysters in the months of May, June, July and August. In the days before modern refrigeration oysters did offer the risk of food poisoning in the warm summer breeding months, which happen not to have an R in their names. Now oysters can be eaten all year round, although normal marketing in Britain still takes place from September to April. As Richard Buttes advised in *Diet's Dry Dinner* (1599):

> The oyster is unseasonable and unwholesome in all months that have not the letter R in their name.

To cheat the rule, people used to eat oysters in August by spelling it 'Orgust'.

Paint the town red, to
To go out and party, to let your hair down and enjoy an uninhibited celebration, to trip the light fantastic, perhaps even to cause some disturbance in town. This phrase of American origin possibly originally alludes to a town's red-light district; that is, the area where prostitutes ply their trade, advertising with a red light in the window of their brothels, and where the cowboys might begin the evening before later extending the party to the rest of town.

Pandora's Box
This is a troublesome 'can of worms' – a gift that seems of great value but is actually a curse, generating all sorts of unmanageable problems. The name Pandora means 'all gifted', because in Greek mythology the gods endowed her with powers which could bring about the ruin of man. Pandora was sent by Zeus as a gift to Epimetheus, who married her, against the advice of his brother Prometheus. She brought with her a large jar – Pandora's box – but, when Epimetheus opened it, all the evils escaped, to afflict the world for ever, while the blessings were lost to mankind. According to some, hope was the last thing that flew out; others believe that hope alone remained in the box. The more modern phrase 'to open a can of worms', which was first used in America in the 1950s, is a euphemism that became popular in the UK in the 1970s. It is a

graphic metaphor for a tangled, squirming, unpleasant, or uncontrollable situation that had not been apparent beforehand.

Pavlovian, a Pavlovian response

This sort of response is an automatic reaction made unthinkingly or under the influence of others, and should not be confused with a fluffy meringue cake with summer fruit and whipped cream which was named after the graceful Russian ballet dancer Anna Pavlova (1881–1931). The Russian psychologist Ivan Petrovich Pavlov (1849–1936) pioneered studies into animal behaviour and discovered the conditioned reflex. In his classic experiment he rang a bell before feeding a hungry dog and showed that, after a time, the dog would salivate on hearing the bell even when there was no sight of food. He called this reaction 'psychic salivation' and the phenomenon became known as the conditioned reflex. Dogs were Pavlov's main focus of experiment but he also used monkeys and mice, demonstrating that the conditioned reflex occurs in all animals, including humans, and can be activated by almost any suggestion or environmental factor. One of Pavlov's less successful ventures, however, was his failed attempt to market an appetite stimulant for humans based on dogs' saliva.

Peace in our time

The most vacuous slogan in the run-up to the Second World War were these words, announced by Prime Minister Neville Chamberlain on 30 September 1938 when he returned from signing the Munich agreement with Hitler, hoping that his concession, which effectively abandoned Czechoslovakia to Nazi domination, would pave the way for peace. Despite any personal misgivings he may have had, he experienced vehement opposition to his declaration to the crowds outside Number 10 Downing Street:

> My good friends, this is the second time in our history that there has come back from Germany to Downing Street peace with honour. I believe it is peace for our time. Go home and get a quiet night's sleep.

According to John Colville in *Footprints in Time* (1976), it was Chamberlain's wife who actually persuaded him to use the phrase, which in fact was 'Peace for [not 'in'] our time'. Noël Coward entitled his 1947 play, hypothetically about England after the Germans had conquered, *Peace in Our Time*. Use of the phrase was probably inspired by the Book of Common Prayer:

> Give peace in our time, O Lord.
>
> Morning Prayer, Versicle

Pete – For Pete's sake

An exclamation of annoyance or impatience. Just who Pete is remains a mystery. The expression is perhaps an oath in the name of St Peter; alternatively it may have evolved from 'for pity's sake'. Nowadays, however, this particular curse is not so frequently heard because the threshold of acceptability for far more blasphemous expletives is far lower.

Pig in a poke, a

To buy a pig in a poke is to buy something sight unseen, to make a blind purchase, usually worthless. This is an ancient form of trickery when animals were traded at market and a small suckling pig was taken for sale in a 'poke', a word shortened from the word 'pocket', which was a stout sack. However, people used to try and palm off the runts of the litter to unsuspecting buyers, and even cats were substituted for pigs. The sale had to be agreed without opening the poke for fear of the lively piglet escaping. If the less gullible purchaser insisted on seeing the contents of the poke the salesman might literally have to 'let the cat out of the bag' (hence that other well-known expression), and the game was up. This form of dodgy market trading has been around for hundreds of years, and is referred to in Thomas Tusser's *Five Hundred Good*

Pointes of Husbandrie (1580). The practice was obviously widespread because other languages have similar expressions, such as the French *chat en poche*, which also refer to the folly of buying something without seeing it first. The Latin proverb *caveat emptor* – let the buyer beware – has a similar meaning.

Pile it high, sell it cheap
This golden rule of Tesco Supermarkets was invented by the company founder, Sir John Cohen (1898–1979). It may have been adapted from the American phrase, 'Stack it high, Watch 'em buy', and is still applied in markets today.

Piper – He who pays the piper may call the tune
Whoever pays the bill commands control of the situation. Although this proverb appeared in the seventeenth century, it probably comes from the story, dating from 1284, of the Pied Piper, who didn't get paid, and might be derived from the phrase, 'Who's to pay the piper?' The Pied Piper was an itinerant musician who agreed to rid the town of Hamelin in Westphalia of an infestation of rats and mice. After he had had completed the task his payment was withheld, however, so he led all the town's children away to a mountain cave where they all disappeared. Another possible derivation goes back to the pipers who used to amuse guests at inns or on village greens, and expected to be paid for their efforts. 'Pay' means to discharge a debt and is derived via the French *paier* from the Latin *pax*, peace, from *pacare*, to appease.

Plain as a pikestaff, as
This alliterative phrase originated in the mid-sixteenth century and means that something is perfectly clear, obvious, unambiguous or unmistakable, although its original meaning was bare or unadorned. A pike is a weapon with a long wooden shaft and a pointed steel or iron head, and was used by the military preceding the bayonet. It later came to mean simply a walking stick, especially one used by pilgrims and travellers. The earlier word for 'pikestaff' was 'packstaff', which was the pole on which a peddler carried his pack and which, through many years of use, was worn smooth and plain – hence the original meaning of unadorned.

Pleased as Punch, as

In the traditional comic puppet show *Punch and Judy*, the pompous Mr Punch gloats smugly at the success of his evil actions and superiority over his shrewish wife Judy. The name Mr Punch probably comes from the Italian *pulcinello* (young chicken), and the show was know as *Punchinello* when it first came to England at about the time of the Restoration in 1660. The present scenario is probably similar to the original by the Italian comedian Silvio Fiorello, dating from about 1600. Although the basic plot varies, it usually involves Punch's enraged bludgeoning of his wife, Judy, their child, and several lesser characters, followed by his imprisonment and escape. Often accompanied by his dog, Toby, Punch is a hook-nosed, long-chinned hunchback whose quick wit is triumphant even over the devil. The violence of the storylines is counteracted by slapstick action and comic dialogue. The British humorous magazine *Punch* was founded in 1841, and the character of Punch is still used as its symbol.

Point blank, to ask something

To ask a direct question. This is a sixteenth-century phrase from the sport of archery. The targets had a white, or *blanc* in French, central spot, so the arrows were pointed at the white, that is *point blanc*. In military, and especially artillery, usage, point blank is a range at which there is no fall of shot due to gravity – in other words, a very close range. Any projectile from a firearm 'drops' from the point of aim as the range increases, which in turn means that the further the target, the higher the weapon has to be aimed above it.

Post early for Christmas

This enduring advice from the Post Office probably dates from the 1880s. The aim of the message is to reduce the pressure on the postal system before the Christmas rush of cards and parcels. 'Post early' was a maxim used in the 1920s throughout the year to encourage letters to be posted early in the day for deliveries to be made later the same day. During the Second World War the phrase was adapted to 'Post early – Before noon'.

Powder – To keep one's powder dry

To be prepared for action, but to be cautious, yet alert; to preserve one's resources. The phrase comes from a saying attributed to Oliver Cromwell (1599–1658), and the powder is, of course, gunpowder. During his cold-blooded and savage Irish campaign of 1649 he is said to have concluded a speech to his troops, who were about to cross the River Slaney before attacking Wexford, with the rousing words, 'Put your trust in God, my boys, and keep your powder dry.' However, it seems likely that the phrase was coined later by the Anglo-Indian soldier Valentine Blacker (1738–1823) and gained the Cromwell attribution through being quoted in 'Oliver's Advice' in E Hayes's *Ballads of Ireland* (1856).

Power to the people

This is the motto of the Black Panther movement in America and dates from 1969. Traditionally shouted with a clenched fist raised, it was publicized by the Black Panther leader, Bobby Seale, in Oakland, California, in July 1969. The Black Panthers were a militant organization notorious for their violent demonstrations and dramatic shootouts with police. It was used by other dissident groups, as Black, White and Red Power were taken up by various other revolutionary organizations. In the revolutionary spirit of the time, John Lennon penned the song 'Power to the People' in 1971.

Pride goes before a fall

An ancient warning for the arrogant to avoid conceit; do not be too cocksure or big-headed, because events may conspire to bring you down. The phrase is shortened from the passage in Proverbs (16:18):

Pride goeth before destruction,
and an haughty spirit before a fall.

'Pride goes before, and shame comes after' is another form of the proverb as it was used in the sixteenth and seventeenth centuries.

It has also been said that 'He who gets too big for his britches gets exposed in the end.'

Probably the best lager in the world
In 1973 Orson Welles' mellifluous tones graced the voice-over to this landmark television commercial for Carlsberg lager. The use of the reservation, 'probably', struck an ironic chord in an otherwise gross exaggeration for a very middle-of-the-road product.

Put a sock in it!
A plea to be quiet, to shut up, to make less noise. It comes from the end of the nineteenth and beginning of the twentieth centuries, when the early gramophones, or 'phonographs', had large horns through which the sound was amplified. These mechanical contraptions had no volume controls, and so a convenient method of reducing the volume was to stuff a woollen sock inside the horn.

Queer Street, to be in
Not to be confused with the gay part of town, this phrase means to be in financial difficulties, in dire straits, or in another thoroughfare, Carey Street (see also **Beam ends**, q.v.). Use of the word 'queer' could be a pun on 'query' because Victorian tradesmen might mark the name of customer with a poor credit rating on the ledger with a question mark. It is more likely, however, that it is a direct translation of the German word *querstrasse*, that is, a road at right angles to the main road. Similarly, to be in Carey Street is to be bankrupt. Carey Street is situated in the City of London off Chancery Lane, and is home to the bankruptcy courts. As an aside, to be in a street, metaphorically, is a neat turn of phrase to evoke an emotional state; for instance, in Elvis Presley's (1935–77) first hit song (1955), 'Heartbreak Hotel' lies 'down at the end of Lonely Street'.

Rabbit – Little rabbits have big ears
A twentieth-century Australian modification of the old proverb 'little pitchers have great ears'. It means that grownups should watch their language when talking in front of small children, who often pick up many a hint that the speaker might wish to pass unnoticed. The 'ear' of a pitcher is the handle, which is often ear shaped, and the phrase 'Asses as well as pitchers have big ears' is also common.

Rabbit – More rabbit than Sainsbury's
Said of someone who is thought to waffle on, or to talk pointlessly. 'To rabbit' means to talk and is thought to come from Cockney rhyming slang 'rabbit and pork'. The singers Chas and Dave gave us the line 'rabbit, rabbit', in a song that accompanied one of a series of TV commercials for Courage Best Bitter in Britain in the early 1980s. The advertisement pokes fun at talkative women who interrupt the pleasures of supping pints of beer. However, according to the *Oxford English Dictionary*, the term to rabbit may come from a French dialect word, *rabotte*, meaning to waffle.

Ragtag and bobtail
The riff-raff, the rabble, otherwise known as the 'great unwashed'; all derogatory terms for the masses or lower classes. This expression was common in the sixteenth and seventeenth centuries as 'the rag and tag'. Rags are tatters or remnants of cloth or clothes, and a ruffian or vagabond is still known as a ragamuffin; a muffin was a colloquial diminutive for a pitiful creature. Rag, Tag and Bobtail were popular characters in the early days of children's television in the 1950s; they appeared on the BBC's *Watch with Mother*, and were contemporaries of Andy Pandy and the Flowerpot Men.

Rain check, to take a

A rain check is the receipt or counterfoil of a baseball ticket that can be used at a later date if a game has been interrupted by rain. It is an American expression and the phrase retains the American spelling of 'cheque'. The phrase is now often used, figuratively, to accept an invitation, put it on hold and defer it until a later date. It is, in fact, a polite way of postponing something indefinitely, with only a minor commitment to rearrange.

Real McCoy, the

This is a common American expression, although it probably originated in Scotland in the 1880s, when it was applied to MacKay whisky. This particular brand of whisky was exported to America and Canada, where people of Scottish origin drank it and kept the phrase alive. In the 1890s, however, there is no doubt that it was applied to a famous boxer, the prize fighter Kid 'the Real' McCoy (1872–1940), and this is the spelling that has remained in use. Coca-Cola, probably the most advertised product in the world, adapted the phrase in the 1970s by describing their product as the 'real thing' in comparison with any rival products.

Red – To see red

To give way to excessive passion or anger, or to be violently moved; to indulge in physical violence while in a state of frenzy. The reference is to the Spanish spectacle of bullfighting and the art of taunting the bull. The phrase 'like a red rag to a bull' is said of anything that is calculated to excite rage. Toreadors' capes are lined with red, although there is no evidence that the colour itself incenses the bulls. Red is one of the primary colours and is the colour of passion; it signifies magnanimity and fortitude in heraldry, and in popular folklore it is the colour of magic. Nowadays it is also the colour of revolution or anarchy, although in the nineteenth century, Lord Tennyson (1809–1892) presaged this when he referred to 'Red ruin, and the breaking up of laws' in 'Guinevere'. Red is the colour of the royal livery, and it is said that it was adopted by huntsmen because foxhunting was a royal sport from the time of Henry II (1154–89).

Revenge is a dish best served cold
Be patient, vengeance will be all the more satisfying if you take your time in getting back at someone. It is said that revenge is sweet, but not when you're on the receiving end. There is an old proverb from 1578 that advises, 'Living well is the best revenge', and according to Euripedes (480–406 BC), 'There's nothing like the sight of an old enemy down on his luck.' When it comes to marital revenge, 'When a man steals your wife, there is no better revenge than to let him keep her,' as Sasha Guitry wrote in *Elle et Toi*.

Revenons à nos moutons
A French phrase that means literally 'Let us return to our sheep,' which has been used for hundreds of years in English to mean, 'Let's get back to the subject'. It comes from the French comedy *La Farce de Maistre Pierre Pathelin*; or *l'Avocat Pathelin* (c. 1460),

in which a woollen draper accuses a shepherd, Aignelet, of cruelty to his sheep. In telling his story the draper continually digresses from the subject in order to discredit the defendant's attorney, Pierre Pathelin. The judge has to interrupt him continuously by saying 'Mais, mon ami, revenons a nos moutons.' The phrase was frequently quoted by Rabelais (c. 1495–1553) and has a facetious equivalent among some English speakers, when asking someone to keep to the subject, in 'Let's return to our muttons.'

Ride, to be taken for a
This colloquial phrase can be interpreted in one of two ways. It refers either to the victim of a light-hearted joke or prank or, in its sinister and probably original meaning – a completely genuine use of the phrase – to someone who is taken for a ride somewhere and does not come back in one piece, if at all. The rival underworld gangs of American cities in the 1920s and 1930s were virtually at

war with each other, and any unfortunate who was unlucky enough to tempt the wrath of the gang leader, or Don in the case of the Mafia, would be literally taken for a ride in a limousine, ostensibly to discuss certain matters or sort out some misunderstanding. He would be very unlikely to return alive, however.

Riot act, to read the
Figuratively, 'to read the riot act' is to attempt to quell chattering and general commotion or misbehaviour, particularly in a group of children, by vigorous and forceful pleas coupled with threats of the consequences if order is not resumed. The original Riot Act became law in 1715, and stated that when twelve or more people were gathered with the intention of rioting, it was the duty of the magistrates to command them to disperse, and that anyone who continued to riot for one hour afterwards was guilty of a serious criminal offence. It was not superseded until 1986 when the Public Order Act was introduced. 'To run riot' was originally said of hounds that had lost the scent, and was later applied to any group that behaved in a disorderly or unrestrained way.

Roaring Forties, the

A mariner's term for the stormy regions between the southern latitudes 40° and 50°, famous for the prevailing westerly winds. In the days of sail these winds often encouraged mariners to return to Europe via Cape Horn, the southernmost tip of South America (named after a Dutch sailor from the town of Hoorn in Holland in about 1616), instead of the Cape of Good Hope, the southernmost tip of Africa (which was first known as the Cape of Storms until 1486, when King John II of Portugal ordered the adoption of its present more encouraging name). The term has also been applied to the North Atlantic crossing between the same northern latitudes. On a different tack, the 1920s were known as the 'Roaring Twenties', to reflect the buoyant and upbeat mood which took hold as people sought to obliterate the memory of the horrors of the First World War (see **Bright youngs things**, q.v.).

Rock 'n' roll – It's only rock 'n' roll

Rock and roll was the pop-music style of the latter half of the 1950s, and was an easy-listening form of rhythm and blues with a heavily accented beat and simple repeated phrasing. It became the accompaniment to a youth rebellion and the parental and establishment shock that went with it. The phrase itself was used from about 1953 by the American disc jockey Alan Freed as a racially acceptable term for 'rhythm and blues', which was essentially black music. Its fans were known as 'rockers' and belonged to the era of the 'teddy boy', so called because of their Edwardian style of dress, after King Edward VII (1841–1910). 'It's only rock 'n' roll' became an ubiquitous graffito in the 1970s after the Rolling Stones album of the same name. In 1977, the punk poet Ian Dury (1942–2000) coined and put to music the much used phrase that summed up the attitude of most rock 'n' rollers, and probably still does, 'sex and drugs and rock 'n' roll'. The term 'rock 'n' roll' was originally American black slang for sexual intercourse.

Rome – To fiddle while Rome burns

To delay or vacillate or do nothing during an emergency or crisis, an allusion to Nero's reputed behaviour during the burning of Rome in AD 64. Nero Claudius Caesar (AD 37–68) was the infamous Roman Emperor whom his contemporaries believed to be the instigator of the fire that destroyed most of the city. As the blaze raged it is said that he sang to his lyre and recited his own poetry whilst enjoying the spectacle from the top of a high tower. Many historians doubt his complicity, however, and Nero himself blamed the Christians.

Rome was not built in a day

Great achievements, worthwhile tasks and the like are not accomplished without patient perseverance and a considerable passage of time. This was originally a Latin proverb and has been quoted ever since, as in:

> Rome was not bylt on a daie (quoth he) and yet stood Tyll it was fynysht
>> John Heywood (c. 1497–c. 1580), *A dialogue conteinyng the number in effect of all the prouerbes in the englishe tongue* (1546)

Rome was the greatest city in the ancient world and, according to legend, was founded in 753 BC by the legendary Romulus (hence the city's name) and his twin brother Remus. However, it is most likely to have been named from the Greek *rhoma* meaning strength, and its other Latin name is Valentia, from *valens* meaning strong. As an indication of its importance in the world, Rome features in numerous old sayings such as 'When in Rome do as the Romans do' and 'All roads lead to Rome' – or 'All roads lead to rum', as WC Fields (1880–1946) put it.

Rose by any other name, a
The name of a person is irrelevant; it is their qualities, their personality, that are important. A mere name has no effect upon the characteristics of the person or thing in question. Or 'A chrysanthemum by any other name would be easier to spell', as William J Johnston once commented. The phrase is from Shakespeare:

> JULIET: What's in a name? that which we call a rose
>> By any other name would smell as sweet;
>> So Romeo would, were he not Romeo call'd.
>>> *Romeo and Juliet* (1594)

Rose-tinted spectacles, to see through
To look at life or to regard circumstances with unjustified optimism, always looking on the bright side of life, as though it were suffused with a gentle pink light. Spectacles of such a hue would show the world in the pink, but it would be misleadingly rosy, bright and hopeful. The French equivalent is *voir la vie en rose* – to see life 'in the pink', which in turn means to be in excellent health, abbreviated from the phrase 'in the pink of health' or 'in the pink of condition', a meaning derived from a flower in its best state.

Round robin
A petition or protest signed in a circular form on the page so that no one name heads the list. The device is believed to have originated in France and the term could be a corruption of *rond* and *ruban* – round ribbon. The round-robin letter or petition is believed to have been first devised by British sailors in the seventeenth or early eighteenth centuries when presenting a grievance to the ship's captain. To avoid punishment the ringleader would arrange for the signatures to be inscribed in a circular fashion around the page – although if the ship's captain was particularly vindictive he would punish all the signatories for insurrection. A round-robin tournament is a friendly sporting contest, such as tennis, in which all participants change partners so that everyone competes against everyone. A round-robin letter, usually sent at Christmas, is a duplicated letter recording one's news and achievements of the year for the edification of one's acquaintances.

Round-table conference
A conference in which all participants are ranked equally, or at which it is agreed that the discussion or dispute should be settled amicably with the maximum amount of 'give and take' on all sides. King Arthur's Round Table, which seated 150 knights, was circular to prevent any rivalry among the delegates, and the earliest written reference to it is in Wace's (*c.* 1115–*c.* 1183) *Roman de Brut* of

1155. The expression came to general prominence in connection with a private conference in the house of Sir William Harcourt in January 1887, with the aim of trying to reunite the Liberal Party after the split caused by Gladstone's support of Irish Home Rule. Other politically notable round-table conferences were those on the future of Indian government held in London in 1931–2.

Round up the usual suspects

Since the film *The Usual Suspects* was released in 1985, this phrase has returned to regular use, and is employed as a jocular instruction to gather a group of people together. It is thought that the line was first spoken in the film *Casablanca* (1943), directed by Hal B Wallis and starring Humphrey Bogart and Ingrid Bergman (although Ronald Reagan and Ann Sheridan were originally named for the leads). Claud Rains, playing the French Captain Renault, Chief of Police in wartime Casablanca, delivers this classic line in the last scene of the movie: 'Major Strasser has been shot. Round up the usual suspects.' When shooting began the script was not finished and towards the end of filming the dialogue was written on demand and literally rushed to the set. According to the film chronicler Leslie Halliwell (1929–1991), the film 'just fell together impeccably into one of the outstanding entertainment experiences in cinema history'. (See also **Bogart – Don't Bogart that joint**, q.v.)

Royal 'we', the

The somewhat superior choice of the collective pronoun 'we' in place of the individual 'I' by a single person. It has long been observed that the Queen has used this style in referring to herself, for instance during her Christmas Day broadcasts, while the frosty comment, 'We are not amused' was attributed to Queen Victoria in 1900. In March 1989, the then Prime Minister, Margaret Thatcher, announced to the world in a famously regal tone:

We have become a grandmother.

Rubicon – To cross the Rubicon

To take an irrevocable step, to burn one's bridges behind one, to go beyond the point of no return. The Rubicon was a small river, possibly the present-day Fiumicino, which formed the border between ancient Italy and Cisalpine Gaul, the province allocated to Julius Caesar. When Caesar, having disobeyed the Senate's order to disband his army and resign his command, crossed this stream in 49 BC he went beyond the limits of his own province and thus became an invader in Italy. With this action he hastened the outbreak of war between Pompey and the Senate, in which Caesar triumphed.

Rule of thumb

A rough guesswork measure, a calculation based on generally held experience in a certain field. This rule is distinct from any proven theory and refers to the use of the thumb to make rough measurements. The first joint of the average adult thumb measures 1 inch or 25mm, and thumbnail sketches are miniature drawings, roughs or diagrams, usually quickly executed. There is also an apochryphal derivation for 'rule of thumb': in the days when it was accepted practice for a man to beat his wife, the stick for this purpose was legally allowed to be no broader than the thickness of a man's thumb; it was illegal for the stick to be thicker and a man using such a stick could be arrested for assault.

Run the gauntlet, to

To be attacked on all sides or to be severely criticized. The expression appeared in English at the time of the Thirty Years War (1618–48) as 'gantlope', meaning the passage between two files of soldiers. It is an amalgamation of the Swedish words *galop* – passageway, *gata* – way, and *lop* – course. 'Running the gauntlet' was a form of punishment used by the Germans, but was said to have originated in Sweden amongst soldiers and sailors. The company or crew, armed with whips, thongs or rods, were assembled in two facing rows, and the miscreant had to run the course between them while each man dealt him as severe a blow as he thought befitted the misdemeanour. The American Indians also had a similar, more brutal, form of retribution, because here the victim was not intended to survive the blows he suffered during his run.

Salt – To rub salt into the wound

To increase someone's pain or shame. The phrase alludes to an ancient nautical punishment for misbehaviour by members of a ship's crew. Errant sailors were flogged on the bare back, and afterwards salt was rubbed into the wounds. Salt is a well-known antiseptic so it helped to heal the lacerations, but it also made them much more painful. An extension of this phrase is the saying 'Don't rub it in', an admission that one may have made a fool of oneself, but people should not carry on reminding one.

Salt – To sit above the salt

To sit in a place of distinction at the dinner table. Formerly the family 'saler' or salt cellar was an ornate silver centre-piece, placed in the middle of the table. Special or honoured guests of distinction sat above the saler, that is, between the salt and the head of the table where the host sat, while dependants and not quite so important personages sat below. Salt is also a significant euphemism, from the early nineteenth century onwards, for one's financial worth, as a play on the word 'salary', or the amount one earned. In Roman times a soldier received part of his pay in the form of a *salarium*, or salary, which was actually an allowance for the purchase of salt (the Latin for salt is *sal*). Salt was not easily obtainable then, and a soldier was not 'worth his salt' if he did not come up to standard, that is, did not deserve his *salarium*. To be 'true to one's salt' is to be loyal to your employers, those who pay your salary.

Salt – With a pinch of salt

To treat information or explanations with great reservation, qualification, scepticism, doubt or disbelief. To make allowance for a mere grain of truth, but not much. To add a pinch of salt to something makes it taste more palatable and helps one to swallow it.

Sands – The sands are running out

A metaphor to remind us that time is short; there will be less time to do what you have to do unless you act now. The phrase is often used with reference to one who has not much longer to live. The allusion is to the sand in an hourglass. The original version of the phrase is 'The sands of time are running out', the first part of which appears in the poem 'A Psalm of Life' (1838) by Henry Wadsworth Longfellow (1807–82):

> Lives of great men all around us
> We can make our lives sublime,
> And, departing, leave behind us
> Footprints on the sands of time.

Or as Robert Burns (1759–96) wrote in 'Tam o' Shanter' in 1791:

> Nae man can tether time or tide.

Sauce for the goose is sauce for the gander, what is

This old phrase seems to promote sexual equality long before it was fashionable. It suggests that the same rules apply in both cases, what is fitting for the husband should also be fitting for the wife. Originally 'sauce', from the Latin *salsus*, means salted food used as a relish with meat, such as pickled roots and herbs. 'Sauce' also means cheek or impertinence, perhaps in relation to the piquancy of such relishes.

Saved by the bell

This is a boxing term thought to date from the 1930s. A floored contestant being counted out (see **Out for the count**, q.v.)might be saved by the ringing of the bell marking the end of the round, giving him the three-minute break between rounds to recover. However, there is another, albeit unsubstantiated, and gruesome theory to explain this phrase. When graveyards became overcrowded in the eighteenth century, coffins were dug up, the bones taken away and the graves reused. In reopening the coffins, one out of twenty-five were found to have scratch marks on the inside, meaning that people must have been buried alive. To guard against this most unfortunate occurrence, a string was tied to the wrist of the corpse, and led from the coffin and up through the ground, where it was tied to a bell. Someone would have to sit in the graveyard all night to listen for the bell – hence the phrase 'saved by the bell'. From the same derivation we have night workers on the 'graveyard shift' and sailors on the 'graveyard watch' between midnight and dawn.

Say it with flowers
This phrase, still used to advertise flowers, was first used by the Society of American Florists in 1917. It is said to have been invented for the chairman of the society's publicity committee, Henry Penn of Boston, Massachusetts. Advertising boss Major Patrick O'Keefe suggested, 'Flowers are words that even a babe can understand', which was a line he had found in a poetry book. Eventually, between them O'Keefe and Penn came up with this winning slogan. The neat phrase has also been the title of several songs.

Scratch, to come up to
To be fully prepared for a challenge, or good enough to pass any test; to make the grade. This is a colloquialism from the boxing ring dating back to the nineteenth century. Under the London Prize Ring Rules introduced in 1839 a round in a prizefight ended

when one of the fighters was knocked down. After an interval of thirty seconds the floored fighter was given eight seconds to make his way, unaided, to a mark scratched in the centre of the ring. If he failed to reach the mark, he 'had not come up to scratch' and was declared the loser of the bout.

Sell (someone) down the river, to
This expression means to deceive or to betray. The phrase probably originated in the first few years of the nineteenth century in the southern states of America. Since by then it was illegal to import slaves, there was an internal trade and they were brought down the Mississippi to the slave markets of Natchez or New Orleans. Therefore if a slave was 'sold down the river' he lost his home and family. The saying particularly alludes to the practice of selling unruly slaves to owners of plantations on the lower river, where conditions were harsher than in the northern slave states. To 'sell' is old slang for swindle or hoax, and a person who has been tricked is said to have been 'sold'. To 'sell the pass' is to betray one's own side; the phrase was originally Irish and is applied to those who turn king's evidence or who betray their comrades for money. The tradition relates to the behaviour of the regiment that was sent by Crotha, Lord of Atha, to hold a pass against the invading army of Trathal, King of Cael. The pass was yielded for money and Trathal assumed the title of King of Ireland.

Sell off the family silver
To dispose of valuable assets or heirlooms that have been passed down from one generation to the next, for a much needed injection of cash, having fallen upon hard times. Many such items are

traditionally silver, and are of great sentimental value; worse, once gone they cannot be retrieved. The allusion was memorably set into a modern context in a speech by the former Conservative Prime Minister, Sir Harold Macmillan, 1st Earl of Stockton (1894–1986), to the Tory Reform Group on 8 November 1985. In it he criticized

Margaret Thatcher's government for privatizing nationalized industries like the railway, gas and electricity companies, when he said, 'First of all the Georgian silver goes, and then all that nice furniture that used to be in the saloon. Then the Canalettos go.' The speech was summarized as 'selling off the family silver'.

Sell-by date, to be past
This term comes from the supermarket and is applied to perishable packaged food on which the date before which, for safety reasons, it should be consumed is indicated. The expression is widely applied metaphorically to almost any short-lived or disposable area of life that may lose its freshness or appeal, such as ideas, fashion, media personalities, relationships; it is sometimes also used of people, especially those in high-profile jobs, such as actors or models.

Send in the clowns
This expression is from the world of showbiz. As it sounds, the phrase comes from the big top, and is a way of saying, 'The show must go on'. In the event of a calamity backstage at a circus the clowns are sent into the ring to keep the audience amused

and distracted until the panic behind the scenes is over. Whatever disasters occur, life must go on as normal and nothing should be allowed to ruin the public reputation of the show. The phrase was used as the title for a song in Stephen Sondheim's musical *A Little Night Music* (1974).

Send (someone) to Coventry, to

To refuse to speak to someone, to ostracize a person or ignore them. At the time of the Great Rebellion (or English Civil War) between 1642 and 1649, it is said that the citizens of Coventry once had so great a dislike of soldiers that a woman seen speaking to one was instantly shunned. Hence when a soldier was 'sent to Coventry' he would get the cold shoulder. During the years of strife between King Charles I and Parliament, Royalists were often attacked and either killed or taken to Coventry, where they would be imprisoned and ostracized, because the city was strongly Protestant and pro-Parliament. Edward Hyde, Earl of Clarendon (1609–74), referred to Royalist prisoners captured in Birmingham who were 'sent to Coventry', effectively into exile. To take this a step further, to refuse to have any dealing with a person or group of people as a means of protest or coercion is to 'boycott' them, which dates from 1880, when such methods were used by the Irish Land League against one Captain CC Boycott (1832–97), a land agent in County Mayo, to try and persuade him to reduce rents.

Serious money

A large amount of money, a substantial fee or a five- or six-figure salary. A frequently heard phrase during the high-earning, high-spending years of the materialistic 1980s, Caryl Churchill wrote a satirical play of this title in 1987. Ambitious, enterprising and successful executives expect to earn 'serious money', and there are many different phrases attached to this sentiment: 'If you pay peanuts you get monkeys' or 'You get what you pay for' or 'We're talking telephone numbers'. (The last metaphor only works provided you are not just dialling the operator – 100 – or other 3-digit numbers.

Seventh heaven, to be in

To be supremely happy, in a state of complete ecstasy. The seventh heaven was defined by the Cabbalists who were students of a Jewish mystical system of theology and metaphysics dating from the eleventh and twelfth centuries, but with roots in ancient Greek teachings. They interpreted passages from the Old Testament based on the symbolism of numbers, devised and decoded charms and created mystical anagrams and the like. They maintained that there are seven heavens each rising above the other, the seventh being the home of God and the archangels, the highest in the hierarchy of the angels. Seven is a mystic or sacred number. It is the sum of four and three which, among the Pythagoreans, were, and have been ever since, counted as lucky numbers. Among ancient cultures there were seven sacred planets, and the Hebrew verb 'to swear' means literally to 'come under the influence of seven things', while in an Arabic curse seven stones are smeared with blood, all of which demonstrate the power of seven as a mystical number.

Sharp end, at the sharp end

Directly involved with the action, positioned where the competition or danger is greatest. The connection is not with the point of a sword, but with the pointed shape of the bows of a ship, which are the first towards the enemy in any engagement or battle. The cry of 'Look sharp!' or 'Sharp's the word!' are both calls to immediate action, whether on the battlefield or in the playground; the expressions also mean to be observant, to 'keep your eye on the ball'. Before the days of large supermarkets and closed-circuit television, if a shopkeeper suspected a customer of shoplifting he would give a coded warning to his assistant by saying, 'Mr Sharp has come in'.

She who must be obeyed

A phrase describing a harridan or domineering woman. It was inspired by its use in John Mortimer's *Rumpole of the Bailey* which was serialized on television in the 1970s and 1980s. The eponymous barrister, Rumpole, famously used this phrase of his overbearing wife. Mortimer's original source was Sir Henry Rider Haggard's (1856–1925) novel *She* (1887), and Denis Healey ironically referred to Margaret Thatcher in this way in 1984. With similar feeling, the phrase ''Er indoors' comes from the 1970s television series *Minder*, that being how Arthur Daley (played by George Cole) refers to Mrs Daley.

Sheep – A sheep in sheep's clothing

An amusing modification of the well-known proverb 'a wolf in sheep's clothing', meaning to be spineless or utterly weak. It is attributed to Winston Churchill in a comment on his successor, the Labour Prime Minister, Clement Attlee (1883–1967), although the British writer Edmund Gosse (1849–1928) first used it when referring to the poet T Sturge Moore (1870–1944) in about 1906. In another political taunt Labour's Denis Healey described an attack on him by the Conservative Geoffrey Howe as like being 'savaged by a dead sheep'. The original phrase linking wolves and sheep probably comes from the Bible:

> Beware of false prophets, which come to you in sheep's clothing, but inwardly they are ravening wolves.
>
> Matthew 7:15

Sheep – Separate the sheep from the goats

To divide the worthy from the unworthy, the favoured from the disfavoured, the good from the not so good. The comparison comes from the Bible, and sheep usually symbolize the meek (and stupid, in certain circumstances); in biblical terms, however, they represent the flock of Christ, while goats symbolize virility, lust, cunning and destructiveness.

> And before him shall be gathered all nations; and he shall separate them one from another, as a shepherd divideth his sheep from the goats.
>
> Matthew 25:32

A similar expression, also from the Bible, is 'to separate the wheat from the chaff', meaning to distinguish good from bad, that is the 'staff of life' from the waste material. The comparison is implicit in certain biblical texts:

What is the chaff to the wheat? saith the Lord.

Jeremiah 23:28

Shoes – Another man's shoes

'To stand in another man's shoes' is to take the place of another person. In similar vein the opportunistic phrase 'Waiting for dead men's shoes' is sometimes thought, if not spoken. Among the Vikings when a man adopted a son, the adoptee put on the shoes of his new father.

Reynard the Fox, a medieval beast epic (c. 1175–1250), is a satire on contemporary life found in French, Flemish and German literature. Reynard, having turned the tables on the former minister Sir Bruin the Bear, asks the queen to let him have the shoes of the disgraced bear. As a result Bruin's shoes are torn off and put on the new hero.

Short shrift, to give

To treat someone peremptorily and unsympathetically, without heeding any mitigating arguments, or simply to make short work of something. Shrift is defined as a confession to a priest and 'short shrift' refers to the few minutes left to a convict between condemnation, confession and absolution, and then finally execution. To shrive a person is to impose penance after confession so that they can be freed from their sins. Shrovetide is the three days just before Lent when people used to go to confession and afterwards indulged in all sorts of partying. Shrove Tuesday is the day before Ash Wednesday and is known as Pancake Day, when the store cupboards are emptied to mark the beginning of a symbolic period of abstinence, as penance during Lent.

Show a leg, to

The summons to 'show a leg' or 'shake a leg' is a morning wake-up call. It is a naval phrase and was the traditional alarm call used to roust the hands from their hammocks. It comes from the days in the mid-nineteenth century when women were allowed to sleep on board ship when the navy was in port. At the cry of 'Show a leg!' if a woman's limb was shaken out of the hammock she was allowed to lie in, but if the hairy leg of a rating appeared he had to get up and get on with his duties. Later in the nineteenth century to 'shake a leg' came to mean to dance, while in America it meant to hurry up.

Sick as a parrot, as

A banality to describe extreme disappointment at an unexpected failure or setback. It suggests several meanings of the word sick, among them ill, diseased or disgusted, and parrots are extremely prone to viruses such as the highly contagious disease psittacosis (parrot fever). In the 1970s and 1980s it was a somewhat overused metaphor favoured by football managers, who often used it to describe their feelings after losing a match. Despite being mocked by the satirical magazine *Private Eye*, and perhaps helped by the absurdity of the 'Dead Parrot' sketch in *Monty Python's Flying Circus*, its imagery caught the public imagination, and it is now used ironically.

Silk purse out of a sow's ear, to make

To attempt to make something good or of great value from what is naturally bad or inferior in quality. A similar old proverb is that 'You cannot make a horn out of a pig's ear'. To make a pig's ear of something is to bodge it, the ear of a slaughtered pig being its most worthless part, no good for anything. This led to a similar slang expression, thought to have been instigated in the 1920s, 'to make a dog's breakfast', or 'dog's dinner', out of something. If a person is described as looking like a dog's dinner, they are considered to be 'done up to the nines', or vulgarly overdressed.

Sixty-four-thousand-dollar-question, the

The ultimate and most difficult question, the nub of a problem. This widely used phrase comes from the 1940s American radio quiz show, *Take It or Leave It*. During the course of the show contestants were asked increasingly difficult questions for prize money, which also increased as the questions became harder. The final question was worth $64. Inflation has affected this expression over the years since it began life as the humble sixty-four dollar question, growing first to sixty-four thousand and recently to sixty-four billion. The expression is used in all English-speaking countries.

Skeleton in the closet

A domestic source of humiliation or shame which a family or individual conspires to conceal from others. Every family is said to have one, and certainly these days it seems that every public figure has one too, whether it is in the form of an ex-mistress or lover, inhaling marijuana smoke, or not, at university, or some ancient but discreditable financial scam. An apocryphal story has it that a person without a single care or trouble in the world had to be found. After a long search a squeaky-clean lady was found, but to the great surprise of all, after she had proved herself on all counts she went upstairs and opened a closet which contained a human skeleton. 'I try and keep my trouble to myself, but every night my husband makes me kiss that skeleton,' she said. She then explained that the skeleton was that of her husband's rival, killed in a duel over her. The expression seems to have been in use at least since the mid-nineteenth century, when it appeared in *The Newcomes* by William Makepeace Thackeray (1811–63):

And it is from these that we shall arrive at some particulars regarding the Newcome family, which will show us that they have a skeleton or two in their closets as well as their neighbours.

Skid row, to be on
An American expression applied to the part of town frequented by vagrants, hobos, alcoholics, or down-and-outs. Hence if you are 'on the skids', it means that you are on your way to that rather grimy quarter of the city, about to skid off the path of virtue. The expression probably comes from the early days of the Seattle timber industry. A 'skid row' was a row of logs down which other felled timber was slid or skidded. Tacoma, near Seattle, became prosperous with the growth of the timber industry, and in due course there were plentiful supplies of liquor and brothels in the town, close at hand for lumberjacks working the skid row.

Sling your hook!
A somewhat forceful command urging a person to leave, or a way of asking someone to go away without resorting to foul language. The expression is probably of nautical origin and alludes to the anchor, or 'hook', which must be secured in its sling at the bow before the ship can cast off. Shortened forms of the expression 'Hook it!' and 'Take your hook!' are also used, perhaps to give more emphasis to one's wish that a person should leave and set about their business. It is possible, however, the hook may be an angler's hook, since to be 'on one's own hook' means to act on one's own initiative – a hook is cast into the water to make a catch or, metaphorically, to achieve something useful.

Small is beautiful
Originally the title of a book (1973) by EF Shumacher (1911–77), this has become a catchphrase for those opposed to large industrial conglomerates and overbearing bureaucracy in government, and who desire economics on a human scale. It is thought that Shumacher, who was subsequently celebrated as a business guru, did not invent the phrase, but that his publishers came up with it, possibly influenced by the power of the phrase 'black is beautiful'. It can now be used in almost any context along with the phrase 'less is more', which implies both refinement and minimalism.

Smoke-filled room

This is a political euphemism (see also **Beer and sandwiches**, q.v.) and refers to the meeting rooms from which political leaders emerge, ideally with a decision or resolution, after many hours of negotiating or horse trading. However, nowadays the rooms are unlikely to be filled with smoke, as the habit of smoking has become extremely unfashionable with its well-known health risks. The original smoke-filled room was a suite in the Blackstone Hotel in Chicago, in which Warren Harding was selected as the Republican presidential candidate in June 1920 after protracted bargaining. The phrase itself appears to have come from a comment by Harding's chief spokesman, Harry Dougherty, and in those days the smoke was likely to have been that of cigars.

Snug as a bug in a rug, as

A whimsical and comfortable comparison dating from the eighteenth century, although a snug is a sixteenth-century word for a parlour in an inn. The phrase is usually credited to Benjamin Franklin (1706–90), who was very fond of children and wrote these words to Georgiana Shipley, the daughter of his friend, the Bishop of St Asaph. As a gift from Philadelphia Franklin's wife had sent the Shipleys a grey squirrel whom they called Skugg, a common name for squirrels at the time. Tragically he escaped from his cage and was killed by a dog. Franklin wrote this epitaph in 1772:

Here Skugg
Lies snug
As a bug
In a rug.

However, there are earlier uses, as in a celebration of David Garrick's (1717–79) Shakespeare festival in 1769, seen printed in the *Stratford Jubilee*:

If she [a rich widow] has the mopus's [money],
I'll have her, as snug as a bug in a rug.

In 1706, Edward Ward (1667–79) wrote in *The Wooden World Dissected*

He sits as snug as a bee in a box.

And in Thomas Heywood's (c. 1574–1641) 1603 play *A Woman Killed with Kindness* there is:

Let us sleep as snug as pigs in pease-straw.

Sour grapes

This is an ancient metaphor for something that seems desirable, but is, in fact, unattainable and for that reason is disparaged or rubbished; in other words, that which you cannot get. The phrase comes from the well-known fable by Aesop (6th century BC), 'The Fox and the Grapes'. One hot day a thirsty fox spotted some juicy-looking grapes hanging from a vine. The cluster of fruit was just out of reach and however hard he tried he could not reach the grapes, and the greater the effort he made the hotter and thirstier he became. Eventually the fox gave up and reasoned that as the grapes were beyond reach they would probably be sour and inedible. The moral of the story is that we can console ourselves with the fact that if some things are unattainable, we probably wouldn't like them anyway. A fine example of the sour-grapes syndrome is by William Penn Patrick:

Those who condemn wealth are those who have none and see no chance of getting it.

And according to Ovid (43 BC–AD 17):

Envy assails the noblest: the winds howl around the highest peaks.

153

Spanish custom, an old Spanish custom

Also known as 'an old Spanish practice', this is the bargaining excuse given by workers trying to bend the rules when it comes to negotiating certain advantages, such as more pay, shorter working hours, more tea breaks, and so on. It is not clear why the Spanish are blamed for this. However, historic national rivalry between the Spanish and the British has led to many light-hearted expressions in the workplace, such as the 'Spanish worm', which is a nail hidden in a piece of wood against which a carpenter jars his chisel or saw. To be given the 'Spanish archer' is to be sacked or given the 'elbow', and Spanish workers, or indeed anyone who procrastinates or takes their time over things, are, whether fairly or unfairly, accused of carrying out their business *mañana* – tomorrow. Perhaps this relates to the custom of the Spanish siesta – which comes from the Spanish words *sexta hora*, sixth hour – when work stops in the heat of the early afternoon and everyone has a nap, during what the British consider to be part of the working day.

Spin doctor

This is an American idiom which was first applied in political commentary in the mid-1980s under Ronald Reagan's presidency, describing his public-relations advisers during promotion of the 'Star Wars' Strategic Defence Initiative (SDI). These so-called 'spin doctors' were on 'spin control', their mission being to give the preferred interpretation of events to the world's media, thereby manipulating public opinion in the desired direction. The phrase comes from baseball and refers to the spin put on the ball by a pitcher to disguise its true direction or confuse the batter. The spin doctor is now a prominent feature in British politics and business in general.

Stand by your man

This is the title of a song by American country and western singer Tammy Wynette (born Virginia Wynette Pugh, 1942–98) and first recorded in 1968:

> Stand by your man,
> And show the world you love him,

Keep giving all the love you can,
Stand by your man.

Tammy Wynette was dubbed 'The First Lady of Country', but despite entitling her 1979 autobiography *Stand By Your Man*, she had five marriages and suffered chronic illness, arson attacks, kidnapping and bankruptcy. The phrase has entered the language, and is used by headline writers when alluding to such stalwart wives as Hillary Clinton and various Tory spouses who stood by their men despite much-publicized philandering by their husbands.

Star-Spangled Banner, the

The flag of the United States of America, otherwise known as the Stars and Stripes. The stripes represent the original thirteen states, and the fifty stars the states that now make up the Union. The flag is also popularly called 'Old Glory', so named, supposedly, by William Driver, a Salem skipper, in 1831. At the outset of the American Revolution each state adopted its own flag; however, in 1776 a national flag of thirteen red and white stripes, with crosses of St George and St Andrew in a canton, was adopted. By act of Congress in June 1777 the new flag had thirteen alternate red and white stripes with a union of thirteen white stars arranged in a circle on a blue field, representing a new constellation; it was apparently designed by Francis Hopkinson. In 1794, after the admission of Vermont and Kentucky, the stripes and stars were increased to fifteen, but in 1818 it was decided to restore the thirteen stripes, and that stars should be added to signify the number of states in the Union; the stars were also squared up for the first time. 'The Stars and Stripes Forever' is the name of John Philip Sousa's most popular military-band tune, and 'The Star-Spangled Banner' was adopted as the official anthem of the United States in 1931.

The words were written by Francis Scott Key (1780–1843) in 1814 and the tune was that of 'Anacreon in Heaven', a popular drinking song composed by a Londoner, JS Smith (1750–1836).

Stiff upper lip
A determined resolve combined with complete suppression of the emotions. This is supposedly a traditional characteristic of the English, especially military officers during the two world wars, their upper lips frequently concealed with a moustache, which perhaps became fashionable because it could conceal any uncontrollable trembling reflexes at the wrong moment. A quivering upper lip is often a sign of emotion. It is not sure when the phrase was first heard, but it appeared well before the First World War in the petry of Phoebe Cary (1824–71) in 'Keep a Stiff Upper Lip':

> And though hard be the task
> 'Keep a stiff upper lip'.

Still waters run deep
However quiet or calm someone may seem on the surface, do not be deceived, there is probably great depth of knowledge, personality or hot temper lurking below. This is a Latin proverb, and the Malayan proverb, 'Don't think there are no crocodiles because the water is calm', means much the same. It is never a good idea to show off or talk too much, because as everyone knows, empty vessels make the most noise. Speech is silver, but silence is golden. Ducks on a pond illustrate this proverb perfectly, in that they glide smoothly across the surface, without a feather out of place, but below their feet are paddling – nineteen to the dozen. However, it can be argued that still waters do not run at all.

Stir-up Sunday
In the Christian calendar, this is the last Sunday after Trinity Sunday and takes its name from the collect, the short Anglican prayer for the day, 'Stir up we beseech thee, O Lord, the wills of the faithful people.' It was an old custom to let everyone in the family stir the Christmas plum-pudding mixture on this day and make a wish, hence the old children's rhyme as a play on the

prayer, 'Stir up we beseech thee, the pudding in the pot.' For best results Christmas puddings should be made well in advance so that the fruit can soak up the brandy and whisky, and the mix requires much stirring. Before electric food processors, involving the whole family in the effort was an efficient way of spreading the work.

Stone, to cast the first

To be first to criticize, to find fault, to start a quarrel, or to cast aspersions on someone's character. To cast means to throw a missile, and the barbaric custom of capital punishment in biblical times was to pelt heretics, adulteresses and criminals with stones and rocks in a public place. The phrase is from John 8:7, spoken by Jesus to the Scribes and Pharisees who brought before him a woman caught in adultery. They said that according to the law of Moses, she should be stoned to death, to which Jesus replied:

> He that is without sin among you, let him first cast a stone at her.

Strike while the iron's hot

To act immediately when the opportunity arises. This is a metaphor from the blacksmith's shop, since iron cannot be easily worked once it has cooled down. The phrase has been attributed to Geoffrey Chaucer (*c.* 1345–1400), although there are many ancient sayings that encourage action today rather than waiting for tomorrow (see **Carpe diem**, q.v.) Pittacus said 'Know thy opportunity', and **Make hay while the sun shines** (q.v.) appears in an early sixteenth-century book of proverbs. More up to date, a women's-lib slogan neatly inverts the proverb in a warning against inaction, 'Don't iron while the strike is hot'.

Suck it and see

Said of anything experimental, the saying alludes to taking a pill which has to be sucked first to see if it works. The expression was a catchphrase of Charlie Naughton of the Crazy Gang (*fl.* 1930s) and probably originated earlier in the music halls. It sounds rather old-fashioned nowadays, with the American meaning of the word 'suck' taking hold in Britain. To say that something 'sucks' is a derisive description of something bad or of someone's failure. A 'sucker' is someone who is easily deceived, a greenhorn; that is, a new-born creature that still suckles at its mother's breast.

Suits you, sir
This is one of many catchphrases that entered the language in the 1990s, and comes from the popular BBC television comedy series *The Fast Show*, starring Paul Whitehouse and Charlie Higson, in which two tailor characters repeat the phrase leeringly, 'Ooh! Suits you, sir. Ooh'. With a further surreal touch, the phrase is now used by the same two characters in a television commercial for a brand of lager. Other daft catchphrases include, 'Does my bum look big in this?' 'I've always admired the music of Frank Sinatra' and 'I'm a little bit weeeeyyyy . . . a little bit tasty . . .'. As comedy writers in the late 1980s, Whitehouse and Higson invented the comic characters Stavros and Loadsamoney for fellow comedian Harry Enfield.

Sunny side up
This is a visual metaphor used to describe how a fried egg should be served. It is a phrase that came from American diners and is urban shorthand when ordering a fried egg. Eggs are served with the yolk 'sunny side up', or can be cooked on the other side and served yolk down, that is, 'easy over'.

Sweet Fanny Adams
This expression is ambiguously used to mean either nothing at all, or sweet nothing. It has a very tragic origin. In 1867 eight-year-old Fanny Adams was raped and murdered in a hop garden in Alton, Hampshire, and her dismembered body was thrown into the River Wey. A twenty-one-year-old solicitor's clerk, Frederick Baker, was

tried soon after and hanged at Winchester. The Royal Navy, with extreme black humour, adopted the poor girl's name as a synonym for tinned mutton which was first issued at this time, and for a while stewed meat was known as Fanny Adams. Sweet Fanny Adams became, as a consequence, a phrase for anything worthless, and subsequently to mean nothing at all. The phrase is still used today usually as just the initials 'SFA' or 'sweet FA', which happen to be the same as 'f**k all', from which most people think this expression is derived.

Sword of Damocles, the

Impending danger or disaster in the midst of great prosperity or good fortune. In the fourth century BC, Damocles, who was a toadying sycophant of Dionysus the Elder of Syracuse (see **Walls have ears**, q.v.), was invited by the tyrant to test his self-proclaimed charm and wit. Damocles accepted and was treated to a sumptuous banquet, but over his head a sword was suspended by a mere hair, intended by Dionysus as a symbolic indicator of the fragility of wealth and power, his own included. This quite naturally inhibited Damocles's performance at the banquet because he was too frightened to move.

Talk turkey, to

To discuss some subject frankly or seriously. The origin of the expression is uncertain, but it may have arisen from the efforts of turkey hunters to attract their prey by making gobbling noises. The stupid birds would then either emerge from their cover or return the call, so revealing their whereabouts. At the turn of the last century, the turkey was considered an amusing bird, and conversations in which one 'talked turkey' were convivial. A young suitor's chat-up lines would also be called 'talking turkey', perhaps because in a fit of nerves he might become tongue-tied and his words would come out like gobbling noises. Later the meaning became more serious and related to stern admonitions. Incidentally, turkeys do not come from Turkey, but from North America and were brought to Spain from Mexico. Benjamin Franklin suggested the turkey should be the emblem of the United States of America – however, the bald eagle was chosen instead.

Tall-poppy syndrome

This expression is believed to come from Australia and means to cut an overtly superior person down to size. The phrase has been current since 1931 when Jack Lang (1876–1975), the left-wing leader of the New South Wales administration, described egalitarian policies as 'cutting the heads off the tall poppies'. It derives from the legend that Tarquin, King of Rome (534–510 BC), symbolically demonstrated his wishes for the captured city of Gabii by decapitating the tallest poppies in his garden; accordingly the leading citizens were executed.

Tango – It takes two to tango

A frequently used axiom that comes from the 1952 song of this title by Hofmann and Manning:

> There are lots of things you can do alone!
> But it takes two to tango.

This satisfyingly alliterative phrase is often used in a sexual context when one partner is accused of seducing the other and it implies willingness on both sides. It is also used more widely in the fields of business and politics, to imply that, in order to achieve agreement between two groups, both may have to compromise.

Tarred with the same brush, all tarred with the same brush
Everyone in the group alike is to blame, all sharing the same failings, all sheep of the same flock. This old saying alludes to the former treatment of skin complaints, sores and the like in sheep, with a brush dipped in tar. In less racially enlightened days, not in fact so long ago, the expression, 'a touch of the tar brush' described a person of mixed race, pointing out the not-quite-white colour of their skin.

Teddy-bear syndrome
This describes the characteristics of someone who gets married or enters a relationship simply because he or she fears being alone and needs the constant presence of a comforter, the function of a teddy bear for many small children. The teddy bear is thought to have been so called after American President Theodore (Teddy) Roosevelt (1858–1919), who enjoyed bear hunting. The toy acquired its name after a presidential bear-hunting expedition in 1903. To ensure the President made a kill, the organizers stunned a small brown bear and tied it to a tree.

Teeth – By the skin of one's teeth
By the narrowest margin. There are several metaphors with the possible meaning 'only just' and many allude to bodily parts, emphasizing the physical danger of a given situation from which one might have just escaped. Teeth have no skin and therefore the action or task that has been achieved has been done so 'by a hair's breadth'. This is a biblical phrase that means to have suffered a 'close shave':

> My bone cleaveth to my skin, and to my flesh, and I am escaped with the skin of my teeth.
>
> Job 19:20

Thick as thieves, as
To be intimate with some person or group, to be in collusion with them. Thieves notoriously conspire and plot together, and devise secret languages so that they can discuss their business in a code that will not be understood by others, a slang or jargon that used to be known as 'thieves Latin'. Cockney rhyming slang itself was originally a closed language to the uninitiated and was created by crafty East Londoners to outwit authority and eavesdroppers. 'Thick' is used in this context to mean closely knit, not in its other meaning of stupid, a bit slow on the uptake. To be 'as thick as two short planks' states the obvious, for when one plank is placed on another the result is twice as thick as a single plank.

Third degree, to be given the
This is to be the object of detailed cross-questioning to get to the bottom of an inquiry, whether it be criminal or general. In America the term is applied to the use by the police of exhaustive questioning in an endeavour to extort a confession or incriminating information from a suspect, criminal, accomplice or witness. 'Third-degree treatment' is also used as a euphemism for torture.

This week's deliberate mistake
A phrase generally used in a facetious way to admit that an error has been made. It dates back to a 1938 BBC radio programme, *Monday Night at Seven*, during which a mistake was inadvertently made. Thousands of listeners pointed the *faux pas* out to the BBC. With some positive thinking, the producer decided to develop the idea and the 'deliberate mistake' became a regular feature of the programme, spawning a new catchphrase, 'Did you spot this week's deliberate mistake?'

Throw in the sponge, to
To throw in, or throw up, the sponge means to give up, to admit defeat. The metaphor is from the boxing world and refers to a second, from the boxer's corner, tossing a sponge, used to refresh his contestant in between rounds, towards the centre of the ring, to signify that his man is beaten. To 'throw in the towel' also means

to concede defeat in boxing, for a second might also literally throw a towel into the ring to show that the game is up.

Thunder, to steal one's

To adopt someone else's own special methods or ideas as if they were one's own. The story behind the origin of this phrase was recounted by the eighteenth-century actor and playwright Colley Cibber (1671–1757), in his *Lives of the Poets*, and was also mentioned by Alexander Pope (1688–1744) in his poem 'The Dunciad'. John Dennis (1657–1734), an actor-manager of the early part of the eighteenth century, had invented a machine to make stage thunder, which he employed in his own play, *Appius and Virginia*, performed at the Drury Lane Theatre in London in 1709. Mr Dennis, whatever his inventive talents, was a not particularly gifted playwright; the play did not fill the house and was soon taken off in favour of a production of *Macbeth* by another company. Dennis went to the opening night and was astonished to hear his thunder machine in action. He leapt to his feet and shouted, 'That is my thunder, by God, the villains will play my thunder but not my play!' Since the eighteenth century the phrase has subsequently been refined to become 'to steal one's thunder'.

Tickety-boo, all tickety-boo

There are many phrases for this enthusiastic statement that everything is 'fine and dandy', or 'all shipshape and Bristol fashion'. 'Tickety-boo' may come from the word 'ticket' as in 'that's the ticket'. In the nineteenth century charities issued tickets to the poor that could be exchanged for soup, clothing and coal. Also at that time, the busy port of Bristol enjoyed a high reputation for efficiency in preparing ships for sea.

To acknowledge the corn

An American expression meaning to confess or own up to a charge, or to admit failure to deliver. In a Congressional debate in

1828 one of the states claiming to export corn admitted that the corn was actually used to feed hogs, and exported not as corn, but inside the animals' digestive systems.

Today is the first day of the rest of your life
Despite the fact that this well-used phrase has a New Age ring, it originated in 1969 at the Syanon anti-drug and alcohol centres. It is believed to have been coined by Charles Dederich, the founder of the centres, and it swiftly became a mantra with a somewhat evangelical flavour, reflecting the 'take-it-day-by-day' approach to curing addictions to anything from cigarettes or food to sex or drugs.

Too many cooks spoil the broth
A well-known proverb meaning that too many opinions on a matter become self-defeating. The adage has been in use since the sixteenth century, if not before. For almost every proverb or nugget of wisdom, however, there is usually another that means precisely the opposite, the usual riposte for 'Too many cooks spoil the broth' being 'Many hands make light work'. Groucho Marx (1895–1977) commented, 'I'm going to stop asking my cooks to prepare broth for me. Over the years, I've found that too many broths spoil the cook.'

Torch, to carry a
To suffer unrequited love. The torch represents the flame of undying love, and the implication is that the emotion is long standing and either not returned or undeclared. A torch singer is (usually) a female who sings sentimental love songs in this vein.

It is thought that 'torch song', in this sense, may have been coined by Tommy Lyman in the 1930s. The film *Torch Singer* (1933) was about an unwed mother who sings in a night club, while *Torch Song* (1953) told the story of a musical-comedy star's love for a blind pianist; later the play *Torch Song Trilogy* (1982) by Harvey Fierstein tackled the more taboo subject of homosexual love.

Turn on, tune in, drop out

This is the mission statement of the hippie movement from about 1967. Turn on to drug use, tune in to new values – reject those of your parents, and drop out – of society. It was used as the title of a 1967 lecture by Dr Timothy Leary (1920–96) and he explored the theme further in his book *The Politics of Ecstasy*. Towards the end of his life Leary attributed the phrase to the Canadian media guru Marshall McLuhan (1911–80). An amusing variation on the theme, known as 'the LSD motto', was:

Turn on, tune in, drop dead.

Turn the tables, to

To reverse a situation and put one's opponent in the predicament that one has been suffering. The saying was recorded in the early seventeenth century and was applied to a popular card game in which a player, if he found himself at a disadvantage, might reverse the position of the board and thus shift the disadvantage to his opponent. The phrase may also come from the old custom of reversing the table or board in games of chess or draughts so that the opponents' relative positions are altogether changed. Another apocryphal theory relates to arguments in Roman marriages. Roman gentlemen were given to buying expensive tables, and if the man had previously chided his wife for making a costly purchase she would 'turn the tables' and remind her spouse of his own extravagance. On a different tack, 'table-turning' is the mysterious phenomenon of the turning of tables without the evidence of any mechanical force, which in the early days of spiritualism was commonly practised at séances. It was said by some to be the work of departed spirits, and by others to be the result of influences such as mesmerism.

Turn-up for the books, a
A piece of luck or unexpected good fortune. This phrase comes from the world of betting on the horses. The 'book' is the record of bets laid on a race and is naturally kept by a 'book'maker, commonly known as a bookie. When the horses do not run to form and the favourite does not win, it's a good day for the bookie and he can line his pockets; for him it's 'a turn-up[wards] for the books'.

Under the counter
This phrase originated during the Second World War, and describes a then very common practice among tradesmen with an eye to the main chance. From the outbreak of the war many items, ranging from the basics like eggs, butter, meat and jam to 'luxuries' such as petrol, silk stockings and chocolate, were rationed. Dishonest tradesmen would keep articles and foodstuffs that were in short supply out of sight or 'under the counter', for sale to favoured customers, usually at inflated prices. This form of trading was part of the thriving wartime black market, and the term is still used today to describe any illicit trading.

United we stand, divided we fall
A political slogan of the state of Kentucky that dates back to the late eighteenth century. The line appeared in a 1768 song called

'The Patriot's Appeal' by Jonathan Dickinson:

> Then join hand in hand, brave Americans all!
> By uniting we stand, by dividing we fall.

The idea can be traced back to 550 BC and Aesop's fable of 'The Four Oxen and the Lion'. And in St Mark's Gospel (3:5) we find:

> If a house be divided against itself, that house cannot stand.

Vorsprung durch Technik
This translates from the German as 'advancement through technology', and was used as an advertising slogan for Audi cars in Britain from 1982. The use of a German phrase which few could understand was apparently designed to emphasize to British buyers that the Audi was a German car and hence a reliable, quality product. In Britain it succeeded as an intriguing slogan, perhaps thanks to the deadpan delivery on the commercial by the actor Geoffrey Palmer, although it only had a minor success as a commonly used catchphrase. The line was used as a morale-boosting dictum to Audi's workers and was written up over the gates of the factory in Germany.

Walk the plank, to
To be put to the supreme test or, worse, to be about to die. 'Walking the plank' is a nautical term for a punishment involving being made to walk blindfold along a plank suspended over the ship's side and eventually landing up in the drink as shark food. It was a pirate custom of disposing of prisoners at sea in the seventeenth century. The practice is probably more familiar in fiction than in fact, however, since pirates would have been unlikely to kill off captives, who could have been sold as slaves or ransomed. In RL Stevenson's (1850–94) novel *The Master of Ballantrae* (1889) James Durie and Colonel Francis Burke enlist with the pirates who capture their ship, but the brigands make their other prisoners walk the plank. And Captain Hook, in JM Barrie's (1860–1937) *Peter Pan and Wendy* (1912), threatened to flog Wendy and the Lost Boys with a cat 'o' nine tails and then make them walk the plank.

Walls have ears, the
This is a warning to watch what you say, or what secrets you divulge, wherever you are, because someone might be listening. In the time of Catherine de Medici (1519–89), certain rooms in the Louvre Palace, Paris, were said to be constructed to conceal a network of listening tubes called *auriculaires*, so that what was said in one room could be clearly heard in another. This was how the suspicious queen discovered state secrets and plots. The legend of Dionysus's ear may also have been the inspiration for this audiovisual play on words. Dionysus was a tyrant of Syracuse (see **Sword of Damocles**, q.v.) in 431–367 BC, and his so-called 'ear' was a large ear-shaped underground cave cut in a rock that was connected to another chamber in such a way that he could overhear the conversation of his prisoners.

Wash one's hands of, to
To abandon something, to have nothing to do with some matter or person. The allusion is to Pontius Pilate's washing his hands at the trial of Jesus. Pilate was the Roman governor of Judaea (from AD 26–36) who tried Jesus. Although he found Christ not guilty, he washed his hands of the matter, bowing to the pressure of Jewish religious leaders, and sentenced Jesus to be crucified.

> He took water and washed his hands before the crowd, saying 'I am innocent of this man's blood, see it yourselves.'
>
> Matthew 27:24

We shall overcome

An American protest slogan since the beginning of the twentieth century. It originated as a part of a song in pre-Civil War times and was adapted in about 1900 by C Albert Tindley as a Baptist hymn, 'I'll overcome some day', which became famous in 1946 when black tobacco workers sang it on a picket line in Charleston, South Carolina. Pete Seeger (1919–) and other protest singers added verses, and in the early 1960s it became the main US Civil Rights anthem:

Oh deep in my heart, I know that I do believe,
We shall overcome some day.

Wham bang, thank you ma'am

This rather vulgar expression was originally used by American forces during the Second World War. The phrase was later employed mostly by women to describe short and meaningless sexual intercourse, or perhaps a one-night stand. It is now used contemptuously for any selfish act of male gratification at women's expense.

What a carve-up

This is an English slang phrase meaning to spoil someone's chances, or to have all prospects ruined. A 'carve-up' also means in criminal circles to share out illicit booty. On the road it means to cut aggressively in front of another driver, one of the actions that has led to the phenomenon of 'road rage'. There are now all sorts of 'rage' situations to describe the frustrations of modern life, such as 'trolley rage' in the supermarket, or 'air rage' demonstrated by drunken passengers on an aeroplane.

What the Dickens?

An exclamation of disbelief, akin to 'What the devil?' There is still some hesitancy in using such a strong oath and the phrase is often shortened to 'What the . . .?' 'Dickens' here is probably a euphemism, possibly in use since the sixteenth century, for the devil, otherwise known as Satan or the Prince of Evil, and has nothing do to with Charles Dickens (1812–70). In Low German its equivalent is 'De duks!' which may have become altered in English to 'dickens'.

> I cannot tell what the dickens his name is.
> Shakespeare,
> *The Merry Wives of Windsor* (1600)

'To play the dickens' is an old-fashioned expression meaning to be naughty, or act like a devil.

What you see is what you get (WYSIWYG)

This is a phrase from the world of computers, usually shortened to the acronym WYSIWYG, and suggests that what ones sees on the computer screen is exactly how the material will look when printed. It has probably been in use since the mid-1960s, although only widely used from the 1980s . Now the expression is used even more broadly by public figures who want to persuade an audience that they are not trying to hide anything or deceive by appearances. President Bush quoted the phrase on the first day of the Gulf War, 16 January 1991, when asked how he was feeling.

Where there's muck there's brass

An encouraging phrase to make one roll up one's sleeves and get to work; otherwise a statement that where there is dirt there is money. Feeding the soil, harvesting the crops, mining the coal may make your hands dirty, but they can produce untold riches. The saying has come to be associated with the grimy mining and manufacturing industries of the north of England, following the Industrial Revolution of the late nineteenth century, many of which brought their owners substantial wealth. Francis Bacon (1561–1626) probably had a more charitable meaning in mind when he wrote, 'Money is like muck, not good except to be spread.' A more modern colloquial phrase is, 'It's a dirty job, but someone's got to do it', but this phrase has more of a 'grin-and-bear it' attitude.

Where's the beef?

Advertising slogan meets political catchphrase. The American Wendy hamburger chain's 1984 television commercial showed a group of elderly women looking at the small hamburger of a competitor on a huge bun – they all admired the bun, but the unimpressed third woman asked, 'Where's the beef?' Later in 1984, when Walter Mondale was seeking the Democratic presidential nomination, he famously quoted the slogan to describe what he thought was lack of substance in the policies of his rival, Gary Hart. In America the phrase is also used to mean 'Where's the problem?'

White man's burden, the

In the imperialistic days during the wide influence of the British Empire, from the mid-nineteenth century, white races, especially the British, believed it to be their duty to govern, educate and generally enlighten the so called 'backward' coloured peoples of the world. It is now inconceivable that such a condescending and racist attitude should have taken so great a hold. The phrase comes from a poem by Rudyard Kipling (1865–1936) of the same title (1899):

Take up the White Man's burden –
Send forth the best ye breed –
Go bind your sons to exile
To serve your captives' need.

To ask someone to 'play the white man', that is to be a 'good sport' or 'good egg' about some minor dispute or misunderstanding, or in some personal crisis, is an ironic reference to the imperial days when a person of honourable character or good breeding was described as a 'real white man'.

Who breaks a butterfly on a wheel?

To put great effort into accomplishing a small or unimportant matter. The phrase comes from Alexander Pope's (1688–1744) poem 'An Epistle to Dr Arbuthnot' (1735):

> Satire or sense, alas! can Sporus feel?
> Who breaks a butterfly upon the wheel?

The allusion is to an ancient form of torture, 'breaking on the wheel', in which the long bones of a convict are broken with an iron bar, counterpointed with the delicacy of a butterfly. Famously,

in 1967 the editor of *The Times*, William Rees-Mogg, caught the public mood when he defended Mick Jagger after his three-month prison sentence for possession of illegal drugs, in an editorial headlined with this quotation. Technically Rees-Mogg was in contempt of court for commenting on the case before it had gone to appeal, but the fact that he was not even publicly admonished testifies to the general support for his stand.

Who dares wins

The motto of the SAS (Special Air Service Regiment) appears to have been borrowed from the Alvingham barony, created in 1929. The SAS was founded by Captain (later Colonel Sir) David Stirling in 1941, and its origins therefore lie in the Second World

War. The motto became famous after members of the crack regiment successfully stormed the Iranian embassy in London in May 1980, ending its occupation by terrorists and freeing their hostages. A feature film about the exploits of the SAS was produced, with the motto as its title, in 1982, and the *Daily Mirror* labelled its bingo promotion 'Who Dares Wins' in the same year.

Willow, to wear the

For those unlucky in love, to grieve for a lost lover, or pine for an absent sweetheart. The willow, especially the weeping willow, has long been associated with sorrow, and is taken as an emblem of desolation or desertion. Thomas Fuller (1608–61) wrote, 'The willow is a sad tree, whereof such as have lost their love make their mourning garlands,s and the psalmist tells us that the Jews in captivity hung their harps upon the willows in sign of mourning':

> By the waters of Babylon, there we sat down and wept when we remembered Zion.
> On the willows there we hung up our lyres.
>
> Psalms 137:1, 2

Wind – It's an ill wind that blows nobody any good

This is an old adage to encourage 'positive thinking'. It means that it has to be a very great misfortune from which someone does not benefit, or in other words that someone will always profit by every loss. It all depends on your outlook in life, the cup is either half empty or half full. The allusion is nautical, and arises because a headwind for one ship will be a tailwind for another sailing in the opposite direction.

Wind – To sail close to the wind

This is another of the many proverbs that come from life on the high seas. It is a figurative expression, still in use today, and means to take a chance, to emerge from an escapade just within the letter of the rule book, or, more riskily, to push the limits of what decency or propriety allows. This nautical expression refers to the practice of steering a ship as near as possible to the point from which the wind is blowing while keeping the sails filled. To 'sail against the wind' is to go against the trend, in opposition to current thinking, practice or fashion. And to 'sail before the wind' is to prosper, to meet with great success, just as a ship sails smoothly and rapidly with a following wind. Similarly, to 'sail into the wind' is to attack or reprimand someone forcefully, or to tackle a task with great vigour and directness.

Wing – On a wing and a prayer
To chance it, to hope for the best and have faith, with perhaps only small chance of success. It is a matter of interpretation as to whether the wing referred to here is that of an aeroplane or a more celestial being. The phrase comes from a Second World War song by Harold Adamson (1943), based on the actual words spoken by the pilot of a damaged aircraft who radioed the control tower as he prepared to come in to land. The song runs:

> Tho' there's one motor gone, we can still carry on
> Comin' in on a wing and pray'r.

Even in his moment of panic the pilot might have been inspired by words from Psalm 104 (v.3):

> Who layeth the beams of his chambers in the waters:
> and maketh the clouds his chariot, and walketh upon the wings
>   of the wind.

Word – My word is my bond

The motto of the London Stock Exchange since 1801. At the Stock Exchange bargains are made on the 'nod' without a written pledge being given, and without documents being exchanged. The motto's Latin form is *Dictum meum pactum*, and the phrase implies a sense of honour, an agreement that cannot be broken without disgrace.

Writing on the wall, the

This is not graffiti, but a bad sign, a portent, often foreshadowing trouble or disaster. The metaphor is biblical in origin and comes from Daniel 5:5–31, where King Belshazzar, while he was feasting, found out about the forthcoming destruction of the Babylonian Empire through the mysterious appearance of handwriting on a wall. The words read in Aramaic, *mene, mene, tekel, upharsin*, literally, 'numbered, weighed, divisions'. Daniel interpreted these words as, 'You have been weighed in the balance and found wanting,' thereby predicting the king's downfall and that of his empire. Indeed, Belshazzar was killed that night, and his kingdom was conquered.

Wrong side of the tracks, to be on the

To be born on the wrong side of the tracks is definitely a disadvantage, for the area was that part of town which was deemed both socially and environmentally inferior. The expression originated in America and refers to the fact that, formerly, poor and industrial areas were often located to one side of the railroad tracks, not least because the prevailing wind would blow smoke and smog in that direction, leaving the better-off neighbourhoods unpolluted; in addition, industry needed to be close to the railroad, and so workers' housing was also established near those areas. The poorer districts of British cities are often east of the city centre for this reason, since the prevailing wind is usually west or south-west.

Years – The first seven years are the hardest

A cliché usually offered as wise advice about a marriage or a new job, implying that the first stages will be the worst and that things can only get better. It probably comes from First World War parlance, 'Cheer up, the first seven years are the worst,' referring to the length of regular service in the army. Seven years is a traditional period for change, and seven is a holy or mystic number: there are seven days in a week, seven ages of man and seven dwarves (see **Seventh heaven**, q.v.). *The Seven-Year Itch* was a play written by George Axelrod in 1952, which became a film starring Marilyn Monroe (1926–62) in 1955. The title has been in use as a catchphrase ever since and is applied especially to husbands, who have a tendency to wander from the marriage after

seven years. The word 'itch' has been used since the seventeenth century as a slang word for a sexual urge.

You ain't seen nothin' yet

This was Ronald Reagan's presidential catchphrase in 1984, which he used repeatedly in his successful bid for re-election. Always happy to quote from movies, he featured the line in his victory speech. It is also the title of a 1974 song by Bachman-Turner

Overdrive, the Canadian pop group, which is the ironic theme tune to 'Smashy and Nicey', the comic radio DJs played by Paul Whitehouse and Harry Enfield in the latter's TV comedy show. The original phrase 'You ain't heard nothin' yet' is most famously attributed to Al Jolson (1886–1950) in the first full-length 'talkie' movie, *The Jazz Singer*, in 1927. It was the title of one of Jolson's songs, written by Gus Khan and Buddy de Sylva in 1919, but he had also used the song title as a catchphrase in his stage act before the film was made.

You are what you eat

An informal slogan with 'alternative-lifestyle' overtones that dates back to the 1960s, and the title of a film shown in Britain in 1969. The idea behind the phrase is not new. In *Psychologie du Goût* (1825) Anthelme Brillat-Savarin (1755–1826) wrote, 'Tell me what you eat and I will tell you what you are.' In 1945 the diarist Sir Henry 'Chips' Channon (1897–1958) fondly commented on the death of Sir Harcourt Johnstone, Liberal MP, bon viveur and Minister for Overseas Trade:

> He dug his grave with his teeth.

You're never alone with a Strand

A classic sixties television commercial with a moody style that is still admired today, although when it was shown it failed to achieve its aim of actually selling Strand cigarettes. In 1960, John May of the SH Benson agency conceived the idea for an advertisement to appeal to the youth market by using a moody Frank Sinatra/James Dean lookalike who strolled through a lonely location in a raincoat and hat. The actor soon had his own fan club and the theme tune became a hit. However, viewers did not rush out and buy the cigarettes, perhaps associating them with the loneliness and rejection of youth. Tobacco advertising on television is now banned in Britain.

You've come a long way, baby

In 1968 it was still perfectly acceptable to smoke cigarettes, and this slogan for the campaign by Virginia Slims was targeted at women, cashing in on the feminist mood of the times. The phrase was then used on Women's Lib posters. To call a girl 'baby' is a term of affection, especially in America; however, in the late 1990s the politically incorrect phenomenon known as 'laddism' resulted in young girls being called 'baby' or 'babe' in a leering, ironic fashion. Fast sports cars are known as 'babe magnets', especially attractive girls are referred to as 'hyper-babes' or '*über*-babes' and Lara Croft, voluptuous virtual heroine of the *Tomb Raider* computer games, is known as a 'cyber-babe'. The phrase is also the title of the 1999 best-selling album by Fat Boy Slim.

You've never had it so good

A strident phrase used by the Prime Minister, Harold Macmillan (later first Earl of Stockton; 1894–1986), in a speech at Bedford in July 1957. He specifically phrased his speech not to sound boastful, but to act as a warning that the prosperity of the post-war years would be difficult to maintain; however, it was taken out of context and used to label him as complacent, interested only in material comforts.

> Let's be frank about it. Most of our people have never had it so good. . . . What is beginning to worry some of us is, 'Is it too good to last?' . . . Can prices be steadied while at the same time we maintain full employment in an expanding economy? Can we control inflation?

Macmillan is said to have adopted the phrase after it had cropped up in conversation with Lord Robens, a former Labour minister, shortly before his speech. However, 'You never had it so good' was already a political soundbite that had been used by the Democrats in the American presidential election of 1952.

Your country needs you

The most famous recruitment slogan ever – inseparably linked with the poster showing Field-Marshal Lord Kitchener (1850–1916) staring out with pointing finger. Kitchener was appointed Secretary of State for War on 6 August 1914, two days after the outbreak of the First World War, and it was his job to build up the numbers of recruits for the 'New Armies'. Eric Field of the small Caxton advertising agency wrote the original line for the posters, 'Your King and Country need you', appealing to all patriots. The idea was widely imitated abroad, and in America, which joined the war on the Allied side in 1917, Uncle Sam pointed his finger out of a poster bearing the legend 'I want you for the US Army'.

CAMBRIDGE
BLACK

Also by Alison Bruce

Cambridge Blue
The Siren
The Calling
The Silence
The Backs
The Promise

CAMBRIDGE BLACK

ALISON BRUCE

Constable • London

CONSTABLE

First published in 2017 by Constable

A CIP catalogue record for this book is available from the British Library.

ISBN: 978-1-47211-963-6

Typeset in Times New Roman by TW Type, Cornwall

Printed and bound in Great Britain by CPI Group (UK) Ltd, Croydon CR0 4YY

Constable
An imprint of
Little, Brown Book Group
Carmelite House
50 Victoria Embankment
London EC4Y 0DZ

An Hachette UK Company
www.hachette.co.uk

www.littlebrown.co.uk

To Broo Doherty – thank you for having faith in Goodhew,
the series and my writing.

PROLOGUE

30 March 1991

'Thank you, Nadine,' the guitarist shouted and the crowd cheered for more but she handed the microphone back to the band. She knelt down to unclip her guitar case, taking her time to remove the strap from her Gibson before placing it in the velour-lined case. Her slowness was deliberate; she loved the singing but hated the fuss. Hated the drunks nearest the stage – not them perhaps but their cigarette-permeated breath and their insistence. And lack of inhibition when it came to pulling at her, or grabbing her into a hug and giving advice and compliments with alcohol-spittled words. She turned her back on them to pack away. It was usually enough for them to disperse.

The Boat Race pub had its music-loving regulars but tonight, hours after the actual boat race, it seemed it had become the place to go to commiserate over the latest Oxford win, and new faces outnumbered the familiar. She glanced up a couple of times and, on the second, caught sight of Theo near the jukebox. He leant back against the wall, typically unhurried. 'OK?' he mouthed.

She rolled up her strap and tucked it away in the space left by the guitar's cutaway body, slipping her capo and picks into the space alongside it. She could sense Theo watching and, inside her head at least, she smiled. Securing the case was another not-to-be-rushed ritual and, by the time she'd clipped the last latch and turned back to face the room, the majority of the punters had moved on.

Carrying a guitar before a gig would always illicit '*go on love, give us a song*' type comments. Afterwards, it seemed to get a little respect; she didn't need to push through the stragglers to reach Theo; people, even the drunk ones, stepped aside or shook her hand and said she'd done well.

Theo took the case from her and she followed him out onto East Road where it was almost as noisy but less congested. 'How was it?' he asked.

'You were there, weren't you?'

'Hiding at the back. I mean how was it for you? It's hard to tell when you're so wrapped up in what you're playing.'

They were walking side by side now and she grabbed his arm and squeezed her face against it. Apart from that, she didn't reply. She couldn't imagine how she looked when she sang; she felt as though it was all written across her face, a transparency – it was never acting and her emotions were so on show that it had to be obvious to anyone watching that they were real. Singing to herself and practising new songs never had the same effect. It was only from the moment that the audience started watching that she had no choice but to commit to the performance. She could sing and play and be barely in the room then, free to touch the thoughts that were too hard the rest of the time. She doubted whether she wanted to know what expressions might flash onto her face. She preferred the idea that there were none.

She didn't ask where they were heading. The evening had become cool but she was content with the idea that they'd take a slow walk and eventually find their way back to Theo's flat.

She wondered whether it always took an unhealthy relationship to make a good one seem valid. Maybe only screwed-up people felt the need to put themselves through that. She slipped her hand into his. 'I can stay over, you know.'

He grinned, 'I was hoping you would but I've still only got a mattress on the floor. It's still pretty squalid.'

'It's not squalid. Just basic. And it's the rest of it that needs to catch up.'

'You're not wrong there. I'll move my furniture in the next couple of weeks.'

'Don't rush because of me.'

Eventually the house would be divided into six letting rooms but, at the moment, his was the only finished floor. 'When Dad offered it for free I imagined it might be unsophisticated . . .'

'You have electric and running water.'

'And I'm just like the live-in guard on a building site.'

'It's not so romantic when you put it like that.'

'Still coming?'

'Of course.' He wrapped his arm around her shoulder and she curled hers around his waist. Neither of them seemed to set the pace but they meandered, each in step with the other until they reached the rise of the Mill Road railway bridge. They stopped and watched a packed train rattle towards the station.

Passengers crowded the aisles, waiting to disembark, to swap a day in London for a night in Cambridge. She rubbed her thumbs against the guitar-string hardened skin at the tips of her fingers. How many train songs were there? Was there a better metaphor for life than a train song?

'What are you thinking about, Nadine?'

'About train songs and wondering which one fits me.'

'I wasn't expecting you to say that.'

She looked up at Theo. 'I'm pretty sure mine's about coming home.'

'I hope so.'

Instead of moving away again, he leant against the metal panel, his back to the tracks now. It was an exposed spot and she shivered. 'Can we go?'

'Of course,' he said, but still didn't move. He seemed to be waiting for something, but she didn't know what.

'Is something wrong?'

'Nothing.' He shook his head slowly; 'I was trying to find the words to tell you how much it means to be here with you.'

'Watching trains?' She always found it easier to deflect serious comments but this time she wished she hadn't. 'Actually, there's nowhere I'd rather be.'

3

He kissed her gently, then his cheek brushed hers as he spoke softly in her ear, 'I love you, Nadine.'

She closed her eyes and let her senses fill with the smell of his skin and the warmth of him. She had been scared that her feelings had jumped too far ahead but now she knew that they both felt the same way.

And, as though he'd read her thoughts, he pulled her closer. 'You don't ever need to worry, Nadine, I've felt like this for a long time.'

'Really?'

'Absolutely,' he grinned and Nadine smiled too. He kissed her again, their lips lingering and the last of the tension melting away. The air no longer felt cold and her earlier unease vanished. Maybe this would be OK. It felt right in the kind of way that she'd never experienced before. And that's what people always said, *you just know.* They took their time walking back to the house in Romsey Terrace. She'd spent the last night there too but now she was more aware of the short street with one terraced house wider than the rest: the only one with a window on either side of the front door, the only one with loft windows and brand new frames.

'It will be lovely when it's finished.'

Theo's gaze followed hers towards the roof, 'I'll have to share it then, won't I? I like this endless building work; it means there's just the two of us.' He slipped the key into the lock and Nadine spoke quietly before he opened the door; all this would be forgotten once they were inside. 'I felt uneasy earlier, kind of restless. Nervous for no reason. Like I shouldn't come.'

'And now?'

'It's gone and I'm glad I'm here. Glad I'm with you. I just wanted to say it before we went in.'

'Speak your fears and chase them away?'

'Something like that.'

He opened the door, set her guitar down in the hallway and reached back to her, 'Don't worry, we're good. Everything's good.'

The stair carpet hadn't been laid yet and their footsteps clattered on the stairs with enough noise for more than two people. The second set of stairs sounded like a distant echo of the first. A few noises made it down after that, the running of a tap, a squeal of laughter, the bang of a door, then silence.

Another hour passed. The other houses stood with curtains drawn and lights extinguished. The bare windows let the sodium orange street light slip into the ground-floor rooms, the open doors letting it trickle into the hallway, picking out the outline of paper and paint and a guitar case standing on the bare boards.

At 3 a.m. the light died and the letterbox creaked open. The fluid trickled, softly splashing onto the coir mat, too quiet for upstairs to hear. A ball of paper was wedged in the letterbox, resting there just long enough to be lit then poked through. It hit the mat glowing then disappeared in the bloom of flame that rose from it. The hall and stairs flushed orange, then black as the smoke thickened. It crept up the stairs as the guitar case slowly melted.

CHAPTER 1

Amy wouldn't recall much about that morning. She remembered ordering a cappuccino and weaving between tables to her favourite at the furthest corner. Her dad was running late so she studied the faces of the jesters, hobos and harlequins on the walls and shelves, trying to pick out any new additions. Many had been here since her childhood when clowns had scared her and she'd stared at the straw bobbing in her milkshake to avoid meeting their gaze.

She saw them differently now, of course, and today it was the clown blanc that caught her eye. He stared sorrowfully, a black painted tear resting on the top of his cheek, his head tilted as though he was ready to listen. Had she felt melancholy he might have seemed sympathetic; instead, she looked towards the door and sipped her coffee as she waited.

It was less than a minute later when the door was opened by a woman wrestling with a pushchair. The sounds of outside burst through for several seconds, with the hum of the city cut through by the siren of an ambulance. Amy moved towards the entrance, curious but not yet concerned. She must have spoken because she could remember the woman looking at her then gesticulating in the direction of the city centre. Then the wave of apprehension. And Amy dashing onto the pavement with silence rushing in her ears and the only thing in focus was the patchwork of paving stones as she ran across them.

He lay on the pavement beside the kerb.

There was no crowd, just a couple of bystanders and two paramedics.

And her dad. He was already on a stretcher, his shirt pulled open with wires and an IV line hanging from him. He lay still, his face bloodied, pavement dust and grit smeared across grey skin and she shouted even though she was close enough to touch the ambulance men.

'Did someone hit him?' When no one replied she added, 'That's my dad,' and repeated it before anyone had the chance to respond. A stocky paramedic knelt close to her father, another, a lanky guy who looked about thirty, had opened the ambulance doors and was now bringing out the gurney.

'What's his name?' he asked.

'Robert Buckingham. I was meeting him for lunch.'

Perhaps they already knew his name because there was no demand for any proof of identity. 'Does he have any existing health issues you're aware of?'

'No, I don't think so.'

The other paramedic looked up, 'Can you travel with us to Adden-brooke's?'

'Of course.' She hadn't taken her eyes off her dad. 'What's wrong with him?'

'We're running checks at the moment. I'm Grant. What's your name?' The paramedic spoke to her father next, 'Mr Buckingham, your daughter Amy's here. Mr Buckingham?'

She saw his mouth move, an attempt to form a word.

'Dad?'

Recognition flickered on his face. Her world slowed and steadied again, she clasped his hand until they loaded him onto the ambulance then strapped herself into the spare seat. Would they let her travel with him if he was about to die? The younger of the two paramedics was driving now while his partner continued to work on her dad. They kept the sliding window open between them and passed comments back and forth. She felt the ambulance take a turn and, glancing forward, could see the traffic on East Road parting to let them pass.

'Amy?' Grant the paramedic prompted. He had a large notepad on his lap now, pre-printed with questions, boxes and the outline of a human body. 'Are you his next of kin?'

'I suppose so, I mean, there's his mum and my mum but my grand-mother's in a care home with dementia and my mum . . .' She stopped mid-sentence.

'Are they married?'

'Not any more. They don't maintain contact.' She studied her dad for a second, then added, 'Unless they have to.'

Grant shot her a wry look. 'Parents, eh?' He reached across to check her dad again. 'Mr Buckingham?'

Amy leant forward. 'What's happening?'

'He's gaining consciousness. Has he had any alcohol?'

'I doubt it.'

He would have had a glass at lunch if he'd made it that far but he wasn't an excessive drinker. At least as far as she knew. 'Did someone hit him?'

'The person who called us said he'd fallen and banged his head. People often say just that, though, it doesn't always mean much.'

'So it's just a head injury?'

Grant pointed to a small square monitor. 'We collect information on the way in, to give the maximum information. Your dad's suffered a head injury but there's ECG activity . . .'

'His heart?'

And all she remembered of the rest of the journey was watching her father's expression, silently trying to communicate, to let him know he wasn't allowed to die young like his own father had. Beneath his tan, his skin had paled to the colour of alabaster and she remembered the clown with the tear on his cheek.

The weight of the day descended in early evening. Amy had spent the afternoon in a bubble; her dad had been wheeled into A & E and throughout the afternoon he had been seen by a succession of staff. Each had done something and asked something else before taking notes and moving on. And she had watched them move between beds, do the same with other patients then, in so-quiet tones, share their details with their colleagues. There was no panic here, no sense of shock or desperation. No windows either and the clock on the opposite wall ticked on calmly. They wheeled him away and left her to wait.

8

Finally, a doctor appeared, a Chinese lady with rectangular framed glasses and a clipboard pressed to her chest.

'You are Mr Buckingham's daughter?'

Amy nodded.

'It seems your father suffered a cardiac incident and a head trauma as he fell.' She stopped speaking long enough to see that Amy had listened and understood. 'He is expected to make a full recovery. He has regained consciousness and you will be able to see him, but briefly. He will be drowsy.'

Amy didn't absorb the rest of the details – she guessed there had been an operation – but she shook her head when the doctor asked if she had any questions. She sat beside her dad's bed and his expression changed just enough for her to know his mind was clearing. The gash on his temple had been patched, the wound itself looked tame but the skin around it was swollen and turning purple. 'You scared me,' she told him quietly.

His right eyebrow twitched but he made no attempt to speak. She took out her mobile. 'I'll phone the agency. I won't go in tomorrow.'

'You don't need to miss work because of me.' His words were monotone and slow, but clear. 'You need that job.'

She shook her head, 'It's just holiday cover, Dad, and it finishes tomorrow. I'll explain and it will be fine.'

'I worry about you.'

'Well, you shouldn't, temporary work suits me.' She sat back in the chair and the PVC upholstery squeaked, 'The doctor said I shouldn't stay too long but I'll come back up in the morning. Obviously.'

'Thanks.' He managed an indistinct nod.

She wanted to ask how he was feeling but it seemed as though it was a question for the start of a visit, an opening question. Instead she asked, 'Can I get you anything?'

He turned his hand over and gently squeezed hers. 'Would you ask your mum to come and see me?'

'Really?'

'I ought to give her the pleasure of seeing me like this.' His brief smile vanished. 'Seriously, Amy, some thoughts are very clear when you are lying in a pool of blood. You should get a regular job. I shouldn't smoke. And, as much as we've never been amicable, your mother and I have unfinished business.'

She caught a bus back to the city centre, the artificial colours and sounds of Addenbrooke's were gone and she was returned to the other end of the same day. It had grown dark outside and the face of the clown blanc seemed to be a memory from another day entirely. Her phone was still cupped in her hand and her hand cupped in her lap. The bus was empty apart from two ladies near the front. Amy sat at the back. She could have called her mum right then but instead she closed her eyes in weariness and chose to speak to no one.

CHAPTER 2

'Mum?' Amy still had the key to her mum's house. She used it whenever she visited but never went beyond the threshold without making sure her mum knew she was there.

'I'm out the back.'

Amy walked through the kitchen and out to the conservatory on the other side. Her mum sat with her back to the window and an open book on her lap. Outside, the sun was strong enough to backlight the clouds and fill the space with a hard grey light.

'Mum?' Amy repeated, quietly this time.

Geraldine smiled as she looked up but that faded as she saw Amy's expression. She set the book aside, her fingers finding the bookmark and the side table in a single, fluid move. 'What's wrong?'

'It's Dad. He's in hospital.' Even after all the years they'd been divorced the mention of either parent to the other caused tension; usually a barely perceptible hesitation. They both tried to show nothing but Amy always picked up on it. This time, though, all she saw in her mum's expression was the need for answers. 'He's had a heart attack. He's conscious.' She started to tremble. 'It looks like he'll be OK.'

'When did this happen?'

'I went to meet him for lunch. He was late but it turned out he'd collapsed.'

'Why didn't you call me?'

'I don't know. I didn't want to call anyone. It didn't feel real and I

11

decided I just wanted it to be me and him if . . .' She didn't finish the sentence; either she'd said enough for her mum to understand or else she'd already think that was as selfish as it had just sounded to her.

'I understand why you didn't phone immediately, Ames, but half a day later?'

'You're not married any more,' she pointed out, then apologised. 'They asked me for his next of kin and I didn't know whether that was me, you or Nan.'

'You as much as anyone, I suppose. Not me in any case.'

Amy took a breath. 'He's asked you to go.'

'To the hospital?'

'Dad said you and he had unfinished business.'

Her mum turned from Amy and stared into her small walled garden but not before Amy had seen the quick widening of her eyes. 'Did he?'

'What did he mean by that, Mum?' Her mum had a strong profile, high cheekbones and features that were neat and in proportion. She was elegant and polished, the sort of woman that Amy thought would find it easy to attract a new man. Amy didn't think she'd ever tried.

'One of your dad's jokes, I expect.' Geraldine laughed lightly as if to prove the point. 'Apart from that, I really don't know.'

'Will you go?'

'Maybe.' Geraldine swung her gaze back to meet Amy's. 'Do you want me to?'

'I think you should.' She almost added *just in case.* 'See him tonight, Mum.'

'I'll go now.'

'I'll come with you.'

Geraldine squeezed her hand. 'I can manage, Ames.'

'I'll see him first, Mum; I feel I should say goodnight.' Amy smiled suddenly. 'And warn him that you've actually turned up. I can get a taxi home afterwards.' She squeezed her mum's hand in reply. 'I won't be a fly on the wall, Mum. I mean, when was the last time you actually spoke to him?'

Geraldine shrugged, 'I don't know; I've blanked it out.'

* * *

12

Visiting hours had long since passed but Geraldine Buckingham hoped that compassion would win over red tape. She spoke quietly when she asked permission for them both to visit and the duty nurse seemed to run a critical eye over them before agreeing. 'As long as he's happy to see you,' she replied, and then called Amy through as soon as she'd checked. Ten minutes later and it was Geraldine's turn.

Robert lay propped up at a forty-five-degree angle. He didn't look as frail as she'd feared but the drip beside his bed and the charts above it were enough to remind her how complicated their lives had become.

'We're not teenagers any more, are we, Gerri?'

She gave a wry smile and shook her head, 'Too much water . . .'

'And too many bridges?' he said, ending a familiar sentence.

'Exactly that.' She pulled a visitors' chair closer to the head of his bed. 'Amy just told me what happened.'

He shook his head as if to say that it didn't matter.

'She said you wanted to talk to me.'

'I said we had unfinished business.' He pushed himself onto one elbow then up into a more upright position. 'I remember feeling faint for just a second or two before I fell. I didn't get sudden pain and didn't know I'd hit my head even though there was blood.'

'Did you know you had a heart condition?'

'Does it matter? I've got one now.'

'So you did?'

'Blood pressure, that's all.' He brushed it away with his cannula-free hand. 'Not enough to make me think morbid thoughts.'

'But now you have?'

'Exactly.'

Gerri could already see where this conversation would be heading. She clasped her hands together – it appeared casual but the fingers on one hand were gripping the others so hard that her knuckles had started to throb.

'What are you planning?'

'To tell Amy.'

'Tell her what?'

'Let me explain something to you first.' He leant towards her further but she didn't reach across to him. She felt her expression set and knew

13

she was glaring. He refocused on the wall behind her and continued to speak. 'What if I'd died? I never felt as though I was going to but I was drifting in and out and Amy was there. It's not right that I could die without telling her the truth.'

'But you're not dying, Rob.'

'But if I did . . . this is my wake-up call, Gerri. It's what I meant by unfinished business.'

Geraldine's anger rose swiftly. She stayed silent for several seconds as she tried to bite back the rage. 'And you're going to tell her what exactly?' she hissed. She was trying to be quiet but her voice had risen to a loud whisper that stabbed the words at him.

'Gerri, shush. You'll get kicked out.'

She had no desire to do as she was told but didn't want to be asked to leave either. 'Amy doesn't need this.'

'Why not? She has nothing to occupy her apart from one dead-end job after the next. It's 2014, Gerri. We've all been living with this for far too long. It's got to stop now. Amy needs to know I never started that fire.'

'You've told her enough times.'

'She needs to know for certain. What have you told her?'

'Nothing. It's between the two of you.'

'Does she ask you about it?'

Gerri pressed her lips firmly shut and shook her head.

He glared back at her. 'Is that nothing or no comment? Because she has lived with this for over twenty years and she asks me questions all the time. Wants to know why we divorced. How can she believe that I'm innocent when she thinks the reason you left was because I was guilty? It's illogical and she knows it.'

'You were guilty.' The words slipped out before Geraldine had a chance to check herself. 'You wrecked our marriage and, if Amy knows the truth about that, how much respect do you think she'll have left for you?'

'I had a fling, I'm not saying "so what" but that isn't the same as killing people, for God's sake.'

'An *affair*, which isn't the same thing, Robert.'

'You could have given me an alibi for the fire.'

'It would have been a lie.'

'Yes, but it would have led to the truth. You know I didn't start it.'

'It doesn't matter. They had evidence, they made the case.'

Robert sighed and let his head drop back against the pillow. He stared up at the ceiling. 'When I was first arrested you told me so often that you knew I was innocent. Do you even believe that any more?' He turned to look at her. There was no frustration or anger now. He was serious and tired. 'We've done each other some serious damage, Gerri. The worst betrayals.'

'I know,' she felt the tiredness too. 'Of course I know you never killed them. I couldn't prove it, though, and part of me . . .' She hesitated and chewed at the top of her thumb. She guessed that she would regret, in the cold light of day, what she was about to say but he was asking for unadorned honesty and it felt like the wrong time and place for any more half-truths. 'I decided to let the justice system carry on. I could have lied for you or gone out of my way to persuade people of your innocence but I would have looked like the disillusioned wife blindly believing her cheating husband, wouldn't I?'

'Maybe,' he conceded.

'So I told myself that whatever you'd got would be karma for what you'd done to me.'

'And if I'd been found not guilty? What would have happened to us then?'

'Same outcome, I guess. There were too many barriers between us by then. You can't run around with other women then complain that your wife wants a divorce, Rob.' Geraldine's gaze met his and they both seemed to be waiting for the other to speak. He'd never been reliable as a husband but perhaps he was still a decent man. A man who loved his daughter and had missed out on years of her childhood. She pushed the thought aside; she knew better than that.

He broke the silence first, 'I'm going to speak to Amy and I'd like you there.'

'And tell her that I always knew you were innocent? It wasn't my job to salvage you from the mess you made. Why try to hurt me now?'

'It's about her knowing the truth.'

'Talk to her on your own. I don't want to be there to see the look on her face.'

'I'll tell her everything, Gerri. Everything that led up to it. She'll understand.'

Geraldine shook her head. 'She won't, Rob.' But as she said it he looked away in surprise. She turned her head too and saw Amy half-way between the doorway and the foot of the bed. She stared from her mother to her father and back again.

'I heard most of that,' she said quietly. 'Whispers carry well in an empty room. The bit I didn't catch is how you're not cruel, Mum.'

'Cruel? Because I wouldn't perjure myself?'

Amy's expression turned stony. 'You let me believe that two people are dead because of him. Did you really hate him that much?'

As Amy had stood at the foot of her father's hospital bed she'd been aware that her view of her childhood had begun to warp and blur. She was the same but they'd revealed a different version of themselves and the ground beneath her had felt as though it was beginning to crumble. She'd been too young to understand anything when her dad had gone to prison. But when she'd started school it had caught up with her; she doubted that she'd ever forget the taunts in the playground and waking in the small hours, her pillow wet with tears. And her mum holding her gently and telling her, 'Your dad did a very bad thing but we'll start again. It will be all right.' Then years later her father asked her to trust him, 'I did nothing wrong, Amy. I need you to believe me.'

The bus travelled back towards the centre of Cambridge. She sat on the front row of the upper deck and closed her eyes against the car lights and street lamps that poked at her through the panoramic front window.

At first, she couldn't remember what she'd just said to them, or what they'd tried to tell her. It seemed as though she'd stood on the one spot for many minutes with the world moving around her and a muffled underwater sound filling her ears. She hadn't decided to walk away; her instincts had decided that on their own. She'd turned and then hurried towards the exit, just short of a run. She'd grabbed the first bus into town. Now, finally, she could feel her breathing settle and her thoughts slowing enough for her to catch hold of them. If everything she'd just heard was the truth . . . she broke off mid-thought to argue that it might not be.

The bus was in Perne Road now; she stared down at the houses. The street was lined with 1930s semis, almost all of which had been altered in some way or another: new windows, replacement doors, paved driveways. All unique, she supposed, but somehow all the same. Her family would never belong there and neither did she, but the idea of a life unblotted by extreme events appealed. If her parents had made up any part of their story she was sure they would have painted themselves in a better light, pretended they had once been the kind of family that had lived a fictitiously contented life in their suburban home.

There was, she concluded, no reason for any of it to be a lie. And, more than that, this new version of events made sense in a way that the version she'd grown up with never had. It felt like the truth.

She ignored the queasy feeling that had stayed within her since the hospital. Suddenly, she had no desire to rush home. She rang the bell for the next stop. She had no one to answer to but she didn't want to bring this back home with her. Right now, she needed space to sift and sort her thoughts and to make sure they remained her own.

Alighting at the Brook pub wasn't a random decision, just a spontaneous one. In secondary school her bus had passed the same way and this bus stop had been part of a regular pilgrimage. It hadn't been the closest stop to the site of the fire but the walk had given her a few extra minutes to shake off whatever the day had held. At each visit, she'd spoken silently to her dad and then visited the remnants of the house she'd thought he'd destroyed. She'd stayed loyal despite the people he'd killed.

It was easy to remember everything about the short street; each detail, from the terrace of houses with front steps overlapping the pavement to the camber of the road and the angle that lamplight shafted into Romsey Terrace, was familiar. She'd been four at the time of the fire, too young to visit, the subject too taboo for her to ask. By the time she'd first come the house had gone, leaving nothing but a layer of its brickwork pinned to the property next door. That's what she'd always stared at, looking for answers in the silent remains.

But this time when she came to the corner she stopped at the head of the street. Her reasons for visiting felt different now. She frowned. The idea that the situation was impossible had been replaced by opportunity.

Once again she stood with the rest of the world drifting past her, but now the shock had faded and it had been replaced by clarity.

Her parents had given her a single, sharp shard of information and the rest had to be up to her. She walked towards home, following the route her bus would have taken; she could have waited at the stop for the next one but her lethargy had vanished and her only instinct was not to stand still any more.

CHAPTER 3

Amy had been halfway home when she'd decided to call Neil Frampton.
She'd waited for him outside the Earl of Beaconsfield, thinking that
they would be able to go inside and find a discreet corner. He pulled
his F-Type up to the kerb, lowered his window. He'd always been a big
man but he'd put on weight since she'd last seen him and he seemed too
bulky to belong with the car.

'Did your mum give you my number?'

'No, I took it off her phone a while ago. I'd like to speak to you.'

'So you said.' Then he waited as if he expected her to have the conversation out here in the street.

She tilted her head in the direction of the pub. 'I thought we could
go in there.'

'I'm not in the habit of slipping out of the house to meet women.
What do you actually want, Amy?' His tone had turned impatient, or
perhaps he'd been impatient all along. His heavy hands squeezed at the
steering wheel. She realised then that the engine was still running and
wondered whether he was about to pull away.

'I'll tell you what,' she began, then hurried around the back of the
vehicle, pulled open the passenger side door and dropped into the seat
next to him, 'we can talk wherever suits you.'

He glared straight ahead then pulled into the traffic without any
further discussion. The interior smelt of leather upholstery mingled
with musky aftershave. They'd driven the length of Mill Road before

the silence became too much. 'I remember you visiting us when I was a kid. But not once I'd started secondary school.'

'I knew you well back then.' He glanced at her, then back at the road. 'But it was time to call it a day.'

'Why?'

'I think you know.'

'Because my dad was being released. What I didn't understand was your relationship with my mum. I knew you weren't having an affair with her . . .'

Amy had guessed where he was taking them and Neil Frampton only responded once he'd pulled up in King Street close to the flight of sloping steps that led to her flat. 'You're correct, I wasn't.'

They were within sight of Clowns and the spot where her father had collapsed just a few hours earlier. 'So why did you help us for all those years?'

'Your mother and I were friends.'

'No, it's not that either, is it? Friendship would have continued, and you like one another but you weren't ever that close.'

Neil shifted in his seat, turning his upper body to face her. 'Amy? You're twisting things round to point in a certain direction. What exactly do you want to prove?'

'I want to understand it.'

'Perhaps it's none of your business. And you didn't get me out here to ask all of this. You said you needed my help.'

Neil was overweight; there was no sign of any great physical strength in him but he still seemed intimidating; a man with high blood pressure and low reserves of patience.

She raised her palms in surrender, 'I'm sorry, this is coming out all wrong. The last thing I meant was to sound critical.' She was messing this up and the fear of the door closing before it had opened made her voice wobble. 'I really need a job,' she stumbled over the words and then bit down on her bottom lip, hoping that her awkward half-truth would be taken as embarrassment at having to ask for help.

'Why ask me now?'

'Because I don't know who else I can turn to.'

'But why today?'

'I've been temping and the contract ends this week . . .'

'And your father has been rushed to hospital this afternoon.' Neil ran his tongue across his teeth. 'Amy, I'm always going to know what's going on with him.'

'That has nothing to do with why I'm asking.'

'You're lying.' Neil's eyes flashed wider. 'Did he put you up to this?'

'No! And he doesn't know I'm here. Do you really think he's in hospital thinking about you? And do you know how hard it is for me to ask you for work?' she reached for the door handle. 'I'm totally at the end of my options.'

He reached for her arm. 'Amy . . .'

But she pulled away and scrambled out of the car and onto the pavement, 'Just tell me one thing. Were you helping us out of guilt?'

'Guilt for what?' She slammed the door and started to walk away. She heard his door open and he shouted after her. 'I said, guilt for what?'

She turned and took a couple of steps towards him. 'You tell me. Seems like a man who helps the family of his son's killer has to be motivated by something. I've thought about it and if it's not sex and not money then guilt seems like the answer.'

'And asking me this on the day he's rushed to hospital?'

'Coincidence. I need a job, that's all.'

He didn't move for what felt like a considerable length of time. Amy waited. 'Go to our yard in Argyle Street tomorrow morning. I'll tell Moira to expect you.'

Amy nodded. 'Thank you,' she breathed.

'Nine a.m.,' he told her and she could feel his eyes on her as she walked towards home.

CHAPTER 4

The flatbed truck drove into the yard, its wing mirrors passing within a couple of inches of the narrow brick entrance. The driver immediately spotted the two figures in the Portakabin as the strip lights drenched the interior in an unforgiving starkness. The window stood out like a huge flat-screen TV in the dull enclosure. He swung left into the gap between scaffold poles and a compact trailer carrying a generator, and then adjusted his rear-view mirror to take another look at the two women. Moira was the finance manager, but the other . . . It was rare to have visitors although, occasionally, a car might pull in. But this woman was younger, not the middle-aged dominant type who'd arrive by Mercedes or Audi and use it to block the entrance and attempt to demand obedience from him or his men. Moira held a sheaf of papers in her hand and the pages flapped like a semaphore flag. She moved towards the spare desk and put her hand on the back of the chair. He couldn't see the newcomer too clearly but she seemed familiar.

He slid down from the cab. He was a big man, a couple of inches short of six foot but solid. The heavy tread of his boots ground mud stains onto the concrete.

When he opened the door their conversation trickled dry. Moira smiled uneasily, 'Stan, this is Amy Laurence, our new temp.'

He wiped his palm on the thigh of his overall and stepped forward to shake her hand. She looked in her early twenties although he knew she wasn't that young. He muttered 'hello' and her grip attempted to be firm but he was aware of overpowering it with his own. 'I didn't know we were employing anyone.'

Moira glanced at Amy then back to him, flat-eyed, 'Neither did I.'

'I see.' Stan stared at Amy but continued to address Moira. 'So who sent for extra help? Neil?'

'Who else?'

Stan grunted and Amy made a point of pretending that she was unaware of his attention but her shoulders were tense and her hands had balled into small fists. Stan went to his own desk and pulled paperwork towards him as he sat. 'Let's see what other shit the day has to offer then.'

Moira slapped her own papers onto her desk, loud enough for him to glance up. She shook her head at him. 'We don't need a bad atmosphere in here, Stan.'

He leant back in his chair and forced the tension away. 'It's a bit of a hangover,' he told her.

She raised an eyebrow. 'Well, don't make us all suffer.'

'I'm happy to make coffee,' Amy offered. 'Would you like coffee?' She had regained her composure very quickly and smiled as though she found the idea of making his coffee amusing for some reason. Perhaps she was about to spit in it.

'Yeah, white with two.'

She seemed to know where to find the kettle. Her eyes were brown and her smile made them sparkle, made her cheeks dimple. Her curly brown hair bounced when she moved. She disappeared towards the kitchenette, her straight skirt doing nothing to hide her figure. He registered all those things but doubted he would ever see beyond the only fact that mattered; this was Robert Buckingham's daughter.

Moira gave her desktop an urgent tap. 'Don't glare at her like that.'

'I wasn't.'

When his coffee arrived he left it untouched. By then he had sent an email across the office and told Moira to meet him at the end of the street. He had almost reached the corner when she drove alongside him. She lowered the driver's window of her Audi A4. 'Get in then,' she told him.

She drove away before he had the chance to put on his seatbelt.

They sped through several back streets until she found an unoccupied residents-only parking space in Vinery Road. He was the first to speak. 'Did you think I wouldn't know her, Moira? What's the idea?'

'I don't know why she's here either. Neil just rang this morning and told me that he'd offered her a job. He said it might be a six-month contract no less.'

'Just out of the blue?'

'She contacted him apparently. She was desperate for work,' Moira raised her hands in despair, 'and he's jumped in to rescue her.'

'Of course he has,' Stan replied. He and Moira had been working together throughout; they'd seen Neil Frampton and the company come back from near bankruptcy. He was a smart man over most things. But not this. 'Where does he think this will end? And how are we supposed to work with her? *Hey Amy, I used to be your dad's mate until he killed those people.*'

'Stan . . .'

'Does she know that payments go to suppliers, not to her own bank account? Sorry, Amy, can't let you loose with a lighter or matches, a cheque book or even a pen.'

'Stan, stop it.' Moira was far better at holding everything in than he'd ever been and watching her restraint now was just aggravating him.

'I want you to admit to being as angry as I am, Moira. Or you can coach me and we can all sit around drinking coffee, sharing stories about the old days.'

'She's not her father.'

'We don't know what she's not. And we don't get a choice either. Thanks, Neil, thanks very much.'

Moira restarted the engine. 'We'll go back, talk to her and clear the air. That's the best way forward.'

Stan exhaled a heavy breath and let his head loll back against the headrest. 'Fucking hell, Moira.'

CHAPTER 5

Three months later.

Sue Gully had curled up on Goodhew's sofa, too exhausted by recent events to worry about politeness or her usual self-consciousness around his home. They'd returned from a funeral and it had marked the end of the previous case in a way that the arrest of the killer hadn't and the conviction wouldn't. This, for her at least, had been the sign-off. She guessed it was the same for Goodhew too; the restless expression that haunted his features during an investigation had gone for now. He'd been sitting on the floor next to her, leaning against his jukebox and telling her about his family, memories of his childhood, even about how he had felt as a young boy when his grandfather had died. It had happened in this very room, the only part of the rest of the house below his flat that Goodhew occupied.

'I may have moved some of my things in here, but I still feel this is his study,' Goodhew now said to her. 'And even though I now know how he died, I still feel that this is a peaceful place.'

It felt right to move onto the floor beside him, but she didn't. Maybe he thought the same because, now, he'd come to sit beside her. It wasn't the first time she'd imagined being close to him. But this was real and she had one inescapable reason why she should not let it happen.

He studied her expression for a single still moment and she felt as though he could read her every thought; she was used to his intensity, but not when she was the absolute focus like this. She held her breath and didn't turn away from his gaze. His fingers touched her cheek, then, as their lips met, he wrapped his arms around her. She pulled him closer. She pressed her fingers against his back, felt the tautness beneath his shirt; the strength she'd watched him regain after his accident. It was the way she'd imagined. Stealing her breath. Making her float. Making anything seem possible. Except she knew it wasn't.

She waited until the moment when there was stillness. She lay in the crook of his arm, her cheek against his chest. They still held each other even though she knew it had to be time to let go. She scoured her thoughts, trying to find the right words, the ones that would explain enough but not hurt, or raise questions or, worse still, leave the door ajar. Her hand rested on his arm and she could feel his warmth through the thin cotton of his shirt.

'Will you stay?' he asked.

She drew a breath. She still didn't have the words but needed to trust that they would come. 'Why now, Gary?'

'Too soon or not soon enough? And does it really matter?'

She shook her head. 'I don't know,' she replied. But she did know and the truth was that there might never be a right time. 'It would be a mistake for us. We work together.'

'Is that the only reason?'

He rolled onto his side and their faces were close. Almost touching. She wanted to kiss him again but instead she pressed her palm against his shoulder. 'We've been to a funeral and then there's . . .' She trailed off, not wanting to raise the subject of exactly what had happened to his grandfather. 'Two shocks, Gary. I get it.'

'This isn't about needing company or not thinking straight . . .'

She knew that. She felt the edge of a void beckoning. If she stayed longer it would only grow more difficult. Her answer had been wrong. She slipped out of his arms. 'I need to go. I have nothing against one-night stands, Gary, just not with colleagues.' She turned away to take her jacket from the armchair. She felt her cheeks flush and was relieved that the half-light hid that at least.

'You know that's not what this is.'

'It always makes things complicated.' It was easier to leave it like

26

that; he didn't know much about her private life; she might have a different bloke every night for all he knew.

She slipped her arms into her jacket but didn't button it. She pushed her hands into her pockets and waited for him to stand. His expression was back to its most unfathomable.

He walked her down both flights of stairs and by then she found the silence too much. 'The thing is, Gary, you don't know me. Not really. I don't want it to get weird between us or to ruin our friendship.'

'I think I know you, Sue. And you know me better than anyone else does.' Without warning he hugged her, kissing her softly on the cheek before opening the door and letting her go.

She hurried down the steps and crossed onto Parker's Piece, walking quickly without glancing back. She concentrated on keeping her speed constant and her step determined until she knew that she was out of sight. She slowed then and took twice as long as usual to reach home and the entire time she could still feel his lips on hers. If her brain worked differently she would have stayed, and damn the consequences, but she'd never understood the throwaway intimacy of a one-night stand. And that was never what she'd wanted with Gary. She doubted there was the possibility of more than that, though, and the thought of him pushing her away later hurt more than ending it before it had the chance to begin.

CHAPTER 6

Goodhew sat on the top step of the short stone flight that led from street level up to his front door. He leant back against the darkly painted wood the weak sunlight had warmed, and he watched Parker's Piece through half-closed eyes. When he was younger he'd believed that the paths crossing the green had marked the centre of Cambridge, like a giant X-marks-the-spot. Unless it was the dead of the night, there were always people crossing it on foot or bicycle; easy to believe that everyone who lived in the city passed through here at one time or another.

His relationship with the city was as complicated as his relationship with this house. He'd grown up with both. The house had belonged to his grandparents but he'd visited most days and had grown up thinking of it as his true childhood home. He'd jumped at the chance to take the rooftop flat when his grandmother had decided to move out. Ownership of the whole building had been passed over to him, but he had continued to live in the flat, leaving the other three floors almost entirely empty.

The ground floor stood half a storey above street level. He had walked down the front steps with Sue, and watched her until she'd disappeared from view. That had been an hour ago and he was still there, trying to re-anchor his thoughts after the shifts and reverberations of the previous few days.

My grandfather was murdered.

That simple sentence had been on repeat since he'd found out. It punctuated every other thought he'd tried to corral. Yes, it had been a shock but not in the same way as if a sudden or violent death had just happened. That shock would be sharper, louder even, the epicentre tangible and the rewritten picture of the future would lie ahead with its debris there to step over and around. This shock was different; it had taken place in July 1992 and the twenty-two years since now looked altered. He had yet to know how far or how deep the rewriting needed to go. His parents and his grandmother had both known the truth and so had DI Marks and potentially any officer old enough to have been part of the investigation at the time.

For the first time in almost six months he'd phoned his sister Debbie. She hadn't known either and they'd spent several long phone calls since dredging up fragments of memory, trying to piece together clues they'd missed. But she'd been nine and he'd been eleven, and he'd been the only one of them who'd seen or heard anything of consequence. He told Debbie how he'd hidden in their grandfather's study when the two men had visited. How he'd done exactly what he'd promised their grandfather he would do and had sneaked back into school and said absolutely nothing.

He'd heard Debbie draw a sharp breath and he could guess the words she'd wanted to say, 'You should have told someone, Gary.'

She'd been right, too, he might have been able to give some kind of description. He'd heard their voices, one sounded much younger, he talked less. The older man had a hard-edged voice, he sounded angry but his tone was thin as though it belonged to a short and wiry body. Goodhew had seen the man's shoes from his hiding place too. Brown leather, the soles newer than the rest. If Goodhew had told the police any part of that description it might have tipped the investigation in a better direction. They were small details but sometimes that was all it took. He'd felt the nausea of guilt.

'If I'd spoken up they might have been caught,' he told her.

'You didn't know there was any investigation and he'd asked you to keep a secret. You just did what he asked, but I'll tell you something, Gary,' she sighed, 'it explains why you joined the police.'

He didn't comment even though the same thought had occurred to him. Being a detective had been a childhood ambition but he couldn't remember having any interest before his grandfather's death. He wasn't ready to admit that, though. 'I'm sure I was younger than that when I first mentioned it.'

'No. You were at boarding school,' she said firmly. 'I clearly remember. I wanted to travel the world and you wanted to stay in Cambridge. It makes sense now, doesn't it?'

It made sense if it really had been bothering him all those years; if, subconsciously at least, he'd always known about his grandfather's murder. He hated it that his grandmother and DI Marks – people he knew and loved – had kept it secret from him. He hated it more that he might have kept it from himself.

His mobile lay on the step beside him and he glanced down at it a moment before it began to ring. His grandmother's mobile number flashed onto the screen. His phone was on silent but the light on the screen pulsed at the same rate as a ringtone. He watched it until the call was diverted to voicemail and the screen faded back to black.

It wasn't that he didn't want to talk to her; just that he didn't know what to say. And, for different reasons, that had been the same with Sue. He could still feel their kiss and the moment he'd realised that she was gently pulling away from him. He picked up his phone and scrolled down to her number before changing his mind and returning the phone to the step.

'Are you avoiding me, Gary?'

His grandmother stood on his garden path. She wore a deep maroon suit and looked like she'd come straight from a wedding; elegant even by her own standards. He saw that she held a leather document wallet; not a wedding then. She'd been to see Mason, her solicitor. Their solicitor actually. 'Not entirely. I didn't know what to say.'

'Isn't that the same thing?' She didn't wait for a reply. 'There's something I'd like to show you, assuming, that is, you're not about to dash off to work?'

Goodhew shook his head. 'I'm in tomorrow. Right now I'm not going anywhere.'

'Can we talk then?'

'I think we should,' he replied, but reluctance swept over him. He felt no rush to go inside the house and didn't move at first. 'Not here though.'

'I thought not. Hobbs Pavilion?' She glanced over her left shoulder at the former cricket pavilion that had housed the Mai Thai restaurant since the summer he'd moved into the flat.

He didn't feel hungry but suddenly realised he hadn't eaten for hours. They crossed the road in silence, glad that the walk wasn't long enough for either of them to feel the need to talk.

They sat at a table laid for four, choosing facing seats and a window view of Parker's Piece. She placed the document wallet on the seat beside her.

He ordered noodles without paying much attention to the menu. The food arrived quickly but he barely noticed; he was more interested in hearing what his grandmother had to say.

'I suppose knowing that I planned to tell you isn't much help?'

He shook his head. 'Debbie and I should have grown up knowing what had happened to him. You and I have always been close and it's a shock to discover that you've lied to me since I was a kid.'

His grandmother watched him for some time. 'How much do you know?' she asked finally.

'That he was beaten to death. He collapsed with a head injury and was rushed to hospital but there was nothing . . .'

She raised a hand to stop him, 'Your grandfather had an old head injury and it was that which ruptured. He may have died if they hadn't hit him, he might have fallen or been in any minor accident and the result could have been the same.'

'He died because they hit him.' Goodhew leant back in his chair and studied her carefully. 'How can you be so calm about it?'

'I'm not.' She pressed her lips into a tight smile, her focus drifted beyond him for a moment and her eyes began to mist. 'Your grandfather and I had an agreement; we accepted whatever time we had together and certain parts of our life, our career if you can call it that, were to be kept secret from almost everyone, including you. No matter what,' she whispered. She blinked quickly and looked at Goodhew again. 'But that was a long time ago and I'm going to let it go now. After all, you made him a promise too and that didn't help. This isn't the time for any more secrets. When I just asked how much you know, I meant about his life, not his death.'

Goodhew shook his head. She reached for the folder beside her. 'What's in there?' he asked.

She moved it on to the table in front of her, one neat hand pressed flat on its tooled cover. Now he could see it more clearly and it was far older than it had first appeared, with little vein-like cracks along the spine where the leather had aged. She lifted her hand very slightly as though prepared to let him take the file but then changed her mind. He could tell that she was hunting for words – precise words. He said nothing, just waited.

He knew that she and his grandfather had loved each other deeply. She'd been in her late forties when she'd been widowed. Forty-nine by his calculations, although her exact age had always been vague. Young enough to have considered marriage again perhaps, but she never had; she enjoyed romance but remained robustly independent. There had never been any sign of frailty or uncertainty about her, not even now as he watched her consider sharing details of her husband's death.

He had no idea what he was likely to hear.

'Mount Kilauea has been erupting every day since 1983, you know that?'

'Yes, but that's not exactly what I thought you would say.'

'I'd hate to be predictable, Gary.' She looked amused for a moment. 'The point is the lava destroys everything in its path, trees, buildings, people if they don't get out of the way, and then you speak to the locals, the ones at the heart of it, they don't see it that way at all. The volcanoes created the land and Mount Kilauea is adding to it. The eruption is about the birth of the island. Your grandfather and I shook things up and we knew it might end badly. But we were happy with the risks.'

She released her hold on the folder and he took it, pushing his half-eaten meal to one side so that he could give it his complete attention. The pages it held formed an inch-thick sheaf, their edges still sharp even though it had clearly been many years since they'd been written and the ink on them had faded. He recognised his grandfather's handwriting at once. The top page was filled with names and comments. Some were ringed and connected by lines. Others were enclosed in boxes and several had been scrubbed through. Goodhew was startled by the similarity to his own way of working. 'What is this?'

'We called those pages firsts because each is the first page of notes he would make on each new job.'

'What kind of job?'

She smiled softly and as she spoke he knew that she was watching to see what his reaction would be. 'We searched for missing people. At the very first meeting with a potential client your grandfather would make those notes. They were like word doodles, they contained key pieces of information but also any thoughts or feelings that came into his head.'

Goodhew shook his head in disbelief. 'And each of these pages is one case? One missing person?'

She nodded.

'How did I never know this?'

'We didn't want you to.'

He turned the first page and then separated the pile at random points. He spotted place names he didn't recognise, scribbled last-known addresses in unfamiliar towns in Bulgaria, Italy, Hong Kong, Thailand, American states and remote Australian towns. 'How many years . . .' he began.

'Always,' she replied. 'We loved it and we were good at it. And, as you can see, we travelled the world. We found runaways, absconders, people who were trying to hide and some that were desperate to be found.' She ran one fingertip down the side of the pile. 'There are more folders than this one, and I want you to see everything now.' There was nothing wrong with the food but neither of them finished eating. She left cash on the table. 'Come with me, there's something I must show you.'

Goodhew followed her outside to find her waving down a taxi. He held the door open for her. 'Where are we going?'

'Hope Street Yard.'

He didn't ask why, he wanted to work it out for himself. He began turning over the pages one by one, trying to spot any clue that would explain why they were about to visit a cluster of units selling antiques and vintage collectibles. The journey would be ten minutes at most so after the first few pages he began to flick through more quickly. He stopped at a sketch of a lion; it was drawn in the style of a heraldic symbol, rearing up on its hind legs with flames dancing at his feet. 'I recognise that. It was on a pen in one of the drawers in the study.'

'Very good. Do you remember what he told you about it?'

Goodhew's grandfather had repeated stories about many of the objects but he couldn't remember anything specifically belonging to this. 'I don't think so . . . he had hundreds of items and he seemed to have stories to go with each of them.'

'All true.'

'Really?'

'Perhaps the odd embellishment,' she conceded. 'He had a sense of drama.' She touched her hand on his. 'We're here.' She let the taxi go and he followed her into the yard. Most of the units stood with their doors open, many with items standing outside. Reclaimed doors and a radiator at one, a rail of second-hand clothes at the next. She passed all of these and headed towards a locked unit in the corner. With her own sense of drama, she reached into her pocket and produced a small key on a large leather fob. She handed it to Goodhew. 'All yours.'

He'd already guessed, or hoped he had. He swung the door open and light fell onto its contents. He had been correct but seeing all the furniture from his grandfather's study still took his breath away. Every item was instantly familiar although not quite as he remembered. The desk looked smaller and the bookshelves less grand; he'd changed, not them. He pushed the folder into his grandmother's hands and reached for the nearest drawer.

'It's all there,' she assured him. 'I didn't know what to do with everything so I took it, lock, stock and barrel, and stored it here.'

'You could have left it in the house.'

'And it would have turned into a museum instead of your home.'

Gently he picked through the contents and among them found a single playing card, a cufflink and the head from a decapitated figurine. 'I remember all of these.'

'One souvenir per case.' She picked up a wooden pawn, long since separated from the rest of the chess set. 'I thought it an annoying habit at first, but I look at these things now and I'm reminded of so many details I might have forgotten.'

In this drawer alone there were more items than he could count. 'That's a huge number of cases.'

'We certainly were busy. People do go missing for very many reasons. And sometimes clients wanted us to find relatives or former colleagues when they'd just lost touch over the years. It didn't all involve anything illegal or underhand.'

'But it sometimes did?'

'Frequently.'

Goodhew opened every drawer and cupboard, taking out items he recognised, remembering fragments of stories that his grandfather had told him. 'What else do you know about his death?' he asked.

'We'll walk back.' She waited for him to finish looking through the drawers and cupboards. He locked up and they walked through the passage to Mill Road. He didn't look at her directly but in the corner of his vision he could see that her gaze was fixed on the street ahead. 'I have another set of keys so you can keep those,' she said.

He wondered whether she hadn't heard his question or had decided to leave it unanswered but either way, he wouldn't ask again until they were back at his flat.

They'd walked for another five minutes before she spoke. 'The skills needed to find a person aren't too different from the ones needed to help them disappear. We knew how to search data trails – different back then, of course, but we made those impossible to follow.'

It took Goodhew a few seconds to grasp what she was saying. 'You helped someone vanish?'

'Once or twice.' She glanced at him. 'Sorry, I was in a train of thought and just started in the middle. You asked what else I knew about Joe's death and there's not much. But about two years before, we'd been contacted by a young history student named Melanie Franks. She was pregnant and already estranged from her family, in debt and desperate to continue her studies. She'd become involved in something illegal, but wouldn't tell us what it was.'

'But you still helped her?'

'I didn't want to unless we knew more, but Joe felt strongly,

35

probably because she was expecting a baby, I don't know. It was very rare that we disagreed about helping anyone; we had rules for which cases we took on and which we didn't. Anyhow, we set it up and she disappeared.'

'Where?'

'To Hereford; the major routes from here are north–south so we liked the idea of the west of England and she took the name Jane Williams. Clichéd as it is, the most common names work best. And that was all we heard from her as far as I ever knew.'

She stepped to the side of the footpath and stopped outside a computer repair shop, her back to the window. 'If Joe was talking on the phone he'd make notes, like the ones in that file. After he died, I found this.' She pulled a folded sheet of A4 paper from her pocket and passed it to Goodhew. He opened it out. There were few words on the page, just a mundane to-do list: renew car insurance, check smoke alarms, *Batman Returns*.

'He took me to see that.'

'June '92. And look.'

She was pointing to the corner of the page but Goodhew was already looking. The name Melanie was written and circled and the ink was several layers deep as if his grandfather had kept tracing the letters as he'd thought about her.

'It doesn't mean she contacted him,' Goodhew said. 'Perhaps someone else was asking or she was on his mind.'

'Maybe,' she replied but shook her head as she said it. 'When the police had gone I checked and every document mentioning her had also gone. There wasn't much, mind you, and nothing that would have given away her new location, but it had all been taken.' She touched the sheet of paper. 'They missed this. And this too.' She removed a bangle from her wrist and handed it to Goodhew. 'I'd never seen it before he died but it was in the drawer with the other souvenirs. I'm sure I knew every item almost as well as he did and he must have acquired it very recently.'

Goodhew took the bangle and turned it over in his fingers. It was some kind of plastic, acrylic perhaps and was transparent with tiny straight fibres, like minute rods of dry spaghetti, suspended in the resin. 'You've had this for twenty-two years?'

'I have. I can't imagine it will tell us much, but who knows.'

'Could he have been working on something without your knowledge?'

'He must have been. And it seems it was connected to Melanie, perhaps proving she was in danger all along. If you can find her without putting her at risk, and if she'll talk to you, you might get your answers.'

'And I have your blessing?'

'Always, Gary.' Without either of them suggesting it, they started to walk again. She waited until they'd finished threading through the traffic on Gonville Place before she spoke again. 'When you mention him, you don't call him granddad any more.'

Goodhew had been very aware of this. He hadn't meant any disrespect but saying *my grandfather* to his grandmother seemed awkward and he found *granddad's murder* impossible to say to anyone. 'I'm sorry,' he replied. 'Would it be wrong to call him Joe?'

'Not at all.' She tucked her gloved hand in the crook of his arm. 'But you'll have to call me Ellie instead of gran.'

'You've never let me call you gran.'

'You say it sometimes and it makes me feel old. Ellie and Joe, please.'

'That will take a lot of getting used to.'

'You'll manage.'

And he had no doubt that he would. He glanced across to Parkside Police Station. There were answers there too and he intended to find them next.

CHAPTER 7

DI Marks wasn't at his desk when Goodhew reached his office. Two orange plastic packing crates stood on the floor and seemed to dominate the room. One was already filled and held the larger objects: several books, a couple of framed photographs and Marks's anglepoise lamp. Each item looked as though it had been packed carefully. The second crate contained fewer items and those seemed to have been tipped straight from a drawer. Marks had left his mug on the desktop, a foot away from the souvenir coaster from Malta. Goodhew wasn't about to check the drawers to see if they were empty but, if this was the sum total of all his boss's years in this room, it wasn't much. He turned to find DS Michael Kincaide standing in the doorway behind him.

'I wondered when you'd appear, Gary.'

'Is Marks around?'

'Do you want to see him or have time to go through his desk?'

Goodhew pretended to weigh it up. 'Both, I suppose. The same as you.'

Kincaide's dark eyes flickered with irritation, '*I* don't need to scavenge for information behind people's backs . . .'

Goodhew grinned. 'So he's on his way up then?'

Kincaide pulled a chair alongside Marks's desk and took a seat. 'Can you wait outside? I need to see him first.'

'No problem.'

Goodhew closed the door behind him and stayed in the hallway until Marks appeared several minutes later. 'I was hoping to ask you a few questions, sir.' Marks nodded towards his office but Goodhew shook his head. 'Kincaide's in there.'

'So you're in the corridor? Five minutes of small talk wouldn't kill either of you.' Goodhew wasn't convinced but didn't comment. He followed Marks back inside. Kincaide wasn't seated now but standing at the window and looking down on Parker's Piece. The mug had been returned to its coaster and Marks's own chair had been replaced neatly into the foot-well of the desk. Would small talk include asking whether Kincaide had really been swivelling in their DI's chair and pretending to be in charge? Goodhew stayed quiet.

Kincaide took a few minutes to run through some paperwork, fussing so much over the small details that Goodhew wondered whether his sole purpose was to hinder everyone else's day.

As soon as Kincaide had gone Marks opened one of his desk drawers and handed Goodhew a thick file. 'Most of this is what I held onto from your grandfather's case.'

'Sue told me about it. Can I have it, or take copies?'

'Take it, and I've also ordered all the documentation up from the archives. It will be here tomorrow or Wednesday.'

'And you finish on Friday?'

'Next Friday, not this. There will be time; you won't be able to take it from the building, though.'

'I understand.'

Marks gave a sceptical grunt. 'Just don't lose it. I might have been more junior back then, but I now know Joe's case well and I'd like to discuss it with you when you're ready.'

Goodhew was ready, but the information his grandmother had given him pressed harder. 'Where would you start if you were me?'

'If I were you?' Marks studied him intently for almost a minute, his gaze impenetrable. 'Somewhere along the line we missed the leads we needed. You might think that you saw nothing of significance but you are the only witness. So, if I were you, I'd sift through everything and see what jumps out.'

'It's not information I should have.'

'My behaviour is beyond improper.' Marks looked unconcerned.

'But I retire next week and this case won't be at the top of anyone else's caseload. You understand that you can't be involved in an official capacity?'

'Thank you, sir. There's one other thing – does the name Melanie Franks mean anything to you?'

Marks shook his head slightly. 'It doesn't ring a bell. Who is she?'

'That's all I have at the moment. She has no criminal record and her name doesn't cross-reference with any other cases.'

'And I'm guessing that this woman's name came from your grandmother?'

'Possibly.'

Marks closed his eyes for a second. Goodhew guessed it was the equivalent of a slow count to ten. 'Have you asked Sheen?'

'He's not in today, I've left him a note.' Sheen was the oracle of all things local; he could often dredge up rumours and connections that had never made it into official documentation.

'He'll also ask who she is . . .'

'Like I said, she's just a name.'

Marks pursed his lips and tapped on the desktop with the tips of his fingers. 'It is still an open case, Gary.'

'And I won't hold back anything that I think is relevant.'

'It's not down to you to decide what counts as relevant, you know. A case is different when it's personal. It really is important that you keep me, or my replacement, informed of anything new.'

'I understand.'

'And Melanie Franks?'

Goodhew tried to look apologetic. 'I'm sorry, sir, as far as I know there's no connection.' He picked up the file and rose to his feet.

Marks stood too and walked Goodhew to the door, 'I always suspected that your grandmother was holding something back. Talking of which,' he nodded at the file Goodhew held, 'I kept a few files, each relating to an unsolved case. All were personal to me in some way or another, mostly because I was close to the investigation and hoped, one day, to have the satisfaction of seeing it resolved. This one was different, I knew Joe before he died; he and your grandmother were remarkable, they helped me several times on local cases.'

Goodhew was startled. 'I had no idea.' Until two weeks ago he hadn't known that Marks and his grandmother even knew one another.

'Not everything in there relates to Joe. I followed your early days and, when I started receiving your anonymous tip-offs for other cases, I filed those in there too. They do need to disappear from Parkside.'

'Was it that obvious?'

'That it was you? It wasn't my greatest feat of detection, Gary. You have Joe's doggedness and a similar mind. And you don't always know when to keep yourself out of trouble.'

Goodhew left Parkside Station and was halfway across Parker's Piece towards his house when he saw his friend Bryn's turquoise and white Zodiac pull up outside. Bryn waited in the driver's seat with his arm out of the window. It wasn't a sign of spring, it was just the way Bryn liked to pose.

Usually when Bryn turned up unannounced it was no surprise but today was different. 'What happened to Prague?'

Bryn reached across and opened the door for Goodhew. 'How about a curry, a few drinks and pool?' Bryn pulled into the traffic the moment that Goodhew closed the door. 'Maya and I have called it quits,' he told him.

Bryn looked and sounded casual but Goodhew doubted that he was. In the years that Goodhew and Bryn had been friends, the relationship with Maya had been the only that had lasted beyond a few weeks.

'When?'

'Yesterday, at the airport.'

'So you never went?'

'We went, but then we caught the next plane home.'

Goodhew waited for Bryn to add more but the conversation stalled until they were at the Earl of Beaconsfield and had taken their drinks to the pool table.

'We were taxiing down the runway and she hates take-off and landing so she's there with her eyes closed and her hands bunched into fists and she says, "It's not working." I thought she meant the seatbelt or something so I asked, "What's not?" And she opened one eye and said, "If we crash right now what hasn't been fulfilled in your life?"

Goodhew broke into the pack and potted a yellow. 'That's deep.'

'That's Maya,' Bryn agreed. 'But if we had crashed I wouldn't have got to hear her list. And if we'd crashed without her saying anything then I would have died happier than I am right now . . .' Bryn potted a couple of reds in silence. He wasn't great at playing and talking simultaneously. 'Apart from being dead, of course.'

'So she just finished with you on the plane?'

Bryn shook his head. 'We talked on the flight and at the airport, and then waited for the next one home.' He leant against the table and suddenly became pensive. 'The funny thing was that I understood what she meant. I thought we were fine but, when she explained, I got it. She doesn't want to spend the rest of her life in Cambridge any more than I want to live mine anywhere else. She wants to travel, to study politics, to become a journalist. I don't even know what I want but it's not all that stuff.' He potted a third ball, then ran the cue ball behind another red to leave Goodhew snookered.

Goodhew aimed the cue ball around the table and managed to pot another yellow. 'I can't believe you sound so philosophical about it all.'

'Yeah, well I wasn't when I went over to my parent's house last night. Last time I cried like that was when I crashed the Zodiac.' The joke didn't sound convincing. 'I was awake most of the night thinking about her and, when I went back to the flat this morning, she'd gone. I'm going to move out too, I don't want to stay there without her.' Bryn paused before taking his next shot, 'How can so much change in a single day?'

Goodhew considered his last twenty-four hours and decided to order more drinks.

CHAPTER 8

Jan Kincaide turned the key in the lock and opened the door an inch or two. She paused long enough to hear the muted sounds of the television in the front room, long enough to face the monotony that hung in the air, to take a breath and nudge herself inside. She dragged her case over the threshold, careful not to scuff it against her suit trousers. It was later than she'd planned by, she guessed, at least two bottles of beer. She dropped her keys on the hall table, leaving her case at the bottom of the stairs and walking towards the kitchen. Her husband Michael was in an armchair, staring at the screen but not watching, a pair of empty bottles on the coffee table beside him. She stopped in the doorway – extending her disapproval from the bottles back to the man.

'Welcome home?'

Michael turned his head a little, dragging his gaze away from the screen, 'Give me a chance. I didn't hear you come in.'

'I don't suppose you saved me any dinner? Or did you eat at work?'

'I didn't bother.'

She knew which he meant and that piqued her interest; her husband was slim but always looked after his appetite. She carried on to the kitchen and returned with coffees, leaving his on the coffee table next to him and still making no physical contact with him. She flicked off the TV and waited until she had his full attention before speaking. 'So, what's eating at you?'

'If you'd been here you would have known.'

'It was a seminar and you could have phoned any evening. And, if you had, I also would have known what was bothering you, so let's skip that self-pity crap, Michael. Unless, of course, you want to piss me off before you've even begun?'

'It was the funeral of that murdered homeless guy today . . .'

'Aaron Rizzo?'

'Yeah, Ratty,' he replied.

She was surprised. 'And you went?'

She saw the tell-tale flexing of his jaw muscles as he clenched and unclenched his teeth, 'Too right I fucking did. Since the last day of that last case I knew there was something going on, some private club that everyone was suddenly a member of.'

'Everyone, like who?'

'Goodhew and Marks, Sheen and Sue.'

'Oh, that everyone.'

Kincaide cocked his head. 'Meaning what? Here I go again? No wonder I don't confide in you when you just dismiss every fucking thing that bothers me.'

She sighed. 'Then say something I haven't heard before, Michael. It always comes back to Goodhew being treated differently, Goodhew getting all the breaks. Who got the promotion? You did. If there was that much nepotism you'd still be a DC and he'd be the DS.'

Kincaide gave a cold laugh. 'There's plenty you haven't heard before and it turns out it was all fucking nepotism, even when they promoted me I bet it was some twisted fucking way of getting me off of Gary's case.'

Jan blinked slowly, an attempt to keep herself calm. She shot an angry glance at the bottles. 'Have you been drinking more than that?'

'I'm not drunk.'

'But you've been at it for a while?'

'I'm a grown man. It's not a fucking crime to unwind with a drink.'

'You're swearing *and* ranting.' She said it as an observation, her tone matter-of-fact.

'Because I finally found out, and I bet I was the last to know.'

Jan dropped into the other armchair with a sigh. 'OK, what did you find out?'

'That Goodhew's grandfather was beaten to death back in 1992 and it's unsolved. Goodhew found out a couple of weeks ago and Marks knew about it all along.'

'You never told me.'

'Because *I* didn't know until a couple of days ago when it was officially reopened and suddenly it made sense. Marks knew the grandfather, he worked on his case; no wonder he's been pandering to Goodhew all this time.'

'Goodhew must have known.'

'Didn't know as a kid and no one filled him in until now.'

'And why's all this your problem?'

'He's like a thorn in my fucking side, Jan. Turns out he's been sitting on a huge inheritance all this time. We struggle for whatever we get and he doesn't even need to work; he's there playing a game while everything I work towards just drops in his fucking lap.'

He'd left his coffee untouched. She reached for hers and sipped it as she studied him. He wasn't hard to measure, for one thing too much alcohol made him swear and it had obviously taken him a while to work himself up to his current state. The bitterness wasn't drink related though, that rippled under his skin 24/7; it seemed to her that her husband enjoyed the role of being hard done by. But this level of anger was new. The question was whether he actually wanted to do something with it or just make her listen ad infinitum.

'There's no point telling me these things unless you're prepared to act on them,' she said quietly. 'I can't fix them for you.'

'I don't want you to.' He stared at her expectantly, though, as if she held all the answers or he was waiting for her permission to act. 'I want to deal with it but I don't know where to start.'

Or perhaps he really did need her to think for him.

She sighed. 'What would actually make you happy, Michael?'

'Goodhew gone . . .' He shook his head slowly as he thought about it. 'No, more than that. I want him to have to leave as a result of his own failure. He needs to be discredited, or isolated.'

Things were changing; she didn't see how that helped but ran through them aloud in any case. 'Marks is retiring, so is Sheen. You and Goodhew will both have a fresh start then.' Her thoughts began to gather momentum. 'He won't have his feet under the table with who-ever takes over from Marks and, apart from him, who else has he got?'

'Sue Gully for one. She was with him today at the funeral. They're always dancing round each other, covering each other's backs.'

Kincaide's lips curled as if there was a bitter taste in his mouth.

'Are they together?'

'Obviously, what else would be going on? He wouldn't bother if there weren't benefits, would he?'

Jan threw him a filthy glare.

'Why the dirty look?'

'I thought it would be obvious.' She fought the urge to clench her teeth.

He looked blank. 'How does Goodhew shagging Sue help me at all?'

'How does your apparently decent IQ leave you so clueless about the way the rest of the population thinks and feels?' Tiredness would not help her patience. 'Sex is not the common denominator in the way all men think towards all women.'

'That's because you don't *know* men, Jan.'

'But you do know the world's not flat, right?'

'Of course I do, and what the fuck's that supposed to mean? The world's not flat, how stupid am I? How clever are you?'

As he redirected his frustrations at her she could see the remainder of her evening being sucked down a drain of accusations and incrim-inations, ending with the expectation of sex, the avoidance of it and the good bits of the day going down the pan with the rest.

She took a deep breath, exhaled slowly and gave up. 'I meant, look at the obvious; Sue helps him, covers for him, he confides in her. She is Gary's Achilles heel. If you can't get to him, get to her. Drive a wedge between her and Gary or her and her job – it will amount to the same.'

He took a few moments to digest what she'd said but she saw him straighten in his chair and a smile begin to form.

'He won't be so cocky once it's just me and him. And I know exactly how to tackle Sue.'

46

CHAPTER 9

Amy had taken a longer lunch and walked across town to visit her mum. The day of her father's heart attack had been the last time she'd been to her mother's house. Geraldine lived in the narrowest house in Fair Street. The strip of front garden had been replanted with box hedging and there were new curtains at the downstairs windows; they'd all appeared since Amy's last visit. Her mum let her in, saying nothing but managing a watered-down smile as she led her through to the conservatory. The rooms smelt of detergent layered over dampness, as though the carpets had been shampooed but the dirty water was still in there, sinking into the pile and drying out in the vain hope of becoming undetectable. Nothing had changed in the conservatory but it was not as she remembered it; what had been a romantic mix of new and old furniture just seemed muddled now. Or like a storeroom. Ornaments and plants and photos that had been comfortably familiar looked dusty and brittle. It had been weeks since the last time she'd been here and those weeks had been difficult; right now she was seeing her childhood home with fresh eyes.

Amy watched her mum reposition pens and a remote control, moving them to one side of the coffee table from the other. A small thing perhaps, but the way her mum expended energy wasn't directionless like this. Ever. She had always been the pragmatist, the capable parent who'd guided her through. And now her mum was feeling vulnerable. Amy wondered whether she should have been feeling sympathy; she didn't, even when her mum spoke and her voice sounded hoarse.

'It's good to see you.'

'Avoiding you wasn't helping.' Amy looked away.

'Do you know what will?'

On the window sill in front of Amy stood a spider plant in a pot that was sun-bleached down one side. New growth sprung out at the ends of the tendrils trailing down to touch the floor. If it had been her plant, she would have binned the entire mess. When Amy replied her voice was clear: 'To discover that there was a genuine reason why you abandoned Dad and lied to me.'

Geraldine stiffened immediately. 'I never thought you would appreciate my reasons. I doubt you will now.'

Amy glared. 'Are you even going to try to explain?'

'We should just move on, Amy. There's no point in going over it, not now, not after so long.'

Amy didn't rush to reply. She forced her breathing to steady. 'Are you about to tell me it's just water under the bridge?' she asked.

She'd always hated the expression but her mum used it regularly.

'I think so, don't you?' Her mum had missed the sarcasm and, very briefly, her voice brightened.

'No, Mum, I really don't. I can't make you talk about it but if you want us to move forward then you need to tell me everything you can.'

'To stir up more trouble?'

'I'm not sure it can, really. And if there's worse then you can't leave it hanging over me. How would that be right?'

'There isn't worse.'

'Well then . . .'

Her mum began to speak but cut herself off before the first word was complete, stopped, then told her 'I just don't want to . . .'

Amy stood. 'Fine, but our relationship won't get over it.'

'Amy, it can.'

'Only from your point of view, Mum. For me, it's a deal breaker.'

'A deal breaker?' she echoed.

Amy wanted to apologise for the choice of words but not the sentiment. 'Yes, it is.'

She hadn't said it for effect or brinkmanship. She expected to leave and to be followed by nothing but silence. Her mum stopped her before she'd made it through the first door.

'OK, Amy. Wait. I'll explain.'

Amy returned to her seat, still expecting her mum to add some caveat to what she was about to share but, instead, her mother's guard dropped and Amy hoped she was about to be told everything she needed.

'I loved your dad, that's the first thing to say, and we had years together when I thought we were complete . . .'

Geraldine meshed her fingers together and squeezed to lock them tightly.

'He and Neil had started the business a few years earlier, your dad put everything into it and cash flow was always an issue.'

Amy shifted in her seat, biting back the urge to ask, 'So what?'

'We stuck together when there was no money, long hours, difficult contracts and tension between Neil and Robert. I was totally committed to him and our family. I thought he felt the same but he'd been having an affair . . .'

'With Nadine?'

'I didn't know it was her at the time. A fling, he said. He broke down when he told me. I hadn't suspected anything, he just came to me and confessed. I was stunned. And the fact that I hadn't seen it coming made it worse.'

She paused again and considered what she'd just said.

'It made it more difficult later when we tried to put it behind us; how would I ever see the signs when I hadn't spotted them the first time around?'

'So this wasn't when you and Dad divorced?'

'No, earlier.'

Her mum sat back in her chair and her thoughts seemed to drift off. 'Years ago, I was in a traffic queue on the M11 when a car behind didn't slow in time. It smashed into a Volvo next to me, throwing it forward and into the crash barrier.' Amy said nothing. 'The first driver was stunned, the driver of the Volvo stood on the hard shoulder telling everyone he was fine, that he just needed to get home. He actually

49

asked who had his keys. His car was a foot too short, one wheel buckled and going nowhere, but he couldn't see that. I found out later that his kneecap was shattered too but he'd still stood there, wanting his life to carry on just as it had before. That was me. I didn't want to deal with what had really happened, to acknowledge the damage or see that it couldn't ever be the same again. All I wanted was to get back to where I thought we'd been.'

'I'm guessing it didn't work out like that?'

'I suppose it did for a while. Our marriage had beaten the odds, come back from the brink, was stronger for what we'd been through – any cliché you'd like to throw at it. In reality, I think I became pretty bitter.'

'Even though you chose to stay?'

'Yes, and if appearances count for anything, I made a good job of it too, but I knew how I felt inside and I should have ended it.'

Amy's summary was pointed. 'So you had an unhappy marriage and decided to let Dad get locked up for it?'

'You make it sound as though I framed him.'

Amy pressed her lips together and waited for her mum to fill the silence.

'I heard he was messing around again and when the house in Romsey Terrace burnt down his excuse was that he'd been working late. I don't know what kind of *working late* that might have been but no one came forward to offer him an alibi. He asked me for one and I could see the fear in him. And I wondered why an innocent man would think he'd be arrested. I made him tell me the truth and I swore that I wouldn't help him if he didn't, so the full story came out. And then, finally, I saw how much I'd given up, and that it was all for nothing. You know, I thought we'd have another child eventually and in the middle of his *confession* all I could think about was how I'd lost that chance.'

She blinked slowly, carefully, as though steering herself through a painful memory. It was the first time Amy had felt anything beyond anger and if they had been closer she might have reached for her mum's hand. She'd never wanted to be an only child and hadn't known until now that her mum hadn't wanted it either.

'Robert was terrified. That's when I discovered it was because

Nadine had been in that house and that's who he was having an affair with. Affair, not fling, not an impersonal one-night stand. He broke down and everything spilled out, how it hadn't been a brief lapse but a full-on relationship, that she'd ended it, not him, that she . . .' Geraldine pulled herself up short. 'And it turned out that the meaningless fling he'd told me about was with another woman, and it wasn't the only one; he'd been persistently unfaithful.'

Her tone suddenly became monotone.

'There was no way that our marriage would bounce back from that, of course, but all I felt was rage; everything I'd suppressed through the previous months crashed in on me. He asked me for an alibi . . .'

She shook her head and leant closer to Amy, and her voice regained its vigour. 'After everything, he was asking me for more. I didn't act out of rage or hatred but I cut him from my life at that moment. I detached myself completely and decided that the police would take the action he deserved.'

'Mum, he was convicted of killing them.'

'And who was I to argue? He'd deceived me time and again.'

'I thought you believed he was innocent?'

'Your father wouldn't have deliberately killed anyone; that much I never doubted. I could believe he might burn a building, but if he'd set that fire and been responsible for those deaths then I think I would have known; he couldn't have handled it.'

'Then you should have spoken out.'

'And been discredited immediately? How could I have given him a character reference when I'd been taken in by his other lies; I had no intention of even trying. He was on his own.'

'And what about the real killer?

Amy stared at her mum in bewilderment; her mum met her gaze, her pupils dilated and her glare became dark and hard.

'That was for the police – you need to remember that my responsibility was to you and to us – I decided right then that the official verdict would be the only one that mattered in our home. It wasn't to spite you, but to protect us both.'

'Someone else murdered Theo and Nadine and by keeping quiet you've helped them get away with it.'

'There's no proof that I could have made any difference.'

'That's a weak excuse. Neil and Stan and Moira all hate Dad and why wouldn't they? But I'm going in there every day and hoping that eventually I'll be able to prove them wrong.'

'You're wasting your time.'

'In your opinion. Perhaps you couldn't have changed the verdict but you should have tried.'

She shook her head slowly and stared at Amy through unrepentant eyes. It seemed as though she couldn't comprehend what she'd done or maybe that she had no intention of trying to see it in any other way but her own.

Her mum's expression didn't change even as Amy gathered her bag and coat and hurried to her feet. When Amy had first arrived she'd thought she'd seen remorse, or at least hope of reconciliation, but now she saw that her mum was too far along her path to turn around. 'You're wrong,' Amy told her firmly.

'And you have a lot to learn about people.' Her mum's voice was cold but it wasn't hard to see the pain in her eyes.

Part of Amy wanted to reach out then but instead she swung her bag onto her shoulder and turned away. It caught the edge of a flowerpot, sending the spider plant crashing onto the quarry-tiled floor. The pot split open and the dry soil scattered. She felt the leaves break underfoot as she stumbled towards the door. She was sorry, but not sorry enough that she was prepared to stop and clear it up.

The plant had been several generations on from the one she'd originally bought with her pocket money. Her mum had kept it going, transferring it from pot to pot, from elder plant to younger plant to retain the link back to the one she'd been given. Amy doubted whether her mum even liked it much and that had made Amy love what it had represented.

But not any more.

CHAPTER 10

Amy returned to her desk at 1.25 p.m. Both Stan and Moira's desks faced hers but neither of them made any comment at her curtailing her extended lunch.

Stan left a few minutes later. 'Do you still want the overtime?' Moira asked once he was out of earshot.

'Yes, please.'

She watched Stan haul himself into the cab of the pickup. She often studied them both when they were unaware of it. She had slight and shadowy memories of them from her childhood. Stan on the local news, outside the court shouting at the camera. She mostly remembered the horrified gasp from her mum when she'd accidentally seen it. She guessed that the way she'd been scooped up and away from the TV had lodged it permanently in her brain.

Stan was only in his forties now but could have been ten years older; his broad frame was still formidable but the years of working outside had left his arms and face crazed with fine lines, his knuckles dark and gnarled like tortoise skin. He seemed the easier one of them to gauge. He was comfortable with being able to use his bulk and gruff manner to deal with everyone from the men working on site to the customers themselves. Neither Neil Frampton nor Moira reacted to him, though, and after the first few weeks Amy's nerves around him had settled. The van left the yard and Amy turned her attention back to Moira.

'Can I ask you something?'

Her only recollection of Moira was like a cardboard dress-up doll where the clothes and the face and hair all have neat edges and it's all precise and two-dimensional. Amy liked the memory; Moira had a precise way of working too and everything she said seemed measured and voiced only after careful consideration. 'Would it be connected to your father?'

'He told me more about the fire.' Amy didn't know what kind of reaction she'd expected. Moira watched her, her gaze steady.

'He's always told me he had nothing to do with it. I doubt that's changed.'

'You say that with conviction.'

'Your father . . .' she paused and Amy wondered whether there was going to be more to the sentence. She rested both elbows on the table top and pressed her hands together. Her hair was neat and straight and ash blonde, just as it had always been and the whole effect was of near perfect symmetry. She blinked slowly. 'Your father burnt down that house. He was guilty, Amy.'

'You were his friend.'

Moira shook her head. 'Meaning what? That I'm not allowed to believe the worst about him? We were friends when we worked together, not when he killed two people.'

'And what if he didn't start that fire?'

'Amy, I knew you'd want this conversation at some point, but I don't. Neil wants you to have a job and that's fine, but don't drag me into any discussion about your father or that fire. There's no point going over it.'

'Not for you.'

'Or for Stan. Drop the subject around us.'

'I know he didn't do it.'

Moira's expression darkened, 'No,' she snapped. She stopped, took a breath and then continued more carefully. 'You're his daughter, you'll see him in a different light, but the Robert I knew wasn't the straightest arrow. He worked hard as a last resort; if he saw a shortcut he'd go for it.'

'That doesn't make him guilty, does it?'

'He blurred the boundaries. He ran up debts that the company had to pay.'

'It was his company.'

'Half his company,' Moira corrected, 'but not his money to screw around with. He was always pushing, living it large as they say.'

'It doesn't mean . . .'

'I used to turn a blind eye to his behaviour; he had charm and I liked to think he'd never do anything too serious. But, looking back, I can see that something had to give. And that house fire would have paid back a substantial hole in company funds.' Moira's expression was resolute. 'I'm sorry, Amy, but I really think you need to let it go.'

Amy looked away. Nothing in the room moved apart from the persistent click of the second hand as it marched around the clock face. 'So you believe he was capable of murder?' she asked quietly.

Moira's voice softened again. 'It's hard to believe that someone you've trusted could do that, but I'm sorry, that is what I think.'

Amy's view of the yard took in three one-and-a-half-storey, red-brick walls broken only by a tight gateway. It would have been more than wide enough for the horses that had originally hauled carts loaded with sacks of coal for delivery to the local houses. She often pictured them standing obediently in this airless rectangle, their lungs thick with the coal dust that had impregnated the brickwork and still left dust shadows on her Portakabin window.

Their vans struggled through the gateway. The entrance gate was striped by gouges and paint scrapes from being clipped by bumpers and wing-mirrors but those horses and their soot-faced drivers were what she pictured whenever she wanted respite from the continual paperwork.

Right now the other desks stood empty, the vans had returned for the night and the halogen lamp over the doorway would shine from dusk. Dusk came sooner to this yard than to the rest of Cambridge.

Her phone vibrated and her gaze slid from the window to the word 'Mum' flashing up at her from her desktop. She let it go to voicemail but after that her thoughts returned to their earlier conversation.

She worked for less than ten minutes after that, but noticed how the darkness was closing in on the yard. She needed the overtime but right now had lost her appetite to be here and on her own. She shifted the invoices to the back of her desk; she'd worked through less than half and done nothing on the other paperwork. 'Shit.' She shook her head. She felt spooked and tried to convince herself that the feeling was irrational; there had been plenty of times when Stan and Moira had left her alone in the office. Why should loss of daylight be a big deal? It was only a little after six. Early evening.

Fifteen minutes, she told herself.

She found the keys to the filing cabinets and rolled open the fourth of the sixteen drawers. She removed a bundle of papers from halfway through the suspension files and took them back to her desk. She read each page. It had taken a while for Moira to leave her on her own in the evenings but each hour of overtime now included quarter of an hour of searching the next document available. She wasn't sure what she needed to find but as long as she worked here then there was the chance of finding something.

But not tonight.

She relocked the filing cabinets then double-checked the storeroom door, knowing that it too would be secure but telling herself that it still needed to be tested just in case.

In the kitchenette she washed the mugs. She had always washed her own but never left anyone else's dirty either and over the past months she'd become the only one who seemed to bother with Stan's. She liked the routine and the feeling that she'd achieved a task, no matter how insignificant, before the end of each day. Her ritual was to leave straight afterwards, to pick up her bag and coat, to scan the room once, turn out the light and lock the door behind her. It felt symbolic although she never understood why.

She pulled on the handle and forced the key to turn. A ripple of movement reflected in the half-glazed door, the distorted shape of a man loomed close behind her. She turned sharply. 'Stan?' Her tone fell halfway between surprise and guilt.

'You're leaving already? I thought you wanted the extra hours.'

'I do.'

He eyed her carefully, as he often did. His expression stayed neutral and, as usual, she found herself trying to guess which way the conversation was about to head. He never wanted her here, she was always conscious of that and maybe that was why speaking to him always felt forced. Sometimes tense and forced, and other times polite but still forced. This time she felt on edge and she was aware of the illogical urge to say the right thing.

'I can come in early tomorrow.'

'What time would you have billed for today?'

'Just the hours I worked, Stan.'

'Because we're happy for you to do the overtime but that doesn't mean we're happy to be taken for a ride.'

She turned so that she faced him more squarely. 'Is that really something you think I'd do?'

'The problem is, I don't know what you will do. Questioning Moira was a mistake. Don't do it again, Amy.' He stepped aside. 'I'll see you tomorrow then.'

'Goodnight, Stan.'

She was halfway across the yard when he called after her, 'There's nothing here for you.'

She kept walking towards the gateway and the street lights on the pavement outside.

CHAPTER 11

Goodhew sent Gully a text, 'Would you help me with something?' And as soon as he received her one-word reply he knocked on her door. He knew where she lived but had never been to her house. She shared with two others but he had never met them either.

A slim woman in her mid-twenties opened the door; she had purple-tipped hair and matching eye shadow and held a pot of Häagen-Dazs. The spoon protruded from her mouth. She stepped aside to let him in.

'I'm a friend of Sue's.'

She pulled out the spoon. 'Gary, right? I'm Zoe. She said it would be you. She's in the kitchen.' She waved towards the far end of the hallway.

Gully was crossing the kitchen with two mugs of coffee, and she set them on the table. 'Or there's beer?'

'This is fine.'

'I didn't say yes to helping.'

'You said "*what?*" and that means you're curious.'

'You could have just phoned. Or did you need to see me in person to check whether things are awkward between us?' She lifted the mug but paused before taking a sip, watching for his response.

'Are they?'

'I think we should keep working together until they're not.'

He barely smiled but could tell she'd recognised that he felt the same. He took a slip of paper from his pocket and passed it to her. 'This needs to be discreet but I want to find this woman.'

Gully read the note then frowned. 'Melanie Franks or Jane Williams?'

'They're the same person. Melanie Franks was a pregnant student in 1991. My grandparents helped her disappear and from then on she used that alias.'

Gully's frown deepened. 'I don't understand.'

Goodhew drew a deep breath and began to explain about his grandparents' work. He was only a couple of sentences in when Gully stopped him. 'Now I get it,' she grinned, 'I always knew your grandmother had a past.'

'Their work was very low-key apparently.'

'I bet it wasn't. So what's this Melanie's story?'

'My grandmother didn't know too much at the time. They relocated Melanie to Hereford and that should have been it but, after his death, my grandmother – Ellie that is – I need to call them Ellie and Joe now – Ellie found a note in his handwriting and she thinks Melanie may have been in touch with him.'

'That's a long shot.'

'I hoped you'd help me track her down.'

'What do you know?'

He flicked the note. 'That's about it. She was studying history and her child would have been born in 1991.'

'And that's it?'

'Pretty much. I'll find her family. They never reported her missing so she may have kept telephone contact.'

'And what exactly do you think I'll be able to do?'

'There's more leeway to look for information while Marks is here. That gives me until next Friday to trawl through as much as possible. You're great with databases and you know your way round the archives.'

She blinked. 'Who told you that?'

'You did.'

'When?' She'd tried to sound casual but there was an unmistakable edge to her voice.

He pretended not to notice and replied lightly, 'When you spotted Joe's case.'

She drained her coffee mug and turned away to put it in the sink. 'Of course I did. I suppose I have a rough idea of the layout.'

She rinsed the mug thoroughly then refilled it with cold water and sipped that as she returned to sit at the table. 'I can look but I'd need a starting point.'

'I know you do. I'll let you know as soon as I find something, then will you search?'

'Yes, and in the meantime, I'll check health and employment databases. Anything I can sneak a peek at.' The pink that had risen in her cheeks subsided again and, to anyone who didn't know her, she would have seemed unperturbed.

'Do you need help searching for anything?'

She had regained full control of herself and didn't react. 'Like?'

He eyed her carefully. 'Whatever took you to the archives in the first place?'

She brushed it away. 'It was a pet project, a diversion. It doesn't matter now, I've finished.'

'If you're sure?'

'I'd rather chase this.' She folded the piece of paper he'd given her and tucked it under her mug. 'I'll start tomorrow. And I'm on earlies so unless there's anything else?'

'Actually, there is.' He passed her the bangle. 'I need to trace this.'

She held it above her head so that the light from the ceiling shone through it. 'Trace what exactly? Who it belongs to or where it was bought?'

'Either. Both.'

'There's no kind of maker's mark. It could be a cheap mass-produced piece. Too late for fingerprints, I suppose?'

'I checked for prints as soon as I got it. I found some but I guess they'll turn out to be my grandmother's.'

'Ellie's.'

'Yes, Ellie's,' he repeated.

'How soon will you get them back?'

'I'll give them to Finn in the morning. He might find something but I'd say it's too late.'

'Yeah, maybe.' She continued to study the bangle, squinting at it now. 'Have you looked under a magnifying glass?'

'I photographed it, then enlarged the shot.'

She screwed up her nose. 'That's more this century, isn't it? And?'

He handed her his phone with the zoomed-in image filling the screen. 'What do you think?'

She held it a few inches from her face and moved her finger across the screen to bring different sections of the picture into focus.

She was studying the 2 mm filaments that were trapped within the acrylic, then looked up, puzzled. 'They're all tiny and pretty much uniform. It looks like hair, but is it?'

'That's what I wondered.'

'Not mass-produced then.'

'Hopefully not. Have you come across anything similar?'

'Locally? No, but I know there used to be a fashion for insects suspended in Lucite. This is the same kind of thing. And Ellie gave it to you?'

'Found it among Joe's possessions.'

She handed it back to him. 'Why ask me what's inside when you already know?'

'I wanted a second opinion before I broke it apart.'

CHAPTER 12

Finlay Beavan had given up on contact lenses; his hours were too irregular and he'd never mastered the right routine. After three months of red eyes and irritation he'd made peace with his heavy-framed glasses and accepted that it was time to embrace his own nerdiness. Contact lenses hadn't been a secret for success with women either. Right now, though, he and his glasses were close to falling out. He dumped them on the workbench and closed his eyes. With his elbows on the work surface he covered his face, using the heel of his hands to block out every intrusive ray from the stark artificial light.

He must have dozed because he heard nothing before he snapped his eyes open at the sound of a familiar voice.

'Finn?'

His blurry vision readjusted. 'Hold on, Gary, hold on.' He found his glasses. 'I dozed off again. I was working but I think over a problem, rest my eyes and bam. Out like a light.'

'Maybe you should go home at night? Being first in and last out doesn't prove anything.'

'I know.' Everyone from his mum to his boss told him the same. 'And it leads to mistakes and depression and loss of the social life that I never had anyway.'

Finn spotted a paper bag in Goodhew's hand, 'What have you got for me today?'

Goodhew passed it across. 'From Sue.'

Finn tucked the bag in the drawer without needing to look. She sent him chocolate digestives as a bribe to fast-track results. He couldn't open them in the lab so it was her way of making him get fresh air and take a five-minute break. A sisterly-type gift, he'd concluded, when the contact lenses had failed to work on her. He still appreciated the biscuits, though. 'Does she need me to do something?'

'No, I do, but she sent them anyway.'

Goodhew took two evidence bags from his jacket pocket and placed them side by side in front of Finn. 'One has some acrylic pieces and the other has the prints I lifted from it. I think they'll be recent. Prints couldn't last twenty years on a surface like this, could they?'

'If the resin hadn't quite set . . .'

'No, after that.'

'Not unless there was a residue of some kind on the fingertips.' Finn repositioned the bag on the work surface and shone a magnifying lamp onto it. 'I'll take a look.'

'I know it's a long shot.'

'This was some kind of bracelet, right?'

'Yes. And I have to level with you, this isn't evidence, it's something I've been given . . .'

'As a gift?'

'If you like. And I want to find out whether it could be evidence.'

'So this is personal?'

Goodhew nodded.

Finn grinned. 'Cool. I never get to do anything that bends the rules.'

'This doesn't.'

Finn's face fell. 'But it might?'

'At a push.'

Finn peered through the magnifying lens at the bangle that lay in three pieces inside the bag. The breaks were clean. 'It's been broken recently. Did you do it?'

'Yes, to see whether it was possible to extract the hairs. Are they human?'

'I believe so. I can extract a sample, put it under the microscope. I can't tell yet how the polymer has bonded to the hair itself. How much analysis are you hoping for?'

'What's possible?'

Finn didn't reply immediately. He knew that Goodhew would sit quietly while he worked. He opened the evidence bag and used a scalpel to scrape away at the plastic until a single hair became free. He studied it under the microscope for a minute or two before risking any kind of answer. 'The hair has been cut at both ends, which will limit some of my analysis. Morphology, for example, may be difficult.'

'Which is what?'

'The growth phase the hair was in when it was lost. There may be no skin cells attached either.'

The hair sample was thin, a pale translucent wisp. 'It's fine hair.'

'I thought that. A child's perhaps?'

'I can't speculate. It might not be head hair. It might turn out not to be human.'

'And what about DNA?'

'Everything's possible on *CSI*. Here, I just do my best.' Finn used several variations on the same comment. Goodhew usually smiled but today his thoughts seemed elsewhere.

'And if it is a child's, can you identify the parents?'

'Familial DNA? Like I said to Sue, it is most conclusive when there is more than one sample.'

'She asked you?' Goodhew asked quickly.

'She's a few weeks ahead of you with that question, though.'

'Why did she want to know?'

Goodhew was studying him a little too closely now and Finn was glad that he didn't have an answer. He wouldn't have wanted to betray Sue's confidence but he wasn't much of a liar either. Finn picked an answer that he hoped was sufficiently vague. 'Just whether two samples would prove a relationship between two people, and I told her, "It depends."' He held up the portion of bangle. 'I'll find what I can but it won't be fast.'

'I know.' Goodhew reached for the evidence bag. 'If I take most of this you'll still have plenty to work with?'

'The more you leave, the more chance there is of a usable hair sample. Your call.'

Goodhew left the two larger sections and slipped the third back into his pocket. At the same time, he pulled out an envelope and handed it to Finn. 'I took my grandmother's prints for elimination.'

Finn double-blinked. 'So this is connected to your grandfather's case?'

'Depending where it leads me.'

This time Finn didn't take the envelope. 'I don't need it. I know Ellie Goodhew's prints are on file.'

'Really?'

'Look.' He moved to his PC, rattled through a couple of menus then pulled up the relevant records, a close up of Ellie Goodhew's right-index fingerprint filled the screen.

'Any idea why it's there?'

Finn shook his head, 'It's from 2009 but was last accessed in October.'

Goodhew didn't comment and there was no sign from his expression that the answer revealed anything. His attention stayed on the display, his gaze darting across it as if checking each whorl, lake and bifurcation.

'Can you print it?' he whispered. 'Not the image, the whole record.'

'Better, I'll email it,' Finn replied and in a couple of clicks it was gone.

CHAPTER 13

A lone coach idled in the bus bays at Drummer Street, the few pedestrians he could see looked unhurried and it was possible to pick out single sounds from the hushed city.

He checked his watch for both day and time. It was Sunday and a little before twelve. No wonder Finn had been working alone.

Goodhew picked up a takeaway coffee from Savino's but didn't attempt to drink it until he reached the market. He could remember when the market square had stood empty and the cobbled area in front of the Guildhall had always looked black and bleak on an overcast day. The current market had begun in a small way, opening for tourists and Sunday browsers; back then it had been more about antiques and curios than everyday needs. Now, it was a permanent fixture, bright striped canopies over fresh food stands and local craft stalls. He often bought fruit and artisan bread here, once he'd bought a painting too, and today he searched the rows until he spotted Kimberly Guyver's work. She drew pen-and-ink backgrounds of Cambridge scenes with women in the style of Al Moore or Gil Elvgren painted in the foreground. Her friend Mule usually looked after her stall but today it was Kimberly herself who stood next to the canvasses. She was one of the most beautiful women he'd ever met and could have modelled for pictures like these but she was only happy behind the easel. She kissed him on the cheek and hugged him. 'How are you? I heard about Ratty. I'm sorry.'

'Thanks. How's Riley?'

'At school and behaving most of the time. He's cheeky, but no vices, no virtues, right?'

'And Anita?'

'The best stand-in grandmother a kid could have.'

'Please give her my best wishes.' He paused for a moment to let the reminiscences drift away. 'I didn't expect to see you here. I thought Mule would be looking after the stall and it was him I was hoping to see.'

'He's back in Wellington for a month, fed up with our weather. What's he done?'

'Nothing. I'm looking for someone who could make a piece of jewellery, with something embedded in it.'

'In a setting, like a stone?'

'No, no.' He handed her one section of the broken bangle. 'Like this, acrylic or resin, or Lucite with the item preserved within the plastic.'

'Is the person who made it in trouble then?' Her dark eyes stared into his and she had a hint of a smile. 'I can't just blab to the police even when it's you.'

'Old habits and all that? And no, he or she isn't in any trouble.'

Kimberly brushed her hair back from her cheek then turned her head towards the Cambridge University Bookshop on the corner. 'You want Crystal; she'll be on the craft market, the one in Trinity Street. She's about my height, in her fifties and usually in the furthest corner from the gate.'

'What's her last name?'

'How would I know? Her first name's not Crystal either, it's a nickname because of what she sells. Like Mule because he makes shoes. Be nice to her,' she winked at him, 'and it's good to see you again.'

Lorraine Martin's best investment had been the workshop at the end of her garden. She'd forgone a car and had cycled to work for two years until she'd saved for it because borrowing the money had been an impossibility. That had been almost fifteen years ago and now she tried to ignore the places where the paintwork had flaked and damp had seeped into the wood, where the grain had swollen and the window no longer fitted the frame. Her plan last spring had been to wait for the summer, then to sand and fill the wood, repainting it with a weather-proof coat again. The last had been guaranteed for ten years and that had flown in the blink of an eye. But the summer had passed and good intentions had achieved nothing.

It was another reason to feel disappointed with herself; her work-shop was her place of comfort, and it deserved to be cared for. Being alone had never been her strength either, but she never felt it here. Solitude yes, but not loneliness. Here, she could lose herself in her work, enjoy the silence, concentrate without listening for the doorbell and without hanging around within grabbing distance of the phone.

She always kept the windows clean though and the step outside brightened with planters, currently filled with lilac and white winter pansies.

Inside measured eight foot square, smaller than she'd originally wanted but just about affordable to heat. She worked in outdoor clothes whenever possible and only turned on the fan heater when her feet ached or her fingers became clumsy. It housed moulds and chemicals, a buffing wheel and an old map cabinet whose shallow drawers she'd filled with an assortment of bezels, clasps and decorative scraps that she thought she might one day have a need to use.

In the corner facing the door she'd squeezed in an armchair draped with woollen throws and sometimes, like last night, she'd fallen asleep to only wake at first light, the windows misted with condensation. She'd wiped them first because she never blocked the view of the garden.

It was bloody cold, but not as cold as standing still for hours at the craft market. She pitied the traders that left warm homes; at least she was acclimatised to it. She packed two boxes into her car; she had time to spare but she still skipped breakfast.

She sprayed herself with deodorant, unable to face the idea of stripping off to wash until she could soak in the bath later. She glanced at the side door that opened into her kitchen; it would be sensible to make up a flask but in truth, even going inside for the essentials held no appeal. Her own home yes, but she had been right to take no part of it into her workshop, to buy someone else's armchair and bench rather than use her own.

She pulled out of her driveway and glanced in her rear-view mirror; it had become her habit to watch her house shrink behind her.

The craft market was located in All Saints' Garden. It was fenced off from Trinity Street by wrought iron railings that flapped with laminated posters advertising local arts events and lectures.

Lorraine's stall was at the back; people generally browsed all the stalls, walking in a circle either clockwise or anti-clockwise. She'd deliberately positioned herself halfway round, hoping to catch customers when they were most immersed.

Lorraine made three sales within the first hour, then nothing for the next few. She bought hot chocolate from the coffee cart and watched the pedestrians on Trinity Street, willing them to come through the gate. A man in his early thirties caught her attention. He didn't meander like most, wasn't laden with tourist shopping or walking with a companion. He was tall and lean and wove between the stalls, glancing at the items for sale but barely pausing.

There was nothing overtly familiar about him but she sensed that he was there for her. She straightened her pile of business cards then continued to fiddle with her display until he reached her.

He picked up a paperweight, turned it over a couple of times before replacing it among the other items.

'They're all handmade,' she told him. It was one of her most used opening lines.

'By you?' He looked up from the table and seemed to study her carefully.

'Of course.'

'Said with pride,' he observed. 'I'm not a customer.'

She didn't respond but she didn't feel threatened by him either. At least, not by him specifically. But her hands were back in her pockets now, with the nail of each thumb digging into the side of the corresponding index finger. She waited for him to speak, trying to keep her mind clear of any panic, even though she had no reason to worry.

'My name's DC Gary Goodhew.'

'Police?' He didn't look like a policeman. He looked like someone's brother. Someone's son. She shook her head at her own lack of logic. He asked for her details but she must have seemed suspicious or bewildered or maybe just slow because he showed her his ID before asking her again.

She murmured her name but was fixed on his. She hadn't registered until she saw his identification. GOODHEW. It could have been a coincidence but for those same green eyes.

She studied him, trying to recall the features too, but failing.

'Are you all right?' he asked.

She nodded, clutching at the thought that his face seemed kind. 'What's happened?'

In answer he held out a section of a bangle. She wasn't sure if she was meant to touch it but reached for it in any case.

'I'm trying to find the person who made this,' he said.

The bangle had been snapped and she ran her thumb over the broken surface.

'Is it one of yours?' he asked.

The last time she'd held this it had been whole, unmarked and barely worn. Would it be surprising if she didn't recognise it now? Or had this young detective spotted the involuntary widening of her eyes and the way her winter-red cheeks must have paled at his name.

'Yes,' she replied, 'it's one of mine.'

'You hesitated.'

'I wasn't sure,' she lied. 'It's so badly damaged. What happened to it?'

He took it from her and was about to speak when he stopped himself. For a moment he looked beyond her, past the railings and along All Saints' Passage.

'I'm not here officially,' he told her. 'You don't have any obligation to answer my questions and this,' he tapped the bangle, 'this isn't evidence yet. But I'm hoping you'll help because . . .'

'Because of your grandfather?' she replied.

And it was his turn to look startled.

The photographer on the adjacent stand had agreed to watch Lorraine's jewellery and they'd retreated to the nearest café. Goodhew noticed that Lorraine Martin often hesitated before she answered questions, long enough to rehearse the answer silently before trying it for real.

The current pause was the longest so far.

'I met your grandfather once, shortly before he died. He brought that bangle to me because he wanted to find its owner. I was shocked when I read about his death.'

'In the paper?'

'Yes, in the death notices. I had promised to contact him if I came across anything. I didn't realise he was ill.'

'He wasn't. It was an assault and I'm hoping to shed light on it.'

'It's a long time ago.' She took a few seconds to consider her own comment. 'But not so long when it's your own family.'

'What do you remember?'

She stirred her coffee and her gaze wandered outside. Memories could prove stubborn after twenty-two years but sometimes the truth was stubborn too. Goodhew needed her to cooperate.

'Obviously I have my grandfather's notes,' he lied, 'but only up to when he spoke to you.'

'I can't remember word for word.'

'As much as you can then.'

'The bangle was a gift, ordered by a girl named Melanie.' He sensed that Lorraine was testing him now.

He leant closer and tried hard to look unsurprised. 'Melanie Franks? Yes, he mentioned her. Go on.'

'He said he needed to find her.'

'Why?'

'I don't know.'

'He could have asked you that without bringing the bangle. Why was it significant?'

'Because I made it, I suppose. I don't know.'

'Maybe because of what's in it? Child's hair or baby hair?'

Lorraine's eyes flickered for a second then met his gaze again.

'Melanie was pregnant.'

'And it's her baby's hair?'

'Yes.'

He wasn't buying it. 'Did she have a boy or a girl?' He fired the question back at her.

And again she hesitated. 'A girl, I think.'

Goodhew's expression hardened. 'I thought you knew her?'

Lorraine sat back in her chair and clasped her hands together in her lap. 'Not really,' she murmured.

'You see,' Goodhew continued, 'according to my grandfather's notes she'd left Cambridge before her child was born.'

It seemed obvious to Goodhew that Lorraine Martin had been quick to give him a false answer but wasn't an accomplished enough liar to sustain the story. 'She phoned me, I suppose.'

'And what? Posted the hair so you could make the bangle? You know that doesn't add up.'

Lorraine knew she'd been caught. She fell silent and chewed her bottom lip.

'It's not her baby's hair, is it?' he pushed.

'No, it's Nadine's baby.'

'Nadine who?'

She shook her head and stared at him thoughtfully. 'I'm sorry, the truth is I can't remember the details. Melanie cleared off and I was hoping you'd let slip about where she'd gone.'

'So let me get this straight.' Goodhew leant across the table and lowered his voice. 'I turn up over twenty years later and you suddenly have the urge to catch up on an old friend? Why would you?'

Lorraine gave a small smile but Goodhew knew he was just supposed to see the sadness behind it. 'For old time's sake, I suppose.' She held out her hands, palms upwards. 'To know she's OK. She was terrified before she left.'

'So the bangle didn't belong to her, did it?'

Lorraine could have stuck to her story but, instead, she was quick to back down. 'No, I made it for her friend Nadine. And, before you ask, I don't remember the rest of her name, but Melanie would.'

'One more question, was this before or after Melanie left the area?'

This time Lorraine's reply was immediate. 'Afterwards.'

Goodhew continued to watch her after they'd parted company. He wondered whether her first action would be to call someone and tell them about his visit. Instead, she stood with her back to the railings and stared at the dwindling numbers of potential customers with no apparent interest. She hung around until the market closed at four then shook herself from her stupor and began to pack away, methodically at first but then with increased haste.

Goodhew grabbed a taxi and sat inside, watching her until she was ready to leave. He'd checked her address by then and followed her to make sure that was where she was headed. He then asked the driver to drop him further along her street. He walked back and waited a little way along from her house. He watched her enter her house, turn on the lights, come back outside to unload her car and then, half an hour later, dim the lights in the front room. The only movement from behind the thin curtains was the perpetual dancing of the light from the TV screen. He walked to the nearest shop, bought a sandwich, then walked back along the street one more time. At 7.30 p.m. he headed home.

CHAPTER 14

Lorraine poured herself a tumbler of red wine and took it and the rest of the newly opened bottle through to the front room. She turned on the TV and channel-hopped for several minutes but despite all the choices there seemed nothing to watch. She left it playing the news channel, hoping it might throw up an item to distract her until the wine took over, but instead her thoughts stayed with Goodhew.

Both Goodhews.

The elder had come to see her and then, just a few days afterwards, he'd died. She'd always wondered about the timing and the rumour that he'd been beaten. If she'd triggered that attack, then she could endanger the grandson now.

If.

And if it had been a coincidence, then keeping quiet to the younger Goodhew now would be a mistake.

If.

And what if she could pass on enough information for Melanie to be found?

Another if.

An hour later the bottle had gone. She went to the kitchen and returned with a second. She remembered Nadine so clearly, not like Joe Goodhew or like Melanie who both existed in her memory as sketches. Nadine had remained a defined image. She'd had old-fashioned features: round face and large dark eyes, small heart-shaped mouth and slender girlish figure. The kind of looks that might have been in vogue in the 1920s or '30s. Lorraine could still see the way Nadine played guitar, leaning back in a chair, picking the individual strings, her small fingers deftly making the shapes of the chords. Lorraine looked at anyone who played and only sometimes spotted that same degree of rapt concentration. Maybe guilt had burnt it into her brain like that.

She phoned her sister then as she always did when she needed comfort. 'I'm going to sleep in the workshop,' she told her. 'Fuck the house.'

'Come to mine. Stay the night.' Her sister tried to sound upbeat and neither of them mentioned the six-plus glasses of wine that had begun to interfere with Lorraine's sentences.

Lorraine could hear herself becoming emphatic, trying to be logical. 'No,' she told her. 'I spoke to Joseph Goodhew and then he died. And what about the fire?'

'Not everything is a conspiracy, some things are just what they are. Bob set that fire.'

'I can see how other people benefited. Even you.'

'Lorraine, listen.'

'I have listened, but who has ever listened to me?'

'Lorraine?'

'I'm going to bed. But I'm not letting it drop. Not this time.'

'Straight to bed?'

'Promise,' Lorraine replied, but her sister's mothering was enough to send her in the opposite direction.

She ended the call. 'Fuck you and your perfect life,' she muttered to no one.

Several minutes passed before she picked up her mobile again. She began to dial but changed her mind and threw it down beside her on the settee. She wanted to be face to face, not fobbed off via the phone.

She grabbed her jacket and house keys and headed towards the city centre. She hurried, head down with her thoughts on everything she needed to say. She imagined the conversation, rehearsed her responses and found Neil Frampton, just as she guessed she would, at his desk in his private office in St Barnabas Road. She tapped the glass and he glanced up from the PC screen. His expression darkened when he saw her, but he gestured for her to wait. It had been a while since she'd seen him but at first glance he looked almost the same; he'd aged but wore the same clothes and the same hairstyle. Still trying to emulate the easy style of the City boy dressing down for the country even though he was too old and the clothes were too tight.

It seemed like a full five minutes before the front door opened. In the hallway light she saw him more clearly. He had more jowl now and an unnatural lack of lines. It might have been a couple of years since she'd seen him last. It might have been longer.

She thought she'd be allowed inside but he held it open by a foot's width. 'Why are you here?'

'I know something about Melanie.'

'What?'

She smiled knowingly.

He ran his tongue around his teeth as though trying to dislodge something unpleasant. 'You're pissed.'

'I know something,' she insisted. 'It's that detective.'

'What detective?'

'The one who died. His grandson came to see me.'

'I don't know what you're talking about.'

'The grandson is in the police. He came to see me.'

'What has that got to do with Melanie?'

'He knew her name and he had Nadine's bangle. I could have told him everything but I didn't. But I want to know something from you.'

'What?'

'Was it because of what I told him?' She could tell by his expression that she wasn't being clear. 'Back then you asked me questions and straight afterwards this policeman's grandfather died. I can tell him that but it depends on you.'

'There's nothing to tell. Go home. Sober up and keep quiet.' He shook his head. 'It's all history and we're not going back there.'

He closed the door and the small pane of glass at the top darkened as he drew the curtain behind it. She swayed a little but, apart from that, didn't move for several minutes as she debated whether to knock again, or shout, or just head home.

This wasn't right. He'd missed the point.

She banged several times on the door with the flat of her hand. 'I know,' she shouted. '*I know.*'

She felt drunk, but within the fuzziness of alcohol there was a crisp clear kernel of sense. A sober eye of her drunken storm, a place where she could see herself with complete clarity. She wasn't a bad person. And that wasn't a new thought. She was a weak person and she knew that too. She continually made herself promises and always broke them because she habitually abandoned good intentions to jump at the easy route. She'd lost count of the number of opportunities that she'd traded for quick money or short-term gains.

But this was a different kind of drunk from her usual slide into stupor. Holding that bracelet had galvanised her. She remembered so clearly when and why she'd made it.

Nadine had been one of the early ones.

She felt in her pockets and pulled out the miniature pen that always hung from her house keys and then found a single business card. She wrote quickly across the back of it then cut through onto Argyle Street with her hands clasped together and the card pressed between her palms.

She was close to the other end when she became aware of a car behind her; its headlights lit the road ahead but it had slowed and seemed to be keeping pace with her. There were few spaces between the parked cars; she passed one gap and expected the vehicle to pull in. After a few yards more she glanced over her shoulder; the boxy silhouette and high wide headlight beams came from of some kind of 4x4. She kept walking, careful to be steady, unhurried, not to panic.

She passed the next parking space and listened carefully, relieved as she heard it swing in and the engine still. But just a moment later the door slammed and a familiar voice called her name.

'Wait up,' he shouted.

She scowled at him but didn't walk away. 'Why are you here?'

'Just passing. Do you want a lift?'

'If I had two broken legs you wouldn't drive me home.' She folded her arms and waited for Stan to respond. He came closer without speaking. She tried again. 'What do you want?'

'Keep away from their house, don't turn up like that again.'

'But they should have listened to me; I wanted to help them.'

'They don't want to know.'

She stepped towards him but wobbled slightly, steadying herself on the nearest house wall. 'I've only ever tried to do the right thing.' She heard the tone of her own voice become more insistent. 'I don't understand why you have a problem.'

'Because *you* are a problem. Nothing is ever left in the past with you.'

'Well, I'm not going anywhere because I know that one day they'll listen.' She waved her finger at him. 'They can turn me away all they like, but one day . . .'

'You haven't got anything they want.' He moved closer and the air around her seemed to still. 'It's Melanie's address or nothing and you don't have it.'

She broke the silence that followed with a short laugh, 'And when I get it? Then they'll change their minds, I suppose?' she shook her head as she stepped away, 'Forget it, I won't bother them again.'

'And I can tell them that?'

'Be my guest.'

She walked away without looking back. After a few seconds of silence, she heard the 4x4's door slam shut and its engine turn over. She held the business card a little more tightly and kept walking.

CHAPTER 15

Amy had worked at Frampton's for enough time to recognise people on her way to work. One or two of them smiled at her now and she smiled back, occasionally said good morning. She could spot anomalies in their routines; the days when the woman in the blue coat from ten-to didn't cross paths with her until five-past. Or when the nervous man wasn't at the bus stop or the lady with the red setter failed to appear from Mill Road cemetery. Mondays were days when people were more likely to run late but this time everyone had been on cue and the day felt comfortably normal until she turned in to Cockburn Street and spotted the first pulse of blue emergency lights from the far end of the road. She could pick out just a single police car at first, parked at the corner of Argyle Street. Her route. Cars still moved freely past her but access to the side road had been barred.

When she reached the junction the officer blanked her at first. His head was tilted as he spoke into his radio; an indecipherable stream of crackling words came back at him. 'No update,' he replied. He glanced along the street behind him and added a comment that she couldn't catch even without the static. Beyond him, at about the furthest point visible, there was another police car and a cluster of activity. The officer finished on the radio and then spoke to Amy. 'Can I help?'

'I work in Argyle Street, can I get through?'

'Where exactly?'

'At Frampton's,' she told him.

'The yard?'

'Yes.'

'Hang on.' He consulted his radio. 'You can go down there, but no further. We will be canvassing local homes and businesses. When were you last here?'

'Friday.'

'OK.' He stepped aside to let her through.

No one she recognised was out on the street now. A few house-holders stood in open doorways and shadows moved in some of the windows. The street was hushed and her footsteps fell noisily. Ahead of her, maybe a hundred yards beyond the entrance to Frampton's, the police had sealed the road. An officer stood facing her, his back to the cluster of vehicles and the people milling between them. A single ambulance had been parked on one side of the street, and opposite it she could see the white top of a tent. She tried not to stare, pretended disinterest for the last few metres before the gateway, then stole a final glance at the scene before turning in to the yard.

Stan stood at the window facing the entrance, Moira a few feet behind him. He actually opened the door for her too. 'What's going on now?' he asked. 'Any developments?'

'I don't know what was happening before, do I?' Amy hung her coat on the back of her chair. 'Just a lot of people behind a cordon.'

'There's a body in an alleyway,' Stan replied. 'The first car was already there before I got in and it's been lights and sirens ever since.'

'Same when I turned up,' Moira added. 'Luckily I decided to leave the car at home today. I'm not sure I would have been allowed to drive into the street.' She held a pile of envelopes and stacked them on the end of Amy's desk. 'At least the post got through.'

'Yeah,' Stan added, 'thank God it wasn't the postie that copped it.'

'Someone did, though.'

Stan moved to his own desk but repositioned his chair so that he was within sight of the window. 'You don't lighten up much, do you?'

Amy grabbed the post and didn't reply at first. She knew from the envelopes which were invoices, which contained cheques or remittance advices. She blotted out the next few comments too. Stan gave them an update each time an official vehicle of any kind passed the gateway.

Moira ignored him too.

Finally, Amy spoke. 'What if we're not interested, Stan?'

'What happened to your dignified silence, Amy?' he smirked.

Her finger was inserted into the next envelope. She ripped it roughly. 'It's none of our business.'

'I bet you looked at what was going on, same as the rest of us.'

'I looked down the road,' she conceded, 'but I'm not standing with my nose pressed to the glass.' She removed an invoice. Mixed with the post was a clutch of advertising literature, the usual supermarket offers and leaflets for solar panels. One of these, an advert for replacement windows, had been folded into a makeshift envelope. 'AMY' was scored into the shiny paper with heavy blue biro. 'I'm surprised you're not out there holding up the police tape.'

Moira shot a warning glance in Amy's direction. Stan leant forward with his elbows on the desk. 'It's not a problem, Moira. No harm done.'

Amy didn't bother replying; shutting up and staying quiet was the best response to his glibness but she'd lost all interest in that conversation anyway.

'Amy.' He had to repeat her name twice before she looked at him.

'What?'

'I'm sorry if I hit a nerve,' he told her. She studied his expression for any sign of sarcasm and saw nothing.

'I was too young to remember much.'

'But even so . . .' he replied, his words petering out mid-sentence, but she knew what he was trying to say.

'Thank you,' she replied.

The 'envelope' contained nothing but a business card. That happened sometimes. Usually a plasterer or a plumber angling for work. But never delivered like this. And this card was ornate, not functional, foil-printed on heavy stock, in an embellished script that read 'Lorraine Martin Designs' and a mobile number. She thought the name meant nothing but a chill ran along the back of her neck. She turned it over. 'Amy, ring me' was scrawled across it in smudged blue ink. She glanced at Stan and Moira but neither had noticed her startled reaction.

She opened the pen tray in her desk and placed the card, logo upwards, among the paperclips and staples.

CHAPTER 16

Gully caught up with Goodhew in the corridor leading to the briefing room. He shot a glance at the closed door in front of them. 'What do you know about this?'

'Suspicious death, female body found in an alleyway in Argyle Street.'

'That's all?' he queried.

'Why, what do you know?'

'The same.'

She didn't reply but they both knew it had to be more than just accident or misadventure.

They pushed open the door. Marks stood at the front of the room and to Gully's surprise there were only a few officers present. She was the only uniformed officer but Marks had warned her this would be the case. The others were out already, going door to door. Maybe he thought being the least experienced officer and the only PC might intimidate her. It didn't.

She'd worked with them all before. DCs Sandra Knight, Kev Holden and Jack Worthington were all old hands but relatively new to Marks's team, Aaron Clarke was on his first day back after a brief secondment to London and, of course, there was Kincaide. DS Kincaide. The DS still made her feel slightly nauseous.

He'd marched through the door a few paces ahead of them and stood to one side of Marks holding papers and an envelope. He probably thought it gave him authority; in her opinion he looked like the magician's assistant.

She and Goodhew took the nearest available seats.

The board behind Marks held two items. The first was a section of map showing a close-up of Argyle Street and its adjoining roads. The location of the body had been marked with a circle of tangerine highlighter. Next to it was a single photo, a crime-scene shot of a woman's body abandoned in a narrow brick passageway. Sue knew the street and could picture the gap that ran between two terraces.

The woman was half lying and half sitting, like a puppet where the strings had been cut, her limbs folding to the floor, her flaccid neck dropping her chin to her chest. In the corner of Gully's vision she saw Goodhew lean closer. She turned in time to see curiosity grow to consternation.

Marks had taken the pages from Kincaide and had just begun to speak as Goodhew cut in. 'Do we know her identity, sir?'

Marks caught his expression immediately. 'Do you recognise this woman, Goodhew?'

'From that picture? I'm not sure.'

Marks turned over the sheet in his hand and held a 10x8 photograph out to Goodhew. There was plenty of time for Gully to look at it too. It showed a close-up of a woman in her mid-fifties. She had tired eyes and deep lines around her mouth. Her hair was mid-brown and shoulder length, badly cut in a style that hadn't suited her and had made her thin face look even thinner. None of that mattered now.

She looked up from the photo in time to see Goodhew nodding. 'It's Lorraine Martin,' he told Marks.

'How do you know her?'

She glanced around; this conversation had an audience.

'She had a stall on the craft market, in All Saints' Garden. I met her there yesterday.'

'Yesterday?' One eyebrow flickered. 'Regarding what?'

'I was asking her advice on an item of jewellery.'

Someone sniggered. It wasn't Marks. He just exhaled slowly. 'A little more information would be useful, Gary.'

'It's a bangle that Lorraine Martin made.'

'And where is it now?'

'Finn Beavan has most of it. I have the rest.'

'It's broken?'

'It is.'

Marks tipped his head in the direction of the door. 'A word?'

Goodhew followed him into the corridor and through the frosted panel in the door Sue could see the dark and unmoving shape of Marks standing with his shoulder close to the glass. They spoke very briefly, then they returned and Marks addressed the room: 'Goodhew will be making a statement.' Then to Goodhew, 'What can you tell us about yesterday that is relevant to this briefing?'

Goodhew explained his conversation with Lorraine Martin. 'I'm sure there was more than she was admitting.'

Marks studied Goodhew carefully throughout. It was an expression that Gully knew well and it didn't miss much, then she saw his expression suddenly change. He stepped back and held out his hand for Kincaide to pass him the rest of the papers. He turned over several sheets before he found the page he was looking for. 'Ms Martin was a divorcee living alone in a house in Selwyn Road. Her only known relative is a sister living in Cambridge and formal identification of the body will take place within the hour. Initial enquiries with the neighbours have produced two independent witnesses who report seeing an IC-1 male, aged around thirty, in the street outside her house at around 7 p.m.' He tapped the page, 'The exact words are "about 6 feet tall, thin and a little unkempt. But too old to be a student." Is this you or an actual person of interest?'

Goodhew winced. 'It's me. I followed her home. I had a feeling she wasn't telling me everything. I thought I might find out more.'

'By stalking her?'

'I didn't. When it looked as though she'd settled down for the evening I left.'

Kincaide stepped forward, 'A word, sir?' Gully wondered whether he thought that echoing Marks's own words gave him some kind of authority. She sensed Marks bristle, although that may have been wishful thinking. Kincaide stepped forward and spoke quietly. She couldn't catch any of the words but Kincaide eventually nodded curtly and stepped back again with his jaw set hard.

Marks looked down at the papers as he turned to another sheet. He read it silently for a few seconds and when he spoke his tone had adopted its usual evenness. 'Preliminary examination indicates that the victim died from strangulation. There were superficial injuries, minor abrasions to the hands and one ankle as well as bruising and further abrasions to the head and face.'

He paused to pass Kincaide another photo to be pinned to the board. The upper half of Lorraine Martin's face filled the entire shot; the skin on her forehead had been scored by two patches of rough grazes. Gully guessed that the victim had hit the brickwork as she struggled. A small amount of blood stained her skin at the hairline.

Marks continued, 'As you can see I received these details only minutes before you all arrived. The alleyway is a fairly confined space and forensics will tell us whether she managed to make contact with her assailant or only with the wall.'

'What was used to strangle her?' Sue didn't look around but knew the voice was Kev Holden's. Gruff and blunt.

'A ligature of some kind. Nothing was recovered from the scene,' Marks replied.

'Definitely not manual then?'

'No.'

'No chance of fingerprints; that's a shame. What about motive then?'

'Nothing conclusive as yet.'

'Unless Gary did it.' Worthington quipped.

'Thank you, Jack, but let's assume it wasn't DC Goodhew, shall we?' Marks didn't appear amused and Gully wished he would glance over his shoulder in time to see Kincaide's expression break into a predictable smirk. 'However, we do have to look at any possible connection to Ms Martin's conversation with Gary. I am no fan of coincidence but it may be just that. As always, pinpointing her movements in those last hours will be key, so Gary's statement will be valuable. Aside from that we will be looking at the possibility of a random attack, possibly sexually motivated. Forensics will be looking for evidence of sexual assault but we already know that her underwear had been disturbed.'

Kincaide's smirk broadened into a grin. 'Couldn't get a date, Gary?'

Marks kept his steely glare aimed at the rest of the room and Sue was certain that no one else dared to smile. 'Gary, stay behind.' He wound up the briefing swiftly then, allocating tasks to everyone else before dismissing them.

Kincaide and Worthington were behind her in the corridor. 'I was only kidding,' Worthington laughed.

'I wasn't. Someone as tightly wound as Goodhew's got to get his kicks somehow. I'd love to pin it on him.'

'Or we could catch the bastard that did it . . .' Worthington grunted before disappearing into a side office.

Kincaide drew alongside her and nudged her elbow. 'Don't mind us, Sue.'

She smiled coldly, 'I don't mind Worthington.'

'You should lighten up, we were just having a laugh.' Kincaide lowered his voice, 'But it wouldn't hurt to put distance between you and Goodhew either.'

She didn't respond but Kincaide carried on in any case.

'He's been unravelling for months, he's become reckless and unstable. He's not going to last in here. If he doesn't get himself killed, he'll be sacked. You watch; he will crash and burn. And then where will you be?' They walked down the first flight of stairs. She hung back to see which direction he would head, planning to choose the other. Instead, he stopped and motioned *after you*, then followed her. A few seconds later he tapped her arm and then lowered his voice again. 'I need to talk to you about something, we'll go to your desk.'

They walked side by side; he was silent until they turned into an empty corridor. He still glanced over his shoulder before he spoke. 'I know why you visit the archives,' he said. 'So how's it going, the search for your dad?'

She glanced at him sharply but he just looked ahead. Thoughts rushed through her mind but none were coherent enough to be spoken. She needed a reply, to show he hadn't shaken her. She managed to say, 'It isn't any of your business,' but her voice sounded fragile and her throat had become tight.

He glanced to his right and saw that the nearest room was empty. He put his arm behind her and seemed to sweep her inside. 'I think it is,' he continued. 'I went down there and checked out your paper trail. It took me a while but it was easy once I saw your mum's name and the date she was attacked. And your date of birth of course. The thing is, I work with you and I'm finding it hard to see you in the same way. I keep thinking of rotten fruit falling from rotten trees.' He screwed up his face. 'Unpleasant, isn't it? And how do you think everyone else will feel about you? Does Gary know?'

Why was this happening? She pressed her lips tight and gave an almost imperceptible shake of her head.

'I didn't think so. Of course, on the face of it, we'll all be understanding. Logically speaking it's hardly your fault.'

'Stop it, Michael.' She kept her voice low; as much as she hated this it was better here than out in the corridor. 'Stop.'

'I read the files, the rape of your mother was extremely violent. Degrading.'

She backed up a little, her brain still scrambling for words. 'There's anonymity for rape victims.'

'Not from us Sue, you know that; we're the ones looking for the bastard.' He grinned. 'The bastard that's your dad. And there's your problem; it isn't your fault but how many of us will, hand on heart, be able to see you in the same way? Nature versus nurture and you can't escape your genes.'

She looked past him to the door.

'You're tainted,' he murmured.

Sue knew she was close to breaking down, but she wasn't going to allow it. Not in front of him. 'What do you want?'

'Just for you to know that I know. To think about how it will feel when everybody looks at you differently, when Gary pretends to feel the same but you know he's secretly repelled. Haven't you had that feeling about yourself?'

She shook her head even though it was true; her parents had made her feel completely loved but her own feelings of revulsion had always lurked.

'Once it's out, Sue, it can't be undone.'

'So what do you want?'

'You should think about your future here. That's all. Like I said before, Gary will crash and burn and I want you to stand clear. I want you to distance yourself from him.' Kincaide opened the door for her then followed her back out into the corridor.

She wanted to reply but found herself retreating wordlessly.

'Don't burn your bridges, Sue,' he called out as she walked away.

CHAPTER 17

The door hadn't finished closing when Marks began to speak, 'Can I see it?' Goodhew handed him the broken piece of bangle. Marks pressed his lips together, narrowing his eyes as he studied it, 'And you broke this, I suppose?' He didn't wait for an answer. 'It needs to go into evidence at once.'

'I know.'

'How did it end up with you, Gary? I'm guessing there's a connection to your grandfather?'

Goodhew hadn't explained it during the briefing but filled Marks in on his grandmother's revelation.

Marks ran back over it, paraphrasing what Goodhew had told him. 'So it was an item that was unfamiliar to your grandmother when she found it in his desk?'

'That's correct.'

'And Lorraine Martin and your grandmother both knew the name Melanie Franks?'

'Is it enough to link the two cases?'

'Tentatively. It's certainly too much to ignore.' He pinched the bridge of his nose and tapped his forehead lightly with his index finger. 'There doesn't seem to be anything in what you did yesterday that could have triggered this attack. But it can't be treated as a random assault.'

Goodhew and Lorraine had stood in the open together at the market. Perhaps someone saw them together then or in the café. Or spotted him standing outside her house. But it would only be relevant if that person also thought that Goodhew posed some kind of threat. He didn't buy it. 'She must have contacted someone.'

'I've made the phone records the highest priority.'

'What about email and social media?'

'No smartphone, no tablet, no PC. Not even Wi-Fi in the house so it was text, phone call or face to face. The old-fashioned way of communicating, not like this,' Marks jiggled the mobile in his hand. 'It's buzzing like a news wire.' He placed it on the seat of the chair next to him. He suddenly stilled. 'Is there anything else you're not telling me, Gary?'

'Such as?'

He didn't reply but didn't look convinced by Goodhew's reply either. 'The files relating to your grandfather's case are up from the archive. I had them sent to Sheen's office, safer there than most other places in this building.'

Sergeant Sheen guarded his desk and accumulated paperwork carefully; Goodhew was the only person Sheen ever accused of snooping around up there and Goodhew suspected that he only got away with it because Sheen let him. 'That's a good idea, thank you, sir.'

'And I want Sheen there when you go through the files. If there's anything that's pertinent to this case, then it needs to be flagged up immediately. As soon as we officially connect the two cases then you are also a witness in both. You weren't acting in an official capacity when you questioned Lorraine Martin so your position on the team is something that has to be handled very carefully. In fact, I'd move you on to something else right now if we weren't so desperate for resources. Don't put a foot wrong. Do you understand?'

'Yes sir.'

'Get that bangle into evidence and your statement done before anything else.'

Marks was right; there was nothing Goodhew wanted more than to start going through those files. But, as Goodhew wrote his statement, he felt himself being drawn elsewhere.

It took him thirty minutes to walk to Lorraine Martin's house in Selwyn Road. There was a patrol car parked in the street opposite her house and a police Transit van blocking her car in her driveway. It was a mid-terrace, built, he guessed, just after the war. He'd seen that much last night but it had been hard to make out the detail then. The daylight revealed that the house was tidy but tired, the once white uPVC window frames were stained to grey, weeds had broken through the sparse gravel and the brickwork had been discoloured by rainwater and the spread of algae.

He hadn't come to look inside, at least, not yet; he kept walking towards the location of her body. There were several routes she might have taken and they only shared the first half-mile. For the rest he chose the route that kept to well-lit roads and avoided the footbridge that crossed the train-line. The route he chose was the one that might have seemed safest to a lone pedestrian. It was busy; easy for her to have made her way unimpeded through to Argyle Street. Despite all that, it was still a two-mile walk so taxi services were being checked too. He made a list of every commercial premises that looked likely to have CCTV capturing footage of the streets. There weren't many, and he knew that it was too soon to know that this was the route she had chosen but he figured that if she had walked this way then people must have seen her.

The junction with Mill Road held promise. Cambridgeshire City Council had its own cameras at several points along the road, pointing in the right direction and recording – providing the spending cuts hadn't switched them off.

There was nothing remarkable about Argyle Street. Like the other backstreets, houses clustered up to the pavements and cars hugged the kerbs leaving narrow channels for vehicles and pedestrians alike. But, unlike the others, access was blocked by a single patrol car. A few bunches of flowers leant against the road-closed bollard. PC Ted Moorey stood to its right clutching a clipboard.

He grinned very briefly when he saw Goodhew. 'How's it going?'

'That's what I came to find out.'

Moorey was of slight build with a teenage complexion and just-out-of-bed hair. 'I was doing door to door but we swapped over and now I'm freezing my nuts off here.' He looked like he should have been at sixth form.

'Any results so far?'

'Nothing much, plenty of residents have gone to work. The family who live opposite the alleyway have a new baby, and when she woke they heard some kind of scuffle, put it down to cats scrapping, but they reckon that was after twelve.'

'That figures. If it had been much earlier I'm sure someone would have alerted us and she wouldn't have been out there all night.'

'It's a narrow alley, though, and plenty of people walk around oblivious.'

Goodhew knew there was a great deal of truth in that. 'Anything on the CCTV front?'

Moorey pointed behind Goodhew to the head of the street, 'There's a shop on the corner with a dummy camera above the door, two that monitor just their entrances so there's a slim chance there and a street cam on the city side of the junction. I logged the number of that one and I'll put in a request for footage from the council as soon as I get back.' Then he turned and faced in the direction of the body as he spoke, his words less audible, 'One down there but they reckon they don't pick up the footpath.'

'You sound doubtful, Ted.'

'Just that it's a builder's yard and it looks like the camera's angled onto their gateway, which would catch part of the footpath too. I'd want a good shot of the entrance if I was them.'

'I'll take a look. What else?'

'The body went a while ago. I relieved Tommo and he's doing door to door with Dawn at the other end of the street.'

Goodhew walked towards the spot where Lorraine's body had been found. An officer he didn't recognise stood outside the tented area that screened off the site of the body. Their investigation had sliced the road in two. Some way in the distance he could make out the shapes of PCs Charlie Thompson and Dawn Marsden as they stood side by side at an open doorway. There was little point in walking down there just to ask if they wanted to double-check that CCTV. Or to find out that they already had. Easier to do it himself.

Goodhew backtracked as far as the yard. A flatbed truck was parked just inside the gateway, dwarfed by a Portakabin that dominated the space. A man stood at one of the windows but he turned away as soon as he saw Goodhew approach. There were a few items of small plant machinery lined up to one side; perhaps there wasn't much to steal but the yard was totally enclosed by a robust and high brick wall. Moorey was right; they had CCTV and no reason to point the camera anywhere except at the entrance and the footpath beyond.

The man introduced himself as Stan Mercer and the two women in the office as Moira Trent and Amy Laurence. Mercer stood between Goodhew and the women and clearly would have preferred to stop the conversation there. 'We've already had some of yours around. That body had been found before any of us arrived this morning.'

'You told my colleague that the CCTV doesn't capture the entrance area. That's exactly where it seems to point. Would you mind showing me some of the footage?'

'He got the wrong end of the stick.' Stan shifted his weight and pushed his hands into his pockets, 'I said it wasn't much of a shot.'

'Can I see?'

'There isn't anything. The camera was switched on but the disc drive is full so nothing was saved.'

'Really?'

'It stopped recording a month ago,' he shrugged. 'I hadn't realised.'

Goodhew stepped forward and Stan had little choice but to let him through.

Moira was a slim woman, probably in her mid-fifties. She smiled, either in greeting or because Stan's failure to keep him out had amused her. Amy glanced briefly. She was younger and as soon as he made eye contact she looked back to her paperwork.

'Who arrived first today?'

'I did,' Stan replied. 'It was cordoned off by then.'

'And prior to that?'

'Friday. I left around six.'

'You didn't come in over the weekend?'

'No.'

Moira spoke next. 'Amy and I left just before that, at a guess, 5.30?' She looked to Amy for confirmation and Amy nodded. 'And we weren't in over the weekend either.' She glanced across again, but Amy had shifted her attention back to a clutch of invoices. 'Well, I wasn't,' Moira added. 'Amy?'

'Sorry, what?'

'Before today, when were you here last? Friday?'

'Yes, I thought I just said that?' Amy seemed slightly puzzled as if she hadn't been completely listening but around her neckline her skin had changed to mottled pink and she held the sheets of paper with rigid fingers.

Goodhew addressed Moira. 'Does anyone else work in here?'

'No. The main office is in St Barnabas Road. We're the overspill,' she added wryly.

Goodhew continued to track Amy through his peripheral vision and waited for her to turn away again. Stan was close to the window, clearly split between not wanting Goodhew there and his own curiosity.

'Mr Mercer, are you aware of any suspicious activity in the area that may have gone unreported?'

'Nothing during the day. I'm rarely here at night. We get takeaway wrappers and cigarette ends left in the gateway sometimes but that's about it. No one's pinched anything from the yard for a couple of years. We heard it's a woman's body.' He paused just long enough to lean in closer to Goodhew. 'Was she local?'

'It's too soon for formal identification.' Moira was watching them. Goodhew glanced at Amy and the way she turned from invoice to invoice seemed mechanical. Stan waited expectantly. It wasn't appropriate for Goodhew to make any comment before the facts were made public. 'There's nothing more I can tell you at this stage,' he said.

'Nothing?' Stan asked sharply. 'You must know what happened to her.' Stan turned to look through the window again. Moira's gaze followed.

'There will be a statement when there's more information.'

Amy glanced at the other two then back at Goodhew. Her gaze was slightly unfocused, as though her thoughts were elsewhere and he was irrelevant. She dipped her head, giving herself the smallest nod then focused properly on Goodhew as she spoke. 'Do you have a card? Just in case anything springs to mind?'

Stan scowled, 'Like what?'

'If I knew what, I'd tell him right now, wouldn't I?'

Goodhew handed a card to her. 'Anything you think of, OK?'

'OK.'

Goodhew thanked them for their time, and left with the feeling that they were still watching him as he walked back across the yard.

CHAPTER 18

Goodhew woke early the following morning, walked across Parker's Piece to swim his regular hundred lengths and still arrived at Parkside for seven. He headed straight to the second floor, and had reached the cul-de-sac of floor space that Sergeant Sheen had commandeered to house his archive of local information when he heard DI Marks yelling his name.

He turned and found his DI close to his heels, bearing down on him.

'Neil Frampton,' Marks announced. He didn't slow but grabbed Goodhew's arm and pulled him out of the corridor towards Sheen's desk. Sheen looked mildly surprised but didn't speak.

Goodhew moved quickly but his expression felt frozen. Frampton's Builders, the yard he'd visited – he made that connection immediately, but Marks didn't know he'd been there. So the name was clearly supposed to mean something more to him. Nothing sprang to mind but Marks had been driven up here by some imperative that obviously related to Goodhew.

'Does the same person get struck by lightning twice?' Marks asked.

Goodhew was baffled. 'Maybe. If they chase storms.'

Marks glared. 'Rarely or no would have done.'

Sheen looked up, his gaze flicking from Marks to Goodhew and back again.

'On the night she died, Lorraine Martin visited Neil Frampton. Do you know who that is, Gary?'

'Frampton's Builders? Apart from that . . .' Goodhew shook his head. 'I don't think so.'

'Neil and Carolyn Frampton?'

Again, Goodhew drew a blank, but he saw Sheen stiffen, then lean back in his chair, poised to witness whatever was about to unfold. Marks's attention was fixed on Goodhew as though he was waiting for him to betray some kind of telltale emotion or admission. 'Lorraine Martin phoned her sister, then went to pay a visit to Neil and Carolyn Frampton. They own Frampton's . . .'

'Builders.' Goodhew completed the sentence. He could picture the livery of their vehicles, white vans and small trucks with the company name in turquoise and black. 'I stopped by their yard earlier in case they had CCTV footage of the entrance. The foreman wasn't keen to help, but nothing stood out.' And, although he couldn't put his finger on it, something that could have been a childhood memory about Frampton's nudged at the edge of his thoughts.

Marks continued, 'Lorraine Martin gave you two names in connection with that bangle, one was Melanie Franks, and the other?'

'Nadine.'

Sheen uttered something that Goodhew didn't catch. Goodhew looked away from Marks to find the sergeant looking stunned. Sheen stared at them both, 'I said Romsey Terrace.'

Goodhew felt mystified. 'What am I missing?'

Without being asked Sheen replied, 'In March 1991 there was a fire at a house in Romsey Terrace. Two people died, they were boyfriend and girlfriend.'

Marks took over, 'Theo Frampton was Neil Frampton's son with his late wife Louise, and Nadine Kendall was Theo's girlfriend. It was arson. Neil Frampton's business partner, Robert Buckingham, was convicted.'

Sheen cut in. 'He'd been poaching money from the firm and the business owned that property. He could have covered up the theft if they'd had the payout.'

'In addition, he'd had an affair with Nadine and she'd threatened to tell his wife.'

They both watched Goodhew as he pulled a chair closer. He sat, and for a couple of minutes was too busy thinking to be concerned about Marks or Sheen. 'So,' he said finally, 'the fire occurred before my grandfather died. The fire involved the Frampton family, and Lorraine Martin's death does too. I saw her about an item in my grandfather's possession.'

'And hence the lightning question,' Sheen added.

Goodhew felt cautious. They all knew from experience that it was easy to head down the wrong route by misinterpreting information. 'Everything does seem to be linked.' And he also knew that it could put his grandfather's case back into the spotlight. 'We'd need to find a link between the fire and my grandfather.'

'I have that already,' Marks said.

'What, in the last twenty seconds?'

'Faster than that.'

Sheen cast a wary look at Marks. The sergeant stayed silent but it was clear to Goodhew that he was the only one in the dark here. 'It's something from before my time?'

Marks gave a humourless snort. 'Only in one sense. From 1989 until your grandfather's death, your mother worked for Neil Frampton.'

'Really?' He had a vague memory of his mum working part-time while he was at primary school. Something in an office. And she'd taken time off during the school holidays. 'I don't really remember.'

'Do you have up-to-date contact details for her?'

'Somewhere.'

'Keep them ready, we'll need them.'

CHAPTER 19

Amy lived in a top-floor flat of a four-storey purpose-built block. It had been designed like a wedding cake with each tier smaller than the floor below, using the leftover roof space to provide a balcony. Some residents used theirs to store bikes and pushchairs, or sun loungers, rusting kettle barbecues and other items that would have wintered unseen in most people's garden sheds.

She often woke earlier than she needed, roused by a sick feeling that balled in the pit of her stomach. Or by the feeling of falling. Or by her heart. She couldn't feel it thump or race; instead it would flutter weakly like the dying moments of a moth at the glass. Today, it was in her gut. She was too tired to move. The idea of proper sleep – restful and dreamless – taunted her. She lay immobile for over an hour until she managed to convince herself that there was no possibility of catching even the briefest nap. Ten minutes later and she was out on the balcony, still wearing her pyjamas and shrouded in her duvet. She stood her mug of tea on the corner of the safety rail and let the steam rise and the drink cool in its own time.

She switched her thoughts to work and let the office conversations between her, Stan and Moira play out in her head.

If she'd met Stan in the street she would have guessed that he might be ex-military, not in the officer-and-a-gentleman way, but in the ex-bouncer, ex-squaddie, stubborn-featured way. He was thickset but probably not as hard or as fit as he thought he was. Even so, she'd noticed that when the other Frampton employees came into the yard they took instruction and held out paperwork with deference. They had minutes in the man's company; she and Moira had all day, every day.

And she was glad of Moira, who diffused Stan's ill temper, brushing it away when Amy would have homed in on the bad atmosphere that he generated and tried to sort it out or, worse still, let it wind her tight with tension.

She knew that feeling responsibility for other people's moods was a weakness. She'd grown up testing the air for her mum's bad days, and more recently had been feeling like the barometer of Stan; between herself and Moira she always seemed to be the first to know when his mood was changing. Yesterday he'd taken too much interest in that dead body and the police activity along the road. She'd prodded at him until he'd finally responded.

He'd torn himself away from the window; what she'd wanted all along was for him to stop drooling at the glass. To anyone else the fascination might have seemed natural but she'd been on the other side of it. She knew how it felt to be on the receiving end of prying eyes and sly gossip.

She'd expected confrontation from him but instead he'd shown the only glimmer of warmth she'd seen from him. Eventually he'd turned to the window again but didn't offer any further comments and she'd tried to busy herself with the mail. She found herself torn between staring at his back and wanting to snatch another look at Lorraine Martin's business card that she'd hidden in her drawer. She'd wished she'd hidden it in her bag instead; it would have been safer there. She slid the drawer open just enough to see one corner of the card. She reached towards a pen, then glanced at Stan. He hadn't moved. Her fingers crept further across and withdrew the card, and then she leant down to transfer it into the side pocket of her bag. She looked up to find Stan staring at her.

'Why are you here, Amy?'

His usual abruptness had returned. She'd slid the drawer closed again. 'I told you, I needed a job.'

And he'd moved closer and stood at the end of her desk, blocking her view of Moira and the rest of the room. 'None of us are daft, Amy, not even Neil. We all know you want more than that.'

'I don't,' she'd begun but Stan had simply shaken his head.

'I thought maybe you were like him and would be trying to screw money out of Neil, but no. It is something, though.'

'My dad was your friend.'

'No, turned out I was his and he was an arsehole . . .' He'd corrected himself, 'Is an arsehole, and you're either a great actress or you have a lot to learn about your old man.'

Amy had pinched her top lip between her teeth and then avoided his gaze and felt ashamed for doing so. He'd left then, slamming the door behind him and she'd stared helplessly at Moira with a lump in her throat and a long pause before she'd risked trying to speak.

'Well,' Moira had said it as if the one word covered everything, then crossed the room to pass Amy a box of Kleenex. 'Stan always had a soft spot for Nadine. He would go over to the main office on any pretext. And he always looked up to your dad and, even though your dad was older, he did think of him as a friend. Imagine the impact the case had on him.'

'I get that.' Amy had thought it over for a few moments. 'Were Stan and Nadine ever a couple?'

'No, they were poles apart. Stan just didn't know it.'

She took her tea and wandered back inside. The flat felt stuffy by comparison with the fresh morning air. She tossed the duvet on to the settee and sat beside it. Her iPad lay on the armchair closest to her and opening the news app was faster than turning on the TV. She wanted to read the latest on the body found in Argyle Street and, after her anger towards Stan for his own prying, she guessed that made her a hypocrite, but that was tough.

She entered her postcode on the BBC site and switched to the local news stories. An involuntary 'oh' escaped her as she read the headline. 'Murder probe after body find'.

Murder.

The photo at the top of the article showed the view down the street from before Frampton's Yard, pointing towards the location of the body. Apart from the police car parked in the foreground the view looked similar to the way it looked every other day.

Police are appealing for witnesses after the body of a woman was found in an alleyway in Argyle Street. The woman's body was discovered early on Monday morning. The body has not yet been identified and a post mortem examination has been arranged.

She scrolled down the page. Two local residents made comments about 'hearing nothing' and it being 'a lovely street to live in'. Until the last line she read nothing that she didn't already know, then a name jumped out at her and she had to rewind to the start of the sentence to be sure that she understood.

Although police have yet to make a formal identification, the victim has been named locally as Lorraine Martin.

'Shit.' Amy said the word out loud and it sounded harsh as it hit the walls of her empty flat.

To Amy, Lorraine Martin was nothing more than the name on the card, but a connection somehow existed. The woman had known where she worked. Anyone who cared enough could have followed her and found out but it was far more likely that someone had told her, and Amy could count on one hand the number of people who knew where she worked: Moira, Stan, Neil and her parents. And possibly Carolyn Frampton if Neil had gone as far as telling his wife. OK, that made six, so not an average hand but still a finite number.

If Moira or Stan had known anything, they hadn't let on, and she'd never heard Lorraine Martin's name from either of her parents. That left Neil, and possibly Carolyn.

Neil had made it clear that she was to work in the yard and to stay in the yard, but within ten minutes Amy had dressed and was heading towards Frampton's main office.

Back in the days when her father had been a partner, when it had been Buckingham and Frampton, the business had bought a large but run-down detached house in St Barnabas Road and used it as their base. Another lost asset, as Amy's mother had been pointing out since before

102

Amy had been old enough to know what an asset was. Once it was no longer theirs, the house prices had risen, the neighbourhood had been rejuvenated and the Framptons had moved in. The office stayed put, but the vans and equipment had been relocated, tucked out of sight in the Argyle Street yard.

The last time she'd walked past had been several years ago in the summer; the wide pavements were baked and the trees and privet hedges were the only signs of life in the heavy silence. She hadn't slowed as she reached their offices but glanced up at the building for enough time to notice that they'd renamed it Frampton House, sand-blasted the brickwork and replaced the aluminium-framed windows with traditional hardwood.

And now it was pretty much as she remembered it. Neil's F-Type Jag was parked in the driveway alongside a Porsche Cayenne and a Suzuki Bandit motorbike. She texted Moira to let her know that she'd be running late. 'Gone to St Barnabas Road, I'll be back as soon as I can.' She switched her phone to silent.

CHAPTER 20

From outside the house, it seemed to Amy that two rooms at the front were used as offices, portioned off from the private, residential part of the building, which had a separate entrance around the side. The door to one of the office rooms was closed, the other open with a desk positioned close enough to the entrance for the woman sitting at it to greet any arrivals. She was in her late forties, tanned and lean in an I-do-yoga kind of way.

Carolyn Frampton.

It took a few moments for Amy to recognise her. She'd seen the wedding photos where Carolyn at twenty had looked like a teenager while her husband had looked old for thirty-seven. She remembered her mother bumping into her on occasion and introducing her as 'Auntie Carolyn' but, apart from that, she hadn't seen her since her father's conviction. Carolyn was still blonde and sporty but now looked mature and womanly rather than girlish.

It was her mannerisms that gave her age away first, the tilt of her head, the way she moved her long fingers when she spoke, the double blink whenever her expression broke into a smile.

'I'm looking for Neil. Is he here?' Amy stepped forward and cast her gaze around the rest of the office. There were two empty desks, one tidy and the other strewn with building plans.

'He's not,' Carolyn replied. 'Can I help?'

'Not really, I just came to see Neil.'

'And you are?'

Carolyn's smile was polite but her expression had the kind of authority that left Amy feeling that she had to answer. 'I'm your temp. From the yard.'

'Amy?' A small 'oh' formed on Carolyn's lips.

'Yes, Amy Laurence.' Amy hesitated; this wasn't how she'd planned it.

'What happened to Amy Buckingham?'

'My mum reverted to her maiden name.'

'Of course she did.' Carolyn seemed suddenly lost for words.

'I know Neil planned to tell you I was working for you.'

'He did, kind of, I just didn't register.' There was a hard edge to the silence that followed, then Carolyn found her voice again. 'Did Neil tell you to stay away from here?'

'Not at all,' Amy lied, 'but I've never had a reason to come over until now.'

'And now with Moira off and Stan out on site . . . I see.'

Amy didn't see but stayed quiet as Carolyn stood.

'Take a seat.' She gestured in the general direction of the other desks and Amy did as she was told and chose the closest chair. Carolyn picked up a couple of pens from in front of her and returned them to the pen pot that stood alongside the telephone, and then tucked her chair back under the desk before leaving the room.

A few moments later, a young man in a heavy plaid shirt entered. He nodded but didn't speak. He crossed to the plan-covered desk and sat with his back to her.

Amy watched the back of the man's shaved head. He had a spreadsheet open and had begun entering data. 'So Neil is here?' she asked perhaps too quietly since he didn't reply. She felt too awkward to ask again and she wasn't sure why Carolyn had left her there or how long she might be. She took Lorraine Martin's card from the side pocket of her bag. If she couldn't see Neil, she'd ask Carolyn to explain about the card; even if it was nothing to do with her, she would see whether Lorraine's name produced a reaction. She held it discreetly and waited.

Everything was different here to the Portakabin where mud scuffs routinely stained the grey nylon carpet and the only item decorating the wall was a laminated year planner. Through this window there was a view of a quiet suburban street and the interior décor included original mouldings, embossed wallpaper and carpet that sprang beneath her feet.

A few more seconds passed, then, from somewhere on the other side of the wall, she heard raised voices. The urgent staccato of a woman. Probably Carolyn. The low rumble of a man's voice. Then shouting. Both voices now. She looked down at her hands folded over the card in her lap and pretended not to hear.

Plaid Shirt's fingers stopped tapping the keyboard. She looked up and this time he turned fully towards her. She guessed he was about her age, maybe a little younger. His shirt sleeves were rolled up above his elbows and a tattoo of a Chinese dragon dancing in red flames covered his left arm, a tiger snarled on the right. 'We can both pretend to be deaf if you want but they're still shouting.'

She screwed up her face. 'That's Neil's voice? I might have caused it then.'

'Flirting with Dad?'

'I'm sorry?'

'That really wouldn't amuse Mum.'

'You're Carolyn's son?'

'You're sharp. No wonder you got the job.' He smiled suddenly; a broad grin that lit his face. He leant forward to shake her hand, 'I'm Alex Frampton.'

'Amy. I'm the temp from the yard.'

'Amy the Temp? Is that double-barrelled?' Then the smile vanished again and his dark eyes studied her for a few seconds. 'So how have you caused that?' He cocked his head in the direction of the shouting. 'Shame the walls are too thick to hear the words. They don't usually fight, you know. Most days they don't even speak.'

'Do you know the name Robert Buckingham?'

'Of course.'

'I'm his daughter.'

'Woah, fuck me,' he gasped. 'No wonder they're pissed.'

'I came here to see Neil. I didn't think it through.'

106

He leant forward, elbows on knees. He seemed more curious than annoyed even though the row still reverberated in the other room. 'And Dad gave you this job?'

'He did, but after I asked him for it.'

'Just like that?'

'Pretty much.'

'How often have you spoken to him since?'

'Not at all. But I'm sure Stan and Moira would tell him anything he wanted to know.'

'Well, you're not dumb, are you?' Alex shook his head. 'My dad still keeps tabs on your dad, you know. He's not going to lose sight of him.'

Amy almost asked why, but Alex answered for her.

'It's an unsettled score. However long your dad spent in prison wasn't long enough in his opinion. He thinks there might be a day when the books get balanced so to speak. He doesn't want to do anything himself but wants fate or the hand of God to step in.'

'Seriously?'

He raised his eyebrows. 'Yes, seriously. I've grown up with it. I know it chapter and verse.' He hooked his thumb in the direction of the door. 'Moment of truth, then,' he said before turning back to his spreadsheet.

Amy stood up when Carolyn reappeared, ready to flash the business card if Carolyn told her it was time to leave. She called Amy over. 'It seems that losing a stepson doesn't give me the same right to complain about you being here as it would if I'd been Theo's mother.'

'I'm here because I needed to speak to him, not cause trouble.' Amy raised her hands in surrender. 'And I'm sorry I've upset you, but I'm not my father. What happened when I was four isn't my fault.'

Alex gave a grunt, 'I wasn't even one. There's no lower age limit.'

'Keep out of this, Alex,' Carolyn snapped and turned back to Amy. 'He'll see you now.'

Neil Frampton was at the window when she entered his office. 'How are you?'

'Fine. I thought you might check up on me, though.'

'I don't need to. I thought you would come to see me when you were ready, and here you are. Do you know what I trust more than any one person, Amy?'

She shook her head.

'My gut. I'll make decisions based on experience but, as soon as my gut tells me something different, I listen. Your gut tells you what your brain's too slow to process.'

She wasn't sure how to respond so she took a step closer to him, ready with Lorraine Martin's card.

'Asking me for a job wasn't just about you needing work as much as you needing something else from me. Your father's heart attack was a trigger and you turned up with the idea that I felt guilty.' His mouth contorted as though the words tasted bitter. He swallowed. 'My first reaction was to throw you out of the car but my gut told me to take a chance and to see where it led.' He cocked his head at the window. 'Now the police are on their way over and here you are. That's not a coincidence either, is it?'

Amy shook her head. 'I don't know anything about the police coming.'

Her bewilderment must have been obvious; enough to make him hesitate.

'The body in Argyle Street?'

'Yes,' she replied, but didn't mention the card or Lorraine's name after all.

'Her name was Lorraine Martin and she's Moira's sister.'

Amy felt herself draw a sharp breath and heard herself say, 'Oh.' Then add, 'I'm sorry, I had no idea.' She smelt the dust and mud from the yard as she felt the crisp edges of Lorraine Martin's business card. 'Why would that be anything to do with me?'

He studied her expression carefully for a few seconds. 'Perhaps it's not,' he conceded. 'It's just my gut that says otherwise.'

She wanted to tell him that he was wrong but she just gripped her bag more tightly and headed for the door.

Alex caught up with her as she stepped onto the pathway outside. 'I'll give you a lift.'

She shook her head. 'I don't think your mother would like it.'

'Are you OK? You look shaken.'

'I'm fine. I need to get back to the yard.'

'Then I'll drive you.'

He reached for her elbow to prevent her from walking away. She scowled at him. 'What are you doing?'

'Please don't walk off. I'm pleased you're here. We need to get to know each other.'

She still scowled and kept moving. 'Why?'

'We have things to talk about, we're like estranged relatives, people who can fill in the picture that the other one doesn't know.'

She didn't stop walking but she slowed, 'Go on.'

'Like I said, I was only months old when my brother died and I don't remember anything that happened, but I know what I've grown up with.'

'Which is?'

'Curiosity, I suppose. Questions I asked that weren't ever answered. Other kids' parents used to stare at me sometimes, but if I caught them they'd look away again.'

'Yeah, I had that too.' Amy stopped and turned to face him. She remembered the expressions at school pickup, the parents who seemed to look straight through her and tried too hard to make small talk when she had walked within earshot. She'd wondered when they whispered to one another whether they had something new to discuss or were just dragging the story out for a fresh audience. She'd thought she had been the only child feeling that way. 'What do you want to ask?'

'Why you think he did it.' He was studying her closely now.

But she was watching him just as closely as she replied. 'I don't,' she said. He didn't look surprised. 'But is it fair to say that to you? Your family don't need to hear it when there's no proof yet.'

'Yet?'

'That's not why I'm here.' She shook her head, then lied. 'I just needed a job. But if there's anything you do know . . .'

'That my parents have never doubted the verdict?' His eyes hardened. 'That your father's as guilty as?'

The spark of camaraderie vanished as quickly as it had arrived. She didn't argue, there would be no point.

A car carrying two men pulled up to the opposite kerb. She recognised one of them as the detective who had visited the yard. He was looking directly at her and she could tell that he'd recognised her too. 'The police are here,' she told Alex, then walked away.

CHAPTER 21

As Marks and Goodhew pulled up outside Frampton House, Goodhew saw the man and the woman walking away from the building. She glanced in his direction and he recognised her immediately. She kept walking but the man with her crossed the road and approached them. 'I'm Alex Frampton. Are you here to see my parents?'

He took them into the building and introduced them to his mother, Carolyn Frampton, who, in turn, took them towards a closed door. Its heavy gloss paint and round, darkly varnished metal handle reminded Goodhew of the formality that still hung in the corridors of local government offices like Guildhall; they might have been modernised but the residue always stayed. And the inside of the room was no different.

Neil Frampton shook their hands, rising from his chair to not quite his full height in order to do so. He was over six feet tall. Carolyn Frampton had to be close to five-eight but she seemed much shorter than that when, very briefly, she stood alongside him. His skin was a blotchy pink, hers lightly tanned. She had a wiry leanness, he had the build of a man who'd made a gradual but dedicated slide towards obesity. He wasn't quite there yet, but it was on the menu.

'Do you want me to stay?' she asked him.

Marks replied, 'It is both of you we've come to see.'

She drew up another chair, placing it at one end of the desk rather than alongside her husband.

Neil Frampton's gaze had settled on Goodhew to begin with, but now he switched his attention to Marks and opened the conversation with a single word. 'So?'

'We're investigating the death of Lorraine Martin,' Marks began. Goodhew watched Mr and Mrs Frampton closely; if Lorraine Martin had been close to them, or they'd been unaware of her death, Marks's approach would have shocked them. Neil Frampton's expression revealed nothing. 'Her sister, Moira Trent, works for you, is that correct?'

'Yes, it is. It was how we heard of her death this morning.'

'And what was your relationship with Lorraine Martin?'

'Casual.'

'How did you meet her?'

Neil Frampton watched his wife answer the first few questions. None of her answers were mirrored with any corresponding nods or murmurs of agreement from him. Some people just weren't emotive, others chose to keep their feelings under wraps. Goodhew was pleased when Marks changed direction. 'Mr Frampton, on the night of her death, Lorraine Martin visited you. Can you tell me about that?'

'I was in here. She banged on the window.'

'What time was this?'

'I don't know. Late. Around ten. I should have been in the house by then but weekends are always spent playing catch-up.' Frampton's gaze strayed from Marks to Goodhew and back again.

'And she banged on the glass?' Marks prompted.

'I opened the front door but just to get rid of her . . . Make her go, that is. She was drunk, virtually incoherent. And she'd phoned Moira too, before she came here, I think. But she didn't say anything much. And then she went.' He stopped as though he hoped that answer would be enough. Marks tilted his head back a little and studied Neil Frampton without comment. Frampton didn't seem quick to take the hint and his wife just studied the desktop.

Goodhew leant forward. 'Mr Frampton, we need to know what she said.'

'She wasn't making sense, she rambles when she's drunk.'

'You've seen that in the past then?'

'Moira has told us,' Mrs Frampton cut in, but too slowly since her husband was already nodding by the time she'd started to speak.

'Mr Frampton?'

The big man rested his elbows on the desk and pressed his face into his hands. He blew a long, unhurried breath out through his mouth and dragged his hands back as far as his temples, stretching out his fleshy features. 'Theo and Nadine. You know all about what happened to them.' He closed his eyes and spoke slowly as though to himself. 'I didn't know what to make of her at first. She wasn't the girlfriend I imagined for him. But what do the parents know? We're the only ones who see our children the way we do and he'd liked her for such a long time before he asked her out.' He paused to inhale then exhale, slow and controlled. 'She worked for us for a while, then moved away. I don't know whether she stayed in touch with Theo, whether he encouraged her to come back even, but at the time we were just pleased to have her working here once more.' Again the breathing. 'She met Lorraine when she was working here the first time. Through Moira, I imagine. I never saw them together when Nadine came back though.' He opened his eyes and sagged back in his chair. 'It was a few months after the fire when Lorraine first turned up drunk. She rambled on about Nadine mostly, how Nadine should never have been at the house, and kept telling us about her weird theories.'

'Such as?'

He shook his head slowly. 'Some comment that Nadine had once made, or a random news item that she'd seen that had meant something to her. She'd piece things together like people do when they're trying to prove a conspiracy theory. Twisting things to make them fit.

'I could see she was struggling – mentally, I mean – but it wasn't my problem. No one else's problems are all that important when you've lost a child. She was erratic; when Robert was arrested Lorraine said she knew he'd done it, but after the court case was over she came and asked me whether Theo had been depressed, whether it could have been a suicide pact. I stopped listening to her then, I couldn't hear it any more. From then on, as soon as I saw her I became angry and I don't know what she said this time, last time or the time before that.'

'Luckily Moira understands.' Carolyn Frampton smiled wearily. 'She intervened as quickly as possible when Lorraine behaved like that. Apart from those times, Moira managed to keep her work life and her private life very separate.'

'Unlike us?' he sighed.

'Yes, unlike us.' She echoed her husband's words and the tension between them seemed to settle. 'I imagine Lorraine's behaviour was hard for her to deal with.'

Marks turned to a fresh page in his notebook, 'Lorraine Martin's body was discovered in Argyle Street, very close to your yard. Do you know of any reason she would have been in that area?'

They both shook their heads. Neil Frampton looked at his wife and she took the cue. 'None. But saying it's a coincidence doesn't make sense either. We don't know why she'd be anywhere near it.'

Goodhew spoke. 'You have three employees there?'

'Yes, plus others that come in either to pick up plant or file paperwork, timesheets for example . . .'

'And how many here?'

'Just us, and our son, Alex.'

'And the woman I saw in the office when we arrived?'

'Amy?' Carolyn replied. 'She is the third person at the yard.'

'Forget Amy,' Neil Frampton cut in. 'She had no idea that Lorraine had any connection to us. And no one would have been at the yard on a Sunday night.'

'Unless she arranged to meet someone?' Marks suggested. 'Who has a key?'

'Moira, Stan and spares here.'

'Stan Mercer?' Goodhew checked, 'What was his relationship to Lorraine Martin?'

'None,' Carolyn replied before Frampton had the chance, but he took over immediately.

'He knows who she is, he's crossed paths with her like we all have. All of us from the time of the fire that is. Don't discount Robert Buckingham, will you?'

Marks shook his head slowly, his expression patient. 'We have no reason to connect Robert Buckingham to the death of Lorraine Martin.'

'Theo and Nadine are the connection. Lorraine didn't have much that wasn't connected to the past. All she ever did was get pissed and rehash events from twenty-plus years ago.'

Marks spoke next. 'To your knowledge, did Robert Buckingham ever threaten Lorraine Martin?'

Frampton scowled but shook his head. 'I wasn't implying that he had. I was just saying that you should speak to him if you haven't already. Moira, the fire, Frampton's; everything that connects us to Lorraine Martin connects to him too. She probably pestered him the way she pestered us.'

Carolyn glanced uneasily between Marks and Goodhew. 'She hadn't turned up like that in a long time. My husband's exaggerating.'

'I'm not, I've said it how it was.'

'Do you have any of the previous dates?' Goodhew asked.

'No,' Frampton snapped. 'It had been often enough.'

'But not this year,' Carolyn added quietly.

Frampton lowered his voice and leant in closer to his wife, 'Something set her off this time, Carrie.' His eye contact remained direct and his voice slow. She didn't look away. 'Lorraine might as well have been left on our doorstep. That's the work of someone who wants to cause problems. Primarily to me and my business. Don't dismiss what I'm saying.'

Carolyn's expression didn't waver. She broke eye contact first and addressed Marks instead. 'My husband seems to think that he is the focus for everything that happens to us.' She stood and offered her hand for Marks to shake. 'Disagreeing with him isn't allowed and, if it was, I wouldn't have let him hire Robert Buckingham's daughter as our temp. I'm going back to my desk as there's nothing else I'm allowed to add.'

'Carolyn,' Frampton began, but she had left the room too quickly to hear more. 'That's not what I meant,' he finished.

'Maybe not,' Goodhew conceded, 'but it was exactly how it sounded.'

CHAPTER 22

They left Frampton House and headed back towards Parkside Station. Goodhew spotted Amy walking quickly among the pedestrians in Mill Road. They drove past her without comment and Marks didn't question Goodhew when, a few seconds later, he asked if he could make his own way back. 'Don't waste the day' had been his only comment as Goodhew got out of the car.

Goodhew turned towards Argyle Street, ahead of Amy. He waited at the final corner, wishing for a phone box or some other prop that would have allowed him to loiter without the risk of a new call to Parkside Station about his suspicious behaviour.

Her tumble of curly hair had been swept to one side and bobbed on her shoulder as she hurried towards him. Her attention was on the pavement in front of her and she didn't seem aware that there was anyone near her until he spoke.

'Amy Laurence?'

The sound of her name stopped her in her tracks. 'Detective Goodhew, right? Were you waiting for me?'

'Can we talk?'

'What's it about?'

'Your father.'

'And his supposed sins? And my sins? Or neither or both?' She studied him as though she were expecting to see something particular in his expression. 'Do I have any choice?'

116

'You do.'

She nodded to herself then seemed to make a decision. 'OK, but not here.' She checked her watch. 'I need to go to the yard first. I'm going to make my excuses and take an early lunch.'

'I don't need long.'

'I need it.' She took a couple of steps forward then paused again. 'Does Carolyn Frampton know you want to speak to me?'

'No.'

'And this is informal?'

'At this point.'

She smiled at that and her cheeks dimpled. 'Keeping your options open?'

'Of course.'

'Good. Can you meet me at half past? At Clowns?'

'In King Street?'

'Yes. Now I really have to go.'

Goodhew remembered Clowns from his childhood and often when he walked past the thought occurred to him that it never seemed to change; the bulbous lettering of the signage had never been updated and the building nestled into the terraces along King Street as if the other businesses had grown up around it. It reminded him of the cafés he'd visited on trips to Florence and Livorno, filled with lively banter and the smells of pasta dishes drifting through the hatch from the kitchen. It felt like Italy, but he couldn't imagine it anywhere else apart from Cambridge.

He'd arrived half an hour early and chose a table at the back with an audience of clowns. By the time Amy had joined him, the café had begun to fill and the surrounding tables were occupied.

'It's busy. We can go somewhere else if you like,' he said.

'No need, it's like the tide in here, people flooding in then out again and I'm sure that no one takes any notice of anyone else.' When she sat she seemed to sag into the chair and he noticed for the first time how tired she looked. Her eyes were a deep brown, and, in the soft light, seemed almost as dark as her pupils. She looked at him intently and it was the only indication that she possessed any energy.

'Have you eaten?'

She shook her head. 'I'm fine.'

'Coffee then?'

'I'm OK.'

'It's no problem, I'm having one anyway.'

She glanced across at the counter then back at him. 'Cappuccino, please, one sugar.'

A couple of minutes later she was stirring her drink and staring down on the dusting of chocolate as it rotated. He waited and, finally, she looked across at him and spoke. 'So you know I'm Robert Buckingham's daughter. What else?' There was no edge to her voice, just curiosity.

'I know a little about his case and about his connections to Frampton's.' He hesitated. 'I've taken a guess about you, and, if I'm right, I think you might be able to help me.'

She withdrew a little, moving her hands from the table and dropping them into her lap, glancing past him to the next table, then across to the exit. 'How?' she asked.

'I think your job at Frampton's is connected to your father somehow.'

She half shrugged, half nodded. 'That's not any great deduction.'

'And either that's on your father's behalf or it's your decision and you're trying to satisfy a personal goal of some kind?'

She didn't reply.

'So I wondered what might have prompted this. I checked back and discovered that your father had a heart attack and was admitted to Addenbrooke's shortly before you started working at Frampton's . . . I'm guessing that was somehow a trigger for you?'

She tried to look calm but he could see tension tightening her shoulders. She glanced towards the exit again.

'I'm sorry, I'm not trying to make you uncomfortable.'

'What then?'

'My grandfather was murdered in 1992 and I've found evidence that his case is linked to your father's.'

'What do you mean by linked? I don't want anyone trying to put anything else on my dad.'

'Amy, that's not what I'm implying.'

'What then?'

'I need to see where it all leads; my grandfather's killer has never been caught.'

There was sympathy in her expression. 'But you're not allowed to investigate a crime linked to your own family, are you?' she asked.

'Not officially. But it's an old case and I've been allowed some leeway.' Amy didn't respond, just waited expectantly until he conceded a little more. 'I'm not to actively investigate but I have access to the files.'

'So this is what? A chat on your own time?'

'It's borderline,' he admitted. 'And I haven't seen the case files yet. I won't until I'm back at Parkside, but I've followed my nose and ended up here.'

'At Clowns?'

'At this connection.'

'When twenty-odd years of investigation didn't?' She shook her head. 'That makes no sense.'

'There was an item withheld.'

'What item?'

'I can't comment, but it led me straight to Lorraine Martin and, from there, to Frampton's.'

'So you had contact with her before she died?'

'I did.'

'And you're now investigating her death?'

'I'm part of that team, yes.'

'And here I am in the middle of both investigations.' She studied him, her expression shrewd. 'What do you think you want from me?'

'I had a feeling about you when I saw you in the Argyle Street yard, then again at the office. Then I discovered you're Robert Buckingham's daughter and I knew I needed to speak to you.'

'You thought we had a connection?' she asked.

'Something like that.'

He saw an amused look cross her face. 'It's a crap chat-up line.'

'That's obviously not what I was getting at.' His reply was out of his mouth before he'd had the chance to see she was joking.

119

'Obviously? Thanks.'

'I didn't mean it like that either.'

She gave a small smile. 'I think I'm safe in here. They know me and I'm sure Genni,' she pointed in the direction of the owner, 'would *know someone who knows someone if you know what I mean.*' She said the last part of the sentence in a patchy Italian accent, then gave a short laugh. 'Sorry, I've been so tense. I don't know the last time I found anything amusing.'

'You're not working at Frampton's at your father's request then?'

She shook her head. 'How do you know?'

'Because I get the feeling that you're keeping everything to yourself.' He leant back in his chair and imagined himself in her situation. It wasn't so hard. 'It must become a strain, a burden and sometimes you wonder whether you're making mistakes because there's no one to ask.'

Without warning, her smile crumbled. 'I've made no progress whatsoever,' she whispered. 'When I started out it was simple. I found out that my dad didn't start that fire and I just wanted to get inside Frampton's and find something that would prove it.'

'I don't understand why they want you there.'

'They don't. I told Neil I was desperate for work. He's a strange man. He helped my mum out when my dad was in prison. He told everyone I was there except his wife; Carolyn found out about me this morning.'

'You weren't supposed to turn up there, I take it?'

'I had no idea that he'd never told Carolyn. My mum switched to her maiden name when she divorced Dad, changed mine too of course. If I'd been Buckingham then Carolyn would have realised sooner.'

Goodhew took another sip of his coffee. 'What did you think you'd discover?'

'How should I know? I even went through their filing cabinets but, of course, there's nothing. It's too long ago and no one would tell me if they did know anything. Why would they? Anyhow, I started off so worried that I might be wasting my time that I didn't realise I don't mind Moira and actually like the work.' She sipped her coffee. 'I don't know how the hell you think I can help you but go ahead, convince me.'

Goodhew explained the background to his grandfather's death, careful to keep to details that were already in the public domain. 'His death came after your father's conviction . . .'

'So Dad's not in the frame for it?'

'No, but that's not what I was alluding to. My mother worked at Frampton's from before the fire until my grandfather died. Your dad must have known her.'

'What's her name?'

'Paula Goodhew?'

She shook her head. 'Doesn't ring a bell, but I was small. Is that the connection?'

'No. What about the name Melanie Franks?'

Again she shook her head. 'Who was she?'

'The details are sketchy, but we know that Melanie knew Nadine Kendall.'

Amy's expression became wary for a second and her voice sharp. 'And?'

'Why the change of tone?'

'Hearing Nadine's name. I don't know, association, I suppose.'

It seemed as though she was fighting to contain some emotion.

'An association with what?'

'Isn't it obvious? I know it wasn't their fault they died, but it was Theo and Nadine's deaths that wrecked my family.'

'And your dad must have been well known to both Nadine and Theo Frampton?'

'Everyone knew Theo. I don't remember but apparently I acted like he was my big brother whenever I saw him. Nadine worked at the office so I know they knew one another but I was too small to remember anything first-hand.'

'So you didn't know there was a connection between Nadine and Lorraine Martin?'

'Oh.' Amy's tone changed again; shocked but muted now. 'No, I didn't.' Her gaze slipped away from Goodhew's and dropped towards the table top. She watched the tips of her fingers tap out a rhythm on the surface. Her lips remained pressed together and even in the artificial light he could see that she'd paled. He didn't hurry her but her concentration seemed so complete that he started to wonder whether he needed to nudge her. 'Shit,' she muttered finally. When she looked up at him deep furrows puckered her forehead. 'Look, I'm going to take a chance on you. Don't be flattered, I just don't know what else to do.' She grabbed her shoulder bag from the floor, hoisting it onto her lap. 'I hadn't decided what to do with this.' She passed him a business card. 'It was delivered to me at work – it arrived by hand the morning that her body was found. I didn't know who she was then, of course.'

It was in Goodhew's hand before he'd had a chance to refuse it, he'd left prints but managed to bag it without handling it further. 'She wanted you to call her. Do you know why?'

'No.'

'When did you receive it?'

'Monday morning.'

'And did you try calling her?'

'No, I was wondering about it when I heard that the body had been identified. She was dead before I could have read it, wasn't she?'

'By hours I believe.' He stared through the evidence bag at the card, the writing on it was small and the three letters unevenly spaced. 'Dropping this in at Frampton's was more than likely the last thing she did. This will need to be logged properly. You'll have to make a statement too.'

'I understand.'

'This complicates things. Your connection to Lorraine Martin will form part of the investigation.'

'There isn't a connection.' She looked at him steadily.

'There's something. Something that Lorraine Martin either wanted from you or had for you. How well do you know Moira Trent?'

'Dad mentioned her over the years and I think I remember her from when I was a kid, but it's only since I started at Frampton's that I've had any contact. And I only found out today that she and Lorraine were sisters.' Her gaze flicked past him. 'Can I tell you why I wanted to meet in here?'

'Go on.'

'It's where I've always come. My mum would see our solicitor, or the police or whoever, then bring me here to cheer me up. It was our thing for a while. She gave up coming but I carried on.' She turned her head to look at the clowns on the shelf to her left. Some of them were ugly – caricatures with distended features or exaggerated expressions. She pointed to a Venetian mask of a woman with liquid eyes and a heart-shaped face. 'She's my favourite. I wanted to be her.'

Of all the clowns this one looked most like Amy. Goodhew didn't comment.

'Some kids have an imaginary friend, I used to make up stories about her. She looks serene today. Sometimes I looked at her and saw a gleam of excitement. Or fearlessness.' She studied Goodhew thoughtfully. 'I'm not fearless, though. I thought I'd achieved nothing since I worked there but since this morning I've been scared.'

'Of what?'

'That I stirred up something that got Lorraine killed.'

'It doesn't work like that.'

'We've both had contact with her and then this? Aren't you worried that it was you?'

He was, but shook his head and lied. 'No, I'm not.'

CHAPTER 23

Goodhew returned to Parkside Station and filed a report on his meeting with Amy, passing the information straight to Marks who passed it straight to Kincaide. Goodhew made his way up to Sheen's desk where the files from his grandfather's case waited. Sheen glanced from his one-finger-one-thumb keyboard skills long enough to greet Goodhew then made a point of turning his full attention back to the computer.

The case files were held in a series of heavy card document boxes. In his mind's eye Goodhew could not have envisaged a situation where he wouldn't have pushed everything else aside to look through these. Instead, he'd followed other leads first. He knew that the contents held the potential for everything or nothing and, even now, felt a reluctance as he opened the box marked '1/5'.

There was no puff of dust or smell of age and it took only a few seconds to see that the contents were in no discernible order. He opened the other boxes too and rifled through the paperwork, trying to find the earliest document. Eventually he found the transcript of the initial 999 call. His grandmother had called it in. Of course, there was no indication of tone, just the words. He could imagine her voice though: precise, determined and taut with pain.

Operator: *Ambulance emergency. Hello, caller, what's the emergency?*
Ellie Goodhew: *My husband's been attacked. I need help.*

124

She gave her address. *I need an ambulance. They've tried to kill him.*

Op: *It is on its way. I will help you until it arrives. Is your husband conscious?*

EG: *No. He's been hit.*

Op: *I need you to check whether he's breathing.*

EG: *He's not, I know he's not.*

Op: *Check in his mouth for any obstruction. Are his airways clear?*

EG: *They're clear. I already checked.*

Op: *You need to start chest compressions.*

EG: *I have. I'm doing them but he's not breathing.*

Op: *You need the heel of your hand . . .*

EG: *I know how. That's what I'm doing. Nothing's happening.*

Op: *Is anyone there with you?*

EG: *It's not helping.*

Op: *Is there anyone there who can take over?*

EG: *No. Where's the ambulance?*

Op: *It's on its way. You're doing well, just keep trying. Two compressions per second.*

EG: *That's what I'm doing. I'm not stopping.*

The operator continued to reassure Ellie, to encourage her to keep going even though his breathing hadn't restarted, even though she had to be exhausted. The transcript ran for another two sheets. Goodhew turned the final page.

Op: *The ambulance is outside now. They need access to your building.*

EG: *We're on the second floor. I don't want to leave him.*

Op: *You have to let them in. Just do it as quickly as you can.*

EG: *Tell them I'm coming. But I think it's too late.*

Goodhew straightened the sheets and read the first page again. *They've tried to kill him.* He leant forward and sifted through the uppermost sheets in the box; there seemed to be no order to any of it and he needed the chronology.

Sheen cleared his throat then pushed his keyboard away, 'You need to unpack them, then spread it all out, like you would with any other pile of information.'

'Have you looked through these boxes?'

'Yes, they're chaotic. That's what happens when people keep poking around taking one more look.'

'People?'

'Marks went over it again when you started here.' Sheen had a broad Suffolk accent and often spoke slowly with long pauses between his sentences. Some of the officers held the opinion that he wasn't that bright; anyone who'd worked with him knew the opposite was true. Sheen just liked to double-check his facts before rushing to speak. 'I think seeing you around here bothered him. We went through every-thing but we didn't find anything new.'

'I see.'

'And in my opinion you shouldn't be let loose on it now; you're too close to it. Even your mother's name's come up, Gary. Marks should transfer you out into the Fens somewhere until it's all done.'

'And I need to read everything I can in case that happens.'

Sheen shook his head. 'Read or photograph, Gary?'

Goodhew gave Sheen a lopsided smile, 'Are you leaving the room for a couple of hours?'

'Long enough to get coffee and then I'll be back, but I don't really think I need to supervise you, Gary. I'll pretend you have been sent to Littleport or beyond and mind my own. What are you having? White coffee with one?'

'Yes, thanks. And can I borrow the flip chart?'

'As soon as two cases were linked I thought you'd be drawing a diagram; when we reached three it was inevitable.'

Sheen returned with the drinks and continued talking as though there hadn't been a five-minute gap. 'I've always been curious about the situation with your parents.'

Goodhew placed his coffee down on the carpet. Sheen hadn't asked a direct question and Goodhew could have brushed it aside, but he had too much respect for Sheen to ignore him. 'I used to spend a lot of time with my grandparents, at their house,' he began. 'Then I was ill, off school for a full term of primary and I spent most days with my grandfather. I carried on going round theirs after I went back to school.'

'Parkside School?'

'Yes, so it was just across the road.'

'And now here.' Sheen's eyes widened as if he'd had enlightenment. 'You haven't strayed more than about 500 yards.'

'I wish. My parents split up after my grandfather died, after they came into his money that is.' It struck Goodhew then that it was easy to talk to Sheen and he wondered why the sergeant had spent so many years behind a desk. 'My mum lost the plot with it and sent us to boarding school.'

'And your father didn't have a say?'

'Dad worked away.' Goodhew had never bought that explanation; there had been enough money for his dad to have worked locally and to have brought up his children at home. He still felt anger at both of them if he dwelt on it for too long. 'That's it,' he added.

He meant it to be the end of the conversation but Sheen didn't take the hint. 'So where's your mum now?'

'On the outskirts of Sydney. When my sister moved out there, my mother followed.' It didn't really hurt to talk about his family after all, he realised, not when Sheen had probably read every detail of his grandfather's murder. 'She remarried a few years back but I haven't met him.'

'And your dad?'

'He's a decent bloke.' Goodhew screwed up his face. 'But we're not interested in my dad, are we?' Goodhew patted the box of documents. 'You're not going to tell me that he's in here too?'

Sheen shook his head. 'No, but there is this one other thing. It might not come up but, then again . . .' For once Sheen seemed to have started talking before he'd thought it through. He paused, made a fist and pressed it to his mouth.

'You can't stop there.'

'I know. I was looking for the words.'

'Sometimes you just have to jump in.'

'You don't say.'

'Sorry.'

Sheen continued in his own time. 'We suspected Neil Frampton of having an affair. It wasn't relevant to the investigation, but it's relevant to you and if it comes up again I'd rather you'd heard it from me.'

'Go on,' Goodhew said. It was obvious what was coming next but he needed it spelt out in any case.

'Frampton hit the booze when his son died. His wife, Carolyn, was busy with their baby and home seemed to be the last place Frampton wanted to be. At least, that was my take on it, and he seemed very close to your mother, Gary. I'm not accusing her, I'm just saying what we all saw.'

'Thanks.' He had only just found out that his mother worked at Frampton's, had never heard of Neil Frampton until Lorraine Martin's death, but believing the story was not a problem. He lifted a pile of documents on to his lap and glanced across at Sheen. 'How well do you remember my grandfather's case?'

'At the time I was pretty well versed. And I've had a little refresher now and then, but no doubt there's plenty that I've forgotten.'

'Did my mum . . . feature?'

'Feature?' Sheen raised one eyebrow, 'Just as the deceased's daughter-in-law,' he assured Goodhew. 'Nothing more.'

'Good. And no, I don't suspect her of anything, I just wanted to understand whether the investigating officers had missed the opportunity to link the two cases sooner.'

'It was that bangle you turned up with that made the link. Without that, it wouldn't have been looked at twice.'

That was true, when combined with Neil Frampton's name it had produced an instantaneous connection for Marks and Sheen. The implication unsettled Goodhew; inadvertently or otherwise his grandmother had helped to ensure that the two cases remained detached from one another. He switched subjects. 'How long before the Romsey Terrace files come up?'

'They'll be here this afternoon. It's connected to an active case now so it'll be quick.'

'Can I ask you a question?'

'Quid pro quo, Clarice?' His accent and attempt at Hannibal's psychotic grin both fell short.

128

'What is Sue searching for in the archives?'

Sheen's smile faded. 'I don't know.'

'She hasn't told you?'

Sheen shook his head. 'I have an idea but it's not my business. Or yours.'

Goodhew ignored the hint. 'But you've guessed? You've worked it out, right?'

'Yours isn't the only family with baggage. Just leave it alone.' Sheen added, 'Would you tell her everything, Gary?'

He liked to think that he would but, in truth, there were things he'd never shared with anyone; Sheen had a point. Goodhew changed the subject. 'I just met with Robert Buckingham's daughter.'

'Amy?'

'Yes, Lorraine Martin attempted to contact her. Amy had no idea who she was and there's no hint to what she wanted so I'm guessing that it's connected either with Frampton's or Moira or, most likely, Amy's father.'

'That third one's a leap.'

Goodhew shook his head. 'Not really, Amy's been working at Frampton's trying to prove her dad is innocent.'

'There's many forms of innocent and I don't think Robert Buckingham qualified. He's served his time, what difference would it make now?'

'You sound like Kincaide.'

Sheen waggled a finger at Goodhew. 'I'm ignoring that.' He turned and pulled a file from the shelf above his desk. After a brief search he passed Goodhew a press clipping. 'That's not how he usually looked. Buckingham loved himself, he was a cocky bloke back then. And too old to be acting like he did.' The photo showed Amy's father as he was led into court. The photographer had caught him looking dishevelled and disorientated, the flash seemed to make his eyes bulge.

The way Sheen had said it made Goodhew expect to see a man in his fifties, a candidate for mid-life crisis. Goodhew studied the picture and then took a guess, 'Mid-thirties?'

'He liked teenagers. And always had to be seen to be doing well.'

'You knew him personally?'

'I met him a few times, the first when he came in here to make a statement. He always dropped things into the conversation that were intended to impress. You know the type?'

It was a rhetorical question; they all knew *that* type.

'They eventually convicted him on a manslaughter charge because there was no clear evidence that he knew the property was occupied. That angered plenty of them here. The end-of-case beer felt more like an end-of-case shandy; watered down and flavourless.'

'What's he doing now?'

'Small-time builder, I believe. He's been out for a while but I don't know where. Of course, his wife divorced him and he lost his stake in the business so I doubt he's as cocky now.'

'And Lorraine Martin? Did she play a role in his conviction?'

'I don't think so. In fact, I don't remember her at all.' Sheen frowned. 'Wait for the Romsey Terrace files and, until then, I'll find you that flipchart.'

But something else had just struck Goodhew. He reached for his jacket, 'Actually,' he replied, 'I don't need it right now.'

CHAPTER 24

Marks had told Goodhew not to waste the day but he had to work with Kincaide at some point. Kincaide was at his desk and, with no one else in the room, he'd rearranged the furniture again, this time so that he was closest to the display board. All the other desks faced his and he was furthest from the door. His desk was clear apart from a neat pile of papers stacked under a container of half-eaten takeaway sushi and a new mug, printed with a picture of handcuffs and the slogan, 'Feel safe at night, sleep with a cop'. Kincaide glanced up long enough to scowl. 'Where have you been?'

'Lunch break,' Goodhew replied, 'and before that I met with Amy Laurence.'

'The admin girl from Frampton's?'

'Yes,' Goodhew echoed, 'the admin girl.' He sat at his desk and powered up his PC. He knew Kincaide was waiting for him to explain but, then again, he was waiting for Kincaide to ask.

Kincaide's patience gave out first. 'So what did she want?'

'I'm about to email it to you.'

'Email what?' Kincaide snapped.

'My report,' Goodhew's voice sounded calm to the point of being inflammatory. It was deliberate but he didn't care.

Kincaide strode across the office then. It was a small space and three or four reasonable steps would have done it. Instead, the carpet between them was swallowed in a couple of strides and his hands slamming down on Goodhew's desk seemed to be his braking method. 'Do you have any idea how much pressure we're under on this one? The fact that you're still on this case when you're involved with the murder victim just shows how fucking under-resourced we are . . .'

'There was no involvement . . .'

'You were meeting up with her and stalking her the night she died.'

'I met with her once in connection with a cold case. A case that Marks knew I was following up.' Which wasn't quite a lie. 'Even you know I had nothing to do with her death, Michael.'

'So what report?'

Goodhew turned to his PC and clicked the screen a few times. 'I've just sent it.'

Kincaide returned to his desk and opened the file. By Goodhew's estimate he'd be fuming by the end of page one. It actually took about six seconds. 'What the fuck?' Kincaide grunted.

'You read quickly.'

'She's Robert Buckingham's daughter and you didn't report it?' He read on. 'And she had material evidence and the first I know is after lunch when you decide to email me?' He spun his chair back to Goodhew. 'What the hell are you playing at?'

'Marks knows all about Amy Laurence. I kept him posted. He said I should update you and I have.'

'You,' Kincaide's index finger made tiny jabbing motions, 'you are someone that needs to get out, out of this department, out of this job.'

Goodhew shook his head, 'You like to threaten people when there's no one else around, don't you?'

'That wasn't a threat, it was a fact. You're reckless.'

'I don't care what you think I am. I care what you do and you threatened Sue.'

'That's bollocks.'

'You told her to keep away from me. That she didn't want to burn her bridges. You shouldn't stand in a stairwell; sound travels.'

Kincaide's eyes had darkened to blackened pips. He rose from his chair and again took a couple of steps in Goodhew's direction. He opened his mouth to speak but Goodhew cut in first.

'Enough. Don't let me see you bully anyone.' Goodhew held his glare then deliberately walked past Kincaide to the board displaying the case photos. 'When's Moira Trent being interviewed?'

There was a lengthy pause before Kincaide answered. Goodhew could feel his eyes boring into the back of his head. He guessed that Kincaide's fists were clenched at his side, his body tense. 'This afternoon,' he eventually hissed.

'I'd like to go.' Goodhew turned slowly and watched Kincaide fight to hold his temper.

'I'm sending Sandra Knight. She'll take someone, but it won't be you.' Kincaide shook his head. 'You don't make the decisions, Gary. You can spend the rest of the day in here following paper instead of people.'

'That's fine.'

'I'll email you as you seem to prefer computers to humans.' His smile was bitter, 'Bank details or phone records?'

'And I thought you didn't love me.'

Kincaide fiddled with his computer for a few seconds then gave the mouse a final double-click. 'You have them both,' he smiled coldly, 'and I'm going with Knight. Email me as soon as you have anything. And email me if you don't, I want you in here until I get back.'

Kincaide left in a cloud of machismo. Point made. Subordinate humbled. Goodhew opened both files and then crossed to the window, looking down in time to see Kincaide and Knight drive out of the car park for their five-hundred-yard journey to Clarendon Street.

He checked the time, ten past two. At worst he reckoned he had an hour.

He slid the papers out from under the sushi. The pile was about three inches thick and, as he'd guessed, contained everything that Kincaide had been copied in on throughout the day, with Lorraine Martin's phone records and bank statements at the top.

'What did you do to Kincaide?'

He glanced up to see Gully in the doorway, leaning on the frame, her arms crossed. 'I might have upset him,' Goodhew replied flatly.

Sue crossed the room, her attention focused on the paperwork in front of Goodhew. 'Did you just manipulate him out of the building?'

'It ended up that way. I really wanted to speak to Moira Trent but Kincaide wasn't having any of it. The best I could do was hope he went too.'

'I was talking to Sandra and he grabbed her by the elbow and practically hauled her out to see Moira Trent.'

Goodhew looked rueful. 'I let him get to me first, though.'

She looked blank. 'Why now?'

'Little things.' And some that were not so little.

She nodded. 'Actually, I wanted to talk to you.'

Goodhew had continued to flick through the papers. He separated a bundle and placed them down on the table in front of Sue. 'What's up?'

'You know I want to become a detective?' She didn't need to wait for an answer, they both knew how much it would mean to her, 'The thing is, there's an opportunity for secondment to the Met.'

'As a detective?'

'No, but attached to a unit dealing with organised crime; primarily people trafficking and forced labour. There's potential for promotion and I'd gain more experience . . .' She fell quiet.

'I understand.' He wanted to ask, *Is it because of us?* Except there was no 'us' and he doubted that Sue thought about him the way he thought about her. 'What about your family?'

She hesitated. 'I was thinking of them, that's why I went for London; it's closer than some of the other options. I just wanted to let you know what I was doing.'

'If you're sure?'

'I think so.' He saw her redden before abruptly turning her attention to the papers, spinning them round so they were the right way up. 'From Kincaide's desk?'

'Ignore bank and phone, he's given me those already.'

'What are we looking for?'

'The best angle for knowing Lorraine Martin better.'

'FORM?' It was an acronym Sue had discovered on a website. It was designed to give topic ideas for making conversation: family, occupation, recreation, money. It worked for building a picture of dead people too and they never objected to personal questions about their finances.

'Yes, and don't think too hard. Just anything that jumps out at you.'

'Uh-huh.' She was already reading. He followed suit and half an hour passed in silence before she pushed several sheets towards him, 'Her medical records going back five years.' She pointed to the medication history, 'She'd been on antidepressants throughout. Plenty of people are, but look.' She turned to a page that contained the standard patient information, a header record with gender, date of birth and NHS number. Below this was a row of short dates with initials beside them. 'This summary sheet dates back much further. These same fields appear on the screen when I visit my GP, so I know that these,' she pointed to the dates, 'represent significant events. The headlines if you like.' There were three entries; 21/06/92 MHA S2, 15/9/01 MHA S2 and 23/1/06 DEPR. 'I'll need to check these abbreviations but that looks to me as though she was sectioned twice then diagnosed with depression in 2006.'

He mulled over the dates. 'Nineteen ninety-two, 2001 and 2006. I wonder if they're significant in any other way. No details, though?'

'Like I said, just the last five years.'

'I'll put in a request for the historic records and hope they haven't been mislaid or mislabelled.' Goodhew was close to the end of his pile of papers. 'You've done better than me.' But his voice slowed at the end of the sentence, his attention settling on the last but one sheet. 'Although . . .' He began to read.

'Gary? It's almost quarter past, we need to stop.'

'OK,' he agreed, then quickly used his phone to photograph the document. He bundled the pages back into their original order, straightening the pile and returning them to their position on Kincaide's desk and crowning the pile with the pot of sushi.

'What was it?' she whispered.

'Last year a neighbour, a Mr Gilligan, made a complaint against Lorraine Martin. He alleged that she was verbally abusive towards him and his wife. He claimed she'd been a problem in the past and that he'd finally had enough. It's worth a follow-up.'

'And what will you do about Kincaide? You can't just go behind his back on either one of these leads.'

'I'm thinking.'

Sue pulled a second chair up to Goodhew's desk. And when Kincaide returned they were poring over bank statements.

'What have you found?' he asked. His tone was reasonable now, filling the post-argument silence with fake politeness.

Goodhew did the same. 'Nothing yet. What about Moira Trent?'

'Says that Lorraine rang her drunk on the night she died. Was shouting about *they* and *them* and sounding paranoid. Not the first time she'd been that way.'

'Michael, I need a word,' Gully reddened a little but carried on. 'I came in looking for something to work on, and I assumed that those papers,' she pointed to his desk, 'weren't restricted since they were out in the open like that. Anyhow, Lorraine Martin was sectioned twice, in '92 and '01, and last year her neighbour made an antisocial behaviour complaint against her. I'm sorry if I did the wrong thing.' She smiled apologetically then pressed her lips firmly together.

Kincaide's expression had darkened instantly. 'One's a dead end. Mr Gilligan passed away three months ago. I didn't know about Lorraine Martin's mental health but her full medical records are on their way to us, so I would have been fully informed by tomorrow. You know what assuming does, Sue, so, for future reference, remember my desk isn't fair game.' Then, as an afterthought, 'Don't do it again.'

'You owe me, Gary,' she said under her breath.

She started trawling through the phone records and Goodhew carried on with Lorraine Martin's bank statements. Her account revealed more by the details that weren't present than those that were; no mortgage payments and few deposits. The money she earned came in infrequently, cash in hand by the look of the modest and irregular deposits. She'd covered her bills and little else.

Goodhew looked over at Kincaide, 'Michael, what did her sister say about her employment status? Was the jewellery her main source of income?'

'Apparently. She said that for spells Lorraine had hosted foreign language students but had knocked that on the head a couple of years ago to work full-time on,' he paused to make quote marks in the air, 'her art.'

Kincaide liked making quote marks so Goodhew made the signs himself and asked, 'Were those wiggly fingers yours or Moira's?'

'Hers. She called it "my sister's hobby". I don't think she approved but then she is an accountant. She wouldn't have seen that as a proper job.'

'Is that what she said?'

'That's what her expression said. Have you found something?'

'Just a lack of income. Is anyone questioning the other stallholders from the market?'

'Worthington's on it.'

'Or the neighbours?'

'Uniform went house to house. What's wrong with deskwork, Gary?'

Goodhew considered the little he knew about Lorraine. She'd owned a tatty Ford KA panel van, tiny with a 1.3 engine. It might have been just large enough to carry her jewellery displays to craft markets and fairs but it was definitely a budget option. The outside of her house had been less than pristine too but he had no way of knowing whether it was down to lack of funds or lack of motivation. He'd met her, of course, and he hadn't seen any sign of money then; her skin had the capillaried look of outdoor living, her hair had seemed unstyled and her clothes more practical than chic. But then again, he wouldn't have known expensive clothes from high-street knock-offs.

'About this deskwork?'

Kincaide had returned to his own paperwork and was reading. Only his eyes moved towards Goodhew. 'Go on.'

'I need to visit her house.'

Kincaide scowled, 'Explain.'

'She either lived very frugally or was receiving other money on the quiet. From her car and what I've seen of the outside of her house I'm guessing the first but I need to be sure. If I find any evidence that her spending outstripped her income, then we'll need to keep looking.'

'You sound like the Inland Revenue.'

'I'd just like to look.'

Goodhew expected him to dismiss the idea out of hand but, instead, Kincaide remained expressionless. 'You'll need to curb that attitude if you ever want to make it to DS.'

'And if I don't?'

'Take the keys and knock yourself out.'

CHAPTER 25

Mr Gilligan had lived in the house facing Lorraine Martin. A two-bedroomed mid-terrace that would have been identical in style to all the others on that side of the street before most people began to update with aluminium then uPVC replacement windows, new roofs and fancy doors. Goodhew remembered biking around these roads when he'd been ten or eleven, sometime in the year before his grandfather had died. Selwyn Road was supposed to be the coldest street in Cambridge. The last place the snow would melt. Back then the best thing to do with a day had been to explore the back alleys and end up at Newnham or Jesus Green or Cherry Hinton Hall. He might have cycled past here then and it might have looked exactly the same with the original windows in sky-blue frames, fussy net curtains and a potted hydrangea on the window sill in the lounge.

He rang the bell and immediately saw movement in the single ground-floor window. After a few seconds the door was opened by a chubby-faced woman in her fifties. Goodhew introduced himself, 'and I realise Mr Gilligan has passed away but I wondered whether his wife might be able to help me?'

'That's Mum. I don't know whether she'll talk to you or not.' She leant close to Goodhew and lowered her voice. 'She's just been diagnosed with Alzheimer's,' she told him and then raised her voice to a conversational level. 'Come in, we can ask, can't we? I'm Maggie,' she added and led Goodhew through to the sitting room.

Mrs Gilligan looked close to ninety and, while there was a strong resemblance between the two women, the mother was daintier. She wore a long-sleeved dress and sat straight with her hands clasped in her lap.

'Mum, this is Detective Goodhew, he's a policeman.' Maggie spoke slowly but without raising her voice.

Mrs Gilligan smiled up at them both. 'Is this about Lorraine? Poor girl.'

'Yes, that's right. I'm hoping you'll be able to answer some questions.'

'And you say you're a policeman?'

'I am.'

'It is only the police that have been in and out of her house so far. I'm waiting for the others to arrive, the young men and women. I have always thought they would one day.'

'Which men and women, Mrs Gilligan?'

'The young men like you. I thought you might be one of them. I'd like to help you but there's nothing to tell.'

'I'm from Cambridgeshire Police.'

She studied him for a moment, her eyes bright. 'Are you looking for your mother, lad?'

Goodhew squatted down near her chair. 'No, I'm a policeman.'

'So you told me.' She pointed at him with a trembling index finger. 'Some will still flourish on rocky ground. And I always thought that would be the case. You seem to have done well.'

'I'm here about Lorraine Martin, your neighbour.' Goodhew glanced at Maggie and she mouthed *sorry* back at him. 'Mrs Gilligan, do you remember your husband reporting her to the police? He claimed she'd been verbally abusive to both of you.'

'Of course I do. Derek said that it was my fault that she lashed out the way she did but I was trying to help her. I thought if she could confide in someone . . . Instead she began screaming obscenities at me. She threatened me, you know, and although Derek thought I was wrong to interfere he always stood up for me, so he decided to have a word. I told him not to but he'd got himself all riled and he wouldn't listen. She came right back at him, screaming and shouting foul language. I tried to pull him away. "Leave her," I said, "she's off again." But he wouldn't let it drop entirely so that's when he phoned you and made a complaint.'

Goodhew nodded. 'What did you mean by "She's off again"? Were these outbursts a frequent occurrence?'

'It had happened before, then other times she was very polite.' Mrs Gilligan's gaze wandered past Goodhew as she thought back. 'I'll tell you something, I went over there later that day and she started crying and I wasn't at all surprised. That's just how it went with her.'

'How long have you lived here, Mrs Gilligan?'

'This house belonged to Derek's parents and we took it on in the fifties so we've been here longer than she has. And how old are you, twenty-something?'

She was a few years out but he didn't correct her.

'Which means,' she continued, 'that we'd seen it all over the years and I knew she was heading for it again. She'd been out the front all morning that day, playing her wireless too loudly and shouting on her telephone. She kept pacing and I went over to see her, not to ask her to turn it down, but to ask her if I could help.'

'You thought she was having some kind of breakdown?'

'I don't know the name for these things but I knew she wasn't right. Derek didn't see eye to eye with all of that, he just saw her anger as an attack on me, thought she should have been able to control herself.'

'Did you have much contact with her after that?'

'Not before my Derek died. I would still say good morning when I saw her, not that that was very often. Then she bought me flowers for the funeral. She was kind underneath it all, you know.' She stared across the street then, reflecting on what she'd just told him.

'And how had she been more recently?'

Her expression brightened. 'There was a man standing in the street the night she died. I saw him and I told the police. I thought he might be one of them too.'

'One of them? Can you be more specific, Mrs Gilligan?'

She shook her head, 'I didn't get a good look at him but I'd say he was your height but younger.'

Goodhew didn't bother admitting that it was him that she'd seen. 'But what do you mean by *one of them*?'

'Lorraine's children, the ones she gave away.'

'Mum! There's no proof.' Maggie had remained in the background until then and Goodhew had been aware of her from the corner of his eye. She'd seemed on edge the entire time: fidgeting with her hands or moving her restless feet, caught between staying silent and the urge to interrupt. 'I grew up on this street, lived here until I was in my twenties and of course I've been back ever since.' She began picking her words more carefully. 'Lorraine always had lodgers, often students, and Mum was a bit nosey. I never thought there was anything strange going on. And I've never listened to this idea of babies. Lorraine didn't have children.'

'So you say, Margaret, but I saw her.' Mrs Gilligan sounded determined. 'I saw her and that's why she went like that from time to time.' She tapped on her temple with her index finger. 'It's all very well thinking that there are shortcuts in life but there's always a price to pay.'

'Which shortcut did Lorraine take, Mrs Gilligan?'

'She should have kept that baby, but she took in those girls and paid off that house. Thought she'd got it free when the rest of us had to slave for it.' She shook her head sadly. 'She paid in the end though, didn't she? Poor, poor girl.'

Goodhew tried asking her more questions but Mrs Gilligan only repeated snippets of everything she'd already told him. Maggie stepped outside the front door with him as he left. 'Mum's clear in her own mind but she's never explained the specifics to me. I've heard these kind of stories time and again but I never had any concerns about anyone but Mum.'

'How long had this been going on?'

'It started after I left home.' She touched her thumb to successive fingertips as she counted back the years. 'That was in the late eighties, I suppose. I can't give you an exact year. It just seemed like nosiness or gossip at first. I thought she was spending too much time at home with an idle mind so I dismissed her as a bit depressed, a bit of a fantasist maybe. And Dad felt the same, bless him. That sounds harsh, doesn't it?'

'A little,' he conceded.

'And I never saw Lorraine with a baby. It all sounded too far-fetched, but since Lorraine died, I'll admit it feels as though there must have been something wrong . . .' Her voice trailed off and her expression became more solemn. 'You're taking Mum seriously aren't you?'

'We're taking everything seriously.' Goodhew shook Maggie's outstretched hand. 'Please call me if she says anything else.' His gaze rested on the house opposite. 'And please thank her again, tell her that she's been a great help.'

CHAPTER 26

The hallway was carpeted in brown with a pattern of cream boxes framing pink roses. It reminded him of a seaside hotel, of more lucrative days now long gone. It was good quality but old, thinner in the centre and faded in the patches where light had fallen through the glass-paned door. The walls were decorated with a heavy embossed paper coated with layers of magnolia emulsion. There were no pictures on the walls, no side table, no curtains at the landing window. And as he walked around the house he found that the rooms were the same; clean but sparsely furnished, the décor good quality but worn and each room tidy because it stood so empty. It was obvious from the start that there was no hidden wealth in the house unless it had been burnt on drugs, alcohol or some other secret obsession.

He wore gloves and began in Lorraine's kitchen. Her freezer and larder were well stocked, her fridge bare apart from milk and cheese. She'd liked soup and pasta and had frozen several kilos of cheese when it had been on special offer. She hadn't been a vegetarian but ate little meat. She'd cooked food in batches and froze them in single portions, bagged and labelled in black pen.

It was a strange way to get to know a person but, from experience, he knew it worked.

He moved from room to room, gathering details and photographing everything he touched even though the crime scene officers would have taken similar shots. It wasn't until he reached the bathroom that the items became distinctly personal. He guessed that when Lorraine Martin had let rooms out to students the entire downstairs had been a communal area, so perhaps she'd never quite re-established herself there.

She had kept her medicines in the bathroom cabinet; here there was an accumulation of prescription blister packs, most were painkillers or antidepressants, some part-used, others untouched. An unfinished course of antibiotics, two years out of date. Two condoms and a small selection of complimentary shampoos and shower gels brought back from hotel stays, all coated with a thin but stubborn film of dust.

The dust continued to her bedroom where the surfaces and handles had been fingerprinted but the curtains and bedspread were dull, their fibres clogged with it. She hadn't been a fan of ornaments or pictures; the only exception he'd seen stood on her window sill; a heavy glass paperweight, hexagonal and set with dried flowers inside. It hadn't been dusted for prints but he could see finger marks on the sides. He turned it over. There was no maker's mark underneath, just the words 'MADE IN ENGLAND' etched into the base. He placed it back down and photographed it, suddenly registering how it had felt in his hand, warmer and with a softer smoothness than glass. Dust-free too.

Lorraine Martin had stood at this window with the paperweight in her hands. This might have been the object that had inspired her jewellery. He looked down on her garden, the barely tended rectangle of grass, the narrow strip of concrete path that looked as though it had been rolled out and dropped on top. Everything about the garden mirrored everything about the house apart from the last few feet before the fence.

The far left corner was occupied by a quarter circle of flowerbed, the far right by a garden building, not quite a shed but not a summerhouse either. It reminded Goodhew of a beach hut with its tongue and groove sides and dark blue window frames that contrasted with the main duck-egg blue body. He could see from the window that the décor of the shed was no less worn than around the rest of the house but, even from upstairs, it was easy to see that the glass was cleaner and that the step outside the door had been kept swept and clear of dead leaves. Plant pots stood either side of the door; one was an old teapot, and the other an enamel saucepan, both brimming with white and lilac winter pansies.

The same pansies filled the flowerbed, too, as though she'd bought too many and they had been planted to use up the surplus. The extras were in the pots, he decided, the others had been planted at regular intervals and provided a dense carpet around the base of a small concrete bird bath. The edge had been made with old house bricks, tilted at a forty-five-degree angle and embedded in the soil.

Goodhew glanced behind him at Lorraine's bed, then stepped back and sat at the pillow end. The window sill was just below his eye level and, from the bed, a large proportion of the view was sky and skyline. And the only part of the garden he could see from there was the beach hut and the flowerbed.

He stayed there for several minutes, trying to see both the room and the view through Lorraine Martin's eyes. Trying to imagine her life in this house, her struggle with depression and how she felt about the home that seemed to have gradually faded around her. Wondering whether anything here had helped her battle the personal ghosts that had visited her for the past twenty-five years.

Are you looking for your mother, lad?

He phoned Kincaide. 'Is there any record of Lorraine Martin having had a child?'

'There's no next of kin apart from her sister.'

'What about a child she lost, or gave up?' He explained Mrs Gilligan's comments.

'And how old is this woman?' Kincaide grunted.

'Old enough to make a reliable statement. Lorraine Martin paid off her mortgage and I'd like to know when. It's been years since this house has been cared for and years since she first suffered from mental health issues, both of which date back to the approximate time of the fire in Romsey Terrace. In my opinion we need to look back that far. If she also gave birth back then . . .'

He was interrupted by another grunt from Kincaide. 'That's all in hand, Gary. What's the situation with her income? Remember that's what you went to look at.'

'There's no money here, she's lived on a shoestring.'

146

'Come back then.'

'I haven't finished.'

'If the finances check out, then you have.' Kincaide hung up.

Goodhew straightened the bed covers and walked slowly downstairs. He wasn't too old to be Lorraine Martin's son and Mrs Gilligan had also said, *I thought you might be one of them.*

He phoned Gully. 'Who's doing Lorraine Martin's pm?'

'Sykes.'

'Can you phone him for me?'

'I thought you were coming back. Can't you phone him yourself?'

'I've looked over the house but not the shed in the garden, I want to do it first and Sykes will be gone by then.'

'So what do you want me to ask?'

'Whether there's evidence that Lorraine Martin had a child, or children.'

'When?'

'Not recently. The neighbour asked me if I was looking for my mother and she thought I was *one of them.*'

'Meaning what?'

'She wasn't specific but she said I was about the right age so I'm wondering whether there might be an estranged child out there somewhere.'

'Or more than one?'

'I know, sounds unlikely, but I can't leave it either.'

'To be your mother she would have been a teenager.'

'Mrs Gilligan thought I was younger.'

'I see, so a pregnancy that was twenty-odd years ago?' Then added dryly, 'I like the timing.'

'I spoke to Lorraine and she also tried to contact Amy Buckingham; I believe her death is related to at least one of those events. But I'm not just homing in on things that date back to 1992.'

'Of course you are. Marks is looking for a connection to your grandfather, so why don't you just tell him what you're thinking?'

'I will, when there's something to tell.'

Goodhew thought she was about to say something and waited but there was silence from the other end of the phone.

'OK,' he said finally.

'I'll phone Sykes then,' she replied before they both hung up.

By the time he returned the phone to his pocket he'd already made it to the beach-hut-shed. The bunch of keys for the house included one for this door too, but the wood was old and the lock rudimentary; it would have been just as easy to open it with a screwdriver.

Inside was small, square and incredibly cluttered. The furniture consisted of a chair heaped with cushions and rugs and a workbench crowded with jars of paints, empty moulds and chemical bottles. The floor was piled with the boxes and display cases of jewellery she'd taken to the craft market. The air was heavy with the smell of solvent and the untreated interior wooden wall nearest the workbench was stained with splashes of pigment; the other walls were covered with bangles and pendants, hanging on tacks from knee height up to the ceiling.

Here there was no dust.

The electric light was concentrated on the workbench and the daylight from the windows was fading; Goodhew had a torch but used the flashlight from his phone to study the items on the walls so he could snap photos too if the need arose. Each piece of jewellery had an item encapsulated in the Lucite, just like the paperweight on Lorraine's window sill and just like Nadine's bangle too; dried flowers or small hand-painted motifs seemed the most popular. He guessed that Lorraine had made them all.

He looked more closely and found that some were visibly flawed with air bubbles locked into the acrylic. He didn't know what he expected to find but still worked his way, item by item, around the first two walls. It was only when he glanced across to the nearest window that he noticed something familiar about the way the light caught one of the bangles hanging there. He photographed it in situ then took it from its hook; he didn't need to magnify it this time to know that tiny filaments of hair were suspended in the Lucite.

Baby hair.

When Goodhew had taken the first bangle to the lab, Finn had only suggested that it might be a child's hair but now Goodhew knew in his heart that this hair was identical and that it had belonged to a baby. He held the bangle in his palm and the grey light of late afternoon fell onto it from the window, then he dropped it into an evidence bag.

When he looked up, he realised that the window was facing the flowerbed squarely. First, he tried sitting in the armchair and then he stood at the bench. Both times, the crowd of mute pansies stared back at him.

He opened the workshop door and drew a couple of deep breaths of the untainted garden air. He could feel the importance of this spot, that it had been Lorraine's sanctuary, but now he was sure that it was so much more. That the carefully maintained flowerbed that she could see from both her bedroom and her workshop was a tiny shrine. But if she had given birth to a child, and that child was now an adult as Mrs Gilligan imagined, then perhaps there would be no baby buried here.

He made two calls to Parkside Station, to Kincaide out of courtesy and Marks out of necessity. As he spoke to Kincaide he crossed the patchy lawn and took a closer look at the flowerbed. Well-kept flowers didn't make a grave; the care given to this little corner didn't make it a memorial.

But by the time he rang Marks, Goodhew was standing in the gap between the workshop and the fence, hooking out a trowel and a metre-long bamboo cane, a garden spade and a black rubber bucket.

'It's Goodhew,' he said as Marks answered his phone. 'Do you have a minute?'

'What's up?'

'If I had the idea that something might be buried, how much evidence would I need for you to authorise a search?'

'It depends what it is and where it is. You can stop being cryptic, Gary. What's this about?'

'The hair locked in that bangle, sir, I wondered if it belonged to a child who'd died.'

'Based on what?'

'Nothing in particular, I was just thinking.' He felt Marks's irritation, imagined his determined lack of expression betrayed this time by the darkening of his pupils and the tightening of his mouth. 'It really is just that and I wanted to know what it would take for me to convince you to look further.' Goodhew took the bamboo cane and slipped it into the soil. It sunk about six inches with little resistance.

'For a body,' Marks muttered more to himself than to Goodhew. 'Proof that a person existed would be a start. Beyond that? Witness statements, evidence of a crime, a confession, something that resembled a grave . . . Where is this location?'

'I don't have one,' he lied, as he tested a couple more points in the flowerbed. 'It was just supposition, in case I got that far.'

'So where are you?'

'In town.'

'It sounds very quiet there.'

'I'm down on Jesus Green. I've been staring at lists for hours and I needed a break.' He held the cane and waited. 'I'm sorry I bothered you, sir.'

'It's fine. Come up to my office as soon as you're back.'

'I will.' Goodhew wished he'd never phoned Marks when he'd known all along that the answer was going to be the same as it had been on so many other occasions; to trust his own judgement.

He sank the cane into the ground at various points; in the flowerbed the soil was less tightly packed and it slipped several inches deeper without effort. He moved the bird bath onto the lawn. It had left a circle of compressed mud, smaller than a dinner plate. He pushed the cane into the ground, and at first it seemed consistent with the rest of the bed, loose earth where the top few inches had been regularly turned and replanted. It was only as he withdrew the cane that he saw a dimple form in the soil, a subtle subsidence where a cavity underground had given way and crumbled in on itself.

He lifted the topsoil away from the footprint of the bird bath, carefully depositing each spadeful on the grass near the fence. He took the trowel, knelt on the pansies and dug down, filling the bucket with the earth he removed.

He had no idea how long it took. There might as well have been nothing else in the world, his thoughts made everything fall silent. The rhythm of the trowel scooping soil into the bucket, the slowly widening wound in the ground, became the seconds and minutes, the ticking of time.

There was no warning when the tip of the trowel first failed to penetrate more than an inch into the soil. There was no sound of it hitting anything hard, it just came to an abrupt stop. He'd dug to just over a foot below the surface and hadn't expected to find anything this soon. At first he could see nothing but dark earth. He used his bare hands to reach down to the bottom of the shallow hole and pushed his fingers into the mud. His fingertips found the obstruction just below the surface, a fold of something soft, slimy from dirt, strong enough to prevent him from pushing his fingers through it. Some kind of fabric.

His hands were now too filthy for him to stop to take photographs and he silently cursed himself as he worked to clear the soil. He freed up a corner of the cloth and scraped away a small section of the mud that clogged it. The texture became visible before the colour; waffle blanket, the kind they wrapped around new-born babies.

He stood up and allowed a few seconds of silence before he went to wash his hands. He'd done enough and now he needed to tell DI Marks the truth.

CHAPTER 27

Marks had spent a long time cultivating the ability to maintain an impenetrable expression, but there were still times when it failed him. Luckily this occasion had been thanks to a phone call from Sykes so no one had seen him scowl and shake his head as he replaced the receiver.

'Goodhew, bloody Goodhew.' He swung by Sheen's desk on the way to Kincaide's. 'Where's Gary?'

'No idea, he went hours ago. Have you tried Kincaide?'

Marks shook his head. 'What did Goodhew say before he left?'

Sheen leant back in his chair. 'Looked over some of his grand-father's papers. Talked about his family a bit. Asked about the Romsey Terrace fire.'

'That's it?'

'How much drama do you want one person to have?'

Marks smiled weakly. 'And Lorraine Martin?'

'Yep, mentioned her too. Wanted to know if she'd been involved in Robert Buckingham's conviction.'

'Nothing about a body?'

It was a rare sight but Sheen looked genuinely mystified. 'What body?'

Marks shook his head; it was too much to explain right now. 'How long are you staying?'

Sheen glanced at his watch. 'A couple more hours. Going straight to the cinema after this.'

That distracted Marks for a moment. 'Really?'

'My grandson wants to see another superhero film. I didn't know the Avengers weren't Purdey and Steed until last time I took him.'

'Hmm.' Marks took a couple of steps to the window and tapped the glass. 'Goodhew phoned a while ago, asked me how much evidence was needed to dig for a body. He said it was a hypothetical question. He told me he was taking a break down on Jesus Green but now he's ignoring his phone.'

'So you don't know where he is?'

'Hopefully back in the building or, at worst, just taking a night off, like a normal person.' Marks still hadn't decided whether he was reading too much into the conversation he'd just had with Sykes, but taking a night off was hardly Goodhew's style. 'Watch his flat and ring me if the lights go on. He's not the only one who can spy from the other side of Parker's Piece.'

By the time Marks left, Sheen was already standing, coffee in hand, watching for movement in Parkside Terrace.

Kincaide sat at his desk with most of the investigating team back in the room. Marks called him and Gully out into the corridor, 'Where's Goodhew?'

Kincaide replied. 'Following up Lorraine Martin's financials.'

'He's here?'

Gully shook her head and Kincaide shifted his weight and looked uneasy. 'No, I told him to come back. Then I told him that if he had a problem following instructions from me then he needed to speak to you.'

'And where was he then?'

'At Lorraine Martin's house.'

'Why?'

'She didn't have any money in her accounts, said he wanted to check out whether there was evidence of funds coming from elsewhere. He wanted to see her house for himself.' Kincaide's expression remained anxious. 'It didn't occur to me that he was lying.'

'I doubt he was but you should have checked with me before authorising him to search that house again.' Marks glared at Sue. 'Do you know anything different from that?'

'No, but perhaps it's something else he found when he got there.'

'Why do you say that?'

'I don't know how he makes connections, but he must have seen something because he rang me and asked me to ring Sykes, to find out whether Lorraine Martin had ever had a baby.'

'Yes, Sykes just told me and that's what rang the alarm bells. I spoke to Goodhew an hour ago and he was clearly having one of his trains of thought.' Marks turned to Kincaide, 'Michael, how much do you know about this?'

'Nothing, but Goodhew doesn't want to cooperate with any of us, does he?'

'Goodhew has the idea that there's a body buried somewhere. Possibly at Lorraine Martin's house. That hasn't come from nowhere, has it?'

Kincaide's expression faltered, 'I don't know, sir. I don't know anything about a baby and it's not my fault if he can't follow simple instructions. He should be back here.'

'Michael, get over to Selwyn Road, make sure the place is secure, then ring me. I want to know whether anything's been disturbed and whether he's still there.'

'Sir, it would be quicker to ask uniform to check. They'd be there by the time I'm out of the building.'

Marks didn't respond.

'I'll grab my keys,' Kincaide said as he ducked back into the office.

Sue had stepped away from them and now she stood quietly, one shoulder against the corridor wall. She seemed in no hurry to go.

'He's right,' he told her.

'Who?'

'Kincaide. That it would be quicker for uniform to check. Depending who.'

She turned her hand over to show her phone. 'I texted him. Asked him if he was still there.'

'Has he replied?'

'Not yet. He will though.'

'And what are you thinking?' he asked.

'That I couldn't second-guess what he's doing right now.'

154

Kincaide's jangling keys came within earshot at the same moment as her phone quietly buzzed. 'Change of plan, Michael,' Marks told him, 'You're right, uniform will tackle it. And I'm borrowing Sue.'

Gully followed him along the corridor and he could see in the periphery of his vision that she was texting one-handed as she walked. 'What did Goodhew answer?' he asked.

'It was a blank text.'

'Which means what?'

'He's got my message, couldn't reply that second. So I've asked him what's happening and told him to speak to you.'

'And?'

'He just texted back, he's going to ring you.'

Marks stopped in his tracks, 'Well, he hasn't yet.'

'I told him to give you a couple of minutes, you were talking to Kincaide.' She tapped rapidly on her phone screen, 'I've put, *now is good.*'

He held his phone ready to answer.

'I'm sure he wasn't avoiding you,' she added as it began to ring.

Marks turned his back to her as he answered, 'Goodhew?'

Marks could hear the sound of footsteps. They halted and Goodhew's voice replied clear but low. 'You need to come.' In the background Marks could hear the distant sound of voices and traffic.

'Where are you?'

'Barton Road, I decided to walk round the block. I needed to clear my head for a few minutes, to make sure that I was certain before I called you.'

'And?'

'There's a body in the garden.'

'You've uncovered it?'

'No, just come, sir, and I'll explain.'

CHAPTER 28

Once Goodhew had found the blanket in the soil he'd stopped digging. He hadn't known that there was a body but had rarely felt more certain of anything. He waited at the house while the work began, positioning himself near the kitchen window so that he was clear of the forensics team but within sight of the activity as they erected their tent and began the slow process of excavating the area.

There would be criticism for the way he'd disturbed the ground but he knew it had been necessary to ensure that the search happened at all. He included that in the report and typed it up on his phone, emailing it to himself for later. The recovery of the body had taken several hours; he'd been there for three when DS Brosner cracked open the back door. 'You were right,' she told him, 'we've found it.'

He'd returned to Parkside soon afterwards and finished his report. It was another few hours before Marks called him. 'Sykes has the body ready. Are you coming?' Then they drove to Addenbrooke's with little further conversation. Goodhew guessed that what they both wanted to discuss was what they had yet to see.

Each set of remains was different, the injuries and circumstances unique, but every autopsy Goodhew had attended had been in the same familiar surroundings. Today, the sterility of the room sat uneasily with him, the tiny form too fragile to belong in a space designed for the largest of human corpses. Both Marks and Goodhew hung back until Sykes spoke.

'If you're going to stay in here you may as well be close enough to actually see something.'

The bones had been laid out in the same order as a body lying on its back, but spaced out to leave at least a centimetre between each joint. They were heavily discoloured and, at least to Goodhew's eyes, the skeleton seemed incomplete. Sykes liked to deliver information at his own speed so neither Goodhew nor Marks asked any questions, they just waited for Sykes.

'I'm not a forensic anthropologist,' he began, 'skeletonisation isn't my field and there will need to be further tests, but let's start with what we do know. Firstly, yes, these are human remains.'

Goodhew glanced at Marks who was studying Sykes through narrowed eyes. Sykes remained unperturbed. 'People bury pets in gardens and I've had plenty of bones through here that belong to a former homeowner's dog, cat or marmoset. They've been brought in by police officers so you can congratulate your colleagues on this occasion.'

'Good to know,' Marks replied flatly.

'So what do we have here?' Sykes didn't wait for an answer. 'Thanks to the synthetic fibre content of the blanket used to wrap the body the bones have been kept together long after the disappearance of the tendons linking them.'

'About the blanket,' Goodhew began, 'what possibility is there that there will be usable DNA from it?'

Sykes scowled at the interruption. 'A waste of time. Anything body-related would have degraded and become so saturated with mud and minerals that it wouldn't stand out. But we're not here for the blanket, are we?' Sykes made a point of recapping his last sentence before continuing. 'The body has been in the ground for some considerable time, certainly in excess of a decade.'

Sykes pointed to two small and tapered pieces of bone with the gloved tip of his little finger and waited until both Marks and Goodhew drew closer still.

Closer inspection revealed that the bones had the texture of dried cuttlefish, or the dehydrated husks of driftwood.

'These are the bones of the lower arm; the radius and ulna. Notice that nothing remains of the hands and feet; the smaller, softer bones have gone the same way as the soft tissue. I certainly cannot tell you anything related to the cause of death, or the age of the baby or even its sex.'

Marks began to ask a question but Sykes immediately interrupted. 'I can, however, tell you that, from the circumference of the skull and the length of the femur, those measurements are within the normal range for an average new-born.'

Marks spoke again, 'But you don't know whether the death occurred pre- or post-birth?'

'That's correct.'

'What's your best guess?' Goodhew began.

'I don't guess.'

'Estimate,' Goodhew corrected himself, 'what would you estimate as the likely age of this baby?'

Sykes looked down at the bones and only spoke after a lengthy pause. 'Somewhere between thirty-two weeks' gestation and the baby reaching two months old.'

'And DNA?' Marks asked. 'Will you be able to recover enough for any kind of profile, or to prove parentage?'

Sykes pressed his lips in a tighter line and shook his head. 'There's almost zero possibility.' He continued to shake his head. 'In fact, I'd call it zero. With just these bones there's nothing we can do to extract DNA.'

Sykes removed his gloves and crossed to the furthest surface where his laptop stood. He began tapping at keys and as the screen accessed the hospital's records system he added, 'But I can tell you who the mother isn't.'

This time Marks and Goodhew moved closer without any prompting. Lorraine Martin's name appeared at the top of the screen and they followed Sykes's finger across to the right-hand column. It read G0/P0.

'Gravidity 0, Parity 0,' he explained.

Goodhew risked a guess. 'She'd never been pregnant?'

'Never past the first two or three months and had certainly never delivered.'

CHAPTER 29

With few exceptions Cambridge buildings rarely rise above a few storeys high and Addenbrooke's sprawls low and wide across the heart of the Cambridge Biomedical Campus on the south side of the city. It took over ten minutes of long corridors and signposted footpaths to make it back to their car. Marks began speaking as soon as they'd left Sykes. 'What made you dig, Gary?'

'Mrs Gilligan wasn't clear but she knew something had been going on at the house, dating back years. She described Lorraine's emotional state and waiting for people to come back . . .'

'How reliable is she?'

'Her daughter says she's been diagnosed with dementia, but the things she said fitted with the picture we have of Lorraine – particularly the emotional outbursts.'

'It's a huge leap.'

Goodhew smiled to himself. The fact was he'd wanted to believe her and he'd tilted what she'd said as a result. Many times he knew it worked the opposite way when the same claims would have been dismissed and, in most cases, that would have been the accurate call. 'I was lucky,' he said, 'her dementia diagnosis is pretty recent and she'd been telling these stories for the past twenty. And you've been to Lorraine Martin's house?'

'I have.'

'Nothing's had more than minimal attention in that time. The only part not neglected was that flowerbed and it was in plain sight of her bedroom and her workshop.'

Marks shot a swift glance in Goodhew's direction. 'Not a case of bury it and try to forget about it?'

'No, it was more personal than that. That's why I thought the baby might be hers. I found another bangle too, it was flawed and kept with other damaged pieces, like a collection of seconds. When I stood where that bangle was hanging I was facing the flowerbed again; I think the baby meant a great deal to Lorraine.'

Marks slowed. 'But why would anyone bury a baby in that way if they cared about it?'

'A concealed pregnancy perhaps. A teenager?'

'But who? And if it wasn't her baby why would Lorraine hide it then treat its grave with so much respect? Why would she choose to look out on it every day unless she was mourning?'

'When Kincaide and Knight interviewed Moira, what did she say about her sister's frame of mind?'

'Little, but that was before all of this. The first thing I'm going to do is visit her again.' He held out his set of car keys for Goodhew. 'You can come if you drive.'

Goodhew took the keys, then neither of them spoke until they were seated in the vehicle.

'Why don't you own a car, Gary?'

'Why do people like that question, sir?' Goodhew slipped it into gear and headed for the exit, 'I drive at work. Apart from that I walk most places and sometimes I use a taxi. It's a valid choice.'

'Don't you feel limited?'

'More like unencumbered.'

'You know people make assessments of others by looking at their car.'

'And that's a reason to own one?'

'Not at all. I was just making an observation; it's just another example of why you're difficult to weigh up.'

Goodhew pulled out onto Long Road and headed towards the city centre. 'Can I ask where we're headed?'

'As in direction or with the conversation?'

'With the conversation, sir.'

'Feels like a cul-de-sac.'

'OK, here's the truth. I've never felt the desire either to buy one or to own one, but that choice seems so alien to so many people that virtually everyone in the department has asked whether I had a bad experience, or can't afford one or whether it's moral or ethical reasons.'

'But it's not?'

'It's not. I just don't have the need for one.'

The traffic slowed and Marks studied the pedestrians who were now able to keep pace with the car. 'I think you feel the need to go your own way, Gary. You don't want to do anything just because it's expected.'

'OK . . . why the analysis?'

'I'd like this closed before I leave. Selfish or not, it would make it feel as though I'd finished at the right moment.'

Goodhew didn't reply; he couldn't see the connection between car ownership and Marks's retirement.

Marks stared at the road ahead although Goodhew had no doubt that he was firmly in his boss's peripheral vision. 'I'm naming the baby Frankie by the way.'

'Why?'

'It's too impersonal otherwise. He or she isn't just a pile of bones.' He let his words settle for a few seconds before he spoke again. 'You found Frankie's body when I told you not to dig.' There was an edge to his voice. 'I trust your judgement, Gary, but if I tell you that I expect you to follow your nose on this one, will you still do it?'

'Despite my personal connection to the case?'

'Despite everything.'

'I'll give it my best.' Goodhew took his eyes from the road long enough to check whether Marks's expression gave any clue. It didn't. 'Is there something you need to tell me?'

'I took another look at Nadine's file. I convinced myself I'd seen that bangle before.'

'And?'

'There it was, in the photos of her flat and in the inventory.'

'The same one?'

'It was in her personal effects, not in the evidence. Her next of kin would have had responsibility for disposal, and the records show that several months after her death all but her family photos were donated to charity. I would like to assume for a moment that it is the same bangle.'

'We can hardly ask Lorraine.'

'Quite.' Marks twisted in his seat and finally looked directly at Goodhew. 'I believe that your grandfather stole it from Nadine's flat sometime between her murder and the disposal of her personal effects.'

'But there's no proof?'

'None, but consider the odds.'

Goodhew already had and Marks was right; Lorraine had admitted that the bangle had been Nadine's and his grandfather had had the opportunity to take it; the probability that Joe had taken it was pretty high. 'How does it help?'

'You tell me. Could he have known of its significance or was it just as the souvenir that it appealed to him most?'

Goodhew didn't know. He pulled up to the kerb outside Moira Trent's house, locked up and was with Marks at her doorstep but still hadn't replied. Marks didn't push for an answer, perhaps he didn't expect one, so they both waited silently at the front door. Goodhew's phone vibrated and he stole a quick glance at the screen, killed the call, rapidly texted Sue in reply and was done by the time Moira appeared.

She wore camel trousers and a cream top, her hair was a muted blonde shot through with streaks of grey. The greyness had seeped into her complexion too. These weren't the details Goodhew usually noticed but the effect was like finding a 1970s colour photo where everything had faded until it was a shade of beige. The interior of the house echoed the same tones. She led them through to her kitchen and gestured for them to sit at the large farmhouse table.

'Thank you for coming,' she said even though their visit had come without warning. She didn't try to smile but pressed her lips tightly shut and waited with her hands resting on the back of the chair opposite Marks.

'Please take a seat, Miss Trent.' Marks waited for her to settle then added, 'You have a different surname to your sister?'

162

'There's the difference between us inspector; I hated our father and used our mother's maiden name after they divorced. Lorraine hated him but continued to use his name to keep the peace. She was more forgiving.' Moira turned her right hand palm up on the table, 'At school she was the one who volunteered her time, and I . . .' she turned her left hand, 'I didn't. Which also explains why I became an accountant and she lived as she did.' She looked across at each of them in turn. 'We were very different but a bond existed nonetheless.' She leant back in her chair. 'I know there's been activity at Lorraine's house.'

'There's been a development,' Marks said. 'A discovery at your sister's home.'

Moira's shoulders stiffened and her jaw set, and Goodhew wondered whether she would be listening fully; the stillness that descended on her seemed forced and he pondered whether her only thought was 'don't react, don't react'.

'A team of officers have recovered the remains of a baby from the rear of your sister's property.' Now it was Marks who became still, watching her, watching him.

She tried hard to show nothing but couldn't help the colour slipping further from her face, or the seasick grey that replaced it. 'She never told me about a baby,' she whispered. She tipped her head back as though she wanted to stare at the ceiling but then closed her eyes. Her lower teeth bit her top lip and she took several heavy, slow breaths. It was a while before she spoke.

'Was it buried near the bird bath?'

'It was.'

'She always kept it so pretty. But I never would have guessed.' She raised herself and then leant forward again, this time resting her elbows on the table and facing Marks squarely. 'I don't know what you're thinking, but Lorraine would never harm a child.'

'We know it wasn't Lorraine's baby.'

'How?'

'Pathology. They can tell when a woman has delivered a child.'

'She wouldn't harm *anyone's* child.' She shook her head. 'Lorraine suffered depression, she lost her job because of it.'

'Which job was this?' Marks asked even though he and Goodhew both knew the answer.

'She was a nurse. At Addenbrooke's.'

'Until when?'

'Maybe 1990, I don't remember exactly.'

The facts matched what they already knew but Goodhew watched Moira more carefully now as he waited for his moment.

'So from 1990 until she began making jewellery, she did what exactly?'

'She had severance pay; it was the stress of the job that had caused her problems. That and the lodgers. I helped her when I could.'

'And you made up her accounts?'

'Yes.'

'So you do have records?'

'Not now. They'd be too old.'

'It will be necessary to search your paperwork.'

'I don't think so.'

'We'll be able to request a search warrant.'

She gave a small, hard smile. 'I have nothing to hide.'

Goodhew leant forward then and they both looked across at him. 'Do you remember any of Lorraine's lodgers, Miss Trent?'

'Vaguely, I suppose. Some Christian names perhaps.'

'Like Nadine?' Marks stayed expressionless. Moira failed.

'What about her?'

'I've just received a message to say that Nadine Kendall lodged with your sister for four months in 1990. Why wouldn't you be forthcoming with that information?'

'I'd forgotten.'

'Really? This is the same Nadine whose bangle is in our labs at the moment, being analysed to see if it contains baby hair. Ring a bell?'

'Of course I knew Nadine. But not the bangle.'

'Are you sure? Because it was made by your sister.'

Moira shook her head. 'I don't know what my sister made.'

'But you know what she used to do,' Goodhew said.

This time her puzzlement looked genuine. So did Marks's.

'What kind of nurse was she?' Goodhew pushed.

164

And the confusion vanished. Moira's eyes snapped shut then reopened slowly, filled with only part of the light they held before. 'She was a midwife,' she told them quietly.

'So,' Marks replied, 'what can you tell us about the baby?'

She stared into her hands.

'Was it Nadine's baby?'

Again she shook her head. 'I don't know. I know Nadine was pregnant and she moved away. As far as I know she had the baby adopted because when she came back the following year it was just her. I don't know anything else.'

CHAPTER 30

Amy and Alex's paths had crossed every day since their first encounter. He'd found reasons to visit the site office: to check costings, to borrow equipment, to look for missing paperwork. Today was no different and Amy glanced up from her computer to see Alex crossing the yard again.

She continued working until he opened the door. 'We don't see you for weeks, now you're here three days in a row. Are you harassing me?'

'You found me out,' he said flatly. He'd crossed the room and dumped a pile of building plans onto Stan's desk. 'He's out on site, right?'

Amy nodded. 'He's back at one.'

'I'll clear off at lunchtime. I need to get through this and I can concentrate here.' He'd unpacked his laptop and set it up to one side of the desk before rolling out the first of the plans, tacking it to the desk with a short strip of masking tape at each corner and settling down to work the old-fashioned way with a scale rule, pencil and notepad. Amy hadn't meant to watch him but when he glanced towards her it had been too late to look away. 'See, I'm not here to stalk you.'

'That wasn't really my suspicion.'

He grinned impishly. 'Hard work is good for me; working hard in front of my parents feels wrong.'

She tilted her head to one side and studied him for a moment. 'You know, neither of those comments suit you.'

'Why?'

'You have that whole tattooed biker thing going on. You should be a mechanic or a bouncer or . . .' She'd tried to think of a third example.

'A guitarist in a heavy metal band?'

'Yes, why not?'

'Because I'm studying to be an architect, you know, just in case Bruce Dickinson needs a house in Cambridge.'

She guessed it was a joke so she smiled then tapped Dickinson's name into Google. A few minutes later she emailed him across the office, 'I don't know a single Iron Maiden track.'

He emailed back, 'Freak.'

They didn't speak for the rest of the morning but a flurry of short emails pinged back and forth across the office. As he'd packed away his paperwork a final email arrived in Amy's inbox. 'Sorry we got off on the wrong foot.'

She replied, 'Me too.'

Sometimes there would be a lull in the afternoons; no drop in work but a period when they all worked silently and the atmosphere in the room came close to harmony. Today, Amy's keyboard made the only sound as she rattled through each successive email. Stan studied a floor plan, transferring measurements and notes onto a separate sheet of paper. A little later he glanced up and caught Amy watching him. 'Is there a problem?'

'I was wondering how well you knew her?'

'Who?'

Stan frowned as he'd asked but she sensed less impatience than usual. 'Lorraine Martin.'

He placed his pen down then spread his broad hands flat on the desktop. 'Well enough, I suppose. She was a face from the past. Like your father. Like Theo. And Nadine.' He concentrated on his hands, perhaps until he was sure that he had them under control. 'I don't know why they've let you stay.'

'Neither do I, but you know them better than I do. It was obvious that Carolyn wasn't happy, but Neil insisted. I'll carry on at least until Moira's back.'

'I know why Neil gave you the job. I've known all along. He likes

167

to keep an eye on things. He told me to watch you and let him know what I saw.'

Stan's heavy features showed no hint of warmth. This was probably the longest conversation they'd had and Amy already knew she preferred the silences. Despite that she still smiled at the arrival of a sudden thought. 'And now he's told you to talk to me? Or was it Carolyn?'

'I tell Neil. Neil tells Carolyn. That's the way it works.'

'But then, there was nothing to tell until Lorraine died. Was there?'

Amy's keyboard fell silent, replaced by the sound of her pulse throbbing in her ears. She needed to believe that she'd done nothing that would have led to Lorraine's death.

'Why would there be a connection, Stan?' She heard a tremor of fear in her voice and his small, tight reply told her that he'd caught it too.

Then he moved from his desk and sat on the edge of hers. 'What did you do?' he breathed.

Amy shook her head. 'Nothing – I'd never spoken to her, never heard her name even.'

'And your father? Did he contact her for any reason?'

'I don't talk to him about work.'

'Bollocks.' He kept his voice low but intense. 'He's not stupid, he'll be watching everything you're doing.'

'He's not well. He's not like he was before his heart attack.' Stan waited and, when the silence became too much, Amy continued, '*I'm* not stupid. I have wondered about the timings, about Lorraine's death coming just after I started here, but I don't have any information.'

'Lorraine died right here.'

'I know.'

'Had you planned to meet her here?'

'Of course not.'

Had Lorraine known that Amy sometimes worked late? Sometimes started early? These were questions that Goodhew had asked. She looked at Stan levelly. 'You and my dad were friends. Haven't you ever considered he might be innocent?'

Stan shook his head. 'I was his mate. He wasn't mine and it took me a long while to see him for what he was.'

168

'He always mentioned you, I remember that from overhearing my parents talk. And I know you gave evidence against him at the trial but when I visited him there was never any resentment.'

'And now I pity you.' He rose to his feet, smoothing down the thighs of his overalls with trembling hands. His mouth trembled too, the words percolating close to his lips, anger leaving him torn between an outburst and a physical reaction. He stepped back, his hands dropping to his sides and forming fists, but he was still close enough to over-shadow Amy. The Portakabin floor creaked under his bulk. 'I pity your blind loyalty.'

Amy was out of her chair and face to face with his before she'd had time to think. 'Tell me why you turned against him then,' she shouted at him. He stepped back again and she imagined him leaving before he'd told her anything. She moved forward until she could feel the heat from his face. 'What did my dad do to you?'

'You don't want to know.'

'Do I look like someone with their head in the sand? I'm here until Moira gets back and I can keep this going day after day if that's what it takes.'

'Don't be ridiculous.'

'Am I? I've had weeks of your bad temper. I'm not scared by it.'

Amy could see plenty of signs of Stan's volatility; it bubbled close to the surface, but she could also see how determined he was to keep it in check. 'I think your friendship ended before the fire, otherwise you would have stood by him. In your mind, he let you down.'

'Not just me.'

'Who then?'

Stan ran his tongue slowly across his teeth before he spoke. 'You heard my name in your house because I was his excuse, his alibi for every time he cheated on your mother. "A lad's night with Stan" and I'd see your mum and she'd say, "Stop dragging him out so often, Stan." And I'd apologise and hope she wouldn't ask any questions about where we'd been or what we'd eaten or even which day I'd supposedly been out with him. Is this really what you want to hear?'

'Is it the truth?' she asked.

He bristled at once. 'I'm not fucking around here.'

'I'm sorry, please go on.'

'He used me to ease things over with your mum, and once in a while we'd have a drink together and he'd act like my fucking mate. I forgot the pecking order for a bit – thought we were equals. Not for long, though. He took money from the business, cheated the firm, and cheated his wife. Think about it – he cheated you. He didn't ever have a conscience.'

'He didn't start the fire,' she responded stubbornly.

'Why not? It could have answered all his problems.'

'Like what? Debt?'

'Debt and more. Some of us think it was money. Some of us don't.'

'Us? Like who?'

'Those who were there. Sitting in court day after day.'

'He wouldn't have hurt people – not intentionally.'

'I went to Romsey Terrace the morning after the fire. Neil asked me to go. He stayed home with Carolyn. Alex was still a baby. I didn't know what Neil thought I'd be able to do. The chief fire officer's report explained about the structural damage, about the ongoing risk, likely causes, et cetera. All I remember is the blackened windows and thinking about Nadine and Theo's last minutes.'

Amy kept very still, careful not to do anything that might interrupt him.

'I remember just one word he said. Accelerant. Then I knew it had been deliberate and the only feeling I remember is wanting to kill whichever bastard had done it.'

Stan leant back against the wall. 'In my mind, Theo was just a kid, I'd seen him grow up. And Nadine . . .' His gaze settled beyond Amy and for one unguarded moment she could see his pain. He looked back at her and returned to his usual opaqueness. 'How did you think I felt when I found out it was your father?'

'Devastated if that's what you believed.'

Stan snorted in disgust. 'Have you ever been to a trial?'

'No.'

'Have you even visited a court room?'

She shook her head.

'When you start out you think that all you need to do is get to the end and hear the right verdict. Either Carolyn or Neil attended every day. Theo's mother too until it became too much for her. You end up hearing everything, you relive the final hours over and over. Experts tell you how slowly they died, how they attempted to escape, the cloth they'd held to their mouths, the skin burnt onto the door handle, the two of them huddled and melted. The jury were handed photos we didn't see but we watched their faces. And, throughout, your father sat there. Expressionless. Didn't even have the balls to look any of us in the eye, and none of it shocked him. Did your mum tell you all of that?'

Amy shook her head. 'No,' she replied, 'she didn't.'

CHAPTER 31

Goodhew returned to Parkside, avoiding Kincaide long enough to make it up to the second floor and to the boxes of information on his grandfather's case. This time nothing diverted him and Sheen kept himself deliberately busy while Goodhew made notes and took photographs. When Goodhew stayed late, though, so did Sheen.

'There's no need,' Goodhew told him.

'Someone has to supervise you. For your own good, if nothing else.'

'If there's a complaint because I've been looking through these documents then I don't think you'll be able to stop the mud sticking.'

'Probably not, but I'm still staying. OK?'

'OK.' Goodhew continued to work, aware that Sheen had moved his chair out from behind his desk and was watching him from just a few feet away. He didn't speak again until Goodhew was done and putting the last of the pages back into the final box.

'What happens now?'

'I read and hope I find something.'

'Then cross-reference, check dates, track lines of enquiry?'

'As far as I can.'

'Just like the investigation then, but with fewer resources?'

'You make it sound pointless.'

'Doing what everyone else can is pointless.' Sheen passed Goodhew a flash drive. 'It's the Romsey Terrace case and it contains everything

I could copy in one afternoon. Now you need to step back and do what you do best.'

'Have you been speaking to Marks?'

Sheen shrugged, 'I often do.'

The longest wall of the former study of Goodhew's grandfather was newly painted in a shade that the can described as Sand Dune. The colour chart had promised *classic* and *serene*. It had lied. As it had dried, it reminded Goodhew increasingly of congealed porridge. The good news was that the wall deserved to be defaced; Goodhew found a fat black marker pen and drew three large circles in the formation of an inverted equilateral triangle.

The top left circle belonged to his grandfather's case, the top right to the Romsey Terrace fire and the lower circle belonged to Lorraine Martin's murder. He filled each with names, dates and key facts; it was a slow process and at 1 a.m. he went upstairs to his flat, returning with a pot of coffee, milk, sugar and a mug. He left it to cool and an hour later drank it cold while he surveyed his work. He continued then, underlining some details in coloured marker, drawing lines to inter-connect others. By 5 a.m. he was done and in the centre of the wall, in the gap between the three circles, he'd written two names.

He phoned his grandmother then. 'Is it too early?'

She sounded fully awake. 'When is it ever?'

'I'm making omelettes.'

'After staying up all night breaking eggs, I suppose? Give me twenty minutes.'

She arrived in fifteen. Her hair and makeup appeared freshly styled, her pencil skirt and cotton blouse looked newly pressed and she wore an expression which said she'd be missing nothing.

'When do you sleep?' he asked her.

'When the mood takes me. Besides, you know I loathe routine.' She immediately redirected her focus to the wall. 'You've been busy.'

'Joe's case is up there,' he said quickly.

She stood in front of the wall for several minutes without comment. He hadn't thought anything of working in here; it was where he pre-ferred to be. But now he was acutely aware that this was the room

173

that had once been the crime scene, the place his grandmother had held her dying husband. He crossed to the window with the words of the original emergency call reverberating in his head.

The police station looked quiet, the swimming pool unlit.

There was no one on Parker's Piece but he could still picture Sue walking away.

This room connected him to everyone and everything that mattered. He turned back in time to see Ellie reach out to touch the place where Joe's name was written before settling herself on the sofa.

'Well, I didn't like that dismal beige anyway.'

'Sand,' he corrected, 'according to the tin.'

'Proof that you shouldn't believe all you read then.' She pointed at the wall. 'Three cases, three circles, that much I understand, but why the two names in the middle?'

'Nadine Kendall is the common denominator, a victim of the fire, ex-housemate of Lorraine Martin and the owner of the bangle that Joe kept. She is connected in some way to every strand of these separate investigations.'

'Plenty to follow up?'

'Yes, but for Marks, not for me. Lorraine Martin's murder is the primary investigation; the Romsey Terrace fire is a closed case and he'll follow up anything on Joe's case but every resource is stretched.' Goodhew pointed towards the second name. 'I need to find Melanie Franks. As far as the investigation goes, she's nothing more than a name on a sheet of paper. I've looked for her through the usual channels. There's nothing.'

Ellie spread her hands on her lap. 'I've looked for her more than once. I can't find any record of her birth, her university admission or anyone of that name living in Cambridge at that time.'

'I thought you wanted her left alone?'

'I do . . .' She pursed her lips for a moment. 'I thought she might have some answers, but, when I couldn't locate her, I decided to come to terms with that. It seemed safer.'

Goodhew knew that there were personality traits that he'd inherited from his grandfather but there was plenty that had come from his grandmother too; like puzzle solving, doggedness and too much curiosity. 'That doesn't make sense. I could just about understand why you never looked for her but, once you'd made the decision to start, you wouldn't have just given up. And there's that thing you're doing with your hands.'

Her hands had remained palms down, one on each thigh. In symmetry. 'What thing?

'When we play backgammon and you do that, I know there's a play you want me to miss.'

She moved, locking her neat fingers together and resting them in her lap. 'And now I know that I'm so readable, I shan't do it again.'

'So?'

Goodhew knew his grandmother well enough to decipher most of her expressions; right now her thoughts had slipped back into the past and he could see her struggling to find the right place to start. He waited.

'Your parents were totally mismatched from the start,' she began. 'I could see why your dad fell for her, though. She was pretty and exciting and clever and all those other clichés of teenage attraction but, more than that, she had this personality that people just wanted to be around. And you know your dad . . .'

She left the sentence to die. Goodhew could have answered that he didn't know his dad much at all, but that was the point. His father's relationships seemed to be mostly with formulae and computer programs; he stayed absorbed in his work to the exclusion of everything else that Goodhew could remember, apart from the instances when he sat patiently with his son to help him with his maths homework. That habit had continued long after Goodhew had begun to excel at the subject but ended when he and his sister had been sent to boarding school. To Goodhew, his father was clever but remote, neither unkind nor warm, a man with solitary habits and an over-productive mind.

'Your dad looked up from his work long enough to be captivated. I think it was the first time he'd ever attracted that kind of attention.'

Goodhew and his sister Debbie had heard the story of how their parents had met but this time it had a totally different slant.

'They seemed to meet, get engaged and then marry very quickly.

175

A wedding reception can be full of truths; drinks flow and people's guard comes down. Her father asked me whether we would be buying them their first home – after all, their daughter had married our only child. I don't know how your mum had found out about our wealth, but here we are, over thirty-five years later, and I remain convinced that she chased him for his money.'

Goodhew didn't argue. His mother had gone on a spending frenzy as soon as his parents had inherited after his grandfather's death. His parents' divorce had come at the end of the money and now, according to his sister, her new husband was a wealthy property developer. Goodhew hadn't been to visit her in Australia. 'How does this connect with Melanie Franks?' he asked.

She waved her hand in a just-wait gesture. 'We didn't buy them a house and your parents lived on what your dad earned. He was soon absorbed in his work again and I can see that her life was lonely at times. She found a job when Debbie was a few months old. We looked after you both so it was easy for me to spot the changes in her; late nights, new clothes, different body language. Suddenly she seemed content with the way your dad seemed so detached.'

'She was having an affair?'

'Not then perhaps, but over the next few years there were several.'

'How do you know?' he asked sharply.

Ellie raised her eyebrows. 'I know how to follow people, Gary.'

'But your own daughter-in-law?'

There was a glint of amusement in her eyes. 'Why should family miss out on the perks of the business? She changed jobs multiple times and the last of those was when she started work at Frampton's.'

'Why couldn't I have a normal grandmother?'

She ignored the question. 'You want the truth? Well, this is it. Melanie contacted us via your mother. They worked together and your mum wanted to help her. After the fire it was your mother who began pushing me for information; it seemed as though she'd had a change of heart about Melanie disappearing and was determined to locate her.'

'But why?'

'All she said was that she wanted to make sure that Melanie knew about Nadine's death, but that never made sense. Your mum and

Melanie both understood that Melanie's disappearance meant cutting all ties. She had another reason for wanting to find her.'

'One that wasn't in Melanie's best interests?'

'I'm not accusing your mother of anything but I think it is fair to assume that she knew more than she let on.' She paused and her determined tone softened. 'But you and Debbie had just lost your grandfather, you'd been packed off to that damn school and your parents were divorcing; I was never going to put you both through more without proof.'

CHAPTER 32

Goodhew left his grandmother and went up one flight to his flat. He stood at his window, watching Parker's Piece as he waited for the call to connect. Sydney was nine hours ahead but he hadn't considered the time difference when he'd picked up the phone and felt slightly disappointed as he realised there was nothing inconvenient about his timing.

He wasn't sure how long it had been since he'd spoken directly to his mother, or to either of his parents for that matter, but he immediately noticed that the Australian edge to her accent had developed since the last time.

'So,' she spoke before he'd had a chance to say more than hello, 'are you finally planning to visit? Your sister would love to see you.'

'And I'd love to see her, but my call's work-related.'

'I see.' She wouldn't have liked that reply and he had a mental image of her standing with the phone to her ear, jutting her chin in impatience and flicking the hair back over her shoulder with a shake of her head. 'Go on.'

'Cambridgeshire Police have tried to contact you.'

'I thought I'd hang on until *you* made the effort.' She said it as if there was a question mark at the end of the sentence. It was a habit she had and when he'd been younger he'd tried to guess at the answer and over-explain himself.

Now he kept it short. 'It's partly about Grandad . . . about Joe.'

'I wondered when this would rear its head again. You've been

178

speaking to Ellie, I suppose? I moved to the other side of the world to escape the scrutiny of that woman.'

Goodhew pressed his hand against the cold window pane and caught the moment when the street lamps on Parker's Piece were extinguished for the day; one of the four bulbs on the Reality Checkpoint was broken and the other three going out restored its symmetry. He took a breath. 'It's about Melanie Franks, I need to find her,' he continued, 'and I know you knew her.'

'I wouldn't know where she lives, would I?'

'Please, tell me what you do know. How you met her. Why you helped her. Why you tried to find her after she'd gone.'

'I worked with Nadine Kendall and I met Melanie through her. Nadine died and it's all too long ago, it won't affect anything.'

'You're wrong—'

'Gary, I'm not going there,' she cut in before he could add more. 'I know you loved your grandad but you were eleven when he died. Hanging onto it for over twenty years isn't doing you any favours.'

Did she really believe that there was a time limit on grief? On finding answers? Goodhew pressed the glass more firmly. 'You knew Moira Trent.'

'What's that got to do with anything?'

'And her sister.'

'Lorraine? Of course.'

'Lorraine was murdered just hours after I spoke to her about Grandad and Nadine.'

Stillness echoed down the phone line. 'Oh, I see.' She added, 'What happened?'

He explained, filling her in on the same details that had appeared in the local papers, before adding the main detail that hadn't: 'Then we recovered the body of a baby from her garden.' He paused until he'd heard her gasp. 'So your help is important.'

'It's not Melanie's baby.'

'Or Nadine's?'

'No.' Her voice wavered. 'At least, I don't think so. Nadine left Buckingham and Frampton's before she had the baby. I never saw it and as far as I knew she gave it up for adoption.'

'But Melanie kept hers?'

'She left the area when she was pregnant.'

'And they both lived with Lorraine? Or just Nadine?'

'Don't you know that?'

'We have records of Nadine using the address, but nothing whatsoever about Melanie.'

'Yes, they both lodged with Lorraine but I don't see why any of this is necessary, Gary.'

'You can't see why we need to get answers? To identify that child and who killed Lorraine?'

She was pacing now. He could hear the clicking of her heels on a tiled floor. Every time she spoke she slowed or stopped, and then moved on again whenever it was his turn.

'Mum? You liked Melanie and that's why you helped her. If she's in danger now we need to find her as quickly as possible.'

'I don't believe she was ever in danger. I bought into a whole sob story about her fearing for her life, about being desperate to start again with her baby. But there are always two sides.'

'Explain what you mean.'

'Melanie was pregnant, not prepared to have an abortion but being threatened by her ex. Well, that's what she told me and, yes, I put her in touch with Joe and he did what he did. Hang on.' The phone was silent for a few seconds, then he heard her cross the room and the sound of her settling into a chair. When she spoke again her tone had become less abrasive. 'To my mind Melanie was quite dull; she never seemed to like much beyond cookery and museums. I met her because I worked with Nadine and, later, Melanie worked in the office too. She wasn't the sort of person I would have chosen as a friend but work pushed us together and I was fond of them both; I suppose I had the big sister role.'

Goodhew's expression stiffened; at least she hadn't said 'I had the mother role'.

'She latched onto me. She was in debt, perhaps she thought I had money.'

'What kind of debt?'

'She was naive. She just didn't know how to manage and her

spending was out of control. I don't think her parents knew any of it. She said she couldn't ask them for help anyway and if she'd told them she was pregnant it would have been worse.'

'What made you change your mind about her?'

'Do you know Neil Frampton?'

'The man you had an affair with?'

'Gary, it wasn't like that.'

'Really?'

'Neil and I were in a similar position: your father was obsessed with work, Neil's wife with their new baby. We spent hours working together and grew close over the following months. We ignored reality for a while; it was more than friendship but we never slept together. It's the kind of thing that happens when people are lonely.'

'Uh-huh.'

'Do you want to know or not?'

The honest answer was that no, of course he didn't. 'Sorry, go on,' he replied.

'We'd been close like that for well over a year and when that house burnt down and his son died I became the one he leant on. He had problems connecting with Carolyn and their baby. He said he found it too painful to be around Alex. That's when we reached our closest; he needed someone and back then I needed to be needed.'

Goodhew was tempted to stick his fingers in his ears and drone la-la-la until it was over.

She kept talking, 'And that's when he told me that Melanie's baby was Theo's. Theo would never have threatened Melanie but Neil was desperate to find her and bring her baby back into the family.'

Goodhew had seen photos of Theo. He had been strongly built with an intense expression, not a prime candidate for timidity. 'You don't know that, people under duress . . .'

'No. Theo was never wired like that. He was a thinker, he was always measured. And always very kind and giving whether it was deserved or not.'

'On the face of it . . .'

'Gary, if Theo threatened anyone then there are no peaceful people in the world.'

Goodhew didn't think he was naturally cynical but he was finding it hard to imagine anyone who wouldn't issue a threat or two in the right circumstances. He didn't push it, though. 'So you think Melanie had been lying?'

'I don't know the truth but by then I was wishing that I'd never stuck my neck out for her. Neil was distraught when he found out that Theo might have had a child and I knew that Melanie had been twisting the story.'

'How distraught? Enough to attack Joe?'

'Distraught at the loss of Theo. He thought the world of him and I don't know how he carried on.'

'I guess he took a lot of comforting?' Goodhew dropped the sarcasm and carried on before she had a chance to respond. 'Were you surprised at Robert Buckingham's arrest?'

She didn't reply and he was about to repeat the question when she spoke. 'Things shifted after that and by the time of the trial Neil and I had drifted apart again. It was just circumstance.' She changed subject and carried on talking with no pause and it took him a moment to focus on what she was saying. 'I wish we'd been closer, Gary.'

'You and who?'

'Us. I sent you to that school because I thought it was the right thing to do – to give you and Debbie stability and a better education.'

And to push two grieving children out of sight of the acrimony of divorce? 'Do you know anything about Joe's death?'

'Of course not.'

'There's a connection between Joe and Melanie and Lorraine, and if there's anything you know, however insignificant it seems, I need to hear it.'

'Only that I didn't give you the time you needed to get over it,' she told him. 'I made mistakes with you and Debbie, but she and I have worked through it. You could visit, Gary, and the three of us could spend time together. It might fix things.'

He closed his eyes and didn't reply.

'And just so you know, I was the one that broke it off.'

He didn't know whether she meant with his father or with Neil Frampton.

'With Neil,' she added as though she'd read his thoughts. 'I stopped it before it went any further. I don't think I did as much damage as you think I did.'

'OK, Mum,' he muttered, 'but that really doesn't matter now. I appreciate your help and I'll call you again if there's anything else.'

CHAPTER 33

They returned to the storage unit in Hope Street Yard. His idea was simple: if the bangle was a souvenir taken from Nadine's flat then Joe would have collected another item the year before when he'd helped Melanie. Goodhew had only learnt fragments of information from speaking to his mother but his disappointment was replaced by a buzz of expectation as he waited for the door to open. He had the illogical thought that everything might have been removed since their last visit, but of course nothing had changed.

A halogen tube was built into the ceiling and drenched the space in bright blue-white light, but the items that lay in the shadows and cupboards were in almost total darkness. Goodhew used the flashlight on his phone, and his grandmother drew a slim chrome-cased torch from her bag. 'A torch won't time out,' she told him. 'How do you want to do this?'

'Was there any logic to the items he kept?'

'They needed to remind him of the person and the case. His idea was that he'd be able to pick up any one of these mementoes and the whole story would come back to him.'

'He could have just written it down.'

The torchlight caught her face and he saw her grin. 'And where's the challenge in that? Besides, rereading the stories isn't the same as retelling them. I'm sure they improved over time.'

Goodhew opened the nearest drawer. All the items it contained were physically small, the size of a matchbox at most. And there were five of those, two were empty, and the other three held individual items of jewellery; a single earring, a signet ring, a tie clip.

She shook her head, 'It's none of those; I recognise them all.'

Goodhew recalled a few but he didn't see how he would be able to locate anything as efficiently as his grandmother could. She seemed to read his mind.

'Remember, Melanie was a history student. Pregnant. Not local. She can't have had connections to Wales or the West Country or Joe wouldn't have relocated her in that direction.'

'Probably not from anywhere south of here or Joe would have picked the north.'

'Exactly.'

Goodhew realised that he was missing the answer to an obvious question.

'You would have met her, wouldn't you?'

This time she nodded. 'Briefly. She wasn't forthcoming with information. I could see she was scared, or making a good job of pretending to be . . .'

'That's when you and Joe disagreed about helping her?'

'People who are desperate can be dangerous. I didn't doubt that she'd had problems but she wouldn't tell us anything of substance and that wasn't good enough for me.'

She'd opened the next drawer and turned her attention to its contents.

'Her story kept changing. She said the baby was a result of a one-night stand, then that the father had threatened her, that he'd wanted to take the baby but then that she didn't know anything about him. I didn't like the situation but for Joe it was enough that she needed our help.'

'My mother said that Theo could have been the father. Did his name come up?'

'No, never.'

'Can you describe Melanie?'

'After this long it's more of an impression. She was in her late teens, shorter than me, about five-five. Apart from being pregnant she was skinny. Perhaps wiry would describe her better.'

185

'So not frail?'

'Not at all, more like one of those outdoorsy types. But I don't see how that helps you; she'd be in her early forties now and it would be a long shot to find anyone who hasn't changed shape in that time.'

'It's not that kind of picture I'm after. Which kid would she have been in the class?'

His grandmother then saw where he was heading. She closed her eyes as she considered her answer. 'In my form she would have been Polly Manby. Polly wore shorts and hiking boots in the summer, she cycled everywhere. I suppose we all cycled or walked but only until we had boyfriends with cars. She embraced it. She took her studies seriously too but she wasn't brilliant, just hard-working.'

Ellie closed the drawer and then paused with her fingers hooked through the handle of the next one. She described Melanie in more detail, her reminiscences of one girl triggering a clearer picture of the other. As she finished she gave a short laugh. 'Funnily enough, it worked out differently for Polly than I would have imagined. Last I heard she'd been caught stealing from her employer.'

'Why?'

'No idea. A shortcut perhaps or maybe she just had enough of being responsible. It happens. She studied history too.'

Her description of Polly had illuminated Melanie Franks, perhaps not accurately, but enough for him to begin searching.

It was a little while later when Goodhew placed three items on the desktop.

'Have you found anything?' he asked.

'There nothing I can't identify,' she replied.

'Here's my shortlist.'

She redirected her torch in his direction then killed it when she realised that the items were lying where the overhead light was more than adequate.

He'd picked a smooth stone, an ornament of a bridge and a segment of a black plastic disc. She picked up the pebble first. It was large enough to fill her palm. She wrapped her fingers around it and passed it back to him.

'This was picked up from Rhossili Bay. I was with him. And this

. . .' She held up the plastic, which at first glance might have been a broken piece of an LP but when it caught the light its surface was far more glossy and shone with the full spectrum of colours.

'It's a video disc. We salvaged it from a burgled flat in Wiltshire. Both cases involved young women, though, so you're getting something right.'

Finally, she held the ornament closer to the light. It was a little over an inch high, painted in grey wash and thinly glazed. 'A three-way bridge? I don't believe I've ever seen this before, but the bridge itself I do recognise.'

She returned it to the desktop.

'Do you know it?'

'No.'

'It's in the centre of Crowland in Lincolnshire. It's a small town and I'm sure we never had a connection with the place. But it's less than fifty miles from here and if that's where Melanie came from it would explain why simply moving back home wasn't an option . . .'

'Because she would have been too close to here to feel safe?'

'Exactly,' she replied. 'How long will it take you to check if that's the place?'

'If she went to school there or has family there I should know within the hour.' He didn't need the ornament now but slipped it into his pocket in any case. 'I really appreciate your help.'

She smiled. 'I'm always glad to give it.'

CHAPTER 34

Crowland's bridge had been built in the fourteenth century at the point where the river Welland met a tributary and in a period when the surrounding flatlands had still been submerged. The community had grown around the dry skirts of the abbey. It might have been hundreds of years since the land had been drained but the fields lay so low that Goodhew could imagine the water rising through the soil and the long straight run of Peterborough Road becoming a causeway.

He drove into the centre of town, finding the bridge within minutes. The river had long since dried and the bridge stood as a worn and dusty tourist attraction, spanning a few metres of history. There had only been two listings for the surname Franks; they lived a short walk from one another and a short distance from the bridge. He'd rung G. and S. Franks and left a message but received no reply. The second call had been answered with the kind of cagey response normally reserved for suspected cold callers. 'Mr Christopher Franks?' Goodhew introduced himself then kept it brief. 'I'm trying to locate Melanie Franks.'

'I'm sorry, you have the wrong number.'

'But Melanie is your sister?'

Christopher Franks hesitated for just a moment then relented. 'Yes, she is. But she moved away and we don't have contact.'

'I see.' Goodhew waited for Christopher to comment further: Have you found her? Is she OK? Has something happened? There were none of those.

Goodhew had replaced the receiver and immediately hired a car. When Christopher Franks answered his door, Goodhew continued to speak as though the intervening couple of hours hadn't existed. 'Most people who receive a call about a relative, even if they have cut off contact, will ask what's happened. You didn't. So my guess is that you know she's safe and well.' Goodhew pointed towards the interior of the house. 'I think we should talk.'

Christopher Franks held the door a little wider. 'Go straight through.' He was tall but when he spoke he bowed his head and spoke in a quiet, clear voice. 'You'll need to tell me what it's about.'

Goodhew waited until they were face to face in the dining room. 'It is important that I speak to your sister immediately.'

'I don't know where she is but I can pass on a message.' A slow smile formed on Franks's lips. 'But I'm not doing that unless there's a genuine need.'

'Do you think that she's currently in any danger then?'

'I think the way she lives her life is working out well and if it ain't broke, don't fix it.'

'I believe your sister may have important information relating to a current investigation.'

'In Cambridge?'

'Yes, a recent murder.'

For a moment Franks looked relieved, 'Trust me, you're wasting your time. She has no connection to anyone there.'

'She knew the victim.'

Franks's eyes hardened. 'Twenty years ago, perhaps.'

'Perhaps.'

'No, there's nothing she could add.'

'I need to speak with your sister, it's not optional and if you refuse to cooperate I could charge you with obstruction—'

'Or get a court order and charge me with contempt? Whatever.'

It was obvious to Goodhew that Franks was close to refusing to continue the conversation. 'I'm visiting your parents next: G. and S. Franks, West Street?'

Franks stepped towards the door. 'They won't speak to you and I'd rather you didn't try. They'll worry.'

'It's not optional that I speak to her but why not save us both time and all the legal shenanigans? Try this: send your sister a message, tell her my name, tell her she can trust me to be discreet the way my grandfather was.'

Franks scowled and shook his head but then gave in. 'OK, but that's all I'm going to do.' He sent the text and then dropped his mobile back into his pocket. 'I'll need your number to call you – assuming she replies.'

Goodhew shook his head. 'Thank you, but I'm going to wait.' He stepped towards the sofa. 'Do you mind?' He took a seat without waiting for an answer.

Franks scowled. 'I do actually and I doubt whether she'll reply.'

'We can leave it a couple of hours then try again. I'm not in a hurry,' he lied.

Franks sank into the armchair facing Goodhew and stared across uneasily. 'I'll give it fifteen minutes then I want you to leave. I know my sister and she won't—' He stopped mid-sentence as the landline began to trill. The handset stood on the coffee table beside him and he glanced at the caller display before answering. He listened for a few seconds. Goodhew couldn't hear any of the words but could pick out a female voice and a barrage of dialogue, which eventually paused. 'Only if you're sure.' Franks replied. He studied Goodhew with interest and then held out the handset. 'My sister.'

Goodhew introduced himself and told her about Lorraine Martin's death.

'And Joseph Goodhew was your grandfather?' Her voice sounded artificially calm. 'What date did he die?'

'The eighteenth of July 1992,' he answered automatically.

'Well then,' she replied, 'we need to meet.'

Goodhew phoned Gully and let her know that she could halt her trawl for traces of the existence of Melanie Franks in Hereford; Melanie was only twenty miles from the city but she'd covered her tracks well. It then took Goodhew just over three hours to drive from Crowland to Monmouth. Learning that he would find Melanie in a small and historic town made sense. From his experience people always hung onto something when they switched lives, and not just hobbies or employment in a parallel career where their own skills would still be useful. It was always more than the practical; they would drink at the same kind of pubs, or move to a house with a similar layout, use the same chain stores or feel at home with the same kinds of views as they'd left behind. He guessed it gave comfort and continuity.

She'd given him an address in Monnow Street, a busy but old-fashioned shopping thoroughfare. He parked at one end close to where her flat was located. She lived above a tearoom and just a few hundred yards from the Monnow Bridge. He looked across at it as he locked his car; this one still had water flowing beneath it and was both older and grander than Crowland's, but similar enough to make him smile as he walked towards her door.

She opened it before he had a chance to knock. She must have been watching him and when he offered her his ID she barely glanced at it. 'I can see who you are,' she told him, then led him up the narrow flight of stairs to her lounge. She turned then and held out her hand for him to shake. Her grip was firm and dry and her hands were rough to touch. She looked older than he had expected with pronounced lines around her pale grey eyes but there was also serenity in her expression. She pointed towards one of the two settees that crowded the space, 'Please sit. I've made drinks.' She left the room briefly and returned with a pot of hot water and canisters of tea, coffee and sugar on a tray with milk and empty mugs. 'Actually, it's a case of helping yourself.'

'That's fine, thank you.' He made himself coffee, and she poured boiling water into her own mug but added nothing. 'Do you live here alone?'

'Just me and my cat.' She met his gaze as if waiting for him to ask her about her child. After a beat she relented. 'And my son, Ben, but he's working away.'

She had strong features and a straightforward way of talking.

'Which name do you use?'

'Officially, Jane Williams. Joe did a good job with the papers, but I still call myself Melanie on a day-to-day basis. It's hard to switch. I tried, but people would talk to me and I would ignore them. And it was tough to start again without people thinking that I didn't have any manners.' She smiled enough to make her cheeks dimple. 'Is there any chance this conversation will be confidential?'

'It's unlikely.' Goodhew shook his head. 'It depends what you know and I do realise that's not an incentive for you to answer my questions. Details of your name and address don't need to fall into the public domain but I can't guarantee that they won't.'

'I see. So no false promises?'

'Lorraine Martin's death has led to many questions. I really need your help.'

She cupped the mug of hot water in one hand and pressed it to her cheek. She pressed the fingers of her other hand to her lips and closed her eyes, effectively cutting herself off from him. When her eyes reopened he could tell that she had made a decision. 'It's wrong if I don't,' she said.

'Thank you. Now, I'd like to start with Lorraine Martin. You were her lodger?'

'Eventually, yes. I met her before that, through Nadine.'

Goodhew had never taken a guess at how Nadine and Melanie had met but his subconscious had planted the idea in his mind that they'd been flatmates first and through that had become friends. Finding out that it was the other way around surprised him more than it should have. 'So how did you meet Nadine?'

'I worked at the Boat Race pub, the one on the corner of East Road and Burleigh Street . . .'

'I remember it.'

'Sometimes they'd have jam nights and she would turn up and play. Guitar mostly but occasionally she'd sing. We struck up this odd friendship. In fact, it was the only friendship I had when I was in Cambridge because I really didn't fit in with any of the other students.' She stared towards the window as she remembered. 'It makes sense to me now. I can see that I was out of my depth in Cambridge and I'd barely left Crowland before that. My social skills still aren't the best but back then I was this awkward, geeky girl who was too needy. I was the first one in my family who'd gone to uni and I'd done that against their wishes. I didn't fit in at the pub either. Nadine must have seen that but she didn't judge and it didn't seem to matter.' Melanie looked directly at Goodhew. 'When I tell you what happened you might think she used me somehow, but she didn't. She had her demons but we always looked out for each other.'

'OK, go on.'

'Nadine had told me that she had a boyfriend. I'd never met him but I guessed that there was some issue, like he was already married or something because I never saw them together and he always took her out of town when they did meet. Eventually she told me that he was a man she worked with, her boss and yes, he was married. She loved him, though, I'm sure of it, but we were both kids . . .'

He poured himself another coffee; he sensed she was about to tell him some of the things that she'd spent the intervening years keeping to herself.

'She got herself pregnant. She did it on purpose thinking that he'd leave his wife for her. But of course he didn't, he just dumped her.'

'Do you know his name?'

A small smile touched her lips. 'Robert Buckingham.'

Goodhew nodded, he'd thought as much.

'He demanded that she had an abortion. She wouldn't. I was just on the side lines then but even with all that drama and heartache her life seemed so much more appealing than mine. And I was in financial trouble, behind on my rent and determined not to jack it all in and go home. I remember envying her at the time, I thought she had it all in hand.' She shook her head at the memory. 'I don't know what planet I was on. If Ben ever got himself into a similar situation I wouldn't blame him or belittle him, I'd just want him to come home.'

'But you didn't go home.'

'No, I did something so stupid . . .'

'Please go on.'

'Robert sacked Nadine. She'd kept quiet about the pregnancy but Robert's business partner knew.'

'Neil Frampton?'

'Exactly. And Nadine was approached by the accountant, Moira. She told her that her sister would be able to help. She said she knew a private adoption agency who would pay all Nadine's expenses and place the baby with a new family and that's when Nadine met Lorraine and moved in with her. I would visit, and it still seemed to me that Nadine had landed on her feet.'

'Was she the only one living there?'

'Initially.' Melanie placed her mug back onto the tray. 'Some other girls had moved on I think, and, after Nadine moved in, others arrived soon afterwards. She had five girls in there at one point.'

'Do you know any names?'

'After this long?' She squinted towards the ceiling as she tried to remember, then shook her head slowly. 'Caitlyn from somewhere, Canada maybe. And there was another they called Renee but I think that might have been a nickname. Apart from that . . . no, sorry.' A moment later though she brightened again. 'There is one thing I know; Nadine was the only one who wasn't a student.'

It wasn't the most specific piece of information but it was still significant. 'Do you think that's how Lorraine found them?'

'Lorraine was offering a service. Do you know how many students there are in Cambridge? How many get pregnant where neither an abortion nor a baby is a viable option?'

He didn't think she expected him to reply but he knew that current figures for the university population ran at about twenty thousand, but finding the answer to the second question was impossible.

She replied for him. 'Enough to keep that house busy. And as I spent more time there it all started to seem normal. Then Neil approached me. Theo was the son from his first marriage and Carolyn was his second wife . . .' Melanie was watching Goodhew carefully, the words frozen on her lips.

'Melanie, what did you do?' he whispered.

'She'd had problems when she was a teenager and she'd been told that she couldn't get pregnant. She was fixated with the fact that Neil already had a child, like she needed to outdo his first wife on every front.' She took a breath. 'It seemed to me that she wanted a baby like someone might want a pet, to just go out and get one. So they paid me to do it, to have his baby and hand it over.'

'Surrogacy?'

'Yes, I agreed to do it. I had no interest in children and it seemed straightforward. I told myself it was no different to what Nadine was doing. I inseminated myself. How's this for irony? I wouldn't have sex with him for money but I'd have his baby. I fell pregnant at the first attempt.'

'So their son Alex . . .?'

'No, I conceived and then, completely against the odds, Carolyn did too. She was just a few weeks after me, but I didn't know that straight away. In fact, I don't remember much until the first scan. I thought it would be exactly what it is, a grainy image of a two-inch blob but the second I was in that room I knew I wouldn't be handing Ben over to anyone.' Her grey eyes brightened as she said his name. 'When I found out about Carolyn's pregnancy I thought it would be easy to get out of the agreement, they were having their baby, they no longer had a reason to want mine.' She shook her head. 'Not a chance. Neil wanted his child. I tried to reason with Carolyn but she didn't waver.' The memory still had the power to make her pale. 'They both made it clear that I didn't have a choice. They had me working at Frampton's for a few hours every day – it was their way of keeping an eye on me. I was never out of their sight for more than a few hours at a time. That's where I got to know your mum and, through her, Joe.'

'And where was Nadine during all of this?'

'She left Buckingham and Frampton's first and when I cleared off she was seven, maybe eight months pregnant. I wanted to keep in touch with her but Joe said that if I was ever tempted to make contact with anyone I had to look at Ben and ask myself whether it was worth the risk.'

'So you never did?'

'Never.'

'Do you know what happened to any of the other girls?'

'One baby was born while I was there. Lorraine delivered a little boy. She left with him soon afterwards, the mum cried and then sat in a daze all evening but by the next morning she'd gone. When I left, I heard nothing else of Nadine until the following year when I read about the fire.' Her expression softened. 'It was a pity she hadn't met Theo first; they would have been good for each other. My first thought was that her coming back after hiding away at Lorraine's had tipped Bob

Buckingham over the edge; he must have felt as though he couldn't get away from her. Maybe that's why he snapped.'

'If he did.'

'Well, I don't think he did it for the insurance money.'

'I'm wondering whether he did it at all.'

It took a moment for the shock to fully register and, this time, her colour drained completely.

'Melanie, why did you contact Joe after the fire?'

'Because I read the reports in the paper and none of them mentioned her baby.' Her voice was barely audible. 'It was Robert's child too and he was the one under arrest, so it seemed to me that it had to be crucial to the case.'

'Why not go to the police?'

'Are you kidding? I was living under a false identity and avoiding contact with my child's father. I didn't want to blow all that so I asked Joe for his advice. He said he'd check out the situation before he involved the police. Told me to sit tight. He contacted me a few days later and said I'd need to be patient. I was and heard nothing. I left it for a few weeks then I tried to contact him again, and that's when I discovered that he'd died.'

'Who told you?'

'I phoned his number and your mother answered. She asked me where I was hiding, said that Neil was desperate to contact his son and wanted me to reconsider.'

Goodhew pushed aside the thought that it was another fact that his mother hadn't bothered to share with him. 'What did you do?' he asked.

'I hung up and never called again.'

'My grandfather was attacked and died from his injuries. And I believe it was connected to you because any papers he had that related to you were taken.'

'No one ever found me.'

'I think he was too careful for that.'

She nodded slowly. 'He was such a good man.'

Goodhew had phoned Marks then. The picture was still fragmented but beginning to form and he'd explained the progress that he'd made.

'So we'll need to track down anyone who lodged with Lorraine from Nadine onwards. My guess is that one of them will be the baby's mother.'

'What about Nadine?'

'Possibly. But not Melanie. I'll bring you a full report.'

'That all stacks up,' Marks had told him. 'By the way, we've just received the background on Lorraine Martin's previous employment: she was cautioned for poor performance and eventually sacked when a couple complained that she was drunk when she delivered their baby. Are you done there?'

'A few more questions.'

'Finish them and we'll ask local officers to take the statement, and I know you're off-duty right now but I'd like you back as soon as you can.'

He'd heard a tense note in his boss's voice. 'Is everything OK?'

'The same as ever: problems with resources,' Marks had replied but his tone hadn't changed.

It had taken Goodhew another forty minutes to finish questioning Melanie and now, as he was about to leave, she reached out to shake his hand. 'I liked Lorraine, I think she was doing the wrong things for the right reasons; I think she set out to help those girls rather than make money. She wasn't much of a businesswoman.'

He didn't comment. There were endless examples of kind people doing bad things and it didn't make them any less guilty. 'Can I just ask, did it work out for you and Ben?'

'Yes, thank you. I would never have thought of myself as the maternal type but it has been the best thing.' She smiled warmly and the years slipped from her face. 'Having Ben has taught me so much and we've muddled through together. I work on archaeological digs, the kind that happen before sites are redeveloped, and sometimes he takes a day off and comes along to help. He's honest and hard-working – everything I wasn't at that age and I'm so proud of him.'

She followed Goodhew down to the bottom of the stairs and by the time she opened the front door she had become serious again. 'What your grandfather did for me . . .' She touched Goodhew's arm.

197

Without warning her eyes misted and she struggled to finish the sentence. 'Sorry.' She took a few seconds more before she could finish. 'What he did for me was immeasurable. The greatest gift. And I'm so sorry for your loss.'

CHAPTER 35

Marks and Kincaide arrived unannounced at Frampton's office in St Barnabas Road and Marks was pleased to note the presence of both Neil Frampton's F-Type and Carolyn's Cayenne. 'I'll do the preliminaries then we'll split them up. I'll take Neil Frampton. Remember, keep it tactful if it's in front of the son; we don't know where this is going and it's the wrong time to be indiscreet.'

Marks entered the building with Kincaide close behind Nothing much had changed; Carolyn and Neil Frampton were at their respective desks and Alex Frampton even seemed to be wearing the same plaid shirt. Carolyn Frampton rose to greet them and gave a smile that achieved the right balance between curiosity and warmth.

'I guess this means that there have been developments?'

'Of sorts,' Marks began. 'We have some questions for you and your husband; we are pursuing some parallel lines of enquiry and need more information.'

Her smile faded as he spoke and her expression grew more cautious. 'We are talking about Lorraine's murder, aren't we?'

'Indirectly, yes.'

Alex Frampton had turned in his chair, enough to watch them through a large bevel-edged mirror that hung from the longest wall. Carolyn glanced at her son then back to Marks. 'I'm surprised Neil isn't out here already; an unexpected visit from the police would still get to him, even after this long.'

Marks finally understood the subtext of her earlier question. 'We're not here about the Romsey Terrace fire or Theo's death but we would like some time with you and your husband.'

She looked relieved. 'Of course, come through.' At the doorway she turned back to speak to her son. 'Alex, if anyone calls, we'll get back to them. The diary's on my desk. Can you get Stan to cover for anything that can't be cancelled?'

'How long will you be?'

She glanced at Marks who gestured that he had no idea.

'A while, I guess,' she replied and led them across the hallway to her husband's office.

Marks squinted at Neil Frampton for a few seconds when everyone else was diverted by the need for a couple of extra chairs. He was trying to blur the man's features enough to see what he might have looked like twenty-plus years ago before grief had visited and before over-indulgence had inflated, reddened and visibly distorted him. It wasn't hard to imagine that he'd been a young forty when Theo had died, but he was a raddled sixty-four now.

Carolyn spun a chair round to the end of the desk, almost along-side her husband, but not quite. She wore a sleeveless white shirt that accentuated her toned and tanned arms. Apart from a watch and her wedding ring she was accessory-free, her makeup low-key but perfect. There could have been thirty years between the two of them, not just seventeen.

'As I explained to your wife, our investigation into the death of Lor-raine Martin is following several lines of enquiry and one of those relates to the discovery of the remains of a baby at her property.' Marks had switched to his briefing voice, the one he used when he was being careful not to be ambiguous. Sometimes it made people talk more, other times they shut down; Neil Frampton's expression had quickly become opaque.

Carolyn Frampton seemed distracted by her husband. 'We saw it in the local paper.' She looked at him warily. 'It's shocking, isn't it, Neil?'

'I don't think Lorraine put the odds in her favour.'

'Meaning what exactly?' Marks asked.

200

'It's just a comment; she drank and she was unreliable, therefore she would have been vulnerable to any random nutter and had no one looking out for her.'

'Do you think this was an unplanned attack then?'

'No, I just meant that she didn't avoid risk like most of us do.' Neil Frampton held a ballpoint pen, a cheap one with the name of a plant hire company printed down one side. He studied it intently and waggled it between forefinger and thumb. 'Lorraine came round here the night she died, but you know that already.'

'Yes, we do. According to your statements, she was shouting . . .' Marks paused to read from his notes even though it wasn't difficult to remember, '"I know, I know".'

'She was a pisshead. Practically incoherent with alcohol.'

'Neil . . .' Carolyn cut in. 'Please . . .'

'I find it hard to have sympathy for that woman.'

'What did you think she meant by that remark?'

Carolyn answered first. 'We've both made statements.'

'We did,' Neil agreed without looking up and he continued to fiddle with the pen.

'When Lorraine Martin said those words, "I know, I know",' Marks continued, watching them both closely, 'did it occur to either of you that she may have been referring to the whereabouts of Melanie Franks?'

Neil Frampton's gaze flashed towards Marks as his hand dropped to the desktop, Carolyn's hand shot up to her mouth and then the room stilled. Marks was the only one who spoke. 'We have questions for both of you and, in the interests of confidentiality, we will speak to each of you separately.' They could have refused, demanded to stay together or sought outside support; it didn't mean anything that they did none of those things. He had caught them off guard and splitting them up was simple.

Kincaide left the room with Carolyn Frampton, Marks stayed in the office with her husband. There had been an instant change in the man and it went beyond the immediate physical response; the stunned expression, the wave of paralysis as time froze then the sudden lurch as it thrust to catch up again.

Neil Frampton leant forward, elbows on the desk, and gave Marks his complete attention. His eyes shone darkly and a healthier colour seemed to have flooded his face. 'Have you found her?' he asked.

Marks blanked the question, 'Can you explain your relationship to Miss Franks?'

'I don't have one.'

'Not currently, no, but I need to understand what it was and why you are clearly so keen to find her.'

Frampton pressed his lips together and the corners of his mouth formed a thin smile. 'I'm sure you know all the key details, detective. Do you want me to go through them all again so that you can pick me up on any discrepancies? Why does it matter whether my version is the same as my wife's, or the same as Melanie's for that matter?'

'Mr Frampton, you are not under caution, but I would appreciate your cooperation.'

'Because?'

'Because it's a murder investigation, because there are multiple strands, some of which involve your business and people connected to it. And because this particular line of enquiry involves you. I would have thought that it was in your interest to see us move on without too much upheaval.' Marks was patient, and he had enough experience to remain so indefinitely. He returned Frampton's smile with his own.

Frampton shook his head and the smugness vanished. 'I'm sorry.' He held up his hands in surrender. 'I didn't like Lorraine, but I do know what it's like to lose a relative to murder. The worst emotions dull but they never go.'

'Understood, Mr Frampton, but my questions are important.'

'So is what I need.'

'And what would that be?'

'To find Melanie.' His tone had calmed quickly but his eyes had lost none of their new-found intensity. 'I've spent years searching for her.'

'I see, so she's chosen to move away and remain untraceable. When did you last see her?'

'Eighth of July 1990. It was a Sunday.'

Marks waited.

'She was having our baby; mine and Carolyn's.' If Frampton expected a reaction from Marks, he would be disappointed. Even if Marks hadn't already known this he was well practised at staying impassive. The silence pushed Frampton on. 'Carolyn couldn't conceive and she was desperate to become a mother.' He paused to consider the statement, 'I think she was insecure and it was her way of cementing our marriage. I'm not going to guess,' he waved the comment away with a flick of his hand, 'but, in my experience, if a woman wants a baby that's an unstoppable force. Some go down the route of throwing money and misery at it, but Carolyn's always been a pragmatist.' He stopped there as if that answered everything.

'So you entered a surrogacy arrangement?'

'We did.'

'And how was the arrangement with Melanie going to work? Were you paying her?'

'Expenses, nothing more.'

'Because that's the terminology that keeps it legal?'

'We didn't do anything wrong and we certainly didn't break the law.'

'And, during her pregnancy, she was to live with Lorraine Martin who, in turn, would eventually deliver the baby?'

'Her pregnancy wasn't secret. She would have gone to Addenbrooke's Hospital.'

'Unlike the other women in her care?'

Frampton stayed poker-faced but kept eye contact for far too long, 'I know nothing about that.'

'Who does then? Your wife?'

'I don't know, but not me.'

'And was Mrs Frampton happy with this surrogacy arrangement?'

'Of course; for one thing, it was her idea.'

'But biologically the child would have been yours and someone else's?'

'No different from an egg donor except that she would have skipped the getting fat part.'

'I think there's more to it than that for most women,' Marks told him dryly.

'You're absolutely right.' Frampton flashed a brief smile at Marks accompanied by an equally brief laugh. 'Those were Carolyn's words, not mine, and when she found out she was pregnant she cried for days.'

'She was facing the prospect of two new babies to care for. That's assuming you planned to keep Melanie's?'

'Of course we did. Back then, I didn't feel that the baby was Melanie's, it was ours.'

'And now? What is it that you're expecting after all these years?'

Frampton rested his forehead to his clasped hands. 'I've always had the feeling that Melanie had a son.' It wasn't spoken as a question but he waited for a reply.

'I can't comment.'

'So you know?'

'I can't comment.'

'I want contact with him. I've never given up looking.' He lifted his head and studied Marks for a moment. 'Do you have first-hand experience of losing a child?'

It was a question that Marks had been asked too many times in the past, one he hoped he wouldn't have to hear once he was retired. 'No, Mr Frampton, thankfully I don't.'

'It was quite a while after Melanie left when Theo died – eight months, to be precise. Melanie's baby had been on my mind but after we lost Theo . . .' He shook his head. 'My thoughts were constantly on nothing but Theo and the baby. Theo and the baby, Theo and the baby . . . going round and round.'

'What about Alex?'

'Carolyn struggled, emotionally I mean, she didn't want anyone near him. I felt detached from him and Carolyn for months, so I didn't bond with him until much later.'

'And hence the affair?'

He blinked a couple of times but apart from that showed no surprise that Marks knew. 'It was barely that and I didn't plan it but it helped me cope until Carolyn and I got ourselves straight again.'

Marks pursed his lips; the man was adept at playing the victim, the victim of crime, of circumstance and of other people's agendas. It would take longer to work out which of his statements were genuine. 'So your interest in finding Melanie is to connect with your child?'

'Of course.'

'When she was pregnant, did she tell you she wanted to keep her baby?'

'No.'

'How do you think you would have responded if she had?'

'Carolyn and I would have been disappointed.'

'Would you have threatened her?'

'Absolutely not.'

'So tell me why she was so terrified of you that she felt it necessary to change her identity? To cut ties with her family and start over?'

'I don't know,' he replied. It was the second time he'd said that and on both occasions he'd been lying.

Marks outranked him so Kincaide knew it made sense that Marks would choose to interview Mr Frampton rather than the wife but he didn't relish the prospect; she was one of those high-maintenance women who looked like she did spa days and probably had her own clothing budget. She looked at him with slight amusement and he couldn't decipher whether it was disdain or her attempt at being alluring.

He followed her through to the other office where her tattooed son was fiddling around with a floor plan. 'Alex?' She had a sharpness to her voice and he responded immediately. 'This is Detective Kincaide and I need to speak to him privately.'

'No problem,' he replied, and less than a minute later they were treated to the throb of the Suzuki Bandit. He revved the engine a couple of times before pulling out into the street. Kincaide and Mrs Frampton waited for the sound to die away before either of them spoke. 'Melanie Franks,' he began. 'You were shocked to hear her name.'

'A blast from the past, as they say. I always suspected she'd turn up eventually. If my husband's anything, he's persistent.'

'He didn't find her, though.'

'He'll have had a hand in it because he always does. I don't see what any of this has to do with Lorraine Martin.'

It already felt as though Mrs Frampton was in the driving seat and Kincaide didn't like it. He settled back in his chair and took a breath before speaking. 'We know about the surrogacy agreement with

Melanie Franks.' He'd had his brief, Marks had been clear about how he wanted this revelation handled and this wasn't it, but he'd said enough to make Mrs Frampton's confidence falter and that had to be a good thing. 'Think back to the time when you and your husband made that arrangement. What did you think that Ms Martin did for a living?'

'She was a midwife.'

'Ex-midwife.'

'She'd gone freelance.'

It was time for Kincaide to employ his own knowing smile. 'Freelance? Was that her word for it, or yours?'

'Hers, I guess. I don't remember.' Mrs Frampton had rallied already and there was a new steeliness in her expression.

'And what exactly do you think that was a euphemism for?' Kincaide didn't usually pay much attention to eyes but Mrs Frampton's were a vivid blue, a colour that looked almost unnatural against her tanned skin. He wondered whether both shades were fake.

'I think she meant that she delivered babies.' The blueness glinted. 'But you're the detective, what interpretation would you put on *freelance midwife*? If you want to ask me something specific, then go for it.'

'How did you first make contact with Lorraine Martin?'

'Nadine had been introduced via Moira, then Nadine came to me and told me about her friend. She suggested the surrogacy option.'

'We have a witness who says that Melanie agreed to go through with it to help herself out of financial difficulty and you paid for this via the . . .' he made quotes with his fingers, '"adoption agency", which turned out to be Lorraine Martin and her . . .' more quotes, '"freelance" business.'

'We paid Melanie's expenses, I was told what those were and handed over the money accordingly. As far as I knew she wasn't making a profit.'

'You thought she was doing it out of generosity then?'

'Why not?' Carolyn clearly didn't care whether or not he believed her.

He didn't. 'So, to clarify, you were aware that Melanie Franks was intending to make financial gain from the transaction?'

'I'm not surprised that she had money left over, the expenses we paid were generous, but I took the advice I was given and had no idea whether or not it was legitimate. Seems to me that Lorraine Martin was filling a niche.' She held out her hands palms upwards as if they were weighing scales, 'Too many babies on one side, not enough on the other. And of course I would have notified the authorities if I had any suspicion that things weren't above board. Please put that in your notes.'

She was lying, she made that clear in the way she said it, but words, not intonation, went into statements and this was even less formal than that.

'How do you feel about Melanie Franks now?'

A shrug. 'Nothing.'

Kincaide took a moment to study her. The detachment seemed genuine at first but then he noticed the way her hands were clasped together, fingers intertwined. He wouldn't want to be either of those hands being crushed by the other. The way to tackle this was all there in those manicured hands. 'I would have thought,' he began, picking his words carefully, 'you would have mixed feelings about being reunited with the person who could have been your child. You can't get away from the fact that your husband is still the father.'

Again with the shrug. 'It's in the past, detective, I dealt with my feelings a long time ago.'

'But it won't stay in the past now. This is the child your husband has spent years searching for. He has some catching up to do.' Kincaide spotted pinkness rising at the sides of her neck.

'Of course he wants contact.'

'Doesn't it bother you that you and your son will have to move over to make room for a complete stranger? Someone who's never had a father figure . . .'

'You're being ridiculous.'

'Am I? Why has he spent all that time and money on the search if it doesn't turn into something more?'

She opened her mouth to speak then hesitated, as if she wasn't sure what to say.

'That's his son and heir, his eldest living child.'

Her lips moved just enough to silently echo the new information. *A boy.*

'Are you ready for your life to change for him?' he asked.

There was a tiny shake of her head and it was all he needed.

'You have dreaded this day, haven't you?'

She looked at him, stricken-faced and wordless.

'Haven't you?' he pushed.

'Yes,' she whispered. Then again more clearly. 'Theo was everything to Neil and I needed to give him a child. Do you know the saying "second wife, second best"? Well, that was how I felt and that's how it would have stayed if we hadn't had a baby.'

Kincaide couldn't follow her logic; the idea of parenthood repulsed him slightly.

'If she'd just done what she was supposed to do then everything would be fine.'

'You had your baby, she had hers. I don't see the issue.'

'Because . . .' She pressed her lips into a hard line and glared at him.

'Because your husband wants his son and you can see your importance and your luxuries being shoved aside by his bastard child.'

This time she found her voice. 'That's not how it is,' she told him.

Kincaide shook his head; he didn't believe her, 'If Lorraine Martin suddenly discovered the whereabouts of Melanie Franks then you had a motive to kill her, didn't you?'

'No,' she snapped. 'And we're done here.' She rose to her feet and brought her face close to his. 'There's nothing more I'm prepared to add to what I've already said and I'd like you to leave now, detective.' She turned away, pulled the door wide and held it open for him.

'Detective Sergeant,' he corrected.

She didn't speak again until the door was closing behind him. 'By the way, detective, most married women have motive to kill, even your wife, but it doesn't mean we do.'

He glanced back long enough to see her tremulous expression and guessed that her bravado was an attempt to hide another lie.

CHAPTER 36

Most days since Amy's first meeting with Alex had involved a work-related email exchange followed by a flurry of short messages containing nothing but casual chat. Both of them had studiously avoided any mention of their parents or the fire. Until now.

Her inbox was open when the new email arrived, the message title simply said 'Please read'. Its contents weren't much longer, 'Who is Melanie Franks?'

'Why?'

'The police are here about Lorraine Martin. They said the name Melanie Franks and some kind of shit hit the fan.'

'Like what?'

'Don't know, I've just been chucked out of the office so I couldn't hear more. I'm coming over to the yard. Will you be there?'

Amy thought for a moment before replying, 'In a bit, I'm going to see my dad and find out who she is.'

Amy was parking up when she saw DC Goodhew entering her dad's house. In itself, the arrival of one junior detective probably didn't mean much, and if she hadn't had the emails from Alex then her senses wouldn't have felt jarred, but seeing Goodhew triggered a surge of unrest. Of anxiety even.

She didn't intend to sneak but found herself approaching the house quietly; she avoided touching the gate and turned the key gently in the lock. She wasn't expecting to burst in and discover any great revelation but she knew from the years when her mum had struggled with depression that the first moments through the door could be the most telling. Her father only had two rooms downstairs, the lounge and the kitchen-diner. Both were visible from the front door. The men sat on opposite sides of the kitchen table and they both looked across at her as she walked in. Her father's face lit up immediately, Goodhew's didn't. He held a thin envelope and, although he didn't seem to be paying any attention to it, he furled it loosely in his grip if to protect it from her. His gaze shifted from Amy to her dad. 'You may prefer this to be a private conversation.'

Her dad's smile faded slightly but he seemed unaware of the look of consternation that had just passed between herself and DC Goodhew. She guessed their concerns were for very different reasons; Goodhew was worried about the conversation he didn't want to have in front of her. Amy was worried that she was about to be excluded from it.

She made eye contact with her dad and held his gaze, 'What's private, Dad?'

'DC Goodhew hasn't got that far.'

'I thought there weren't any more secrets for me to worry about.'

He shook his head. 'There aren't.' The reply had been a reflex and it sounded defensive rather than genuine.

'Not convincing, Dad.' She turned and had every intention of walking away.

'Amy, don't.'

She hesitated, her back to him.

'Please, there's nothing you can't hear.'

She turned back to them. If anything, Goodhew seemed to have tightened his grip on the rolled envelope.

'So, I can stay? No matter what this is about?'

Her dad's reply was to pull back the chair next to him and beckon her towards it, 'No more secrets, Amy, I promise.'

Goodhew held an envelope in his hand and a backup plan in his pocket. Amy's arrival had the potential to complicate this meeting but Goodhew needed Robert Buckingham to tell him the truth and couldn't let Amy's presence jeopardise that. She had settled down next to her father and neither of them had any intention of asking her to move. He unfurled the envelope and laid it on the kitchen table making sure that the label displaying the sender's name was clearly in sight. Goodhew was pretty certain that Amy had no idea what was coming but Robert Buckingham was harder to gauge.

'Mr Buckingham, you knew both Theo Frampton and Nadine Kendall.'

'Of course.'

'Your previous relationship with Miss Kendall was investigated as a possible motivation for you setting fire to the house in Romsey Terrace.'

Buckingham shot an apologetic look at his daughter. 'Yes, it was. But I didn't start that fire.'

'Why was Nadine's baby never mentioned?'

Buckingham's surprise appeared genuine. 'What baby?'

'She was pregnant at the time of your affair and we have a witness that states that you put pressure on her to have a termination.'

Goodhew was conscious of Amy staring at him but he kept his attention firmly on her father.

'What witness? That's an absolute lie.'

'Which part?'

Amy interrupted, 'I know about your affair, Dad.'

After a short pause Buckingham replied. 'If she was pregnant, it wasn't mine.'

'And was she?'

As a liar his voice was convincing. He could have pulled it off in a telephone conversation but everything about Buckingham's body language was on the defensive. 'What do you want to pin on me this time?'

'Nothing. We just need some straight answers.'

'I don't have to listen to this shit. Or deal with your questions.'

Beyond Goodhew was the front door and Buckingham directed his gaze towards it. Perhaps he would have headed that way if Amy hadn't been here. Or refused to answer anything. He couldn't do that when he'd promised her no more secrets and Goodhew was suddenly pleased that she was in the room.

211

Amy reached across and placed her hand over her dad's. 'I think you should just tell him what he wants to know. If everything's in the open . . .'

'What? It will be for the best?'

'Dad, the police are with Neil and Carolyn right now.' Buckingham's attention shot towards his daughter, then to Goodhew.

'Is that true?' he asked.

'It is.'

Buckingham shook his head. 'I don't know who got Nadine pregnant and I regretted ever getting involved with her. I certainly didn't feel jealous of her relationship with Theo. Good luck to them, that's all I thought. I don't understand why all that matters now.'

'A baby's body was found at Lorraine Martin's property.'

'That's not . . .'

He stopped.

'Not what? Not yours? You knew about it then?'

Buckingham's hesitation had been more telling than if he had finished the sentence.

'Do you know if her baby was delivered safely?'

'If she'd had a baby then the autopsy would have shown it.'

'Except you know that their bodies were beyond any analysis like that.' Goodhew slid the envelope closer, 'Now tell me, what happened to Nadine's baby?'

'It's nothing to do with me.'

'Lorraine Martin has been murdered. This isn't about what's convenient for you to answer; we need every detail to try to identify her killer. You just told your daughter that there would be no more secrets so right now I need to know what happened to your baby.'

The bombshell took a moment to explode. Amy's eyes widened and she sagged back in her chair, her hand falling from her father's arm.

Buckingham glowered and hissed, 'It wasn't mine.'

There were plenty of people like this who would stick to their stories in the face of irrefutable evidence. Goodhew slipped his hand into the envelope and pulled out a section of broken bangle. 'This was an item of jewellery made by Lorraine Martin for Nadine. Do you recognise it?'

Buckingham barely glanced at it but shook his head.

'It is made from a form of acrylic and Lorraine Martin specialised in making pieces like this with small items embedded within them. In this case . . .' Goodhew held it out towards Buckingham, 'those small flecks. They are trimmings of baby hair.'

He let the words settle.

'Perfectly preserved.'

Amy's face had grown ashen. 'So there's DNA?' she whispered.

Goodhew tapped the envelope and saw her focus for the first time on the printed label and the words 'Forensic Laboratories'.

'Mr Buckingham, I have just been to pick up these results and I want to know what happened to your baby.'

Buckingham ran his fingers through his hair and stared at the envelope. 'Like I said, the kid wasn't mine.'

'And when you were facing a murder charge for killing Nadine Kendall it didn't occur to you to mention this other man? He would have been the perfect person to have cast doubt on your guilt.'

Buckingham took too long to find an answer. 'I didn't know his name.'

'That wouldn't have mattered, someone else would have done . . . if he'd existed.' Goodhew rested his hand flat on the envelope, 'Do you know the odds on a DNA match coming up against the wrong person?'

Robert Buckingham brushed it off. 'You've fiddled with the results. Someone's trying to set me up for this just like they did with the fire.'

'Dad?' Then more urgently, 'Dad? Stop it.'

'Stop what, Amy? Standing up for myself?'

'You said there wouldn't be any more secrets.'

'There aren't.'

'That's your baby, though. It's bloody obvious. I'm not stupid, there's evidence right here.'

'I don't believe it, Amy.'

'Listen to yourself. They have a hair sample, actual hair from Nadine's baby that proves you are the father. But if you can't bring yourself to own up at least think about me. That child is my sibling.'

Buckingham glowered at the envelope, then replied, 'She had a girl and it died. That's all I know. I never even knew the baby's name.' He looked across at Amy then but she was already on her feet and heading for the door.

Robert Buckingham didn't call or chase after his daughter but he stood at the window and watched her until she'd disappeared from view. 'Are you pleased with what you've just done?'

'You could have asked her to leave,' Goodhew replied.

'You could have held back.'

'And what happened to "there's nothing you can't hear"? Or did you forget that you had another child?'

'I never wanted that baby. I gave her money to get rid of it but she decided not to. And when it died it felt like the best outcome.'

Robert Buckingham's expression was filled with a combination of distaste and indignation. To Goodhew it seemed childlike, only a breath away from shouting 'it's not fair'. 'Mr Buckingham, forget about what you'd prefer to whitewash from your past. Tell me about the baby.'

'For fuck's sake,' Buckingham muttered but, when he realised that Goodhew was planning to sit it out until he answered properly, he began to talk. 'Nadine was refusing to have an abortion, I don't know why because I'd finished the relationship and she knew we weren't going anywhere.'

'Perhaps she didn't agree with it.'

'I told her it would be less hassle in the long run.'

'And that didn't sway her?' Goodhew asked dryly.

'No. Everyone at Buckingham's knew.'

Goodhew silently corrected it to Frampton's.

'Moira and I were good friends and she told me about her sister. I knew Lorraine was a midwife but I didn't know about the adoptions until then. Moira spoke to Nadine and it seemed to be the answer to everything; we'd both be able to move on as if there'd never been a baby.'

'And you really believed that?'

'Why not? If she'd had an abortion it would have been the end of it. I didn't get a say in that and it was her choice alone to carry on with the pregnancy.'

'Therefore the baby was nothing to do with you?'

'Exactly.'

Buckingham was clearly convinced of his own logic and for several seconds Goodhew felt lost for words. 'So Neil and Carolyn Frampton knew about the baby and never spoke up at the trial?'

'They had their reasons.'

'The surrogacy?'

'You don't miss much. That, and the fact that they were busy distancing themselves from me. A criminal investigation doesn't do much for business. It was the fact that his son died that bought him some goodwill.'

'Did you know where the baby had been buried?'

'I didn't want to know but as soon as I heard about the grave in Lorraine's garden it was obvious.' A mocking smile played on Buckingham's lips. 'Don't expect me to feel any more than you people do.'

'Are you trying to bait me, Mr Buckingham?'

'Why would I do that?'

'I don't know but I doubt that Amy would think so much of you if she could hear you now.'

The amusement vanished. 'I missed out on Amy's childhood because of people like you. Yes, sometimes I can lack subtlety, but who wouldn't after losing all those years to the sodding prison system?' His scowl deepened and there was sincerity in his voice. 'And one thing about Amy; she's always loyal. She's annoyed right now but she's always going to be there for me. And for her mum. She can't help herself; it's the way she's wired.'

Goodhew nodded slowly. 'Mr Buckingham, do you know who killed Lorraine Martin?'

'No, but she pissed someone off, didn't she?'

'Like who?'

'Her problem was getting an idea into her head and never letting it drop. And alcohol made her mouthier. But even if I knew who'd done it I wouldn't tell you; I will never do anything that helps you do your job. You've done your damage and I'd like you to leave.'

'I'm afraid I'll be here until I've written this up and you've signed it off.'

* * *

215

Buckingham had scowled but hadn't argued. Goodhew called Marks and gave him the key points, then settled down to take Buckingham's statement. He had expected it to become prolonged by Buckingham's increasingly bad mood and him picking over every sentence, but in the end it went the other way and Buckingham had hurried through each point, keen to see Goodhew leave as soon as possible.

Despite this, it had still taken nearly two hours to complete and Buckingham's expression had been set to glower for the duration. Finally, Goodhew folded the signed statement and tucked it away.

'Will that become public?' Buckingham asked. 'I don't want the press turning up on my doorstep.'

Goodhew didn't reply at once. He picked up the section of bangle from the table as he stood to leave. 'Did you notice how the baby hairs were just tiny trimmings?'

'So?'

'From a new-born baby all that gives us is mitochondrial DNA. It was enough to make a familial connection to the mother but it wasn't enough to identify you as the father. Your confession did that.'

The words winded Buckingham. 'You're kidding?' he breathed.

Goodhew allowed himself a small smile, 'I appreciate your cooperation, Mr Buckingham.'

Goodhew drove the unmarked car away from Buckingham's house, turned the first corner and immediately saw Amy waiting ahead. She sat on a garden wall and moved slowly to her feet. It was now two hours since she'd left her father's house. He lowered the passenger side window and leant across to speak to her. 'How long were you planning to wait there?'

'As long as it took.' She folded her arms, 'That wasn't the way I should have found out that I had a sister.'

It hadn't been his first choice either. 'I know, and I'm sorry. It might be better than never knowing.'

'You think he would have kept it secret?'

Goodhew turned off the engine and left the car at the kerb. 'Yes, I do, but my opinion doesn't really matter.'

'Except it does. I've set out with this idea that I could find out something that would prove his innocence. He might not have started the fire but he's not innocent of much else. I've spent so many years imagining that I could make our family right again . . .' She began to walk and he fell into step alongside her. 'But you know what it's like to have your family screwed up by a crime. At what point do I let it go?'

'I haven't worked that out yet.' His natural instinct was to stop there but Amy was waiting for more and he was conscious of the link, however tenuous, between the cases and their situations. 'My grandfather's death affected me, still affects me, and I suppose I'm the same as you and think that I need answers before moving on.'

'What if the truth makes it worse?'

He liked her directness. 'It won't,' he assured her.

'And it's as simple as that?'

'I believe so.'

'So I just found out that, however briefly, I had a sister and that's fine because it's the truth? I just forgive my dad and it's all OK again? Good old dependable Amy.' Her eyes shone darkly, brimming with anger. 'He promised me that there were no more secrets . . .'

'In his eyes it's in the past and he never expected anyone to find out—' Goodhew had no idea why he was saying anything in the man's defence. Amy cut him off sharply.

'He had no right to keep it from me.'

'He might have been afraid to—'

'No. It wasn't fear, it was cowardice. He didn't tell me because it wasn't convenient for him and he's a fool if he thinks it'll all blow over. Not this time.'

CHAPTER 37

In the first minutes after walking out of her dad's house, Amy had felt a now familiar surge of anger. Most recently it had been directed at her mum but now it was her father's turn and she paced the pavement just out of sight of her dad's house as she worked to dispel it. Two hours had been enough to tame it and by the time she'd started speaking to Goodhew she knew there had been a shift in the way she saw her father; the trust had gone, the respect wrecked.

She'd refused Goodhew's offer of a lift and her anger dissipated as she walked back towards town. Maybe she was shocked because the calmness had come in waves and in between she'd seen her situation with clarity; this was what was meant by a pivotal moment and it couldn't be undone or denied. And, because of it, certain things had run their course.

She'd had a mile to go when she'd made a call to Alex. 'I'm sorry, I never asked my dad about Melanie.'

'It doesn't matter, I know the answer now.' A pause. 'What's wrong, you sound weird?'

'I had some news. Look, I'm walking back from my dad's, would you mind giving me a lift?'

'Of course.'

He'd ridden into view within ten minutes. He'd brought a spare crash helmet but removed his own before offering it to her. 'I don't know what's happened to you but, personally, I could do with someone to talk to; can we get a drink?'

Perhaps he'd meant alcohol but she agreed and asked to go to Clowns. And now they sat facing each other across the same table where she'd met with Goodhew. 'So,' she concluded, 'you're not the only one with an extra sibling. Only yours is alive. It's a shock.'

He blew into his tea and didn't reply immediately. In the end he put the mug back down onto the table without drinking from it. 'It's a parent's job to fuck us up but ours have really done a job of it. From birth in my case.'

'At least they're consistent.'

Neither of them smiled.

'Are you going to leave Frampton's?' he asked.

She shook her head. 'I don't know. My reasons for everything seem to be changing daily. If anyone's going to prove my dad's innocence it will be the police, not me. I not even sure if I care any more.'

'But you still need a job.'

'Of course.'

'Why move unless you have to?' He made it sound like a casual question but it didn't feel like it. Plenty of the clowns on the shelf behind him had eyes that followed her; usually she didn't mind.

'I like the work,' she admitted. 'And some of my colleagues.'

He grinned impishly. 'Am I on that list?'

'No, you're in File 13 with Stan.'

'Ouch.'

'Just kidding.' They smiled across at each other until Amy realised that the eye contact had continued for too long. She hadn't even had a date in the last year. She felt an unexpected jolt of emptiness. 'I'm sorry, Alex. I think I should go home.'

He looked disappointed but smiled. 'Sure.'

'If you speak to Stan, tell him I'll be there tomorrow and I'll work late to make up the hours.' She dropped some coins onto the table. 'Thanks, that's for the tea.'

She was already leaving by the time Alex was only half on his feet. 'There's no need . . .' was the last she heard before heading out onto King Street. She drew a deep breath of the outside air and hurried towards the Brew House pub, planning to take the shortcut behind it that led to her flat. She'd only walked a few yards when she felt a hand on her arm.

'Amy?' She stopped and he turned her gently towards him. 'Can I get you dinner? Or we could drive somewhere?'

She shook her head.

'A drink then?'

'No, I don't think so.' But his hand was still on her arm and she didn't step away. She hesitated then said, 'There are things I need to do right now.' She closed her eyes and leant her forehead into his shoulder. 'I like you, Alex . . .' He wrapped one arm around her.

His mouth was close to her ear, 'It's a bit soon for the I-like-you-but speech, isn't it?'

She shook her head, 'No, it was going to be "I like you a lot." Or "I like you despite this mess we're in." I just hadn't decided.'

'It's our families that are in a mess, not us.'

'We are our families aren't we? We're right in the thick of it and maybe I like you because we're kindred spirits right now and when all this passes . . .' She could feel his warmth through his shirt and the urge to slide her arms around him.

'You've been in my head since you walked into the office,' he said, 'and that was at least five minutes before I knew who you were. And that was when I thought my family was the same dysfunctional nightmare that it had always been. I'm attracted to you, Amy, but not because of the situation.' He ran his hand across her hair and cupped her face, his fingertips made her skin tingle and she felt his breath close to her face.

'I'm sorry but I do need to go to my mum's.' She slid her hands around his neck. 'It's not an excuse, though.'

He kissed her softly on the lips, 'I know,' he grinned. 'I'll come and find you tomorrow and we won't settle for the pavement outside a pub.'

'OK,' she kissed him. 'You choose.'

CHAPTER 38

Amy took the direct route to her mum's house and was within sight of Fair Street in less than five minutes. The Hopbine pub stood halfway along the short road. She didn't want a drink but needed a few minutes to gather her thoughts so ordered half a cider. Orchard Pig apparently. She guessed it would have tasted good if she was tasting anything at all. She felt detached from everything. What she needed were some opening words for her mum; 'Just because I'm here doesn't mean I've forgiven you' wasn't going to be the best start. Her mind remained blank.

She finished drinking with the glass close to half full and left it on the end of the bar. She still had no idea what she would say but decided that she would have to trust the words to find her when the moment arose.

It was 8.05 p.m.; too early for her mum to go to bed, but heading towards nine when her habit was to settle down in front of the latest crime drama on the television with a glass of red and both house phone and mobile set to mute or diverted to answerphone.

Amy knocked. The door opened and her mum didn't wait for her opening line. 'Amy, come in.' She managed the same watery smile that Amy had seen on her last visit. Her mum swung the door wide and then walked back into the heart of the house leaving Amy to close the door and follow her to the lounge.

The TV was already on and a half-drunk bottle of Malbec stood open on the coffee table. 'Would you like a glass of something, Amy?'

'Sure, thanks.'

'Same as me?'

'Yes, please.' She turned off the TV while her mum was out of the room and chose to sit at the other end of the settee; not too close but still within touching distance.

Geraldine filled Amy's glass but stopped pouring her own at the three-quarters mark. 'I'm ahead of you.'

Amy smiled politely but the right words still weren't coming.

Her mum found hers first. 'I've missed you.'

'I'm finding it hard to accept what you did, but I understand Dad more now too . . .'

'And we're both a disappointment?'

Amy thought about it. 'Maybe my expectations are unreasonable.'

The glass had been close to Geraldine's lips, but she placed it back on the table without taking a sip. By the time she looked back at Amy she was frowning. 'Your expectations are too low, Amy, not too high.' Amy opened her mouth to protest but Geraldine spoke first. 'That's not a criticism of you. Trying to put things right is in your nature. So is having broad shoulders. They are strengths but I haven't shown you how to draw the line. I drew that line with your dad but you wouldn't have seen it like that.'

'You should have told me what he was like.'

'By the time he was freed we had our own life. I didn't have a need to tell tales on him; I wanted you to form your own opinion.'

'I thought he'd been unfairly convicted. I couldn't see anything beyond that except an image of what our family could have been if he hadn't been in jail and you'd tried harder to love him.' She took a hefty swig of the wine. 'I think the reason I've never had a relationship that's lasted more than a few weeks is because of the way things were between you and Dad.'

Geraldine looked startled but didn't comment.

'When I was small, preschool age I suppose, I can remember how desperate you were for the divorce to come through and how many times you told me that we didn't need a man.'

'But I wasn't aiming to make you feel like that about your own relationships.'

222

'Each time I've had a boyfriend I've known that it's going nowhere. You've always said that all men are the same but I don't believe that any more.'

Geraldine slid an arm around Amy's shoulders and pulled her close. Amy nestled her head under her mother's cheek and listened to the words spoken softly in her ear. 'I thought I was protecting you by teaching you to be independent, teaching you that you don't need to be in a relationship to be happy.'

'I don't need one, but maybe I'd like one.'

Her mum straightened and studied Amy's face for a moment. 'Have you met someone?'

Yes, Neil Frampton's son.

'No,' Amy lied, 'not yet. But I want my life as straight as it can be first and that means dropping this obsession I've had with Dad's case.'

'Really?' Geraldine's face flashed with sudden optimism, 'What's brought this on?'

'The police. They were at Dad's today . . . don't look worried . . . they came to speak to him in connection with Lorraine Martin's death and I found out some things.'

'What things?'

She squeezed her mum's hand. 'It's OK, they didn't arrest him or anything.'

'Thank God, I wouldn't want to go through all that again . . .'

'Listen, I'll tell you, but the first thing you need to know is that as I walked out of Dad's I thought, I can't do this any more. He's lied to me too many times now. And it's not because I don't care, or because I'm disloyal or . . .' she shook her head and fished around for the rest of the sentence. 'I've just had enough, Mum. I won't stay long but I wanted you to know.'

'I'm really sorry about everything. About your dad and the way I behaved.' Geraldine exhaled slowly and reached forward to top up Amy's glass and refill her own. She drank half immediately. 'What else do you need from me, Amy?'

Amy smiled weakly. 'Peace? Sanity?'

'Have you eaten?'

Amy became serious again and shook her head, 'I am tired but I need to tell you the rest too.'

She didn't speak immediately and Geraldine must have sensed her apprehension because she too began to look worried. 'Go on.'

'I know about Nadine's baby.' Amy couldn't bring herself to say 'Dad's baby'. 'You should have told me . . .' The suggestion of blame hung in the air but she was beyond caring about that. 'I would rather have known.'

'I understand, but to tell you about her would have meant telling you about your father's affair. It would have been a mistake. Why should I dump all that on you when you were small? Why tell you when you're older?' she said when she finally spoke. 'She died.'

'I know, but it proves so much about Dad. And she should have had a funeral. Dad knew she'd died and he didn't care. Did you know she was buried in Lorraine Martin's garden?'

'Not then. When I saw the baby in the news, I guessed.'

'What if she'd lived, would anyone have told me then?'

'No. She would have been adopted. He was doing everything he could to deny anything about Nadine. He would never have wanted her to keep the baby.'

'I don't understand how you're so calm about it.'

'I'm not calm because I know that we're about to get dragged through the papers again, your dad will be in the frame for Lorraine's murder, and the story of baby and Nadine will be smeared across every tabloid.'

'They won't arrest him, will they? He wouldn't have killed her.'

'Give him an alibi if you're sure. Or refuse to because of everything else he's done. Exactly the same dilemma I faced and it's tough.'

'I see,' Amy said slowly. There had been no suggestion that her dad was under investigation for Lorraine Martin's murder and she wouldn't be prepared to lie for him even if he was. 'It would have been wrong for you to cover for him, wouldn't it?'

'I think so.'

'It makes sense now and I'm really sorry, Mum, I shouldn't have blamed you. Would you do something for me?'

'Of course.'

'Tell me the things you can remember, the small details; I need to put all of this in one clear picture and then I think I can deal with it and leave it behind.'

In reply Geraldine slipped her arms around her daughter and hugged her tightly. Amy leant against her mum and felt the wine and the effects of the day start to overtake her. She closed her eyes.

Geraldine picked up the two glasses and the empty bottle. 'We'll talk, I promise, but right now you need to get some sleep. The spare bed's already made.'

'Thanks, Mum.' Amy opened her eyes enough to watch her mum leave the room. She knew she needed to rouse herself before she fell asleep on the settee but it was only when she stood that she realised that her mum was in the hallway waiting. 'Mum?'

'It is just a small detail; her name was Abigail,' she whispered, then carried on towards the kitchen.

CHAPTER 39

When Goodhew returned to Parkside, Jack Worthington was alone in the office. 'Where is everyone?'

'Everyone? You make it sound like there's a decent number of us on this one. Kincaide went with Marks to see Moira Trent, the others have gone for the day. I'm just leaving, I've been in since seven.'

Goodhew checked his watch: the day had disappeared into evening and he hadn't noticed. 'I won't stay long either,' he said, but he was still going through paperwork when Marks and Kincaide returned an hour later. 'What happened with Moira Trent?' he asked.

Marks held up a sheet of copier paper. Goodhew was too far away to read the details but he could see the shape of the printed characters forming two columns that reached three quarters of the way down the page. 'She admitted that she knew about the babies but claimed that Lorraine had told her that it was cash-in-hand money for looking after the women.' Marks passed the page to him. 'Dates and amounts, it's the money that Lorraine gave to her to look after.'

The font size was small, eight point, no more. The entries were chronological, the first dated 27 May 1987 and the final entry 4 April 1996. Goodhew counted forty-two lines. 'One line per adopted child? Four or five per year – it's possible.'

Kincaide spoke next. 'Moira Trent wouldn't be drawn on that and tried to stick to the story that the fees were for accommodation.'

'Over £200,000? That's a lot now, it would've been a fortune back then.'

'She carried on denying knowledge of anything even though we knew that both Robert Buckingham and the Framptons claimed they'd met Lorraine through her and that she'd introduced her as a midwife.'

'And?'

'We heard back from the NHS. Lorraine had been sacked for drinking on duty in February 1985 and struck off the nursing register later that year on a charge of gross misconduct. She had no right to be practising. Moira knew about the drinking but nothing else so when we dropped that bombshell she became slightly more forthcoming,' Marks reached across to point to 1990, halfway down the sheet. 'She was told that Nadine's baby was stillborn. She claims that she didn't know that the baby was buried in the garden, that she never knew its name or sex.'

'So Frankie is Nadine's baby?'

'Yes.'

'That's forty-three babies.'

'And Lorraine started drinking again after Nadine lost her baby. From there on out it was a cycle of sobriety, relapse and a succession of breakdowns.' Marks tapped the sheet, 'and forty-two illegal adoptions. This will all belong to the Major Crimes Unit by tomorrow.'

'Lock, stock and barrel,' Kincaide smiled. 'You could call it in now?'

'In the morning, Michael. First thing, when I'm not too tired to think straight.'

Goodhew took a copy of the list and it was still in front of him an hour after the others had gone. Everything was too tightly interconnected, Major Crimes would take Lorraine Martin's case too, and his grandfather's. The mass of detail would belong to other officers and it would be for them to continue or drop the current leads, to pick up on elements Parkside had missed, and, worst of all, also miss the clues that the current team were missing too. And, in the case of his grandfather and the fire, the things that had been overlooked back then.

His gaze fell on the boxes of information from those previous cases. They'd been brought in and stacked by the wall. He wondered how many had been recently searched or if they had done what the next team might do and assume that there was nothing to find?

He wandered across the room and removed the lid from the first box. Lying on top was a note from DC Knight, 'Box 2. Cross-referenced everything in here and in boxes 1, 3, 4 and 5.' He lifted the lid on a couple of the other boxes and found a version of the same note in each. He wasn't surprised; she was incredibly thorough with documentation. But there'd been no mention of the sixth and final box. He squatted beside it and noted that it was still taped shut as it had been when it was moved up from the archives. He grabbed scissors from the nearest desk and slit it open. It contained nothing but a small box of DAT tapes and a few sheets cataloguing the contents of each. 'Only one way to find out,' he said in reply to his own silent question, then he picked up the box and left for home.

Goodhew owned a DAT player. If he'd visited his grandfather's storage unit, he probably could also have played back most audio formats from PlayTape and Microcassette onwards. He realised that his need for gadgets was yet another part of his personality he had probably inherited from Joe.

He took the DAT player and tapes to his grandfather's study and sorted them into chronological order. All interviewees bar one were names he recognised. The first tape was marked 'Steven Powell'. Goodhew read the accompanying notes then listened to the recording. Mr Powell had lived in the adjoining property and had been alerted by shouts, which he could hear through the party wall. 'I had the TV on and wasn't paying too much attention to them at first, but I suddenly realised that the tone of their voices was wrong. Panic-filled. So I turned down the volume and moved outside – out the front I mean, into the street. It wasn't shouts by then but screams and other people came out of their houses too and we could see smoke at the windows. "Call the fire brigade" I shouted and someone else grabbed a ladder and we propped it up at the front. We didn't get any further; we could hear the sirens but the screaming had stopped.' He seemed to say it all in a single breath and every subsequent question about anything suspicious he'd seen in the days preceding the attack drew a consistent and monotone negative response.

The next tape was Neil Frampton's. Goodhew scanned through the others; unsurprisingly about half of them were labelled as interviews with Robert Buckingham, their frequency increasing as they drew closer to charging him. But date order made the most sense and he lay back, closed his eyes and waited for the familiar voice of Neil Frampton to speak.

'I last saw Theo that afternoon.'

A male voice with a soft Scottish accent prompted him. DS Montgomery according to the notes.

'Sorry, I mean 30 March 1991.'

Goodhew's eyes drifted open again – it was hard to match this voice to the Neil Frampton he'd seen this week. The tone sounded familiar but he spoke more rapidly then with words that were clipped and more driven.

'I was in the Cow and Calf on Pound Hill with my business partner, Robert Buckingham. Theo popped in, had a half and then left us to meet Nadine.' He'd hesitated as he spoke his son's name and the second syllable wobbled and for the rest of the sentence his voice shook.

'We barely spoke. He was quiet but we chatted to Robert for a few minutes. I asked Theo if he wanted another. He said no and that was the last time I saw him . . . until afterwards.' Frampton had identified Theo's body then.

'He seemed fine. In good spirits actually.'

Montgomery again, 'And between him and your partner?'

'That business between Robert and Nadine was a long time ago.'

'I'm sorry, what business?'

Goodhew listened as the first seeds of doubt were sown.

After that DS Montgomery seemed to look for links to Buckingham. He interviewed Geraldine Buckingham. He questioned her about Theo and why she'd failed to mention that he had visited her house.

'I forget. He came to see my husband who'd gone out.'

'Was it usual for Theo to visit your home?'

'The only time as far as I know.'

'Did he tell you what he wanted?'

'Just to speak to Robert.'

'Was he agitated?'

'No.'

229

'How did your husband react when he found out that Theo wanted to speak to him?'

'I don't remember.'

'Were you aware of any problems between your husband and Theo?'

'No, but I don't think he would have told me. My husband doesn't always share his thoughts.'

And then the interview with Carolyn Frampton. She'd been twenty-four then and still had a girlishness to her voice and vocabulary. She claimed that she'd last seen Theo at home the night before. 'He was keeping himself to himself. He'd just hang around sometimes, brooding over stuff.'

'How was your own relationship with him?'

'Fine. Yeah, it was pretty good. We hadn't worked together since I had the baby and that helped too.'

'So you and he had had issues?'

'Sometimes he'd get on my nerves. But Neil says that's how it is if you work and live with someone.'

'And you both worked for your husband's company?'

'Yes, that's right. Theo started a couple of months before I went on maternity leave.'

'Was the age gap between you and Theo ever an issue?'

'It was only five years.'

'But you're married to his father.'

'It wasn't a problem.'

'Fair enough. And how was he with the other employees? It was his father's business, were there any conflicts with management; with Robert Buckingham for example?'

'With Robert?' He thought he could hear a smile in her voice. 'It's hard to comment when they're never in the same room at the same time.'

And so it went on. Goodhew changed tapes again and waited for Stanley Mercer to be led down the same path.

'When was the last time you saw Theo Frampton?'

'On Friday,' he replied.

Before Goodhew could think his hand had shot forward and hit the stop button. He rewound and played it again. Goodhew listened and his blood ran cold.

CHAPTER 40

It was 4 a.m.

The only person he knew he could ring at that time was his grand-mother. *Ellie*, he reminded himself. But Ellie was the one person who didn't need to know. Not yet anyway.

He called Sue instead. Ellie usually answered with a sharp comment and gave the impression that she'd already been wide awake. Sue grunted, 'What's happened?'

'I need to talk to someone.'

'And not over the phone?' Another grunt then the sound of a drawer being hauled open.

'At mine. I'm sorry.'

'It's fine, I'm not complaining. I sound like this when I talk in my sleep.'

'There will be a taxi outside yours in a couple of minutes.'

'You just assumed I'd come straight over?'

'I booked it online, confirmed it just then when I heard you getting dressed.'

'No one should be that alert at 4 a.m. You're abnormal.' She hung up and ten minutes later he met her at the front door. 'Normal people sleep, Gary.'

'Ellie does that.'

'What? Sleeps?'

'No, starts the conversation, hangs up, then walks in and carries on as if there hasn't been a fifteen-minute gap in the middle.' He meant it as a throwaway comment but, as he spoke, he knew that his voice sounded hollow.

Sue reached out and caught his arm, 'What's happened, Gary?'

He tipped his head towards the stairs and she followed him up to the second floor. She sat beside him on the settee and he placed the DAT tape player between them. 'I need to put this in context.'

'OK.'

'I've been playing the interview tapes from the Romsey Terrace case. It seemed to be the only box file that Sandra Knight hadn't been through. They had Robert Buckingham in their sights from the start and I was listening and trying to put myself back there, hearing it all for the first time so that I was in the shoes – in the mind-set – of the team back then.'

'OK,' she repeated.

'Then I heard this.' He pressed play. Montgomery asked the question and Goodhew felt his chest tighten in anticipation of the reply. He held his breath even though the audio had been repeated relentlessly and he knew every beat and breath in the detective's question and Stan Mercer's reply: 'On Friday.'

He pressed pause.

'He sounds different now, doesn't he?'

'From two words?'

He pressed play again and let her hear a few more seconds.

'Yes, he does.' She then agreed, 'Age, smoking and years of yelling at people I guess.'

Goodhew nodded. 'Stan Mercer is one of the people I heard when I hid in my grandfather's flat. I didn't recognise his voice when I met him, but from this,' he tapped the tape player, 'I have no doubt. He's either an accessory, a witness or the one who struck Joe.'

'Phone Marks.'

'No. As soon as I do that these tapes will be out of my hands. Last night, the Lorraine Martin murder just turned into the Lorraine Martin baby-selling scandal and Marks reckons Major Crimes will be taking it all from us tomorrow.'

'Shit.'

'Marks will be in at seven at the earliest. Help me check these tapes. If there's anything else here, I need to find it.'

Sue stared at the pile. 'What are we looking for?'

'I have no idea.'

'Great. There's one tape player and a pile of DATs, it's not like we can take half each.'

'Sue?'

'What?'

'I'm glad you're here. I could go through the rest on my own, but I'd rather have company.' Her skin was pale with tiredness and her hair was untidier than usual. 'I'm sorry I dragged you out of bed.'

She supressed a smile. 'I don't mind. Not really, Gary. I just don't do well on three hours sleep.'

'Well, I'll nudge you if you doze off.'

'Don't you dare.'

Neither of them flagged but by quarter to seven all they had were notes and questions, and still no answers. 'I keep looking out for a link between Stan Mercer and the fire or even Lorraine Martin's murder.' Sue sat cross-legged on the floor. She moved her notes around on the floor to see if changing the order helped, 'It all looks different now we know that he was involved with Joe's death but I'm not seeing a way forward.'

Goodhew looked at his own notes. 'Yeah, I keep seeing bias against Robert Buckingham but who's to say that they weren't right when he was arrested the first time. He's unpleasant. And a liar; one of those who'll say whatever gets them off the hook.'

'Unpleasant isn't a crime, Gary, but I do wonder what he and Theo talked about in that pub. Could have been something that wound him up; Theo and Nadine were dead within hours.'

'I'll ask whether Buckingham can be re-interviewed.' Goodhew checked his watch. 'We need to get in soon and update Marks.' They gathered up their papers and he didn't speak again until they were ready to leave his flat, 'Sue, you know I don't want you to leave Cambridge, don't you?'

'And you know I've made up my mind.' She took a step closer to him and he took hold of her hand.

'I do but I need to say this anyway. Last year when I heard that an officer had been killed, all I cared about was that it wasn't you.' He squeezed her hand and neither of them looked away. 'At that moment I knew that it has been you all along. And when we kissed . . .'

'I know and at that moment we both felt the same.' She began to withdraw her hand again but he held onto it. 'Gary, it won't work out.'

'My grandfather said Ellie was a better reflection of himself. Suddenly I understood what he'd meant. For me, that's you.'

'Gary?'

'It's OK, I just wanted to make sure you knew, that's all now. But it shouldn't be your reason for leaving.'

Finally, she looked away. 'It isn't, not entirely.' She squeezed his hand this time and then let it go, turning away and taking her phone from her pocket. 'I'm going to call a taxi.'

'For 200 yards?'

'I don't want to get spotted coming out of here, it'll look like I'm doing the walk of shame. I'll get a cab home then come back in as soon as I've changed.' She placed the call then stood with her elbow resting on the jukebox and looked around the room. 'You were here when Joe told you to hide, and here when you played the recording. It's come full circle.'

CHAPTER 41

Abigail. The name conjured up a freckled face with brown eyes and long brown hair. The image was a child's drawing at first, cartoon-like and just the approximation of being human; the ears were level with the eyes and the nose and mouth were just two dots and a straight line. That was 3 a.m.; by six Abigail's image had become a Facebook profile photo, she was tanned, wearing a vest top and holding a piña colada with the straw to her mouth. Amy was glad she'd woken and pushed the pictures from her mind.

Abigail. Perhaps she would have been Abbie by now. Amy washed and dressed quickly while mulling over the name-shortening possibilities. Abbie or Abi or Abby. The dream had been mundane and had wedged itself into her short-term memory in an eerie impersonation of real life.

She brushed her teeth then splashed her face with cold water. 'Wake up, Amy.'

She'd asked her mum for the small details, the minor facts that no one would bother fabricating. She figured that they were the ones that hovered in the background and either validated or disproved the rest of any story. She awoke in the middle of the night and realised that she had some of those facts too. She checked her watch.

Over an hour before work and it was time to visit Moira Trent.

From Fair Street to Clarendon Street was a short walk. In June it was the route to Strawberry Fair from town, and back again. It would be packed with revellers, waves of them in each direction, painted and tawdry and loud in every way. Today, the road was grey and silent. Milk bottles were on the doorsteps of the houses that still took deliveries and a lone cat crossing between the parked cars was the only movement. Moira Trent lived in the same sash-windowed terrace that Amy remembered from visiting as a child. She rang the bell then stepped back to the roadside edge of the hop-scotch-paved footpath, and remembered her dad telling her that it was good manners not to crowd an entrance. She watched the half-circle of frosted glass above the door and straightened as soon as movement rippled the light seeping through it.

There was a pause and Amy guessed she was being observed through the spyhole. When the door opened, it was easy to see the weariness on the older woman's face.

'I'm sorry about Lorraine.'

Moira acknowledged the comment with a dip of her head but then moved straight on. 'Why are you here?'

'I need to speak to you. I'd like to come in.'

It wasn't a question and Moira obediently stepped back to allow Amy inside. Amy walked towards the kitchen at the back of the house where she'd often sat at the stripped pine table reading or doing her homework while Moira and her father discussed the accounts. The kitchen hadn't changed much. It had the same mushroom walls and red-tiled floor. The wooden units had been repainted cream. She'd hated sitting in here. Mushroom, she'd decided then, was the colour of boredom. Now its familiarity warmed her. She reached for the nearest chair. 'I hope you don't mind?'

Moira shook her head and pulled out a chair so that she could sit opposite Amy.

'I asked Neil for the job because I wanted to prove that my dad never started the fire.'

'I guessed that.'

'It hasn't exactly worked out the way I'd hoped and I might not have tried if I'd known everything in the first place, like about my dad and Nadine . . . Then I realised that, while those things are important to me, they might not mean so much to someone else . . .' Her words faltered. In her mind's eye coming here had been a good idea, but now she wasn't sure. She spread her hands flat on the table, took a breath and carried on staring down at them as she spoke. 'I want to tell you something in case it's important to you and ask you something else because that's important to me.'

'OK,' Moira replied gently.

'The police know but I started thinking about how I've been kept in the dark . . .'

'Go on.'

'Lorraine tried to contact me.' She didn't wait for Moira to respond. 'She posted a card through the door in the yard, said she wanted to speak to me but, by the time I saw it . . .' She hesitated and softened the words she was about to use. 'By then it was the following morning and she'd already been found.'

Moira stared at her, bewildered. 'Why would she?' she mouthed the words, more to herself than to Amy.

'I think she was going to tell me about my half-sister, about Abigail.' It was enough to startle Moira.

'You know?'

Amy nodded. 'The police confronted my dad yesterday; he didn't want to admit it but in the end he had to own up.'

'And he told you her name?'

'No, that was Mum.'

'I see,' Moira murmured. She gave Amy a sympathetic smile and reached across the table to squeeze her hand. 'Maybe Lorraine was going to tell you something else.'

'Like what?'

'I don't know.'

'Did Abigail die because Lorraine made a mistake?' Amy felt Moira's fingers stiffen. 'I'm sorry, that was tactless.'

'No, it's fine,' she replied, but Amy knew it wasn't; she could see a new hardness in Moira's expression. 'We won't know that, but I'm sure that burying the baby in the garden must have troubled her. Perhaps that was what she was going to tell you. The place where they found the baby was well tended, I really don't think she buried the baby to forget about her. You said you wanted information from me? About your dad?'

Amy hesitated. Moira's mood had shifted and she was conscious that she'd hit a nerve. 'You were there at the time, I just wondered if you'd tell me . . .'

'About your dad?'

'About any of it. You and he were friends.'

'And even after everything, you want someone to speak in his favour?'

'I want a balanced picture. I want to see my parents clearly.'

'OK, well I thought we were friends . . .'

'Just friends?'

'Yes. Absolutely. But maybe that's why I hadn't seen that other side of him. I thought I knew him pretty well until I saw the way he treated Nadine. She knew he was married and should have had her eyes open but she fell for him and he used her. She was his lunchtime shag, nothing more.'

Amy grimaced.

'Obviously that's not how we like to think of our parents but there you go. The pregnancy was her biggest mistake. He dumped her and she hung on. He really, truly despised her in the end. Wouldn't acknowledge that the child was his so I'm surprised he even knew her name.'

'No, I told you, Mum did. My dad didn't know it.' She paused to think. 'I don't know how she knew.'

Moira didn't respond.

'Well,' Moira said finally, flicking the comment away with her hand, 'I kept making excuses for Rob until his arrest. And then those rose-tinted glasses of mine fell and smashed. Of course he killed them; he hated Nadine. I made too many excuses for Lorraine too. Recurrent hypermetropia.'

Amy looked blank.

Moira leant forward and whispered, 'It means that I couldn't see what was right in front of me.' She smiled but her expression had become taut. 'I'm returning to work today. Will you be there?'

'Yes, in the yard.'

'Good.' Moira's intonation changed suddenly. 'Now I must get ready.' She left the room and returned with a makeup purse. She applied foundation in her compact mirror and began on her eyeshadow.

'I could give you a lift?' But her tone was brusque and the real question was 'Don't you think it's time you went?'

Either way the answer was the same. 'Thanks, but no.' Amy rose to her feet but waited, thinking that Moira might say something else. But Moira finished adding shadow to one eye and switched to the other without a word. For the first time, Amy saw that the hand holding the eyeshadow brush was shaking.

'What's wrong?'

Moira paused but didn't look at her. 'I need you to go now.'

'OK.' Amy took a step back. 'I didn't mean to upset you.'

'I just need you to go,' Moira snapped back, spelling out her reply syllable by syllable. She reached out to put the makeup on the table but fumbled and brushes and a lipstick rolled from the purse and clattered on the floor. 'Shit.' She reached down for the lipstick but it slipped from her fingers.

As Amy bent to pick it up Moira grabbed her arm.

'Don't you understand? My sister has been murdered and this is my first day back at work. That's big enough without you coming in here and swamping me with all this other stuff. Now go.'

Amy stood and began to apologise when Moira swept the rest of the makeup onto the floor. She grabbed Amy again, this time at the elbow, and manhandled her towards the hallway. 'Just get out,' she shouted until Amy had been propelled back onto the street. The door slammed behind her and, from the other side, she heard Moira sob.

Moira gathered the makeup items from the floor and lined them up on the kitchen table and then she cleansed her face and started again. Have I misunderstood? That was the question that mattered beyond all else. Her hands had stopped trembling and her breathing had settled but she wasn't ready to speak to anyone yet.

This time the foundation went on evenly, the eyeshadow subtler. She turned her head from left to right and checked it in the mirror from multiple angles. There was a tiny amount of puffiness left from crying. She paused to make eye contact with herself and tried to decide whether she was now looking at an intelligent woman or a foolish one. Neither, or both, she told herself, then reached for the phone.

The call was answered and she spoke without any preamble: 'Amy came to see me. She knew that Nadine's baby was called Abigail. Geraldine told her, but I don't know how she knows.' Moira had already gone through the potential explanations and, unless there was something she'd missed, had narrowed it down to a single possibility. She waited, imagining the same logic unfolding at the other end of the line and nodded to herself as the same inevitable conclusion was reached.

'What do you want me to do?' she asked.

The instruction was brief and clear. Hang up and wait.

CHAPTER 42

The box of DAT tapes sat on Marks's desk next to the player. Marks released the pause button. It was the third time that he'd listened to the same two words: 'On Friday.'

He stared at Goodhew. 'And that was enough?'

'Absolutely.'

'Without a shadow of a doubt?'

'None whatsoever.'

'But you didn't recognise his voice when you met him in person?'

Goodhew sighed. 'That's right, sir. He's forty-four now but sounds at least a decade older; he was only twenty-one on this tape. You can hear the difference, can't you?'

'Devil's advocate, Gary. I need to make sure this stands up. His accent is the same and there's bound to be an expert who'll swear that his patterns of speech haven't changed, but, in all honesty, I wouldn't have thought it was the same man.'

'Well then,' Goodhew replied.

'I need a statement from you formally identifying Mercer's voice. But without a confession, all we'll have is a witness statement with an identification based on two words heard twenty-two years ago. And the fact that you were just eleven at the time won't add anything to its credibility. I hope you can see the issue with that.'

'Of course, and it's a greater problem because I can't name the second man.'

'About that,' Marks tilted his head and looked at Goodhew over his glasses, 'I'm thinking that Stanley Mercer is more likely to be the second man . . .'

'To Neil Frampton's lead?'

'Exactly.' Marks agreed. 'Frampton had the motive to visit Joe . . .'

'Taking Mercer for support . . .'

'But we don't have a scrap of evidence.' Marks rewound the tape and played it one more time. He steepled his fingers as he weighed up the options. 'We'll bring in Mercer and simultaneously question Frampton – all we can do is keep him occupied so Mercer and he can't collude. We'll put pressure on Mercer and hope that he places both of them at the scene.' Marks removed the tape and handed it to Goodhew. 'Get that copied and then filed. And as a witness you won't be involved with interviewing either of them. We do have another bonus.' Marks tapped a sheet of paper too far from Goodhew for him to read. 'A local resident, Stuart Whitt, puts Mercer in Argyle Street with Lorraine Martin shortly before her estimated time of death.'

'And he's just come forward?'

'He was leaving for the airport when he saw them. He's back now and just caught up with the local papers.'

'How reliable is he?'

'Solid. And very precise with the timings.'

Marks had arrived in Argyle Street, his unmarked car chasing the tail of the leading response car; their arrival wasn't intended to be subtle. The gates to Frampton's yard had been open and a Transit pickup stood just inside the entrance. PCs Thompson and Marsden had waited at the gate while Marks and Worthington approached the Portakabin. Walking alongside Worthington felt similar to turning up in the company of a pit bull. Their whole entrance had been rather on the showy side for Marks's liking but then he'd seen Mercer glance out through the window. If a single expression could have been captured and put forward as evidence, then they would have been able to charge Stanley Mercer on the spot.

They'd read him his rights and had him back at Parkside and in an interview room within fifteen minutes.

Now Mercer's initial shock had subsided and he sat glowering at Marks from the other side of the table. 'Your solicitor is on his way,' Marks told him.

'This is bollocks. You can't bring me in on some random charge.'

Marks levelled a cold stare in his direction. 'There's nothing random, Mr Mercer, we have two witnesses that connect you with two separate crimes. One who connects you to Lorraine Martin's murder. And the other who puts you at Joseph Goodhew's house at the time of his attack.'

'I have nothing to do with Lorraine's death. Who's said that I do?'

'Mr Mercer, if you want to start the interview immediately then that's possible, but if you want to wait for your brief then I'm not having this conversation now.'

'I'll wait, but it's all bollocks. I never touched her.'

'Interesting,' Marks mused. 'Two denials over Lorraine's death and no mention of Joseph Goodhew.'

'Because there's no point; Detective Goodhew is a relative and you all look after your own.'

'You'd be better off wondering who's not looking after you.'

'Meaning what?'

'The witness claims he was in Joseph Goodhew's flat with you on the day Goodhew died.'

'Who?' Stan Mercer's complexion had been darkened by the years he'd spent working in the open air, but that couldn't hide the way the colour drained from his face. His glare barely wavered but if Marks hung around he guessed he'd start to see him sweat. 'What witness?'

Marks gathered up his notes; some people were easy to read and Mercer was the kind of man who liked an audience, liked to be heard as long as it was at no one's convenience. Hand him a microphone and he'd be as good as mute. He didn't like Marks breaking eye contact and made a predictable grab for attention before Marks reached the door. 'You're bluffing, otherwise you'd tell me.'

Marks opened the door then turned back and gave Mercer a deliberately pitying smile. 'If I were bluffing, how would I know that you were in Joseph Goodhew's flat? That there were just the two of you and the victim. The witness isn't the dead man, is it now?'

Marks stepped out of the room and closed the door behind him; he'd leave Mercer to sweat and then see what that shook loose. The moment of optimism was short-lived. Gully hurried into the corridor and he immediately saw her worried expression.

'What's wrong?'

'They arrived at Neil Frampton's house to bring him in but he'd taken off already.'

'When?'

'Obviously before Kincaide arrived at his house, before anyone at the yard could have tipped him off that we were coming. But I don't know more than that. His car's gone and there's no trace of it so far on traffic cams.'

'So where's Kincaide now?'

'Back at his desk.'

'And he sent you to find me? Why the hell aren't I having this conversation with him?' He hurried down the corridor, heading for Kincaide. 'That was rhetorical by the way,' he grunted as an afterthought.

'I guessed,' she replied.

He pushed open the door and shouted across the office, 'Michael, get Carolyn Frampton on the phone. Now.'

CHAPTER 43

Geraldine Buckingham had slept later than she intended. She planned to be out of bed by the time that Amy was waking up, envisaging the kind of sit-at-a-sunny-table-style breakfast that only seemed to exist in American TV shows. Obviously without the pancakes and maple syrup; who ate desserts at 7 a.m.?

But when she'd first heard Amy stir it had been much earlier and after a few minutes of moving around she had heard Amy open and close the front door and then listened to the sound of her daughter's footsteps gradually fading as she walked away. She'd cancelled her alarm then and drifted off again.

Now she stirred enough to follow the sounds that travelled up the stairs and across the landing: Amy had returned and she was boiling the kettle, making toast, washing her hair. Geraldine lifted herself onto one elbow and discovered that her head throbbed each time she moved. 'Amy,' she called. 'Amy?'

'Coming.'

Amy nudged the door open a few moments later. Her hair was damp and hung over her shoulder leaving a damp patch on her T-shirt, 'OK, Mum?'

'Headache.'

'I'm not surprised. What do you need?'

'Paracetamol and codeine from my bag. I'm sorry, love.'

Amy came back with the tablets and a glass of water, and sat on the edge of the bed until Geraldine had taken them. 'Are you still up for breakfast?'

Geraldine winced at the idea of food. 'Where did you go?'

'I popped round to see Moira; I'm going in at ten. What do you fancy, fried eggs, greasy bacon?' Amy raised an eyebrow. 'Or toast?'

'Toast. Now let me get dressed, I'm coming down.'

Amy closed the door and a few seconds later Geraldine heard her in the kitchen again. She sat on the edge of the bed and cradled her head in her hands. She tried to remember how much of the wine she'd drunk. Probably most of it. And it had been much stronger than her usual Pinot Noir. She doubted she would have drunk it all if Amy hadn't come home and, conversely, she wouldn't have drunk at all if she'd known that she'd have company.

She screwed up her eyes and focused on their conversation. The details began rushing back to her then. Amy's disgust with her father and Geraldine's own relief at having her daughter back in the fold. Amy claiming to want to leave the past and her dogged determination to pick over the details. She'd always been like that; picking at the minutiae, returning to a subject, chewing it over, then asking for more.

And there had been something more. Geraldine pushed her memory . . . something she'd said to Amy, hoping to impress her perhaps. Her eyes snapped open and brightness of the room made her cringe.

Abigail.

'No, no.' she gasped. Why had she said anything? 'Amy?' she called out to her daughter just as the doorbell rang. She scrambled to her feet as a wave of nausea hit her. 'Amy,' she shouted. 'Come up here, don't open the door.'

Amy's light-heartedness vanished as she headed back downstairs. She was glad she'd patched things up with her mum, and now that she'd begun to understand the depths of unhappiness that had existed in her parents' marriage she could see that Geraldine had done an excellent job of shielding her from it. Amy hadn't grown up witnessing endless rounds of fights and recriminations or been dragged through the trauma of prison visits.

She made herself tea, well brewed but with plenty of milk. The way she'd always liked it. From where she stood she could see into her mum's tiny walled garden; it had been her favourite spot when she'd lived here. *This* had been her childhood; a tranquil home and just the two of them.

She opened the back door and stood on the threshold. Weak sunlight was coming over the back wall and the pale brickwork and dense shrubbery vied for attention. It wasn't spectacular but she found it beautiful.

She smiled to herself then. What she was searching for wasn't spectacular either, just a version of her family story, one that she could accept as fact and know that it wouldn't change. Then she'd be able to confine it to the past and let it go.

She could feel that point was close and it didn't scare her. She tried to remember the exact conversation she'd had with DC Goodhew about truth. Just then she heard her mum calling her and the train of thought was lost. 'Hang on.'

She'd made it as far as the foot of the stairs when she saw the outline of a person through the frosted glass door. The bell rang as she reached across to open it. She'd twisted the catch by the time she registered her mum's voice.

Don't open the door.

But it was already flying towards her, the back of it simultaneously smacking her in the face and the side. Her right arm was flung wide and glanced off the banister, her ankle twisted over and she crumpled to the floor. The back of her head seemed to bounce on the tiled floor and she found herself staring in the direction of the landing. Sound separated itself from image. There was shouting. Her mum's legs on the stairs. And the taste of rust in her mouth.

CHAPTER 44

Marks stood next to Kincaide's desk and was using that desk phone to call. Carolyn Frampton picked up on the first ring. 'Mrs Frampton, this is Detective Inspector Marks, we need to speak to your husband urgently.'

The office had stilled and he didn't need to check the room to know that everyone was listening to him make the call. They could only hear his end of the conversation and not her replies.

'He's not here.'

'Can you tell us where to find him?'

'I don't know where he's gone. He had a phone call on his mobile but I didn't hear any of it,' she said. 'The next thing I knew he'd gone.'

'We've attempted to contact him on that number but his phone isn't responding.' Marks did his best to sound patient. 'I need to go over it again with you. Did you actually hear him leave the house?'

She sighed. 'I heard the car start, he over-revved it and reversed out onto the street too quickly. I heard the exhaust scrape the ground.' She sounded as though she wanted to add yada, yada, yada to the end of the sentence.

'Is that how he usually drives?'

'No, not these days, and never in that car.'

On the edge of his field of vision Marks could see the doorway. Goodhew entered the room now and stopped just a few feet from Gully. She moved to his side and whispered to him.

'What were his plans for the morning? Did he intend to go out?'

'No. He was supposed to be here, in meetings. And you're not letting me phone out so everyone from customers to planning officers are going to turn up and find us closed. My son's a no-show, our accountant's a no-show and the yard is calling and I can't pick up.'

'Alex and Moira?' He said it clearly and gestured to Kincaide to follow it up. Marks quickly covered the mouthpiece, 'Locate them both.' Kincaide immediately began directing the officers at the nearest desks.

'Yes,' Carolyn Frampton continued, 'Alex and Moira, Amy and Stan for all I know.' Without warning her tone had changed from frustration to weariness. 'Now please tell me what's going on.'

Marks nodded. It was time to give her something. 'We're following a lead we've had in relation to a separate murder investigation. Does the name Joseph Goodhew mean anything to you?'

She sounded cautious. 'I remember the case.'

'We have a reliable witness who can identify at least one of the two men present.'

'Oh.'

There was a long pause. Marks glanced towards the door. Goodhew had gone.

'Mrs Frampton?'

'Are you planning to arrest him?'

Marks hedged. 'I'm sorry, I can't comment. But I would like your help.'

This time the pause lasted longer. 'OK, but I need to speak to you in person.'

CHAPTER 45

'Alex and Moira.'

When Marks spoke the names and the room broke into activity. Goodhew stood for a moment amid the sudden flurry of activity and weighed it up.

Alex had been a toddler when Joe had died. He might be with his father or know where he might be but Moira was the better bet. And she lived closest. He made his decision and ran.

He left the rear of Parkside and took the route through the smaller streets before cutting down the footpath at the rear of Elm Street. He guessed it was a quarter of a mile and he was in Clarendon Road before he'd heard any siren. Moira's house came into view just as she stepped outside. The door slammed behind her and she hurried across the pavement, pressing the remote to unlock her car. She had the driver's door open before he reached her. 'Ms Trent?'

'I need to go out,' she mumbled. 'I'm supposed to be at work.'

'No. We need to speak to you.'

All colour had faded from her face and she'd clearly been crying. She stared into the interior of the car as though she was still contemplating driving somewhere. 'I don't understand what's happening.'

'Where's Neil Frampton?'

'I don't know.' She looked along the street and then back towards Goodhew; her focus had drifted off into a thousand-yard stare.

'Moira? I need to find him.' Goodhew pushed, 'You know him well; where would you look?'

She didn't seem to have an answer.

It was no great leap of logic to work out that she'd been the one who had phoned Neil Frampton. 'You called him this morning.' Goodhew didn't wait for confirmation. 'What did you say?'

'I didn't know how he'd react.'

'Moira, what did you say?'

Moira rubbed her forehead with the side of her hand and gathered herself enough so that she could concentrate. 'Amy came to see me. She knew that Nadine's baby was called Abigail.'

'So?'

'When Nadine came back to Cambridge she never mentioned her baby. Not to anyone apart from Theo; it was a closed subject. She wanted to blank it out.' Moira snorted at the irony. 'She was too young to realise the naivety of that idea. But it worked for a while. After the fire we each had our own reasons not to mention it. Neil just folded in on himself.'

The first response car had arrived in the street, the officers held back but the seconds were ticking away. 'Moira?'

'Neil and I never really talked until my sister died and suddenly we've been talking like we used to. That's when I found out the baby's name. And, in all those years, no one else knew. Not even Carolyn.'

'And Amy?'

'She said her mother told her. I didn't think that Geraldine ever knew about Robert's baby back then, but she must have done because the only people who could have told her the name were Nadine and Theo.'

Realisation hit him; the clue had been on the very first interview tapes and everyone had missed it. Theo hadn't been to the Buckingham's house to visit Robert, he'd gone to see Geraldine. Geraldine's refusal to provide Robert with a fake alibi had been her masterstroke.

And now Neil Frampton knew the truth.

Moira's expression reflected his own. 'I didn't think he'd do anything,' she gasped.

Goodhew grabbed her by both shoulders, 'Where does Geraldine Buckingham live?'

Moira glanced over her shoulder. 'Fair Street.'

'Number?'

'Fifteen.'

Goodhew took her keys and tossed them at the nearest constable. 'Ms Trent is a witness.' He turned away, shouting into his radio as he ran, 'Fifteen Fair Street. Assistance required.'

Clarendon Street to Fair Street was a two-hundred-yard sprint but this time a police car arrived at the head of the street as Goodhew came in via a footpath at the other end. Kincaide jumped from the first vehicle as Goodhew reached the front gate. Goodhew banged on the door with his fist.

'They've gone,' Kincaide told him, then shouted over his shoulder at Holden, 'Quick as you can.'

Holden swung the Enforcer out of the vehicle and strode towards the door, holding it in both gloved hands.

'We've found Frampton's Jag,' Kincaide told Goodhew as Holden reached the door. 'He's swapped it for one of their own Transits. We're searching for it now.'

Holden lined the Enforcer up to the lock, swung it back then into the door with full force and on the second strike the frame split. He pushed the door wider with the flat of his hand.

The hallway was dark and narrow. Even with the light from the open door the blood streaks on the floor were barely visible against the dark red tiles. A mirror that had hung from a hook on the wall now lay smashed at the foot of the stairs with shards of its glass scattered the length of the hallway. Here the blood stood out against the bright fragments.

They moved quickly through the house disturbing as little as possible as they checked from room to room. Each stood empty and the only signs of disturbance were at the entrance.

Kincaide decided to state the obvious, 'So they came and left this way and at least one of them was injured in the process.'

'Nothing reported by the neighbours?' Goodhew glanced along the short street and realised that there were only a few properties within sight.

Kincaide did the same. 'I'm leaving you here to secure this place,

Gary, and I'll send you a couple of uniforms and a SOCO.' He turned the car keys over in his hand. 'Keep me posted.'

Holden was staring at the damaged door and pretending not to listen.

'No chance,' Goodhew replied and ran back the way he'd come.

Stanley Mercer had demanded a solicitor with a smug expression. Perhaps he thought that he'd bought himself time with a get-out-of-jail card waiting at the end. The reality was different; sometimes 'I want a solicitor' worked better for the police than no solicitor at all; the seemingly endless wait made the suspect sweat and it took a strong mind to deal with the boredom of four walls and no view.

Marks opened the door and Mercer's relief was palpable; he'd had too long to think and no longer cared enough to wait. Marks cut him short. 'In the last couple of minutes, I've been informed of a significant development and I need a fast decision from you.' Marks had received confirmation that Robert Buckingham was safe but the whereabouts of his ex-wife and daughter remained unknown. He could see he'd hooked Mercer's interest but knew he needed to tread carefully. He decided to start the conversation at a less direct angle. 'Carolyn Frampton's about to make a statement. You can pre-empt her or not . . .'

'She's your witness?' Mercer stood with his hands folded and his back straight; attempting and failing to make himself appear bigger. 'She doesn't know anything.'

'Well, I mentioned Joseph Goodhew and she volunteered to come in.'

The corners of Mercer's mouth curled downwards. 'You're bluffing.'

'You like the idea that I might be bluffing, don't you? She's had enough of the lies and she's ready to make a statement. We have a witness who places you in Joseph Goodhew's house at the time of his attack. That's two people against you.' Marks hoped that Mercer would still picture Neil Frampton as the second. 'This is not the time for misplaced loyalty.'

'It's not misplaced,' Mercer replied.

'No one is protecting you now.'

The two men stood toe to toe for several seconds.

'Fuck,' Mercer growled and drew a heavy breath, tipped his head back and stared up at the ceiling. 'It was a single punch.' He exhaled slowly, shaping his mouth into an 'O' and blowing loudly. 'The old man was an accident, but it wasn't me. Neil lost his temper and hit him.'

'Neil killed him?'

'Yes.'

'And now I have the situation where Neil Frampton is at large and considered a risk to two members of the public.'

'Wait. Neil's not the witness?' Stan did a double take as he realised he'd been misled. 'You bastard.'

Marks continued, unfazed, 'You're an accessory, it's a serious charge. You have the chance to help us.'

'With what?'

'I need to find him before anyone gets hurt. I want you to cooperate with us, but it needs to be right now.'

Mercer's eyes narrowed. Part of him wanted to deflect whatever Marks had to say but his focus drifted off to his left before returning to Marks, 'Who's in danger?' A moment later he put his hands out, making the stop gesture. 'No, forget it. Robert Buckingham is the only person that Neil has ever wanted to hurt and I wouldn't interfere with that.'

'Robert Buckingham isn't in danger but two women are.' Marks drew closer to Mercer. 'You've just admitted that he's a killer. What's he going to do next, Stan?'

'Nothing.' Mercer shook his head. 'Why would he?'

'What if he thought that Robert Buckingham was no longer the answer?'

Mercer looked mystified. 'Then who?'

'Stan, what would he do if he thought he had found the person who set the fire and it turned out to be someone he knows well, someone who's been above suspicion for all these years? Someone he's supported even? He's going to want revenge, isn't he?'

'No, he'll want justice.' Stan shook his head. 'And I'll tell you what he won't do.'

'What's that?'

'He won't leave it to you.'

CHAPTER 46

As far as Amy knew, the journey had been brief and silent and dark. She was aware of them moving, of tilting in directions she couldn't predict. She lay on some kind of plastic sheeting, a crumpled pile of it that rucked uncomfortably under her back. It was dusty and she was aware of trying to cough but only achieving something between a gag and a spit. She felt a hand on her arm, a soft squeeze and it felt like her mum.

They stopped moving and she began to hear again. Her mum repeating her name, telling her she needed to wake up.

She opened her eyes and found that it was possible to see a few details in the gloom. A small amount of light was seeping through from the driver's cab and she could make out the wood boarding on the walls of the van, pieces of equipment and the silhouette of her mum leaning over her.

'I'm so sorry,' her mum whispered.

The side panel door opened, rattling against the van's bodywork. Amy expected light to flood in but outside was only slightly brighter. Neil Frampton stood in the doorway. His skin shone with sweat and his expression had become blank and disconnected. He shone a torch into her face. 'You're awake, now sit up.'

She began to raise her head, then dropped it again as she was hit by a wave of nausea. 'I feel sick.'

He grabbed her upper arm and pulled her upright. When he released his hold she began to sag backwards. 'No,' he growled and dragged her straight again. His fingers left her arm throbbing.

'Neil, you're hurting her.' Her mother's voice was a mixture of desperation and fear.

He shone the torch on to Geraldine. Her mother looked terrified and, for the first time, Amy felt it too. 'Mum, what's happened?'

Geraldine's hand found Amy's and squeezed it tightly. She was shaking. Her entire body trembled, her mouth quivered as she tried to speak.

'Tell your daughter what you did.'

Geraldine started to cry, heavy sobs wracking her body.

Neil stepped back then slammed his boot against the side panel of the van, 'Tell her. Fuck you.' He kicked the van again and again, 'Fuck you,' screaming the words and kicking the metal with each syllable. 'Tell her what you did.'

Geraldine started shouting through her sobs. Just distorted and unintelligible words at first. Spit flying from her mouth.

Amy managed to decipher, 'It was Robert. He pushed me and pushed me.'

'Mum, tell me, talk to me.'

'I couldn't stand living with him.'

Neil reached towards Geraldine but Amy cut in. 'Do you want her to talk?'

Neil lashed out with the flat of his hand and caught Amy across the side of her head. 'Then talk, Gerri, or I swear I'll hurt her.'

This time it was Amy gripping her mother's arm. 'Take a breath, Mum. Talk to me.'

Her mum continued to pant heavily as she spoke. 'I wasn't going to leave him. We would have lost too much; I would have lost too much of you to him. And why should we have been punished for the things he'd done?'

'It's what happens in divorce, Mum.'

Suddenly Geraldine's expression changed. The fear was still there but mingled with a new steeliness. 'Amy, I wanted him to die. I took money from the business, made it look as though he'd used it. I researched different methods . . .'

'You *hated* him that much?'

'You have no idea. And then Theo came to see me . . .'

Neil hadn't stood still but had remained agitated and restless. He stiffened at the sound of his son's name.

'He told me about the baby. Abigail. I never knew about the pregnancy until that moment. He wanted me to know that Nadine was sorry.' She pursed her lips. 'Your dad stopped having sex with me when he was shagging her, even though he knew I wanted another child. She got pregnant and I didn't. So Nadine's sorry and, what, everything gets erased? Reset? Forgotten?' She shook her head. 'How could I kill Robert when I suddenly had a visible motive? I had no intention of living the rest of my life with that man.'

Staying silent finally defeated Frampton. 'Tell her, Geraldine.'

Geraldine looked at Amy and smiled. It was a calm expression, proud even. 'I set fire to that house and your father went to prison.'

Neil began to shout but Amy couldn't keep the nausea at bay any longer. She closed her eyes. Covered her ears and sank slowly to the floor.

Sue Gully stopped beside Jack Worthington's desk. Worthington could be abrupt and was usually taciturn but he always answered her. 'Have the ANPR cameras picked up the van?'

'Not yet.'

'I was thinking, swapping the car for the van didn't make Frampton anonymous because we had the registration number straight away.'

'It bought him time and he's moving people; it's discreet.'

'He's only gone a short distance or the cameras would have picked him up. And it cost him time to swap vehicles . . .'

Worthington frowned. 'What exactly are you thinking?'

'That there's a reason it needs to be a van? Or there's something a van can do that a car can't?' She shrugged. 'I thought I had something for a second.'

Worthington stared at her, his frown deepening. He picked up the phone and she saw him dial the number for the custody suite. 'Is anyone in with Mercer?' Worthington checked his computer screen, 'Ask him about Ford Transit Hotel-Golf-5-7 . . .' He finished reading out the rest of the registration number. 'Is there anything about it that makes it different to the other vehicles that were on site? Maybe the spec or what it's carrying?'

Worthington waited.

He listened to the reply and was on his feet before he'd finished replacing the receiver. 'We need to speak to Marks. It's the only one that carries welding gear. It's loaded with gas canisters.'

Amy lay still and just listened. She felt no panic or fear at that moment, just the sensation of feeling detached from everything around her. Was this, she wondered, how survivors of massacres felt when they played dead?

Without warning Neil Frampton lunged at Amy, grabbing her hair. He pulled her head straight and slapped her hard across the face with the palm of his hand. She inhaled with a shuddering breath.

Geraldine, wide-eyed, shook her head and mouthed 'I'm sorry.'

He gripped Amy's hair at the scalp and began to drag her upwards. Amy yelped.

'Neil,' her mum breathed, 'let her go, please.'

'I need you to confess properly, Gerri.'

'I will,' she told him, 'I promise.' But in her mum's face was a look that she hadn't seen for many years. She flashed back to the days she'd walked home from senior school. She'd been fourteen before her mum had stopped meeting her at the gate and she'd been teased for that too. But once she'd started walking home alone she hurried every step, worried about the trouble she'd be in if she arrived home late. Worried that a couple of minutes talking to another kid would be seen as a slight by her mum.

Her heart would beat harder when she crossed the threshold.

'Why, Mum?'

'Look at him,' Geraldine pointed to Neil. 'He's beyond seeing reason and it's my fault. That's how I was when I found out about the baby; out of my mind.'

'Don't compare us,' Neil snapped, then without warning his voice dropped to a harsh whisper. 'You killed my son and then you came to his funeral. You sat in court with us. You apologised for Robert and then let him go to jail. And for all those years I helped you.'

'Out of guilt,' Amy said softly. This was the only thing she had worked out. 'You saw us as victims of my dad, just as you and Theo had been.'

He just stared back at her but she knew she was correct. 'What did any of us do to you?' he asked her mother.

Geraldine shook her head. 'It wasn't about you, Neil. When Theo told me about the baby I snapped. I reached the edge and went over. I don't have a word for the way I hated Nadine then, I would have taken my bare hands and twisted her neck.' Geraldine's hands briefly formed claws before she clenched them into fists.

'At any point you could have confessed.'

'Robert was going down and Amy needed me.'

'Amy needed you?' Neil stepped back from the van. 'I killed Joseph Goodhew because of you. I hit him and he died. I wouldn't have been so desperate to find my other child if Theo had been alive. I wouldn't have even been in Goodhew's house. So that's on you too.' Neil glanced at his watch and then shook his head. 'Every fucking thing I've done wrong is down to you, right up to today. But this one will be all mine.'

He slammed the door. It was followed by the muted peep of the doors locking and then they were in darkness again.

They both listened for a moment before Geraldine began to bang on the sides. 'Neil. Neil.'

'Mum, stop,' Amy said, then continued in a low voice. 'There must be a way to open this from the inside.' She shuffled across to the side door and felt for the catch, 'Check at the back.' The edge of the door was in complete darkness and she used her fingertips to feel along it. She found the location of the catch in seconds, she moved closer, attempting to see any part of it. 'It's broken,' she whispered.

A boot slammed against the metal on the other side, 'Of course it's broken,' Neil shouted. He yanked open the door just wide enough to come face to face with Amy. 'That's why you're not tied up. No one can hear you either. Now shut the fuck up while I get this ready.'

CHAPTER 47

Gully was the first person Goodhew saw when he pushed open the doors at Parkside. 'Have they located them yet?'

'No. But the Transit he's taken carries gas canisters. Worthington's with Mercer and he's listing every location Frampton might use.'

'Good. Where's Marks?'

'With Carolyn Frampton, Room 2. And Sandra's with Moira Trent in Room 3. They're all asking the same thing . . .' Gully broke off to look over his shoulder and they both turned as Sergeant Norris opened the door between them and the front desk.

'I've got an Alex Frampton out here, asking for DI Marks.'

'Thanks, I'll deal with him,' Goodhew replied. He and Gully followed Norris into the waiting area.

Alex stood holding his crash helmet in one hand and his leather jacket in the other and his feet firmly planted on the tiled floor. When he spoke his voice was calm but firm. 'What's going on? No one's telling me anything and, to be honest, I'm worried about Amy.'

Goodhew pursed his lips, made a fast assessment and decided that breaching confidentiality was the least of the risks. 'We believe that she and her mother are with your father. We're concerned for their safety.'

For a moment Alex appeared bewildered and studied Goodhew's expression for a sign that he'd misunderstood. His puzzlement rapidly became consternation. 'What the hell has triggered it?'

'You're not surprised?'

'Yes and no. He's complicated. Volatile.'

'He believes Geraldine Buckingham killed your brother and Nadine Kendall.'

Alex drew straighter, 'How accurate is that?'

'He may be right,' Goodhew conceded. 'He's picked a Transit van containing gas bottles and we're pretty sure he's somewhere in town. We haven't heard from him and at least one of the women is injured.'

'Which one?'

'We don't know. Can you think of anywhere we might find him?'

Alex's face drained of colour. 'Somewhere they can burn.'

Holden followed Kincaide back into the building. 'Let it drop, Michael.' If he said it one more time Kincaide swore he'd swing at the man. 'The man's a suspect in the Joseph Goodhew murder, you couldn't leave Gary on the doorstep.'

Kincaide stopped in his tracks, spun around and jabbed his finger into Holden's body armour, 'Back off, Kev.'

They carried on up to the office in single file, Holden saying nothing until they were at the door. 'Now let it drop,' he told Kincaide and pushed through the door in front of him.

Kincaide darted through after him but was immediately sidetracked by Worthington who was standing at Kincaide's desk and pointing to the phone in his hand. 'I've got DS Jerram on the line. Frampton switched on his phone.'

Everyone else in the room looked around too.

'Where is he?'

'He switched it on, sent a single text then switched it off again. They've triangulated it to within 500 metres of the north-east end of the Cambridge Retail Park.'

Kincaide reached across and took the phone from Worthington. 'We need to narrow it down more than that.'

The voice at the other end was male and droning and his reasoning involved multiple acronyms. 'So if it is switched on again and for longer we will have more data.'

'Can't you recalculate what you have?'

'No.'

'What was in this text?'

'We know that it went to a mobile registered to his wife. He sent a single message and, judging by the packet size, I would be happy to speculate that it contained data other than text.'

'A picture?'

'Possibly.'

'Can you retrieve it?'

'No.'

He shoved the phone back at Worthington. 'That's as good as useless. I need to speak to Marks.'

'I'm here.' Marks had just entered the room, urgently pressing buttons on his phone as he did so. He then held up a sheet of paper. 'This is a copy of the picture that Mrs Frampton just received on her phone. I was with her at the time and she is not able to shed any light on her husband's location. The picture is of a handwritten note which I have just forwarded to all members of this team.' Around the room several phones were already pinging and buzzing. He paused for a moment to give everyone the chance to look. 'We now have a narrowed search area; we have vehicles on the way and you are all to make finding Neil Frampton your absolute priority. This may be the only opportunity we have to find him.'

They'd just moved into a side room conveniently furnished with three chairs and one badly defaced table when a text arrived at both phones simultaneously. Gully glanced at hers first. 'From Marks,' she said as she opened it.

'Same,' Goodhew echoed.

Opening it must have also been in unison because Goodhew tensed at the same moment she realised what she was seeing. The photograph was of a sheet of ruled paper, from an exercise book, she guessed, judging by the size of the letters compared to the gap between the lines. It was being held between a man's finger and thumb with just a thin strip of dark background visible on each of the four sides. The penmanship was messy after the first couple of lines, produced by someone whose hand was hurrying faster than they were able to form words. In several places words had been crossed through and rewritten in an attempt to make them more legible.

Carolyn.

Hand this over afterwards. I was never going to be arrested for killing Goodhew without killing Robert first but it was never him.

Geraldine Buckingham killed Theo and she will be punished.

He didn't sign off and Goodhew guessed he'd just given up.

He finished reading but continued to study the photograph. Gully looked across and met Alex's eye. 'It's from your father to your mum.'

Goodhew looked at her sharply. 'Hold on, Sue.'

She shook her head. 'This one's my call,' she said and turned the phone to face Alex. 'Is it his handwriting?'

Alex winced as he read, 'It's erratic but yes, it is.'

'He was somewhere near Cambridge Retail Park when he sent this,' she explained. 'Does the company own any property near there? Are any projects located there?'

Alex began to shake his head then stopped and rose to his feet. 'Oh shit. Behind the retail park is the railway line and behind that is a road of old industrial units – warehousing and workshops. He'll be down there.'

He was talking about Coldham's Road, a half-mile stretch with both current businesses and the shells of long-forgotten ones.

'Where exactly?'

'Halfway down, further maybe. It's an old vehicle-repair shop, block walls, sheet roof. It's empty; Dad's been trying to buy it for years.'

Goodhew grabbed Alex's arm and propelled him towards the door. 'Is your bike outside?'

'Yes.'

'Spare helmet?'

'And with a full tank.'

'Then show me the building.' Goodhew turned for one second and looked back at Sue. 'I'll use my earpiece. Keep me posted and tell Marks what I've done.'

She hurried to find their DI, pushing aside the phrase Kincaide had used, the one that was trying to play on repeat inside her head. *He will crash and burn.*

Crash and burn.

* * *

263

Goodhew shouldn't have allowed Alex Frampton to leave the building. Shouldn't have allowed him to ride a bike either. But here they were; riding from East Road onto Newmarket Road in less time than it would have taken him to unlock any of the cars.

They had just over a mile to go but Sue would be directing the officers that were already in the vicinity towards the workshop. He prayed they were there already. That it was the right location. That is wasn't too late.

And behind them he could just make out the sound of more sirens too. He glanced back and saw a couple of response cars keeping pace.

Alex and he were just the backup plan and he expected to hear an update via his earpiece at any moment. They swung into Coldham's Lane, as usual clogged with vehicles. Alex slalomed between the cars, narrowing the gap between them and the turning they needed. A police helicopter hovered ahead of them near the junction of Coldham's Lane and Coldham's Road. That had to be a good sign but still nothing came through the headset.

As they crossed the railway line Goodhew glanced down from the bridge and saw Coldham's Road running in a thin line parallel to the train tracks. The furthest section visible was dotted with blue lights and strewn with vehicles and men. The road usually appeared bleak but today it looked desperate.

CHAPTER 48

Both Amy and her mother had stayed still and quiet since Neil had shouted. They listened instead and for the first few minutes only whispered when one or the other thought they'd heard something.

'He'll come back eventually.' Amy noticed that her voice had stopped shaking even though her heart continued to thud. 'We need to decide what we're going to do.'

'I can answer that; nothing. We're locked in and he knows what he wants.'

'I can talk to him. Or try to. I'm not going to give up. You should tell him you're sorry.' Amy paused to think about her statement. 'Are you sorry?'

'Does it make any difference? At the moment I did those things I didn't have a choice. You know what it's like to have compulsions, Amy, with your fact collecting and constant poking at the past. Same thing. That's how it starts and it takes over.' She looked pensive then cocked her head to one side a little. 'I killed Lorraine Martin.'

Amy clapped her hand to her mouth but managed a muffled 'Why?'

'She banged on my door. Kept saying that she knew.'

'Knew what?'

'About Nadine. She said that she was going to tell you. I was too slow and I let her go. I thought she was going to tell you about the baby but, when her words sank in, I realised that she might have meant that she'd worked out that I'd set that fire. I couldn't risk it, could I? I knew I had to find her. So I drove to your flat.' Geraldine's hands formed the fists again. 'Then I realised that she didn't know where you lived and was maybe looking for you somewhere else. I drove to her house and back again but when I saw Stan driving out of Argyle Street, I guessed where she might be.' Geraldine's eyes shone, proud of her deduction.

Amy thought of Alex and under her breath mouthed the words, 'I don't want to die.'

In the silence that followed, she could hear the distant throb of helicopter blades cutting the air. Slow and rhythmic.

Amy jumped when the central locking was released. The driver's door rattled open. 'Neil, please talk to us,' she shouted. 'You don't have to do this. You can let us go.'

Neil Frampton had considered letting one of them live. Like the pied piper who'd left a crippled child to tell the tale. There were two options and each depended on how much Geraldine loved her.

He thought about releasing Amy but remembered how many times he had wished he could have taken Theo's place. He couldn't risk Geraldine dying with a half-smile on her lips and the knowledge that her child was safe. And releasing Geraldine only worked if she truly loved Amy and the pain of losing her was absolute. It seemed to him that Geraldine loved Geraldine more than she loved her daughter; some people didn't love their children as much as they ought.

In the last few minutes he'd found a happy compromise.

He felt a pang of guilt then. He had obsessed over Melanie's baby, the child he'd never met, the one who, in his mind's eye, might have become Theo's replacement. It had been a nonsense, a fantasy. And he hadn't loved Alex as much as he should because that fire had burnt out his own ability to feel anything but the gap Theo had left. It had taken him a long time to understand that Melanie's baby couldn't have filled it. And neither could Alex; he'd never given him the chance.

He unlocked the van and took a bottle of vodka and a can of diesel from the foot well on the passenger side. He placed both on the ground near the side door and then opened the van.

The kick hit him from nowhere and sent him sprawling on the

grease-soaked floor. Geraldine scrambled from the van and he saw Amy stagger to her feet too. Clutching the doorway.

Neil scrambled upright and went for the mother, grabbing her and bringing her down before she'd made it halfway across the concrete. She fell hard and grunted as the air was knocked from her lungs. He punched her full in the face and fought back the urge to choke the life from her.

'Mum!' Amy shouted.

He dropped Geraldine's lifeless arm and leapt across to grab Amy. He pressed a hand across her mouth, bundled her back into the van and listened. The police were out there somewhere but if they'd been close the commotion would have been their signal to burst in. The helicopter wasn't overhead yet and the sirens sounded still too distant. He spoke into her ear. 'I'm calling it a *happy compromise*,' he told her. He dragged her back down onto the floor of the van and used his free hand to grab the vodka and then his teeth to break the seal. 'You won't know much, I can live with that. Or not.' He climbed on top of her prone body and used his weight to pin her arms. There wasn't much fight in her but she still gagged and tried to spit out the alcohol. It became easier after the first couple of involuntary swallows though and her movements quickly lost their coordination.

He dragged Geraldine back to the Transit and hauled her inside. She was semi-conscious and limp. Her listless eyes followed him as he pulled the gas canisters from the van and slid them underneath. He was pleased to see her eyes widen very slightly; she needed to know. 'Think of a cooker. Then think of Theo's last minutes.' He closed the door and swigged from the vodka himself. Then he grabbed a thick pile of yellowed newspapers from one corner of the workshop floor and piled them a few inches from the diesel and the gas canisters.

The helicopter was closer now. Blue lights flickered through a Perspex panel situated a few feet above the full-length doors. An amplified voice spoke to him through the wall, 'Neil Frampton, this is the police.'

'If you open the door I'll kill them,' he shouted. 'I need to speak to DI Marks.'

Timing was everything. He lit the papers and watched the lazy flame take hold before he climbed in with the women. He stood his torch on the floor with the beam pointing up at the roof. He swigged more from the bottle and watched Geraldine's face as she realised she would be paying for what she'd done.

The other response cars and the fire engine pulled in next to Alex and Goodhew. Already there were four cars at the scene, all uniformed officers and only Ted Moorey who knew anything of their investigation. 'He wants Marks,' Moorey shouted as Goodhew removed his helmet.

Kincaide stepped from the nearest vehicle. 'I'm in charge until Marks arrives.'

Goodhew checked his earpiece and tried speaking to Sue. 'What happened? I couldn't hear you.'

'I'd have told you if it was over. I stayed silent because you just needed to get there. I'm connecting you to Marks right now.'

Marks's voice took over seamlessly, 'I'm two minutes away. What can you see?'

'An old-style repair shop, large doors, solid walls.' Pretty much what Alex described. 'It's locked and we can't see in. Frampton is confirmed as being inside. He has issued threats if we try to enter and he's asked for you.'

'Keep him talking,' Marks told him and cut the connection.

Goodhew grabbed Alex's arm, 'Come on,' he said and moved closer to the unit's door. 'Mr Frampton,' he shouted, 'your son is here.'

He nudged Alex. 'Get his attention.'

'OK,' he replied, then turned to face the door and shouted. 'Dad, it's Alex. You need to listen to me. I need you to let Amy go . . .'

'This is DS Kincaide.' Kincaide was a few feet away with a megaphone and his voice swamped the end of Alex's words. Kincaide stared resolutely at the closed door but Goodhew's attention immediately switched to a sudden movement from the fire crew.

Their commander banged his hand on the appliance door to get police attention, 'We have a heat source in there. He's started some kind of fire.'

Kincaide lowered the megaphone. 'How much time do we have?'

'None. It's a fire.' He swore under his breath. He instructed his crew and they swarmed past Kincaide and the other officers to reach the door. 'And everyone else get back, we need a safe perimeter. You,' he shouted at Kincaide, 'sort it out.'

Beyond the fire engine another siren died and a door slammed. 'Kelday, what have we got?' DI Marks ran across to the crew commander.

He showed Marks the screen of their thermal imaging camera. 'The fire is beside the vehicle, it's not huge yet but there are three people in the vehicle and the engine is running. It's belt and braces: if the fumes don't get them the fire will.' He pointed to the small door in the nearest wall. 'That's the quickest way in. We need a hose in there right now before the canisters blow.'

Two firefighters swung a battering ram between them. After the third attempt it hadn't budged. 'It's reinforced,' they shouted.

'Shit.' Kelday raised his hand. 'Check the building for any other points where we can force entry,' he instructed and moved forward to examine the lock.

Goodhew's gaze scanned the building too. 'That's the only door,' Alex told him.

Goodhew pointed up to an off-white rectangle above the entrance. 'What's that?'

'It's for light. They're on the roof as well.'

Goodhew took a breath, 'OK,' he replied and grabbed the crash helmet from Alex. 'I'll try.'

CHAPTER 49

The roof had a low gradient and was lower at the rear of the building. Goodhew moved Moorey's patrol car to the back of the building; he wasn't bad at shinning drainpipes but starting from the roof of the Ford Focus made it a whole lot easier. He threw a tyre iron up first then followed with the crash helmet hooked to his belt.

There were half a dozen panels in the roof. He guessed they'd once been clear but were now opaque with age. He plumped for the most central of the three in the lowest section of roof. He struck it with the metal bar. The second attempt broke through and the sun-damaged Perspex split into brittle lines. He kicked at the rest and found himself directly above the ground and about eight feet behind the van.

The opening in the roof drew the fire upwards, it's burble beginning to roar.

He put on the crash helmet and closed the visor before lowering himself through the gap. He waited until his arms were fully extended then he dropped. He landed on his feet but hit the ground hard, pain from an old injury jolting the length of his spine. The air was thick with exhaust fumes and smoke but he reckoned the crash helmet contained one good clean breath; he drew it in and held it then ran for the cab.

He jumped into the driver's seat and rammed it into gear. Black smoke billowed past the passenger side window as he swung the van in a tight semi-circle away from the fire and towards the entrance. He sounded the horn and accelerated, smashing the van against the large metal door. It bent but held.

He released his breath and coughed as the thick air hit him.

He checked his mirrors. Small blue flames had begun to dance on the floor and the burning pile of newspaper was slowly crumbling towards the fuel can. He reversed towards it and then straight into first gear to hit the door again. He butted the van up to it and powered against the panelling but it wouldn't give.

He looked back. The flames had reached the canisters now. He saw the newspapers hit the fuel can, there could only be seconds now. He slammed the van into reverse and drove backwards in an arc, stopping at the back wall. The fire burnt between him and the door. The floor was alight now and the canisters smouldered. He revved the engine and hit the accelerator. He cut a path straight through it all. The fuel can exploded behind him and the first canister erupted as he hit the door. This time it gave way and the burning van careered into the light and crashed into the yard's perimeter fence.

Foam hit it first. Then Goodhew pushed open his door and was pulled clear. An oxygen mask was held to his mouth and his eyes stung from the smoke as he fought to keep them open. He saw the Transit doors open and firefighters pull the three people out one by one.

He was carried away from the fire and put on a stretcher. 'I'm fine,' he insisted but was strapped to the trolley and loaded into the ambulance in any case. He lay still and listened to the voices outside trying to work out what had happened to Amy, Geraldine and Neil. 'Are they OK?' he asked.

The paramedic checked his blood pressure. 'No one's dead. I hear that's a bit of a result.'

The van doors opened and Amy was hit by daylight and foam, acrid air and confusion. She only had to turn her head to see Neil or her mother but she couldn't bring herself to look at either of them. She kept her eyes on the space above the doorway where she could glimpse a patch of sky until she felt someone lift her clear.

They inserted a drip and began cleaning her wounds. A paramedic leant over her and shone a torch into her eyes, 'What did he give you?' he asked.

She managed the word. 'Vodka.'

'Anything else?'

She replied, 'Nothing,' but could hear him talking to his colleague. Weighing it all up. They could pump her stomach; she didn't care. She reached out and managed to tap his arm. 'I need to call someone.'

'You'll have to hang on for that, Amy.' His expression was calm and reassuring. 'You have a few bumps and bruises to deal with first. Hang on.' He disappeared from view for a few seconds and almost instantly she felt herself begin to doze. Then she felt his fingers tapping on the back of her hand, 'Amy? Amy love? Stay awake. Alex is here, he wants to sit with you. Is that OK?'

She nodded.

Alex stood beside her and held both her hands in his.

'We have shitloads of baggage between us, don't we?' she whispered.

'I'm not my father,' he told her.

'And I'm not my mum.'

'Well then, we're sorted,' he joked gently. One side of her mouth managed to smile. 'Our families are really screwed up, Alex.'

He kissed her softly on the lips. 'And we can't undo any of it.'

'That's depressing,' she murmured as she kissed him again.

'Absolutely,' he replied. 'Or it's the best thing for us.'

'Maybe it is,' she murmured and began to drift off, sure that he'd be there when she awoke.

Marks watched the third ambulance pull away and surveyed the mess left in Goodhew's wake. Four fire engines were still at the unit, although there was nothing to save and the risk of it spreading seemed to have passed. The remains of the Transit had been loaded onto a recovery vehicle and his officers were finally leaving the scene. The last ambulance was Goodhew's. 'I'll go back with you, Michael,' Marks told Kincaide. 'Let me speak to Goodhew first.'

He climbed the steep step into the back of the vehicle. 'What the hell was that, Gary?'

Goodhew squinted at him. 'I don't know. Spontaneity? How's Amy?'

'All three of them have gone to hospital. They're all in a bad way but not life-threatening. And you'll have your day in court with Frampton.'

'His airbags don't work.'

'You're a mess, Gary. And I may as well tell you that my final report will be damning: your behaviour, bad attitude, reckless endangerment of the public. Oh, and driving skills. The list goes on.' He placed his hand on Goodhew's shoulder. 'But Joe would be proud.'

'Thank you, sir.'

'Don't miss my retirement drinks either. If you're not there I won't believe that I'm finally rid of you.'

He stepped back out into the smoky afternoon and into Kincaide's car.

'I think you're psychic, Michael.'

'Really, sir?'

'Was that the kind of crash and burn you had in mind for Gary? You see, I have spoken to Sue. Do you really think I hold with the view that colleagues have to stay quiet in the face of unacceptable conduct from their superiors?'

Kincaide didn't reply.

'That's not a rhetorical question,' Marks added.

Kincaide reddened. 'No, sir.' Then added, 'Goodhew constantly undermines me, sir.'

'Goodhew constantly undermines me, but do you hear me whining or crying "he started it"? I have few regrets but seeing you promoted has become one of them. You have the makings of a decent DS but you choose to throw it away at every opportunity.'

Kincaide stared at him.

'My replacement will be fully briefed but, until then, grow some balls, Michael.'

EPILOGUE

Three days later.

The doors stood open on the unit in Hope Street Yard as Goodhew and Ellie watched the furniture being loaded into the removals lorry.

'You're sure about this?' he asked.

'If it feels like the right thing for you, then I am delighted.'

The second-floor room had always been his grandfather's no matter where Goodhew positioned the jukebox or how he painted the walls, and he planned to put the desk and bookcases back the way he remembered them. 'I'm going to move my furniture out of the attic and have everything together on the first floor.' He took the piece of broken bangle from his pocket. 'And this will go back where it belongs.'

Neil Frampton had been charged with his grandfather's murder, Stan Mercer as an accessory. 'How are you feeling?' he asked her.

She knew exactly what he meant. 'Lighter. And I've been thinking of Joe a lot more, remembering things about him. We had thirty excellent years, plenty of people aren't that lucky. And I don't mean that in an I'm-calling-it-a-day way. Doors open, Gary, and Joe encouraged me to go through them. I always loved that about your grandfather.'

Goodhew's own memories had been stirred by the recent events. 'By the way, I've been thinking and I understand why you kept Joe's murder from me; you tried to protect our childhood. In fact, the more

I look at it, you and Joe made our childhood. All the best memories I have are in that house.'

'Really?' She tried to sound casual but couldn't hide her pleasure at the thought. 'We both loved you and your sister so much.'

'I know.'

He nodded towards the entrance. 'Happy to walk?'

'I'd prefer to; I've heard your driving's poor, especially exiting garages.'

'It's abysmal. But I don't think they'll sack me this time.'

'Never on DI Marks's watch, Gary.' She smiled. 'But it doesn't mean you have to stay. You could do what Sue's doing and relocate.' She squeezed his arm. 'With Marks, Sheen and Sue all leaving . . . it won't be the same.'

'You're too smart. You already know I've made up my mind, don't you?'

'I guessed, although I thought Kincaide might make you stay.'

The junction with Parker's Piece lay ahead and soon he'd be within sight of the station. 'I knew I was at a crossroads; I could feel it. The reasons that drove me to join in the first place didn't exist any more. The way I worked was wrong. My ambitions for promotion were non-existent. But I couldn't imagine not being part of Parkside either.'

'So?'

'So I resigned anyway. For good this time. I want to move on.'

She didn't seem surprised and he wondered if this outcome had looked obvious to her all along, the way so many decisions did from the outside looking in. 'And Parkside?' she asked.

'I reckon I'll visit when I need to.'

'Like Joe and I used to do?'

'Something like that,' he replied. 'I just need someone I can trust on the inside.'

'Have you told Sue yet?'

'No, we haven't talked so much recently, but we will. I thought I'd tell her tonight.'

'Sometimes there isn't a right time; you need to make it.'

He didn't comment and they walked the rest of the way in silence. As they passed the Reality Checkpoint he looked across to his house and saw Bryn sitting halfway up the flight of steps to his front door.

Ellie followed his gaze. 'Coffee at Savino's for me I think. I'll see you this evening though.'

'At Marks's leaving drinks?'

'He tells me it's my round.' She grinned. 'Besides, I wouldn't dream of missing it.'

'Are you happy sitting there?' he asked Bryn. He was wearing jeans and a shirt and looked relaxed.

'Always a good view from here,' he grinned. Goodhew followed his gaze to the group of young women crossing Parker's Piece.

'I have furniture coming from Hope Street Yard. I'm hoping you'll help me move my jukebox again.'

'How many flights of stairs this time?'

'Just one.'

'Up or down?'

'Down.'

Bryn pretended to weigh it up. 'OK, but please tell me what the deal is with the music on that thing? Every time I look at it I think that it can't all belong to one person. Was it full of crap when you bought it?'

'No, I've filled it with the records that I like and the songs that remind me of people.'

'Really? Like what?'

'"Come On Eileen" reminds me of you.'

'How does that work? I don't even like the song.'

'Me neither, I hear it, I think of you and it disturbs me actually.' Goodhew grinned. 'I'll tell you some other time – definitely after you've moved it.'

'Great.'

'And by the way, I've decided to get a lodger. I'm moving down to the first and the top floor will be available. I need someone I can rely on.'

Bryn raised an eyebrow, 'Reliability isn't my middle name and being sociable isn't yours.'

'We've both improved, haven't we?'

'No, we're both pretty shit but yes, I'd love to.'

At the end of the afternoon Marks called everyone into the office for their final briefing. 'Drinks in the Grain and Hop Store tonight,' he reminded them. 'And well done to you all, the last couple of weeks have been difficult, but what a result.'

Holden used his football-terrace cheer.

Goodhew was standing near the back of the room when Sue approached him. She looked serious.

'Are you OK?' he asked.

She stepped to one side and pulled him with her. She turned her face away to shield herself from the rest of the room and kept her hand on his arm to keep him close. 'Marks called me in this morning; he wanted to wish me luck.'

'And?'

'We talked for a while. He thinks the world of you, by the way.'

He waited, knowing that wasn't all she had to say. 'He gave me some advice and I have thought it over, and he's right.'

'What advice?'

'There's something I should have told you before, Gary.' She looked worried. 'And now you'll find out along with everyone else. But not because I didn't want you to know.' Usually she blushed but this time the colour faded from her face.

'You can tell me.'

'I know that, but there isn't time.' She looked across the room and acknowledged Marks. 'He's letting me do this and it has to be right now.' She crossed the room and stood by their DI's side. 'I realised that this might be the only opportunity I have to speak to you all. Initially I wanted to announce my transfer to the Met, to tell you all at one time and DI Marks kindly agreed that I could do it now.' She paused and swallowed. 'That was the plan until this morning.' The room was still. 'He pointed out another way, and how many times do we deal with cases when those involved could have taken a different path?'

She made eye contact with Goodhew.

'Marks told me that the best way to tackle bullying was straight on and this is my response.' She paused and took a deep breath. 'I am the biological daughter of the man who raped my mother.' She looked away from him then and allowed her gaze to drift around the room, 'I am not going to leave here because of that fact, and I am going to support the police in any way possible to ensure that he is eventually apprehended.' Her gaze stopped on Kincaide. 'I'm not interested in attacking anyone who has put pressure on me to leave but it stops now.' She took another breath then exhaled. 'And on that note I would like to thank DI Marks for all the help and encouragement he has given me.' She turned to him and they hugged, 'Thank you so much,' she whispered.

'Be fearless,' he replied.

Then she looked back towards Goodhew, read his lips and smiled.

ACKNOWLEDGEMENTS

At this point, it is great to be able to look back over seven books and thank the people who have been there throughout. Top of the list are Krystyna Green and Broo Doherty, who have championed the Goodhew series all the way from *Cambridge Blue* to *Cambridge Black*. Equally important is the support I've received at home from Jacen, Lana and Dean, as well as my lovely step-daughter, Natalie, and my amazing sister, Stella.

During the writing of this book, the following people were generous with their time or expertise and often both. Thank you to: Dr William Holstein, Alison Hilborne, Richard Reynolds, Genevieve Pease, Lisa Sanford, Jane Martin, Kelly Kelday, Ian who prefers to remain anonymous, the members of the Newmarket Reading Round and fellow writers Lynn, Tracey, Jenna, Charlotte and James. Thank you to Rebecca Sheppard, Amanda Keats, Howard Watson and the very talented Poppy Stimpson at Little, Brown. Thank you to James Linsell-Clark for a cold but successful photoshoot – I love the front cover. And, as always, thanks to Christine Bartram and Claire Tombs.

Thank you to the Royal Literary Fund for your support and for the privilege of inviting me to return as an RLF Fellow.

This book contains several characters who have been named thanks to generous donations in aid of CLIC Sargent children's cancer charity. Thank you to Gary and Sue Franks, Alex Frampton and Tony Jeevar for supporting this good cause.

Finally, I'd like to thank all the readers who have followed Goodhew and have contacted me at various times over the years. It has been an absolute pleasure to release each book and to have the conversations that have followed at events and on social media. I hope you enjoy *Cambridge Black* and my future books.

THE SOUNDTRACK FOR
CAMBRIDGE BLACK

For each book in the series, I have listed the twelve songs that were played the most while I was writing. Each book is different, and so each playlist is different, too. When I think of Goodhew's jukebox, these eighty-four songs are all there.

'Baby, Please Don't Go' – Billy Lee Riley
'Dance For Evermore' – Si Cranstoun
'Don't' – Elvis Presley
'Forever's Much Too Long' – Go Cat Go
'Haunted Skies' – Lana Bruce
'(I Just Wanna Make You) Mine' – Nik Lowe
'Let's Fall In Love' – The Five Stars
'Mother Of Lies' – JD McPherson
'Oh What A Night For Love' – Roy Tyson
'Panic Cord' – Lana
'Pin-Up Girl' – Jacen Bruce
'You Don't Love Me' – The Go Getters

For more information please visit www.alisonbruce.com or find me on Twitter @alison_bruce.